D0584946

The
ELTON JOHN
Story

MARK BEGO

BOOKS

First published in Great Britain in 2009 by
JR Books, 10 Greenland Street, London NW1 0ND
www.jrbooks.com

A catalogue record for this book is available from the British Library.

ISBN 978-1-906779-21-4

1 3 5 7 9 10 8 6 4 2

Printed by MPG Books, Bodmin, Cornwall

TABLE OF CONTENTS

Introduction

Sir Elton John

PLACE: The Monte Carlo Sporting Club, Monaco

DATE: August 1, 2008

MARK BEGO, author: "So, Bill, have you thought of a quote for my Elton John book?"

BILL WYMAN, former member Rolling Stones: (laughing) "You mean Reg Dwight of Watford?"

GARY BROOKER, Procol Harum lead singer: (rolling his eyes) "You mean 'Sharon?'"

Elton John represents many different things to many different people. To rock & roll devotees, he is the creator of the classic album *Goodbye Yellow Brick Road*. To English rock musicians who have known him since the early 1960s, he is still chubby Reg Dwight of Watford, England. To film buffs, he is the outrageous "Pinball Wizard" of *Tommy* fame. To British subjects and the royal family, he is now "Sir" Elton John. And, to those close friends who've always known about his gay/bisexual personal life, he is still jokingly known as "Sharon." But as crazy and outlandish as he can be, it is his pop and rock music that has made the most enduring and lasting impression on the world. Legendary songs spanning five decades such as "Crocodile Rock," "Your Song," "Daniel," "Island Girl," "Bennie and The Jets," "Goodbye Yellow Brick Road," "Don't Let the Sun Go Down on Me," "The Bitch Is Back," and "I Guess That's Why They Call It the Blues," are all part of Elton's incredibly prolific musical catalogue.

He has sold over 200 million records and CDs worldwide, endured the rise and fall of disco, New Wave, and synthesizer rock, won five Grammy Awards, one Tony Award, and an Academy Award, outlasting enough one-hit-wonders to fill a football stadium. As recently as 2007, Elton was still scoring Top Ten albums on both sides of the Atlantic. No one has had a musical career quite like the self-proclaimed "Captain Fantastic." He has had so many incarnations that he has had to invent dozens of personas to accommodate his many moods, including both male and female pseudonyms for himself. Through it all, whenever someone announces that "The Bitch is back," there is no doubt that they are talking about Elton John.

Elton has never been shy about expressing whatever is on his mind—no matter how controversial it is at the time. His collaborations with songwriters such as Bernie Taupin, Tim Rice, and Gary Osborne have produced songs about topics that are deeply personal to Elton: "Someone Saved My Life Tonight," about his own suicide attempt; "Empty Garden," about the death of John Lennon; "American Triangle," about the murder of Matthew Sheppard; and "The Last Song," about a man dying of AIDS. He recorded a song about his own self-centered behavior ("Ego"), an ode to his own self-endurance ("I'm Still Standing"), and even a bawdy ballad about having gay sex with a sailor on the top of an amusement park ride ("Big Dipper").

In the 1970s, his string of Number One albums, including *Honky Château* (1972), *Don't Shoot Me, I'm Only the Piano Player* (1973), *Goodbye Yellow Brick Road* (1973), *Caribou* (1974), *Elton John: Greatest Hits* (1974), *Captain Fantastic and The Brown Dirt Cowboy* (1975), and *Rock of the Westies* (1975) made him one of the most recognizable stars on the planet. His first *Greatest Hits* album spent two months at the top of the American album charts, and his *Captain Fantastic* album was the first LP ever to enter the *Billboard* charts at Number One. By the end of the 1970s, Elton John had delivered an astonishing 20 albums and 37 singles.

The hits haven't stopped coming for Elton. In his incomparable career he has managed to chart a Top 40 single in England and/or the United States every single year from 1970 to 2005. He has logged seven consecutive Number One albums on the United States charts. Eulogizing Great Britain's Princess Diana in 1997, he and Bernie Taupin revamped one of their biggest hits, "Candle in the Wind," selling over 37 million copies worldwide. It became—almost overnight—the biggest-selling single in the history of recorded music, hitting Number One in the U.S.,

England, Germany, France, Australia, and dozens of other countries. According to *Billboard* magazine's 2008 list of the 100 Greatest Artists of all times—on the publication's Hot 100 singles chart—he is surpassed in hit singles only by Madonna and The Beatles. This makes Elton the top-selling solo male singles artist ever.

In a marketplace which regularly creates "disposable" pop icons, Elton has not only been able to maintain his global popularity as a rock star, but he has grown and developed his talent into new arenas of expression, including composing the hit musicals *The Lion King*, *Aida*, and *Billy Elliot* for Broadway and The West End, scoring film soundtracks, and garnering a whole new generation of fans via his gaudy and bawdy Las Vegas extravaganza *The Red Piano*.

True, during his five decades as a recording artist, he has suffered temporary slumps in creativity and sags in album sales. From time to time he has fallen out of favor with critics. But through it all, Elton John remains the most remarkably beloved rock and pop artist of rock history.

Meanwhile his personal life has been no less dramatic. Often Sir Elton is portrayed as a tasteful twenty-first century George Gershwin. In reality his life more closely parallels that of a modern-day Oscar Wilde. Wild, glitzy, boozy, and unconventional, Elton's story is filled with addictions, affairs, bouts with depression, a sexual-identity crisis, bulimia, drunkenness, and a pair of ludicrous suicide attempts.

After years of depression, failed gay love affairs, a masquerade of a marriage to a female recording engineer, and excessive drug use, Elton had a watershed moment in the 1990s when a *Rolling Stone* magazine reporter finally squeezed out of him the confession that he was indeed gay. Newly sober and drug-free, the singer found himself speaking frankly and publicly about his sobriety and his sexuality for the first time. He found self-confidence and a new direction. In 2005, during the global controversy surrounding the legalization of gay marriage, Elton and his longtime boyfriend David Furnish joined in a legal union in England, making him the first major rock star to have been married to both a woman and a man. Always outspoken, Elton has become vastly generous, using his time, his money, and his fame to raise funds to fight AIDS.

Elton's scandal-filled life of rock & roll excesses continues to be both colorful and fascinating. His stylistic versatility, combined with his flamboyant stage shows and outlandish costumes, makes him into a flashy combination of Liberace, John Lennon, Noel Coward, Billy Joel, and Barry Manilow. There is no one quite like Sir Elton John, and this is his story.

CHAPTER ONE

Reg Dwight of Watford

It was in Pinner, Middlesex, England, on March 25, 1947, that Reginald Kenneth Dwight was born. His mother, Sheila Harris, and his father, Stanley Dwight, had lived in Pinner since marrying in January of 1945, twelve months before World War II ended. Dwight was a flyer with the Royal Air Force—both during and after World War II.

The couple had very little money, so they set up housekeeping in the home of Sheila's parents, Fred and Ivy Harris. The house was a semi-detached little dwelling located at 55 Pinner Hill Road. After little Reggie came along, all five of them lived together under one roof.

As Elton recalls of his humble beginnings, "I was born in a council house, which is government housing, in North London. And so I grew up in my grandmother's house."[79] Indeed it was a modest existence for the lad who was destined to grow up to become one of the wealthiest men in show business.

There were many hardships for British citizens in post-war England, including food shortages and rationing of every commodity. It was here, amidst these circumstances that young Reggie grew up in a totally suburban setting. He was an only child and was somewhat doted upon and spoiled by his parents. Sheila had secretly hoped for a girl when Reginald was born, and for a long time she refused to cut her son's blond curls, having him pose for some rather girlish baby photos.

The year that Reggie was born, Stanley was promoted to flight lieutenant. He was stationed in Iraq for a great deal of his son's first four years. Sheila, alone with her son much of the time, raised Reginald by decidedly feminine standards. She was overly protective, and he was not allowed to play with other children or to get his clothes dirty. Instead he was forced to play alone in the backyard, where he couldn't get into any boyish mischief.

It was his mother, his grandmother, and his aunt who first encouraged him to play piano as a youngster. As Elton was later to recall, "My father was away most of the time in the Royal Air Force, and I was really brought up in fairly humble circumstances by my mother, grandmother and auntie. We always had music in the house. My Auntie Win used to play the piano, and my grandmother and auntie used to put me on their knees, I'm told, when I was very young and I'd play. The radio was always on, my mother collected records, and I grew up really with a background of Nat 'King' Cole, Kay Starr, Dean Martin, Guy Mitchell, Rosemary Clooney, all of those sort of people. It was really a good environment."[78]

When Reginald was just three years old, his parents heard him tinkling with the piano keys one day and realized that he was playing a rather accurate version of "The Skater's Waltz," by late 19th century French composer Emile Waldteufel. Sheila immediately recognized that her young son had the ear and the musical aptitude to mimic songs that he had heard on the family's piano.

From that point forward, Reggie was looked upon as the family's musical child prodigy in-the-making. His mother always treated him as being a special child, and she made certain to show off her son's talents to her family and friends. On several occasions, when she was going to entertain guests in the evening, she would put Reggie to bed in the afternoon for a long nap. That way she could wake him up when the party was in full swing and have the young boy entertain her guests with his keyboard mastery. While most four-year-old boys might be shy or embarrassed at such a display in front of an audience, not Reginald Dwight. Not only was he not shy or reticent, he was downright self-confident.

At first, Stanley was pleased at his son's interest in music. As Elton would later explain, "He was a trumpeter in a band. I mean, he did influence me. Used to play me George Shearing records. A four-year-old listening to George Shearing is a bit off."[55]

When he was five years old, Reggie had his first formal piano lesson. According to him, "I played piano by ear, and then when I was—I can't remember the exact age—my parents said, 'You should have lessons.' I went to a woman called Mrs. Jones in my hometown: Pinner."[78]

He very quickly devoured all of Mrs. Jones' piano lessons and found that her instructions magnified his own natural musical talent. By the time he was six, when asked what he was going to be when he grew up, he would instantly reply that he was destined to become a concert pianist.

There is a photo of young Reginald from this era, which appears in the booklet that accompanies *Don't Shoot Me, I'm Only the Piano Player*, his 1973 album. He is seen seated on the bench of his parents' upright piano. He has his hands on the keys, and he is looking over his left shoulder, his head turned flatteringly towards the camera. By the confident and cherubic look on his face, you can tell that he already knows that he is destined to become a piano star.

When young Reggie was six years old, another of his lifelong passions was instilled in him: his father took him to see the local Watford soccer team play. As deeply enthusiastic as the young boy's love of the sport became, so did his affection for the Watford team itself.

In 1953, Stanley was further promoted to become a squadron leader. Finally, he could move his wife and son into a rather prestigious four-room house of their own. Located at 111 Potter Street, Northwood, it was a mere two miles away from Pinner.

Elton was often to complain publicly that while growing up he found his father to be cold and unloving as a parent. Perhaps, since Sheila was such a warm and loving person, Stanley's attempts at fatherly affection went unnoticed. Elton would later whine about his strained relationship with Stanley, "My father was so stupid with me it was ridiculous. I couldn't eat celery without making noise. It was just pure hatred."[55]

In spite of any negative feelings Reggie had for his father, Stanley did help to nurture his son's interest in music. It wasn't all Sheila's influence. Elton explains, "My dad was a trumpet player, so I must have got my musical ability from his side. When I was about seven, my dad gave me a copy of Frank Sinatra's *Songs for Swinging Lovers*, which isn't the ideal present for a seven-year-old. I really wanted a bicycle. He bought me the Nat 'King' Cole Trio, with him playing piano not singing, and George Shearing.... So I grew up with as wide a selection of music of the time as could be before rock & roll."[78]

In the late 1950s, as rock & roll swept around the world, new role models presented themselves to the future "Elton John."

In 1958, Elvis Presley placed five different songs in the Number One slot, virtually dominating the radio airwaves around the world. The newly crowned King of Rock & Roll had a profound effect on Reggie.

According to Elton, "I remember the start of rock & roll perfectly. I went to have my hair cut, and while waiting I picked up a copy of *Life* magazine. There was a picture of Elvis Presley in there; I'd never seen anything like it. I remember it vividly. That same weekend my mom came home with two 78s—'ABC Boogie' by Bill Haley and 'Heartbreak Hotel' by Elvis. She used to buy two records—78s—a week, and someone told her these were wonderful. I said, 'Oh, Mom, I just saw this bloke in a magazine.' It was just weird that it happened the same week. That changed my life."[78]

That was the same year that Britain's own Lonnie Donegan became a huge hit with his folk/rock "skiffle" song "Rock Island Line." However, it was the American rock & rollers who really piqued Reggie's imagination. They were such dramatic showmen, especially when compared to the more reserved Englishmen like Donegan.

Elton was later to recall, "All the people I idolized were Americans. Everybody in Britain was copying the Americans anyway. Well, there was one person in England I admired: a black lady named Winifred Atwell. She was enormously fat and played two pianos, and I used to try and imitate her."[70]

The dramatic piano playing of rockers like Atwell, Jerry Lee Lewis, and Little Richard instantly attracted Reggie. Both Lewis and Little Richard were flamboyant in their ability to play the piano with tornado-fast precision. It was Little Richard that Reggie would most closely try to emulate when he became a rock star a dozen years later.

Sheila was responsible for getting Reggie hooked on rock & roll at an early age. Elton remembers, "She brought the records home and said they were different from what we had been hearing. She thought I would like them. Well, I couldn't believe how great they were. From then on, rock & roll took over. I used to play Jerry Lee Lewis and Little Richard things on the piano to myself, just thump them out."[77]

As rock & roll hit Great Britain in the late 1950s, it was welcomed with open arms, as though it was an energetic breath of fresh air. The pain and loss of World War II were easing. As Elton recalls, "We were ready for it in England. Up until that point, the songs we heard there were very prim and proper. Then we got things like 'All Shook Up,' which, lyrically, were far and away different from Guy Mitchell doing 'Singing the Blues.' All of a sudden you had Bill Haley singing 'Rock Around the Clock,' Little Richard screaming on 'Tutti Frutti'—lyrically it was a whole new ball game."[55]

Reggie's eye was also caught by the television performances of flamboyant American pianist, Liberace. A closeted gay man who played "popularized" arrangements of classical songs on a grand piano, with an elaborate candelabra in front of him, Liberace mesmerized Reggie when he saw the showman on television.

It was in 1957 that Reggie took possession of the first recordings that would become his own personal record collection. As he recalls, "The first 45s I ever owned were 'Reet Petite' by Jackie Wilson and 'At the Hop' by Danny & The Juniors."[76]

A year later, in 1958, at the age of eleven years, Reginald Dwight won a scholarship to study at The Royal Academy of Music, a highly prestigious music school. His talent for music grew in new directions as he was forced to concentrate in new ways. As he explains, "Then I passed the examination to go to The Royal Academy of Music and went from 11 to 15 years of age."[78]

The Academy's course director, Margaret Donington, immediately found Reginald to be a student of great promise. During a test of his ability to "play by ear," another teacher played a piece by Handel, which was four pages of sheet music in length. When she turned the piano over to Reggie, he proceeded to play the piece, with near note-for-note accuracy. From that point forward, the young boy's Saturdays were filled with lessons at The Royal Academy of Music. Not only was Reginald accepted for the Academy's classical piano playing classes, but he also sang in the Academy's choir.

While Reggie was excited at first about attending the Academy, he soon grew bored of the regimentation of having to learn and play the classics. For him, it represented attending school a sixth day of the week, which—for an 11-year-old boy—is not a fun prospect. It wasn't long before he was skipping his lessons. According to him, "I kind of resented going to the Academy. I was one of those children who could just about get away without practicing and still pass; scrape through the grades. Sometimes, when I didn't practice, I used to go up to Baker Street, which was where the Academy is, sit on the Circle Line train, and go round and round on the Circle Line. Then go home and tell my mom that I've been to school. So, I was not the perfect person."[78]

The punishing schedule of regular school combined with music lessons could have left young Reggie isolated from his peers. He had some friends at school, but as he tells it, from "Monday to Friday I went to school. Saturday was the Royal Academy of Music. Sunday I had to sit home and practice and do my homework.... I was very introverted and had a terrible inferiority complex. That's why I started wearing glasses—to hide behind. I didn't really need them, but when Buddy Holly came along, God, I wanted a pair like his! I began to wear them all the time, so my eyes did get worse."[55]

Hiding behind his unnecessary glasses, he felt that he was something of an outcast. "As a kid I was always on the fringe of everything," he explained. "I wasn't part of the gang. Going to the cinema with mates, I was always the last one to be asked. I think being raised by women shaped my personality because I spent a lot of time on my own, in my room, playing records. It made me a loner. It made me shy with other kids. I created my own world. I was immersed in music and records even at that young age."[73]

His weight added to his self-esteem problems. In spite of his growing musical expertise, he worried that he would never be admired like the sports heroes of the day. His cousin Roy Dwight became known locally as something of a sports star. Roy had helped the Fulton team win the FA Cup semi-final game that season. After that he was signed to play for the First Division Nottingham Forest team. He was paid the astronomical figure of £15,500. The future for Roy looked bright on the soccer field when the 1958 to 1959 season opened. Roy performed like a true star during that season, taking the Nottingham Forest team to the FA Cup Final. Even the Queen and the Duke of Edinburgh were in the audience for that particular championship game. However, thirty three minutes into the match, Roy sustained a compound fracture in his tibia, or shin bone.

Although that injury pretty much ended Roy's high-profile soccer career, Roy's success left a lasting impression on young

Reginald. If Roy could suddenly become the family's star, what were the possibilities that lie ahead for little cousin Reggie? Even if his feelings of inadequacy very quickly led to the loss of any interest he previously had in playing on his own school's sports teams, there was always music.

The way he felt about himself as a child was later interpreted into the kind of adult Reggie became. When he was in his twenties, Elton John was determined to make up for all he felt that his former persona—Reggie Dwight—had lacked. He became outrageous onstage, explaining, "I'm catching up for all the games that I missed as a child."[68]

In the early 1970s, one of Elton's schoolteachers granted a magazine interview but wished to remain anonymous. The teacher expressed shock over the fact that polite Reginald Dwight had morphed into the flamboyant rock star known as "Elton John." Recalled the teacher, "He was always very amiable and chatty, and always smiled when we passed each other in the corridor.... My memory of him is in short trousers with this protruding little bum and his blazer tightly buttoned over it. The last thing he could have been called is 'flash.' So I nearly died when I saw him perform at the Albert Hall, and this creature in a yellow satin tailcoat came rushing out and jumped on a piano!"[71]

Three years into his Royal Academy of Music studies, Reggie's cousin, Roy Dwight, got married. At the ceremony, the hired band was late in arriving. To fill in the time before they showed up at the event, Roy asked Reggie to entertain the wedding party with some of his classical piano work. Always up for an impromptu concert, young Reginald gladly complied. This was another turning point for him as he found himself on a stage playing for people who loved him, especially his own icon Roy Dwight.

From the time Reggie first heard American rock & roll, it was the music that possessed his soul. Feeling a bit like an outsider amongst his own classmates, he immersed himself in music. He would sit alone in his bedroom, listening to his record player. For him, the recordings that he heard were his closest friends. As he explains it, "I got involved with music, used to listen to records all the time. I would buy records and file them. I could tell you who published what, and then I would just stack them in a pile and look at the labels. I like my possessions. I grew up with inanimate objects as my friends, and I still believe they have feelings. That's why I keep hold of all my possessions, because I'll remember when they gave me a bit of happiness—which is more than human beings have given me."[55] Collecting records became a lifelong obsession with him.

By the time Reggie reached his teenage years, his parents' marriage had begun to crumble. He would lock himself in his bedroom when his parents argued. The atmosphere affected him greatly. "My father would come home and there would be a row. I expected it. And lived in fear of it. I don't think I had a dysfunctional background, but when your parents aren't getting on, you tend to go into your own world. Mine was music, and that became my life. Every performer starts with a cry for attention: 'I love doing this, but I want applause and verification that I'm good.'"[74]

Amidst the tension at home, teenage Reggie found himself more confused about the world around him and his own changing body as he reached puberty. While his classmates bragged about their budding sexual experiences, they may as well have been speaking a foreign language to young Master Dwight. The entire subject of sex mystified him.

"At school I used to have crushes on people, but not really any sex at all, male or female…. I never had any sex education when I was at school. Sex was never discussed," he was later to explain. "The first time I masturbated I was in pain. I was so horrified. And my parents found out because I'd used up all my pajamas. And then I got ripped apart for doing it. Sex was completely frightening. At school everyone boasted about sex. Meanwhile, I was dying to be molested by someone. When I [years later] went into therapy, my therapist said, 'I have to ask you if you were molested.' And I said, 'No, actually.' But I was dying to be molested by someone—just to teach me, just to find out, you know?"[75]

He was overweight, confused, frustrated, and he felt awkward in his own skin. Before Reginald could burst forth and become the show business butterfly he longed to become, he was wallowing in his own 13-year-old cocoon of confusion. Locked in his bedroom, playing music from his own meticulously arranged record collection, young Reggie began to dare to dream that he might one day break free from his inhibitions to become a piano-playing rock legend himself.

CHAPTER TWO

Crocodile Rock

In March of 1961, Reginald Kenneth Dwight turned 14 years old, and that was the year his life was destined to change drastically, especially on the home front. He was bored with school, and he resented his father's constant harping to do his schoolwork and his edicts about what his son "would" and "would not" do. Elton was later to recall that what he wanted most was a pair of Hush Puppies loafers. It was the era in which the casual pigskin suede shoes were all the rage. Stanley told teenage Reggie that he was forbidden to get a pair. In Reggie's eyes this was nothing short of a barbaric demand from his dad.

A short, pudgy, and not-very-attractive teenager, Reginald was riddled with so many self-doubts. With his Buddy Holly–like spectacles, he looked like the very personification of an introverted "geek." He had to find an outlet for his frustrations and his musical aspirations. His deep fascination with rock & roll music made him wonder what his career options could be. Would he go into classical music? Would he become a music teacher? Would he manage the piano department at a department store? The very idea of becoming a rock star seemed a long shot.

Then something really life changing happened. His parents announced that they were going to get a divorce. At the time, Stanley was posted by the Royal Air Force to Harrogate, a base located in Yorkshire. While Elton claimed that Stanley was having extramarital affairs at the time, it was his mother—Sheila—who asked for a divorce.

Sheila had spent so much time away from Stanley, due to his postings with the military, and she resented their recent arguments. She longed for a man in her life who was more agreeable and was more supportive. Sheila found just such a man in Fred Farebrother, who was a contracted builder and house decorator.

Reggie immediately liked Fred, and Farebrother took an instant interest in Sheila's awkward teenaged son. Fred became the supportive and understanding father figure that Reggie felt Stanley was not. Reggie liked to joke around with Fred. He has always affectionately called Fred, "Derf"—Fred's given name spelled backwards. So close was Reggie to Fred that it wasn't long before he was referring to Fred as "my dad" in conversations. The divorce and transition were not without disquiet for Reggie. When the divorce was finalized, he expressed some of his concerns to a teacher at the Royal Academy of Music, Helen Piena. According to her, Reggie confided that he thought his days at the Academy might be numbered. And, even more stressful to him was the threat that he may never get the new piano that Stanley had promised him if his grades improved. As it turned out, Reggie was not forced to withdraw from the Academy, and he did eventually get his new piano—"a secondhand upright pianoforte by Collingwood, walnut finish," from Hodges & Johnson's music store in Romford, Essex.[83]

Not long after the Dwights' divorce was announced, like Sheila, Stanley found a new love. In 1962, he met a 33-year-old woman by the name of Edna Clough. She worked in the medical profession as a lab technician. When they announced their intention to marry, Reggie apparently approved.

In a letter dated December 2, 1962, Stanley wrote to Edna: "In the afternoon I met Reggie and told him about us, pet, and he was very pleased. Indeed, he was really delighted. He took the news exactly as I said he would, dear, and said that all he wanted was for me to be really happy and now he is really looking forward to meeting you—especially as you play the piano. He saw your photographs, pet, and said, 'Yum! Yum!' Cheeky imp! Ha! Ha!"[84]

Another letter from Stanley to Edna mentions a wedding present Reggie gave them: "This weekend Reggie came over and brought us a nice magazine and newspaper holder for our wedding present, dear."[85]

Following Stanley and Edna's wedding, Reggie wrote a four-page letter to his dad. In it, the aspiring teenage pianist announced the occupation that he most deeply wanted to pursue as an adult. According to Reggie's letter to his dad, "I also know what I want to do when I leave school. Actually I have known for a long time but I have never said so before because I thought everyone would laugh at me. I want to entertain—that is, to sing and play the piano. I know that it is not easy to become an entertainer and I appreciate that it takes a lot of hard work and of course luck, but I know I would really enjoy doing it. I hope you don't think I'm foolish but I thought I'd tell you anyway."[86]

Therein the friction was to lie. Although Reggie was quite serious about launching a career as a pianist, Stanley instantly frowned upon what he saw as folly. He fancied that his son would find a more stable and steady profession, rather than becoming something as frivolous, at best, as a struggling musician.

When Stanley didn't react well to his goals, Reggie was disappointed. According to him, "My dad was a musician. He used to play trumpet with Bob Miller & The Millermen before he joined the Royal Air Force. He frowned upon what I was doing...you see, he was a bit snobbish. But my mother always encouraged me and, when she remarried, my step-father also encouraged me."[25]

Unlike Stanley and Edna, Sheila and Fred lived together a full ten years before marrying. Together with 14-year-old Reggie, they moved into an apartment house in Frome Court, where they lived in flat 30A.

Like any teenage boy in the 1960s, being transfixed by programs on television was a very normal mental state. Reggie found himself in love with the silly BBC comedies of the day, including *The Goon Show*, *Take It from Here*, and *Round the Home*. One of his favorite programs of the day was *Steptoe & Son*, an original situation comedy series about the owner of a junkyard and his modern-thinking son. It was later adapted into the American television series, *Sanford and Son*. *Steptoe & Son* included a horse by the name of "Hercules," a name that would make a lasting impression on Reggie.

After Stanley and Edna were married, they opened up a small stationery and toy store located in Chadwell Heath, Essex. On occasion Reggie would come and visit them.

Edna was later to recount, "Reggie enjoyed himself when he came to stay with us. We were both busy a lot of the time in the shop, but he seemed quite happy upstairs, playing my piano or picking out letters on a portable typewriter we had. One day I saw that he'd typed over and over again, 'Stan Dwight is my father, Sheila Dwight is my mother.' I felt a great sense of sadness that at such an impressionable age, a boy should be separated from one of his parents, and wondered if this had been preying on his mind as he sat there typing."[87]

From this point forward, Elton had an on-again/off-again relationship with his father. Over the next several years, Stanley and Edna had four children together. This bothered Reggie deeply. In a 1976 *Playboy* magazine interview he claimed, "At 14, when my parents got divorced, there was a point when I did feel bitter because of the way my mom was treated. When they got divorced, she had to bear all the costs. She more or less gave up everything and had to admit to adultery, while he was doing the same thing behind her back and making her pay for it. He was such a sneak. Then he went away and five months later got married to this woman and had four kids in four years. My pride was really snipped, 'cause he was supposed to hate kids. I guess I was a mistake in the first place."[55]

Stanley Dwight later declared that this was not the case at all. According to him, he paid for all of the divorce costs, and he split the profit from the sale of their house at 111 Potter Street with Sheila. Furthermore, he gave her the family car and all of the furniture in the house. Stanley claimed that all he took were his clothes and two photographs of Reggie in silver frames.

It was Fred Farebrother who really stepped up to the plate when it came to encouraging Reggie in attaining his dream of a career in music. He provided an important link to a weekly gig for young Reggie. In 1961, a married couple by the name of George and Ann Hill took over the bar at The Northwood Hills Hotel, which was located just outside of the Pinner city limits.

The Hills had previously managed a bar called The Hare, located at Harrow Weald. It had been a big success, so they were up for the challenge of turning the larger Northwood Hills Hotel location into a moneymaker as well. They knew that one of the keys to drawing and keeping a drinking crowd was to have music in the tavern. At first they employed an older woman who played honky-tonk piano; then they booked an energetic albino pianist who put on a lively show. After a couple of weeks, he began to complain that he had to travel too far to perform, and he quit.

Fred Farebrother saw an opportunity for his stepson and asked to talk to the man who ran the tavern. He met George Hill and asked him if he needed a piano player. George informed him that he just so happened to have such an opening. That was all it took. Fred instantly lined up an audition for young Reggie.

Ann Hill was to recall, "He was only about 15, still at school. His hair was cut very short. He wore a collar and tie, and grey flannel trousers. And this Harris tweed sports jacket that was kind of gingery color. He was very shy."[87]

Since they were without entertainment for the bar, the Hills had nothing to lose by giving the young boy a chance. At the time Reggie was very much into Ray Charles' recent Number One album *Modern Sounds in Country & Western Music.* Two of the most prominent songs on that album were the hits "I Can't Stop Loving You" and "You Don't Know Me." That was the kind of music that Elton decided to try out for the crowd the first night.

Naturally, Sheila and Fred came to the opening night performance. According to George Hill, the future Elton John was anything but an instant hit. "They gave him terrible stick," he recalls. "They'd shout 'Get off!' or 'Turn it down!' He'd have empty crisp packets and ashtrays thrown at him—we only had tin ones, so they didn't hurt. Or somebody would sneak up and unplug the leads of his PA system. I think he had quite a few pints [of beer] emptied into that piano as well."[87]

For the next year and a half, though, this was Reggie's weekly gig. He was paid a pound a night and had a box that was passed around at the end of the evening. As word spread, Reggie drew more of a crowd and could earn up to £25 a week.[25]

Reginald Dwight became known as something of a local prodigy. To have a regular moneymaking gig was quite an accomplishment for him. As he recalls, "I used to sing Jim Reeves songs, Cliff Richard songs, anything that was popular—and also play things like 'Roll Out the Barrel,' Cockney songs, 'When Irish Eyes Are Smiling'...you had to play 'When Irish Eyes Are Smiling' otherwise you'd get a pint of beer slung over you. Al Jolson songs were also very popular."[25]

How odd to think that in the year 2009 people have paid thousands of dollars to see Elton John at the end of his record-breaking run at Caesar's Palace in Las Vegas. Yet in 1962 you could wander into the pub located at 66 Joel Street in Northwood Hills, England, to see the yet-to-blossom singing legend, for the cost of a pint of beer. No one at the time could have predicted the massive success that would befall the young bespectacled lad behind that piano.

The confidence that Reggie gained from playing at the Northwood Hills Hotel pub drove him to branch out further.

During this same period he joined his first band. They called themselves The Corvettes, after the sports car that was all the rage among teenagers. Reggie played piano, Stewart Brown played the lead guitar, and Geoff Dyson was the bassist. The drums were played by a fourth member of the group, whose father owned a local pub. The Corvettes, in spite of their "cool" name, didn't last very long. When their drummer suddenly left the group, Reggie and his fellow band members quietly disbanded.

Not long afterward Reggie joined several friends to form a new group who called themselves Bluesology. When he wasn't in school, or studying at the Royal Academy of Music, or performing at his hotel pub gig, Reggie was rehearsing with Bluesology.

The music scene itself was changing around Reggie, and suddenly England was on the map in rock & roll terms. In 1963 and 1964, the infectious sound of The Beatles changed everything in the music business. First they swept England in 1963. Then, in February of 1964, The Beatles appeared on the American television variety program, *The Ed Sullivan Show*, and suddenly the U.S. was eating out of their hands. The Beatles ushered in not just "a sound" or "a look," they created an incredible multi-media phenomenon. It truly was Beatlemania!

Suddenly, right before his very eyes, Reggie saw how easily unknown British teenagers could become huge singing stars overnight. Reggie was so enthusiastic about The Beatles that he dragged his cousin and good friend, Paul Robinson, to one of The Fab Four's concerts. "We'd gone up to London to see a schoolboy's exhibition. That was boring, so Reg said, 'Do you fancy seeing The Beatles?' They were doing one of their Christmas shows at Hammersmith Odeon. Another great eye-opener was to see John, Paul, George, and Ringo prancing around the stage in pantomime fancy dress, even coming on in drag. No one had thought of putting pop together with slapstick fun before."[87]

According to Elton, "Before The Beatles, pop music in England was sort of an isolated thing. It was for older people. But The Beatles were like the boys next door. We all wanted to be like them."[77]

Thanks to The Beatles, the year 1964 marked the beginning of the American phenomenon known as "The British Invasion" of the U.S. record charts. The American Top 40 was populated with hitmakers from England including The Rolling Stones ("Time is On My Side"); The Animals ("House of the Rising Sun"); Peter & Gordon ("A World Without Love"); Manfred Mann ("Do Wah Diddy Diddy"); Herman's Hermits ("I'm Into Something Good"); The Kinks ("You Really Got Me"); and The Zombies ("She's Not There").

The Beatles and other British pop and rock musicians were an inspiration to Reggie Dwight. They represented everything that he longed to become.

CHAPTER THREE

Bluesology

For a while, in the early 1960s, Reginald Dwight had several overlapping projects at hand. First of all there was his academic life, as a student at Pinner Grammar School. Then there were his studies at The Royal Academy of Music. At the same time, he was the featured performer at The Northwood Hills Hotel pub. And, he was a member of his new band, the R&B group Bluesology. It wasn't long before everything else that was occupying his time would be pushed aside for him to pour all of his concentration into Bluesology and his dreams of finding success and fame in the music business.

One of the first things to be removed from his schedule was his study at The Royal Academy of Music. Even his instructor, Helen Piena, could feel him slipping away from her influence. Clearly he was focused on rock & roll and popular music and not the classics that the Royal Academy taught. Piena recalls, "About that time he began to realize what it was he wanted to do. He told me afterwards that he had formed a jazz band of his own, and that's what he was doing. He wasn't doing that much for me. I gave him one of the most wonderful things I could think of, some Mozart. I just wanted to cajole him and make him do some practice. I knew there was a lot of music in him that I couldn't bring out. That was one of the things I pride myself on, being able to bring out the gift that was in them. And I couldn't [with Reggie], because I was doing the wrong kind of music."[88]

Piena also recalls that when Reginald first told her about his thoughts of stopping his formal education all together, to chase his pop music dreams, she tried to talk him out of it. "I used to look at him on the stool next to me," she says. "I remember sitting there for three-quarters of an hour trying to persuade him to go to university. And he said, 'No, none of my family has ever been to university. I'm not going to university.' And, I couldn't make him change his mind."[88] It wasn't long before he dropped out of The Royal Academy of Music.

Whatever his ups and downs at the Academy, he was later to admit, "I'm very glad to have had the experience of having a classical background, because it makes you appreciate all sorts of music. It also helps you as a writer because, as a keyboard player, you tend to write with more chords than a guitar, and I think that has a lot to do with my piano playing and my love of Chopin, Bach, Mozart and my love of singing in a choir. I think my songs have more of a classic leaning to them than other artists who haven't had that classical background, and I am grateful for that."[88] Indeed, The Royal Academy of Music gave Reggie the musical polish that became a basis for his future as a musical composer. Interestingly enough, two of his later life collaborators were also students of The Royal Academy of Music: orchestral arranger Paul Buckmaster and record producer Chris Thomas.

With quitting the Academy, Reggie's focus shifted to Bluesology. He actively saved up his money to afford an amplifier of his own for performing in clubs. He often used the stage of the pub for Bluesology rehearsals.

The original four-member band chose their name for stylish Belgian-born Gypsy jazz guitar man Django Reinhardt and his instrumental masterpiece: "Djangology." Since Reggie and his new bandmates were playing the blues, "Bluesology" seemed like the ideal name to describe them and their sound. The original lineup of Bluesology included bass player Rex Bishop, guitarist Stuart A. Brown, drummer Mick Inkpen, and Reginald Dwight on keyboards. As their expertise as a unit grew, they saw it necessary to add a sax player, by the name of Dave Murphy.

At first, Bluesology was little more than a glorified pub and bar band. They would take any gig that they could get. As Elton recalls, "We played in scout huts and at youth club dances—just one ten watt amplifier with the piano unamplified. But we were always playing the wrong stuff. Bluesology were always two months too late—or three years too early. Never playing the right thing at the right time. We appealed to minority tastes and we always thought we were hip because we were playing Jimmy Witherspoon songs."[71] Witherspoon was a black blues man from Alabama who was known for songs like "Ain't Nobody's Business," "Big Fine Girl," "No Rollin' Blues," and "Times Getting Tougher Than Tough."

But in 1965, as Bluesology struggled along, seventeen-year-old Reginald Dwight received his lucky break in the music business. His cousin Roy Dwight produced a possible lead on a job in the music publishing business.

After Stanley Dwight's divorce from Reggie's mother Sheila, cousin Roy had stayed in touch with Sheila and Reggie. Through a friend, Roy knew Pat Sherlock, who worked for a company by the name of Mills Music. Pat agreed to interview Reginald Dwight.

According to Sherlock, "I can see him now, sitting in my office. I remember thinking what small hands he had for a piano player. He had this nervous mannerism of pushing his glasses back up his nose. And, a funny little pouting look."[87]

Reginald was such an eager interview subject that Sherlock offered him an immediate job as the office boy for Mills Music. The job paid £5 a week. With that offer on the table, Reggie made the most dramatic decision of his young life: he was going to drop out of school for this low-paying job working for a West End music publisher.

His decision caused a huge rift in the Dwight family. Naturally, Stanley was aghast at the idea that his son planned to quit school, just months short of graduating. However, Reggie had made up his mind. Looking back on this era, Elton was later to explain, "There was a period like that when I was still at school. I've still got a letter from my dad…which says, 'He's got to get all this pop nonsense out of his head, otherwise he's going to turn into a wide-boy, and he should get a sensible job with either BEA or Barclays Bank'…. Actually, I did go for an interview with BEA…but my mother never discouraged me at all."[25]

Regardless of what his father thought, on March 5, 1965, Reginald Kenneth Dwight attended his last day of classes at Pinner Grammar School, and he never looked back. If he were really serious about launching a career in the music business, then he would surely have more leverage working for a legitimate music publisher.

When Reggie told Bill Johnson, his history teacher, of his plans, Johnson gave him a piece of sound advice: "I told him if he really wanted to be in the music business, this was probably the most sensible way. 'When you're forty,' I told him, 'you'll either be some sort of glorified office-boy or you'll be a millionaire.'"[87] Fortunately, it was the latter path that Reggie was to take.

The publishing house Reggie worked for, Mills Music, was the London branch of an American company. It was famous for publishing music by legends such as Fats Waller, Leroy Anderson, and Duke Ellington. The London wing had several hits by British rock crooner Cliff Richard and some of Russ Conway's piano pieces.

The office was in the rear of the Mills Music warehouse in Denmark Place. At the time, Cyril Gee was the managing director of the company. Years later, when he was asked if he had any memories of teenage Reginald Dwight, Gee recalled "this podgy kid" who would always address him as "Sir." According to Gee, "I remember him coming to me one day and asking if he could play one of the arrangers' pianos in the lunch hour."[87]

It was not the most glamorous job in the world, but it was in the music business, and it made Reggie feel like an entertainment industry professional. His title was "Tea Boy" because making tea for everyone was one of his tasks. According to him, "I used to take all the parcels to the post office, which was a mile away. I'd work in the packing department wrapping up the parcels and take them on a wheelbarrow to the post office in Kingsway near the Oasis swimming pool…. Looking back on those days, I had a thoroughly good time working there. They were nice people, and we always used to have a laugh."[25]

Being a messenger, or a "tea boy," was about as entry level as one could be in London's music publishing world. Another young man whom Reggie became friendly with during this era was Caleb Quaye. At the time, Caleb was an office boy who worked for Paxton's wholesale music delivery company, located on Old Compton Street. He made deliveries to Mills Music every day. Over the next dozen years, Caleb was to become instrumental in several of Reggie's budding musical ventures.

For a while, Reggie's regular gig at The Northwood Hills Hotel pub had overlapped with the existence of his new band, Bluesology. It was hard to give up a regular income, but it soon became necessary to pour all of his time and energy into Mills Music and Bluesology. Reggie decided to continue the gig just as long as it took to save his money for better equipment. When Georgie Fame had a hit with the song "Yeh Yeh," suddenly the sound of the electric piano was the latest thing. Reggie longed to own one, and at one point he asked pub manager George Hill if he could borrow £200 to purchase one. Hill told him that he could not afford to make the requested loan.

It was drummer Mick Inkpen who was responsible for bringing a more serious investor into the picture. At the time Inkpen was working at a London jewelry manufacturer. His boss, Arnold Tendler, was in his thirties. When Tendler was invited by Inkpen to one of the band's gigs, at a Pinner church hall event, he was impressed. After that, Arnold Tendler became Bluesology's first manager.

Tendler was later to recall of Reggie, "At the piano there was this little roly-poly boy in clothes even I called 'square.' But when he played, he was marvelous. Even then he used to kick away the piano stool and play sitting on the floor."[87]

Now that Bluesology had a real manager, things began to happen at a much quicker pace. The band accepted any booking they could get. "God, we used to work," Elton was later to explain. "Once, we did four gigs in one day. We played an American Servicemen's club in London and then went to Birmingham and did a double—two ballrooms. Then at about six in the morning we went back and did The Cue Club, which is a black pub in London."[55]

One of the most dramatic things that Arnold Tendler brought to the table was money for Bluesology's first recording, a "demo" recording of two of the band's most popular songs. The first song was recorded on June 3, 1965, at a recording studio in Rickmansworth. This studio was run by the son of Jack Johnson, a famous English bandleader.

What was most exciting for Reggie was the fact that the song was his composition, "Come Back Baby." Not only did he write it, but he provided the lead vocal on it as well. And it was Mills Music, the company where he was still employed as "Tea Boy," who published the music and lyrics of the song. Reggie sang lead instead of the group's usual lead singer because his voice was better suited to it. Stuart Brown's was too deep, but Brown did sing the second number that Bluesology recorded.

The next step was to interest a record company in releasing the single. Reggie was not wasting any time, and it was he who sought out Philips Records. As Elton was later to recall, "First I wrote this song and.... I don't know how the hell I got the

audition.... I went to see Jack Baverstock at Philips Records and
played him the demo I'd cut at Jackson's Studio and he liked the
song. We went into the studio and cut 'Come Back Baby' and the
B-side, Jimmy Witherspoon's 'Times Getting Tougher Than Tough'
in three hours."[25]

And how did this sit with Brown? According to Elton,
"Stuart, who was the singer in the band around that time, was a bit
jealous. Sure, I wanted to sing, but for a start, I didn't look like a
singer." When the song was finally released, radio stations played
"Come Back Baby," more than the Witherspoon tune. The first
time that Reggie heard the song on the radio, he nearly fainted.
According to him, "I can remember sitting in the car and hearing
the record being played on Radio Luxembourg and saying, 'Hey,
that's me singing, folks!' I was really chuffed because that was the
very first time that I'd really sung anything."[25]

Once the single was released, Bluesology suddenly found
themselves in demand. Says Elton, "I remember doing nine or ten
gigs a week. We used to get £15 each a week, and out of that we had
to pay all our own expenses: hotel, petrol, HP payments and repairs,
but yet we still managed to survive somehow."[25]

One of their most memorable gigs was at the famed Cavern
Club, the Liverpool nightspot famous as the place where The
Beatles got their start. As Elton recalls, "We played The Cavern Club
in Liverpool twice and it was definitely one of the worst places for
getting your gear nicked, so bad that we had to keep someone
placed all the time. And the overflow from the men's toilet was so
disgusting...but it was still a great place to play."[25]

Bluesology actually had three different phases to their
career. The first chapter was when they were a band hoping to
become a huge hit on their own merit. But after "Come Back Baby"
failed to burn up the record charts, Reggie, Mick, Rex, Stuart, and
Dave began to explore some new inroads to stardom. A second
chapter in the band's life opened when they started to be booked
as a "pickup band" for visiting American singers. Their third
chapter, still to come, was as the backup band for British blues/rock
singer Long John Baldry.

In 1966, they first started to back up American performers
who were on tour. Elton was to recall, "We did an audition for Roy

Tempest at the Gaumont State, Kilbum, and he said 'Yes.'.... Roy Tempest offered us a job backing Wilson Pickett...and we rehearsed...and he [Pickett] said we were lousy and went back to America. As you can imagine, we were really disappointed."[25]

After Pickett's people turned Bluesology down, it was Major Lance who gave them their big chance as a professional touring band. At the time Major Lance had a string of hits including, "The Monkey Time" (1963), "Hey Little Girl" (1963), and "Um, Um, Um, Um, Um, Um." For Bluesology, this was truly the "big time." It was a great opportunity to put their music in front of fresh new audiences.

After Major Lance, the band went on to back up Patti LaBelle & The Bluebelles twice, The Original Drifters, Doris Troy, The Ink Spots, and Billy Stewart. When they weren't working with other musicians, they toured Germany, France, and Sweden on their own.[63]

It was Billy Stewart who really "worked" Bluesology. Stewart was a total professional who had been discovered by Bo Diddley in the 1950s, and he had made his first recordings in 1956. He expected Bluesology to really "turn it out" onstage, and he wasn't about to accept any slacking on the job. Elton was later to appreciate Stewart's demands for sharp arrangements and succinct playing onstage.

Working for Roy Tempest and the acts that he booked became a "trial by fire" kind of situation. Often, the soul acts that he brought over to England were on the last legs of their careers. Tempest was also using his own apartment as a hotel to house the groups during their stay in London, and he would charge the group members for their modest lodging.

Another of Tempest's ploys was to have "fake" groups come in, and he would add the word "Original" to the advertising to avoid copyright infringement. He would call a "soundalike" group "The 'Original' Drifters" to masquerade the fact that the singers had nothing to do with the real hit-making group known as "The Drifters." Elton recalls, "Tempest's doubles were amazing, and how we ever kept to those schedules I still don't know.... Tempest eventually got exposed in the Sunday papers for bringing over all these phony American acts.... I even remember 'James Brown Jr.,' 'The Original Supremes' and we even backed 'The

Original Drifters' a couple of times. The one group that I really felt sorry for was The Ink Spots because the kids thought they were going to be something like The Drifters."[25]

Without a doubt the most exciting group that Reggie and his bandmates played with during this era was Patti LaBelle & The Bluebelles. The Bluebelles—Sarah Dash, Nona Hendryx, and Cindy Birdsong—and Patti LaBelle were four girls from the south New Jersey/Philadelphia, Pennsylvania, area. They had been singing together since 1962. They had a hit with "I Sold My Heart to the Junkman," and with their recordings of popular middle-of-the-road standards like "Danny Boy," "You'll Never Walk Alone," and "Over the Rainbow" from *The Wizard of Oz*—the film that would later inspire Elton's *Goodbye Yellow Brick Road* album.

For Patti, Nona, Sarah, and Cindy, their 1966 trip to England represented a certain level of fame for them. Even in the United States, Patti Labelle & The Bluebelles had not had the kind of chart hits that The Supremes or Martha Reeves & The Vandellas achieved. However, for The Bluebelles the best was still yet to come.

In 1967, Cindy dropped out of the group to replace Florence Ballard in The Supremes. That became her major ticket to stardom. Left as a trio, Patti, Nona, and Sarah stuck together and in 1970 changed their name to "LaBelle."

Sarah Dash, Nona Hendryx, Cindy Birdsong, and Patti LaBelle met Reg Dwight for the first time when they arrived for their 1966 extensive British tour of clubs and nightspots. Sarah recalls, "We met him, and he was in a band called Bluesology. He was a little chubby guy with glasses. He was a delight. He was upbeat and he was just a delightful kid, because he was a couple of years younger than us.… And, he was so excited to be working with a group from America. I, at the time had no idea that he was such a prolific writer of songs. I don't remember how good the band was, but we always remember how well he played. I remember him as being the one in the band who could pull it together. There were some moments of frustration, but we had to go on."[98]

Not only did LaBelle and Bluesology play at several places in and around London, their tour extensively zigzagged its way across the English countryside. "We were playing clubs—a lot of clubs there—up north, there was a lot of work to be done," says

Dash. "Because we were there for so long, we rented an apartment. We were there for the first time—three weeks—and we had to put shillings in the heater to make it work. It was quite a culture shock for us. Of course, as time went on, we came in more luxurious ways."[98]

She also remembers that she and the other three members of her group all became great friends with Reggie Dwight. "We did our rehearsals," says Sarah. "They played for us. Backstage we were bored because we had traveled to Manchester and places like that. The biggest thing that Patti loved over there—her and Elton—who we called 'Reggie' at that time—were the ginger snap cookies. I have to find that picture. It's a picture of both Patti and Elton with ginger snaps in their mouths like they were circular plates in their mouths. They're holding the ginger snaps; both of them. He was just ever so respectful. It was just a really nice time. He was just this chubby little bright-eyed kid."[98]

What was it like to suddenly be backing up acts like Patti LaBelle & The Bluebelles? According to Elton: "Hard. I mean, to begin with, we weren't the very best of bands. At that time, LaBelle were doing slow things like 'Over the Rainbow' and 'Danny Boy' which was completely the wrong kind of material for them to be doing around the clubs. The things that they went down best with were 'I Sold My Heart to the Junkman' and 'A Groovy Kind of Love' and 'All or Nothing.'… Let's face it, we were just an average backing group and if you interview Patti LaBelle now, she'll admit that when she first came over, Bluesology weren't the best backing group around. And she'd be correct!"[25]

Actually, Patti had nothing but great things to say about Elton. "At the beginning of the tour, we hooked up with this fierce English group, Bluesology, that was working as a backup band for a lot of visiting American R&B artists. After our shows, they would come over to our place and a bunch of us would get drunk and play cards. The piano player, Reggie Dwight, could play keyboards like no other white boy I have ever heard."[92]

One of the favorite backstage activities was an ongoing game of cards. The gambling game that Patti preferred was called Tonk, a variation of the game Rummy. Patti LaBelle humorously recalls, "For some reason he thought he could play cards like he played that piano, and he wouldn't give up until I had won what little money he had. 'Come on, Patti,' he would say in his cute British accent. 'One more game of Tonk, and I will win back all my pounds.' Of course, the only thing he ever won was my sympathy. I might have sent him home with an empty pocket, but I never let him leave with an empty stomach. After I won all his money, I cooked Reg the biggest, spiciest dinner he'd ever tasted. After we ate, we sat around and talked—about music, about the States, about his dreams."[92]

There was a second British tour for Patti LaBelle & The Bluebelles several months later. Again they played with Reg Dwight and Bluesology as their backup band, but by now Bluesology was changing yet again and there were new guys surrounding Reggie Dwight. Sarah Dash recalls, "We went back again, and he wasn't with the same guys, he had a different group with him."[98]

The third and final incarnation of Bluesology came about by way of the rocking bluesman who billed himself as Long John Baldry. He became instrumental and influential to Reg Dwight's emergence and transition into becoming Elton John. It was Baldry who gave him his next batch of musical experiences, introduced him to one of his lifelong best friends—Rod Stewart—lent him his name, and was the first person to look Reggie in the eyes and tell him that he has no luck with women—because he is gay.

Like Elton John, Long John Baldry's musical career had many different phases. He took many paths towards mainstream recognition and had many career peaks. As a rocking legend he started out playing the blues, had a sudden pop hit, "discovered" both Rod Stewart and Elton John, and watched both of them flourish in careers that by far eclipsed his own musical accomplishments. Then, at the height of Rod's and Elton's initial superstardom, they both came back to help Baldry out, by co-producing the two most famous record albums of Baldry's entire career.

Long John Baldry got his nickname because he stood six-feet seven-inches tall, and he cut quite a dapper and imposing figure wherever he went. Born on January 12, 1941, in London, the tall boy with the resonant voice first sang in his church choir, until at the age of 12 he discovered the blues. Black American bluesmen like Muddy Waters, Willie Dixon, and Huddie "Leadbelly" Ledbetter forever changed his musical focus. When he was just 15 years old, the young Baldry made his London club debut at Acton Town Hall. He also became adept at playing the 12-string acoustic guitar and toured Europe with folk icon Ramblin' Jack Elliot.

In London, he frequently performed with guitarist Davy Graham, and, along with Cyril Davies and Alexis Korner, Baldry frequented the famed folk club The Roundhouse on Wardour Street. In the early 1960s Baldry moved to Denmark, and then upon returning to London he continued to perform on the club circuit, dazzling the likes of Eric Clapton and Spencer Davis with his blues guitar prowess.

Elton John knew of Baldry from his music and his stage act. According to him, "He really was a fantastic blues guitarist, just him on his own, singing Leadbelly stuff. It was just amazing. He was definitely a pioneer and at the forefront of British blues music; he was right up there. Without John there wouldn't have been a blues scene as such. He was up there with Alexis Korner and Cyril Davies. And he always wore very smart suits and ties. He was this incredibly tall, imposing man who had this fabulous fashion sense."[93]

There was a certain club circuit in London, where everyone who was destined to make it in the music business in the 1970s seemed to be running into each other. One of the most famous places to play was the hotel on Eel Pie Island, in the London borough of Richmond. While headlining there, Baldry rubbed elbows with all of the solo performers and bands who were struggling to establish an audience for their blues, rock, and jazz music, including The Rolling Stones.

Located in the middle of the Thames River, Eel Pie Island became famous as the spawning ground for a whole new brand of British pop music. Bill Wyman, the original bass player for The Rolling Stones, has fond memories of Eel Pie Island: "There was a great rock club there. We used to play The Eel Pie Island Hotel. It used to be a jazz club, that was before we started to play there. It was The Rolling Stones who were responsible for bringing rock & roll to Eel Pie Island!"[91]

Baldry put together several bands in search of stardom. In January 1964, he met Roderick David Stewart on a train platform, on his way home after a gig on Eel Pie Island. The two connected immediately, and Baldry invited Stewart to join him onstage. He formed a band called The Hoochie Coochie Men and shared the lead singing chores with Rod. Then came the addition of Brian Auger and Julie Driscoll. They christened their group "Steampacket." When Steampacket failed to find mainstream success, Baldry broke up that band and began to look for a new group.

One night he went into The Cromwellian Club, and there onstage was a band calling themselves Bluesology, complete with the studious-looking, electric keyboard-playing Reginald Dwight. Reggie and the rest of his bandmates recognized Baldry from the London rock club scene. The next thing everyone knew, Baldry hired Bluesology as his new backup band.

Of that fateful night at The Cromwellian Club, Elton John recounted, "John Baldry came along and said, 'Would you like to join up?' I said, 'Well, at least it's a step in the right direction.' So we backed John for a year, starting off with a soul package, really. It was our singer, who was Stuart A. Brown, Marsha Hunt, another singer called Alan Walker, and Baldry. Baldry had just finished with the Brian Auger thing, and Julie Driscoll: The Steampacket, with Rod Stewart."[63]

Reggie Dwight really liked and admired John Baldry, and they were to remain lifelong friends. Baldry was homosexual, though that was only known in his inner circle. According to Eric Clapton, "He was very elegant and incredibly flamboyant, combined with this highly acute sense of humor. I think I found out much later that he was gay. I think when I was very young, in the early days, I didn't really know what 'gay' meant anyway." Eric also admits that there was a certain "guarded" sense about Baldry's personal life: "There was a darkness to him, too, that I didn't really get to know very well. I just could sense that the guy was troubled, you know? I'm not sure, at that stage of his life, if he had really come to terms with his sexuality. It was much more open in the '70s and everything, once he had kind of 'come out,' although I don't know if he ever 'came out' publicly. But he was definitely 'out' on a personal level."[93]

Elton claims that he was clueless about the tall singer's sexual orientation, let alone his own: "I cannot believe I never realized that he was gay. I mean, I didn't realize I was gay at the time, but, looking back on it now, John couldn't have been any more gay if he tried. It wasn't on my radar at that time. Of course when I [later] came out of the closet, John was very, very happy about it."[93]

In June of 1967, as The Beatles released their psychedelic masterpiece, *Sgt. Pepper's Lonely Hearts Club Band,* the season officially became known as the "Summer of Love." Suddenly everyone was going "hippie chic" with colorful outfits and love beads around their necks. Baldry got it in his head that Bluesology should jump on the bandwagon as well. As Elton John recalls, "This was at the height of Flower Power and we'd suddenly gone from playing Jimmy Witherspoon numbers to Flower Power stuff. I remember we were playing Scarborough Floral Hall with Baldry and he made us all go out and buy bells and beads and caftans— and it was all so horrible. So overnight we switched from wearing frilly satin shirts to that 'Love & Peace' thing."[25]

Like everybody on the club circuit—including Reggie Dwight—Long John Baldry longed for his own big lucky break. For Baldry, it came in 1967, in a chance to record a big schmaltzy pop single called "Let the Heartaches Begin."

Elton John explains, "When Baldry got his hit 'Let the Heartaches Begin' he quickly got rid of Marsha and Stuart and Alan, because it was just uneconomical. Baldry was the fairest man I've worked with. I love him and the only reason I stayed so long was because he was such a great person to work for."[25]

By then, the Bluesology lineup had changed again. Neil Hubbard was on guitar with Freddy Gandy on bass and Pete Gavin on drums. Elton Dean played sax and Marc Charig played trumpet. Of course Reggie Dwight was still on piano. Baldry and Bluesology continued to tour on the strength of "Let the Heartaches Begin."[25]

The "B" side of "Let the Heartaches Begin" was Reginald Dwight's composition, "Oh Lord, You Made the Night Too Long." For every copy of the single that sold, Reg got a payment as a songwriter. He later said, "I got amazing royalties from that, and I still get the odd check for four pence from Italy when another few copies are sold!"[135]

Despite the success of Baldry's single, Reggie Dwight was getting restless being the keyboard player for Bluesology and Long John Baldry. He felt relegated to the background, and this particular group was not pushing him far enough up the entertainment business ladder. He wanted to do rock & roll of his own, and Bluesology seemed to be at a creative standstill. Elton later explained, "I began to get totally frustrated with Bluesology, because nobody had any ambition…. It was held together by loyalty."[71]

Feeling that he had gone about as far with Bluesology and Long John Baldry as he could go, twenty years old, and seemingly stuck in the middle of the London music scene, Reggie sensed that it was time for him to make another forward leap. He decided that his lucky break would come only if he became a successful songwriter.

CHAPTER FOUR

The Songwriting Years

It was transition time for Reggie Dwight. He decided that he had to take chances, and he longed to change just about everything in his life. He dared to dream of one day becoming a solo star on his own, and he felt that the time had finally come to do just that. Reg had witnessed first hand as his bandmate Long John Baldry suddenly hit Number One on the charts with "Let the Heartaches Begin." He saw how one record can suddenly change a person's career forever, and he longed for that opportunity as well.

He was already plotting his exit from Bluesology. Looking back at his life circa 1967, he recalls, "I just wanted to be on the stage to show people what I could do, and that's why I got very brought down by Bluesology, because I was just nothing. There's so many people going round in bands who are afraid to take the plunge or don't get the chance. They really want to break out but they daren't; the only reason I did was because I was [so] desperate and miserable that I just had to."[94]

For a while, Elton thought that his escape from Bluesology would come in the form of landing a gig with an established band, by becoming their lead singer and front man. On two separate occasions he auditioned for bands in search of a leader—for the avante garde rockers King Crimson, and then again for artsy rock band Gentle Giant. Answering their "casting calls," he was subsequently turned down by both bands. Things could certainly have turned out quite differently if he had successfully joined King Crimson. Nowadays we might all be listening to Elton John singing that group's psychedelic favorite—"Larks' Tongues in Aspic"— instead of hearing him belt out "Your Song."

Some major changes had to happen before Reg could soar to the heights he longed to achieve. The first obstacle that stood between him and success was his name. Who in their wildest dreams could envision a rock star by the name of Reginald Kenneth Dwight? Especially, if this particular Reg Dwight also looked like a bookworm in thick eyeglasses?

It was time to completely change his persona. He decided to start with his name. He took "Elton" from his bandmate, Elton Dean, and on the suggestion of Caleb Quaye, he used Baldry's name as a last name. Elton John was born. And, that was it. From that point onward, only the people from his past would refer to him as "Reg." This was the sudden birth of the rock star who would henceforth be universally known as Elton John.

Now billing himself under his new "stage name," all Elton had to do was completely reinvent his career. He realized that he wasn't in a position to quit one job before he found a new one. He applied for other jobs including one as a record-plugger for Philips Records. They turned him down, but he saw an advertisement that Liberty Records was looking for new talent. He remembers, "At this time, I was still with Baldry but I fixed up an appointment and went along and told [Liberty] that I thought I could write songs but not lyrics. Then they asked me if I could sing and I told them, of course I can sing. I went along to the Regent Sound Studios in Denmark Street to record five numbers. As I never sang in the band, the only songs I could remember were the ones I used to sing in the public bar of the Northwood Hills Hotel, so I did some Jim Reeves material.... 'I Love You Because,' 'I Won't Forget You,' 'He'll Have To Go'.... I even sang 'Mammy.' Of course, once they heard them, Liberty shrieked with horror and said 'No.' But someone stepped in and said, 'There's this guy in Lincolnshire called Bernie Taupin who writes lyrics.' I got some of them, looked them over and thought they were alright, quite good."[25]

At the time Bernie Taupin was a seventeen-year-old boy, slight of build, with a vivid imagination. He was born on May 22, 1950, and he grew up in the lush English countryside with a deep love of literature including the authors Someset Maugham, Oscar Wilde, and Christopher Isherwood. He also loved to read about America and was especially fascinated by the tales of the Old West. Cowboys, pioneers, and the old South of the 1800s intrigued him and became recurring themes in his writing. Musically, he was very influenced by country singers like Marty Robbins—who was famous for the songs "El Paso" and "A White Sports Coat (And a Pink Carnation)"—and folk singer Woody Guthrie. Of the current rock stars, Bernie also listed Jimi Hendrix and Bob Dylan as among his favorites.

According to Taupin, "Contrary to Elton, I was raised in a very rural area in the north of England in Lincolnshire. My father was a farmer, and my mother had a very literary background because my grandfather was a college professor. She encouraged me to read, and I loved to read, especially narrative poetry. When I started listening to radio—which is where I first heard music—I listened to what we called the American Forces Network, and the first kind of music that I really loved was what we used to call 'skiffle.' There was this guy Lonnie Donegan who used to cover all these great Leadbelly and Woody Guthrie songs. I always thought Donegan wrote them, these great narrative songs like 'John Henry's Hammer.' Then I got turned onto people like Johnny Horton and Johnny Cash and their story songs."[78]

One of the keys to Bernie Taupin's success as a songwriter was the fact that every song seemed to tell a story or lyrically sketched out a vignette or a scenario. Whether he was writing about emotions or events, his words took the reader or the listener on a voyage. "I got into long, narrative poetry, Coleridge and stuff like that, the way other young people got into pop music…. I loved stories. To write a story and put it to music, I thought that was wonderful. Then I got obsessed with Americana, and from there it was a natural progression to country music and people like Woody Guthrie who documented American social life," he explains.[45]

As Reggie Dwight, now known as Elton John, was applying to Liberty Music, Taupin had also seen the ad in *New Musical Express*. He wrote a reply but then apparently got cold feet when it came time to drop it in the mailbox. His mother saw the letter in the wastebasket and mailed it. Bernie's letter arrived on the desk of Ray Williams at Liberty. When Ray was meeting with Elton, who could write music but not lyrics, Ray told Elton to hook up with Bernie, who could write lyrics but not music. With that was born one of the most successful songwriting teams of the 20th century!

The pair eventually signed with Dick James Music. Elton quit Bluesology for good when Dick James promised Bernie and Elton £10 a week against royalties. Unfortunately, Bernie and Elton didn't find overnight success. There was a lot of "trial and error" between the meeting and the stardom.

It wasn't always easy for Elton to figure out what to do with Bernie's lyrics. According to him, "When he originally started, his words would never be in verse form; there'd just be 115 lines and I'd think, 'Where the fuck do I start?' But it didn't seem that difficult once I'd got used to it. In those days, the songs were much more complex because the form in which Taupin wrote wasn't the verse chorus style."[25]

It wasn't until after composing music to several of Bernie's lyrics that Elton finally met the man himself. According to Elton, "After Liberty turned us down, Ray Williams said, 'I have an interest in a publishing company called Gralto over at Dick James Music,' so I went over there. I started doing demos of the songs and Caleb Quaye was the studio engineer. One day while we were recording, this bloke suddenly appeared and sat down in a corner and after we'd finished he said, 'I'm Bernie Taupin,' and I said 'Hello.' Then we went and had a coffee in the Lancaster Grill on Tottenham Court Road and decided that we would write songs together."[25]

As a songwriting team, Elton and Bernie were signed to Dick James' music publishing company in 1967. After finishing up a couple of performing engagements with Long John Baldry, Elton was suddenly a full-time songwriter along with his new buddy Bernie.

The Dick James operation was quite interesting on its own. Born in 1920 as Isaac Vapnick, James changed his name and became a crooner. He even had a hit of his own in England in 1956, singing the theme for *The Adventures of Robin Hood*. He took his knowledge of the music business and started up a successful eponymous music publishing company.

In 1963, a record producer by the name of George Martin was frantically shopping for a publisher to handle the music written by an up-and-coming group he was representing. The then-unknown group called themselves The Beatles. It seemed that every music publisher in the Denmark Street area of London turned him down. That was until he entered Dick James Music (DJM) at 71-75 New Oxford Street. Becoming the music publisher of The Beatles catalogue, under the title Northern Songs, was one of the biggest jackpots in James' entire career. In addition to having the music of The Beatles under his company's umbrella, James quickly sought out other potential rock & roll songwriting legends. One of the other groups he nurtured was The Hollies. He set up a music publishing label using letters from the three main members' names—Graham Nash, Allan Clarke, Tony Hicks—and came up with the moniker that became Gralto Music. Elton and Bernie were signed to Gralto first.

From that point forward, Elton John and Bernie Taupin were pretty much inseparable. In the 1970s, when Elton's fame was at its initial monumental heights, the natural question was as to whether or not the pair were gay lovers. Surely, Elton must have been attracted to Bernie on several levels. He had never seemed to have such a close and long-term mate as he and Taupin soon became. Did Elton fall in love with Bernie? "I did," he later admitted. "But it was never a sexual thing. I would never leap on him. I just adored him, like a brother. I was in love with him, but not in a physical way. He was the soul mate I'd been looking for all my life."[88]

When Bernie decided to move to London to concentrate on his songwriting with Elton, he had no place to live. Sheila and "Derf" came to rescue. They moved Taupin into their small two-bedroom maisonette they owned on Frome Court. So that there would be room for both Elton and Bernie in Elton's tiny, record album–stuffed bedroom, they purchased bunk beds. Elton was twenty, and Bernie was seventeen. They lived together, they wrote music together, and they worked hard to establish themselves in one of the most competitive businesses on the planet.

Although they were incredibly close, Elton and Taupin actually wrote separately. As Elton recalls, "Oh, yes. Even back then, when we lived together, he'd give me lyrics and I'd go into the next room and play. I could never do my songs with him in the room. I'd be embarrassed. He's never sat down on the piano stool next to me and said, 'Well, I don't like this or that.' Sometimes he'd say, 'Well, that came out different than I imagined it.' He's been constantly surprised at how songs turn out. But I just leave the lyrics to him."[55]

With regard to his working relationship with Bernie, Elton claimed, "I think we are the only people who write this way round—Bernie doing the words and me just the music, except for Keith Reid and Gary Brooker [of the group Procol Harum] who do it like that. It takes me about 20 minutes to write the music of a song, but Bernie spends much longer on the words."[135]

It was hard work, trying to predict which songs would be successful. Occasionally they would get very discouraged, as they cranked out dozens of songs every month. Elton claims that it was his mother who would get them back on track. "Every time Taupin and I felt like giving up she'd say, 'Right, piss off...go on, there's a job going up the greengrocer's,' and we'd mumble something about, 'That's not what we want to do,'" Elton explains. "The people who did encourage us in the first place were Steve Brown and Lionel Conway and Roger Cooke and Roger Greenaway who all worked at Dick James Music."[25]

Two of the first Elton John/Bernie Taupin successes were the songs "The Tide Will Turn For Rebecca," which Edward Woodward recorded, and a song called "I Can't Go on Living Without You" for Cilla Black. Another high-water mark came for the duo when Dick James submitted a song of theirs to the Eurovision Song Contest, and it was recorded by Lulu to represent England's entry into the competition. Elton recalls, "In those days we'd do anything for our ten quid a week while 'I Can't Go on Living Without You' was just a fluke. It was one of our old songs that was lying around the office and Dick entered it in for the Eurovision Song Contest and it got into the last six and came last. It was an awful song for which I wrote the lyrics because Taupin wouldn't have anything to do with it. Those lyrics—they were really awful: 'I can't go on living without you, oh yeah, baby / Oh no, I can't go on living without you.' It was bloody terrible."[25] However, both Elton and Bernie knew that all it took was one hit song, and one's fortunes could dramatically change for the better. In the meantime, they were still trying to polish their craft and find a winning formula for success.

It seemed that everyone working for Dick James—Elton and Bernie included—was staying late in the office to sneak time in the recording facilities, laying down tracks for the songs that they were hoping to sell. When James found out that his recording equipment was being used without his authorization, he began to fire people right and left.

Recalling this bloodbath, Elton explains, "We originally must have written 50 or 60 songs. You see, originally we were signed to Gralto and they didn't do anything with that material. Then one day, there was a mass clear-out up at Dick James Music because a lot of groups were going in there and cutting demos for nothing without Dick ever knowing about it. When Dick eventually discovered what was happening he had this great purge and Caleb more or less went into Dick's office on his knees and said, 'Reg and Bernie are worth fighting for' and so Dick signed us to a contract, after he had heard some of our songs. So we've really got Caleb to thank for that."[25]

James wasn't interested in Elton becoming a solo star. He wanted the duo to pen some moneymaking hits for the likes of Cilla Black and Engelbert Humperdinck. As Elton recalls, "To give him his due, he did give us a lot of freedom but on the other hand he did keep on saying, 'You've got to write Top 40 material for Cilla and Engelbert,' which we wasted two years of our lives trying to do."[55] One of the songs Elton describes as "very, uh, Engelbert Humperdink," was "I've Been Loving You." Though credited to both John and Taupin, it was Elton who wrote the lyrics as well as the music.

Bernie and Elton were stuck doing this type of music until Steve Brown joined the company. He told the pair that they weren't "quite there yet" in their songwriting.[25] Elton recalls, "It wasn't as good as we could do and he asked us the reason why: so we told him that half of us wanted to write things that we really wanted to write while the other half had to do what Dick wanted us to do— and that was write hit songs. For the life of us we couldn't write a hit song. So in the end, Steve said, 'Fuck Dick' and told us to write what we liked. The first thing we wrote after that was 'Skyline Pigeon' and then 'Lady Samantha,' and from that point on we've never written a song that we haven't liked."[25]

"Lady Samantha" was recorded and released as a single in 1968. It wasn't a complete success. Elton remembers, "I took a bit of time. I wasn't doing gigs. I hadn't got a band together. In fact, when 'Lady Samantha' came out, it was 'a turntable hit,' not a real financial success. And then 'It's Me That You Need' came out, followed by *Empty Sky*, and they got good reviews but didn't sell. I also made another single called 'Rock and Roll Madonna,' which was a bit of a disaster."[55]

During this same period, Elton's personal life was becoming something of a soap opera. On Christmas Eve 1967, at a club in Sheffield, Elton met a young woman he immediately found fascinating. Linda Woodrow was the daughter of the owner of the Epicure pickle company. It is outrageous, and yet comically fitting, that Elton would fall madly in love with a pickle heiress. Not only did they briefly live together, but Elton also moved his inseparable companion, Bernie, in with them. As Elton explained, "It was a girl I met when I was in Sheffield one miserable Christmas doing cabaret with John Baldry. She was six-foot-tall and going out with a midget in Sheffield who drove around in a Mini with special pedals on. He used to beat her up! I felt so sorry for her, and she followed me up the next week to South Shields—this gets even more romantic folks—and I fell desperately in love and said, 'Come down to London and we'll find a flat.' Eventually we got a nice flat in this dismal area. It was a very stormy six months, after which I was on the verge of a nervous breakdown. I attempted suicide and various other things, during which Bernie and I wrote nil: absolutely nothing. I tried to commit suicide one day. It was a very Woody Allen-type suicide. I turned on the gas and left all the windows open."

Recalls Bernie, "He'd only turned the gas on to low, and he'd left the kitchen window open. And he'd even thought to take a cushion to rest his head on too."[45] It was Bernie who told Linda what happened. "I remember when I told Linda, and said, 'My God, he's tried to commit suicide!' And she said, 'Why he's wasted all the gas!'"[63]

This strange and completely crazy suicide attempt was just one of several desperate cries for "help" that Elton John would stage over the coming decades. He harbored a deep sense of insecurity combined with a sexual-identity crisis.

Elton's ill-fated love affair with Linda eventually became the basis for his 1975 Top Ten hit "Someone Saved My Life Tonight." As Elton explains of that famous song, "Some people think that's about me with my head in the gas oven, but it's actually about Long John Baldry, of all people, and, 'ahem,' my troublesome sexuality. I was living with Bernie in a flat in Islington and I had a girlfriend, as you do, who I was gonna get married to and have kids and the whole thing."[47]

How did Baldry save his life, and what was Elton's first affair with a woman like? Elton recalls, "It was just like six months in Hell. I got the flat, I bought all the furniture, the cake was made, it was three weeks away, Baldry was going to be best man, and in the end Baldry, we were out in…The Bag of Nails…Baldry was there, and one of The Supremes. One of The Supremes used to go out with the singer of Bluesology, how about that for a piece of gossip? Cindy Birdsong used to go out with our singer. Anyway, we're there at The Bag of Nails and Baldry is saying, 'You're mad, man, you're mad. You don't love her.' And, I was saying, 'I do. I do.'"[63]

As the liquor flowed, so did Baldry's insistence that Elton was making a stupid mistake even harboring the idea of marrying Linda. "He knew I was gay and told me I had to get used to it or else it would destroy my life," Elton recalls.[47]

Elton had to admit it was far from a match made in heaven. "She hated my music, hated everything about me, and I was completely dominated by her. It was like my father all over again. This was about a year after I first met Bernie, and we were living together in a flat in Islington. The thing that destroyed me was that she hated my music. Everything I'd write, she'd put down. Her favorite record was actually Buddy Greco singing 'The Lady is a Tramp.'"[27] Linda's hatred for Elton's music should have been a clue right from the start.

Thankfully, Long John Baldry sat him down and gave him the facts straight and to the point. "Oh, my dear, for God's sake, you're getting married?" Baldry demanded. "You love Bernie more than this girl. This is ridiculous. Put a stop to it now, Reggie. If you marry this girl you'll destroy two lives—hers and yours."[88] Elton knew it was a silly notion to begin with. He was no more in love with Linda than he was going to fly to the moon. It just seemed like a logical step to him, to marry someone stable.

It was Baldry who finally cut through all of the formalities, looked him in the eye, and told Elton that—whether he admitted it to himself or not—he was gay, and he would eventually have to deal with the fact. Elton recounts, "He was the first person to bring it home to me. I respected his opinion because he had no reason to tell me I was wrong, other than he really liked me. So, I went home at four o'clock in the morning and I told her the wedding was off." [29]

Linda was in shock to hear this. She even tried to tell Elton that she was pregnant in a final bid for them to stay together. Elton wouldn't hear of it. The following morning, "Derf" Farebrother came around to help Elton pack up all of his things and to move him back home. As he tells the story, "In the end, my Dad came with his Ford Cortina, and how he managed to cram all that stuff in there, I don't know." When they got back to the house, Sheila weighed in with her opinion as well. He claims, "My mother said, 'If you marry her, I'll never speak to you again!' Oh, it was amazing."[63]

Apparently, as a fiancé and a boyfriend, Elton wasn't exactly a Casanova when it came to lovemaking. In fact Linda found him to be uninspired and uninterested when it came to sex with her. She was later to state to the press, "Looking back, and when I'd had other boyfriends after Elton, I realized something was not right with that side of things. He was inexperienced and lost his virginity to me. But even allowing for that, he didn't show much interest in me sexually, and didn't pay me very much attention. We didn't have sex very often. But I just thought that was the way it was at the time. He never took me out for meals or treated me. He spent most of his money on clothes, records and drinking. He seemed to assume I'd pay for everything else."[88]

Although that was the last Elton was to see of Linda, he did hear from her lawyers. As he recalls, "I was sued for breach of promise and it was a horrible experience to go through. It was a fiasco!"[29]

One day he was engaged, and the next day he was back at the modest home of his parents, with Bernie once again in residence with him. That was the end of his affair with Linda Woodrow and the end of his personal involvements with women for several years.

Meanwhile, in an effort to do anything to earn extra money, Elton began to take odd jobs on the London recording scene. This included working with The Hollies and with Tom Jones. In 1969, Elton was the recording session piano player on The Hollies' recording of "He Ain't Heavy, He's My Brother." He recalls, "Back in the early days I supplemented my meager earnings from Dick James Music by playing on sessions—paid in cash! My specialty then was backing vocals—I'm on Tom Jones' 'Daughter of Darkness,' 'Back Home' by The England World Cup Squad and even some of the Barron Knights' stuff. Fucking hilarious they were. I worked on that 'Here Come the Olympics' spoof ['An Olympic Record'] they did at Abbey Road. In wanders McCartney—he was in Studio 2 and thought he'd pop in and see what the peasants were up to. Me and Bernie Taupin just froze and made some mumbling noises and he said a few things, then sat down and started to play the piano, told us it was the latest thing the band had finished and it was 'Hey Jude.' Blew my fucking head apart!"[47]

Another source of extra income came to Elton via his performances on several "cover" albums he recorded in 1968 and 1969. Budget record labels were in the habit of hiring "soundalike" singers to make "cover" versions of the latest Top Ten hits. They paid royalties to the song publishers for use of the music, and they paid flat fees to the "session singers" whose voices were heard on their albums. In that way, labels like K-Tel, Marble Arch, and even Top of the Pops could release albums comprised of nothing but nonstop hits. They weren't the real recording artists singing the hits, but they were a close facsimile and cost the consumer a fraction of the price of purchasing the original hits.

Several different labels, since the 1990s, have rereleased these newly discovered tracks under titles like *16 Legendary Covers From 1969/70 As Sung by Elton John*. The albums are fun time capsules and curiosities to hear, especially knowing that at the time of their original release, Elton wasn't even credited as the voice of some of the songs.

Among the most enjoyable songs that he did are the Elton John versions of Norman Greenbaum's "Spirit in the Sky," Bad Finger's "Come and Get It," The Four Tops' "It's All in the Game," Creedence Clearwater Revival's "Travelin' Band," Lou Christie's "She Sold Me Magic," and even Cat Stevens' "Lady D'Arbanville."

The recording sessions were done very quickly, and at the end of a day's work Elton left the recording studio with a check. Although those "cover" recordings added to Elton's personal income, finally in 1969 the push was on for him to concentrate on his recording career. He found that he had a really strong ally in Steve Brown, who worked for Dick James. He was the one who saw the potential in Elton and Bernie's writing and could envision a bright future for Elton as a recording artist. It was Steve who produced "Lady Samantha," and the tracks that were to become Elton's first album, *Empty Sky*.

The *Empty Sky* album was recorded in late 1968 and early 1969, in the eight-track demo studio of Dick James Music (DJM) with Steve Brown producing, Frank Owen as the recording engineer, and Clive Franks as the tape operator. The musicians included several recurring characters in the Elton camp: Caleb Quaye on guitar and congas, Tony Murray on the bass, Roger Pope doing drums and percussion, Don Fay on tenor saxophone and flute, and Graham Vickery playing harmonica. The drummer on "Lady What's Tomorrow" is the longest-running and widest-time-spanning Elton musician of all time, Nigel Olsson.

Quaye and Pope were members of the group Hookfoot, who were signed to DJM as recording artists. Murray had worked with the The Troggs, and Olsson was concurrently playing with The Spencer Davis Group.

Originally, the *Empty Sky* album was released in Great Britain only. It hit English record shops on June 3, 1969. It never made the album charts, and no singles were released from it. Intended more as a songwriter's demo, it became just that. With the exception of later appearing in "import" shops in the U.S., it wouldn't receive an American release until 1975, with completely different artwork on the cover.

The title track, "Empty Sky," provides the album's most rocking moment, although it really doesn't have much of a "hook" to make it as memorable as the songs that were to follow for Elton John and Bernie Taupin.

As an album, *Empty Sky* would have been a much stronger package if "Lady Samantha" had been included on it originally. The 1995 compact disc reissue of the *Empty Sky* album adds "Lady Samantha," as well as "All Across the Havens," "It's Me That You Need," and "Just Like Strange Rain."

"It's difficult to explain the amazement we felt as the album began to take shape," recalls Elton. "But I remember when we finished work on the title track—it just floored me, I thought it was the best thing I'd ever heard in my life."[97]

Elton has always had a fondness for *Empty Sky*, mainly because it represents the naïve and innocent point in his career in which it was recorded. According to him, "The title track rocks so much. The guitar sound is unlike anything I've heard since. We got it by putting Caleb Quaye out on the fire escape at the top of the studio with a microphone at the bottom to get that incredible echo. That's how things were done then, a wing and a prayer and a lot of invention."[47]

Though *Empty Sky* was originally a complete sales "bomb," it still shows off flashes of the many sides of Elton that were later to be developed and magnified. The songs have "zero" focus, and there are no "hooks" or catchy chorus lines to really distinguish them. Yet, there is a certain charm to Elton's singing style and keyboard work.

Elton admits that *Empty Sky* was very much an experimental album for them to get their feet wet in creating an album. From this point forward, each of Elton's successive albums had something of a theme running through them—whether that theme was dictated by the era, the musicians, or an artistic thread.

They say that artists create art so that it can live on and give them some sort of creative immortality. Elton totally bought into that way of thinking. In 1969 he told *Jackie* magazine, "I always wanted to be famous—the old ego bit. I never wanted to be a movie star, because in fifty years' time if you mention an old film star's name they'll just say, 'Who?' But they'll still be playing Gershwin."[135]

In spite of the sales failure of his first album, others were responding to Elton and Bernie's songwriting skills. It was the multi-million-selling rock group Three Dog Night who were first responsible for exposing American and international audiences to the duo's music.

Three Dog Night's self-titled debut album was released in 1968, and the group became an instant success with the Top Ten song "One [Is the Loneliest Number]" which was written by Harry Nilsson. A seven-man unit, Three Dog Night was comprised of lead singers Danny Hutton, Cory Wells, and Chuck Negron, and a band of four made up of Jimmy Greenspoon (keyboards), Floyd Sneed (drums), Mike Allsup (guitar), and Joe Schermie (bass). There was something of a competition between the three lead singers to find great songs for the band to sing. Much of Three Dog Night's success came from their work with the cream of the era's up-and-coming songwriters, including Laura Nyro, Dave Mason, Randy Newman, Neil Young, Steve Winwood, Joni Mitchell, Billy Preston, Hoyt Axton, and Paul Williams. Elton John and Bernie Taupin were another of their discoveries.

From 1969 to 1974, Three Dog Night placed 12 consecutive albums in the Top 20, all of them certified Gold, and created Number One hits such as "Mama Told Me Not To Come," "Joy to the World," and "Black & White." The first *Three Dog Night* album was such a huge success that the band had to quickly scramble to find some great new songs for their second album, which was ultimately titled *Suitable for Framing*.

In the early part of 1969, Three Dog Night came to England, and Danny Hutton met with aspiring songwriter Elton John. "We went to England in '69 to tour," recalls Danny. "We just did little clubs basically, little venues touring behind 'One'—our first tour over there. So I phoned up Dick James Music and said I was looking for songs. They sent over Reggie Dwight up to my place. I got along great with him. He played me a song called 'Bad Side of the Moon.' I still have the demo. It had someone else's name on it, but it was crossed out. Not Cliff Richard, but Cliff somebody."[101]

Jimmy Greenspoon, the keyboard player for Three Dog Night, recalls, "The first time I remember seeing Elton and Bernie was when they showed up at one of our showcase performances in London, peddling their songs, and we thought, 'Who the hell are you guys?' I'm not sure what club we were doing. It was either The Speakeasy or The Roundhouse, but we were doing our first-ever Three Dog Night junket tour over there. We left the hotel, and we went down to the club. I remember standing around outside, waiting for them to let us in the back door, and these two guys showed up and said, 'Hey, we heard about you guys, and we're songwriters…' And we thought to ourselves, 'Yeah, right…sure.' Then one of the guys said to us, 'Hi, my name is Reggie, and this is my friend, Bernie. He writes the lyrics and I write the music.' We said, 'Hey that's cool.' So then Danny said to them, 'Hey just be cool, and pretend you are with us. You can pose as "roadies."' So we handed them something to carry, and they came into the gig and had a drink, and watched the show for free."[210]

According to Greenspoon, "After the gig that night we went over to Dick James Music. They opened up the offices at night so we could listen to some of their music. There was Danny, and myself, and our 'handler,' Steve Barnett. He worked for Lillian and Jerry Bron from The Bron Agency. I remember—at that point being quite drunk—and listening to songs that they had written. It was basically everything that was going to be on Elton's very first American album [*Elton John*]. I remember that the very first songs that we really glommed onto and put a 'hold' on, were –of course— 'Your Song,' 'Border Song,' and 'Take Me to the Pilot.' Actually, we never did 'Border Song.' We recorded 'Your Song,' on our third album. We did go into the studio and put a track down for 'Take Me to the Pilot,' but it is 'in-the-can' somewhere and remains one of those unreleased Three Dog Night rarities."[210]

Danny loved Elton and Bernie's songs, and he very quickly became friends with them. Although it was Danny's first year of rock & roll fame, in Elton's eyes Hutton was a big American rock star. Hutton recalls of 22-year-old Elton, whom everyone still referred to as Reggie: "He was just a really sweet guy. Then we were playing at The Revolution, a really small club in London, and I invited him to the show. You could see everybody in the audience from the stage, and I didn't see him during the show. The bouncer came up to me afterwards and said, 'Oh there's a guy named Reggie, and he's here to see you, but he wasn't on the guest list, so I didn't let him in.' So, I went downstairs, and they had a little pub and restaurant down there. And, he was there with Bernie, and he was great. I really apologized. He was sitting there and music was playing, and he was kind of singing along with it. I said to him, 'You have a great voice.' He said, 'Ahhh! I'm a writer, I'm not a performer.'"[101]

Danny laughingly recalls, "Then we had a gig at The Marquee Club, a famous place where The Stones had played, and these other great bands. We weren't really big enough to have a big guest list, so we snuck Elton in with us as a 'roadie.' So, technically, Elton was a 'roadie' for Three Dog Night!"[101]

When Three Dog Night got back to the United States, Elton kept in touch with Danny. "Then he sent me a bunch of letters and he sent me demos, and 'Lady Samantha' was one of them," Hutton remembers.[101]

When Danny heard "Lady Samantha," he knew that it could become a hit record. He also thought that it was an ideal song for him to sing. "I was bugged when we got 'Lady Samantha,' Hutton recalls. "I brought it in, and then Gabriel Meckler, our first producer…he said, 'Well, you all should try singing it, and then I'll pick the lead singer. So he picked Chuck. And, Chuck's voice was not really the right voice—I don't think—for the song. But, who am I to say? I felt a little territorial too, because I had found the song. Later on it wasn't like that: we'd go in the studio and say: 'That's my song! I found it! It's mine!' We were a little more open and liberal about it then."[101]

When *Suitable for Framing* was released in July of 1969, it included "Lady Samantha," hit Number 16 in America, produced two Top Ten hits—"Easy to Be Hard" and "Eli's Coming"—and sold a million copies. Although Elton and Bernie's song was not a single on its own, over a million people in America were listening to it. The Three Dog Night version of "Lady Samantha" has the distinction of being the first Elton John/Bernie Taupin song to be released in the United States, perfectly setting the stage for 1970—the year that Elton John became an overnight star in America, and subsequently the world.

CHAPTER FIVE

Your Song

The year 1969 was an era of major regrouping, plotting, planning, and activity for Elton John and Bernie Taupin. They continued to write songs and did everything they could to sell their songs and compositions to anyone who would listen. Encouraged by the experience that they gained from recording the *Empty Sky* LP, they were already plotting their next album, which they intended to make bigger, better, and more accessible to radio programmers and the public.

Placing "Lady Samantha" on Three Dog Night's *Suitable for Framing* album was a real coup for Elton and Bernie. When the album became a big hit in America, a series of nice royalty checks arrived for the songwriting duo. Elton was blown away over the fact that they had finally gotten one of their songs on a hit album. According to Danny Hutton, "I have a three page letter from him thanking us as a group, so much, for paying he and Bernie's rent!" [101]

That was such a success for Elton that he immediately mailed off another package of John/Taupin demo recordings to Danny for consideration on the next Three Dog Night album. "He sent me a whole stack of them," Hutton recalls, "and it was basically *Tumbleweed Connection*, which I didn't know. He sent me 'Your Song,' and all that." [101]

Three Dog Night was so hot at that point that their record company very quickly recorded and released an in-concert album entitled *Three Dog Night: Captured Live at the Forum*. It hit Number Six on the American charts and was certified Gold. The group was already working on their next studio album, *It Ain't Easy*, and they recorded another one of Elton and Bernie's compositions, the ballad "Your Song." Danny loved the song the minute he heard it. *It Ain't Easy* was released in March 1970. The first single off of it, "Mama Told Me Not to Come," hit Number One in America, and the album was certified Gold, peaking at Number Eight on the album charts. It was the second recording by

Elton and Bernie to be released in the U.S. Again, they were due a sizeable amount of money for their songwriting skills.

Meanwhile in mid-1969, back in London, Elton and Bernie were doing all that they could to make ends meet. In addition to trying to sell their tunes to American rock groups, and Elton lending his voice to the "soundalike" albums, Elton took a job as a sales clerk at Musicland record store on Berwick Street in Soho. He was paid a small salary, and he received discounts on his record purchases. Another way Bernie and Elton tried to make extra cash was by selling their tunes for television commercial jingles, film music, and radio advertisements. There was a company called Essex Music, run by David Platz. Essex Music purchased songs from aspiring writers and paid them an up-front fee.

Elton John was one of the dozens of songwriters who went to the offices of Essex Music to meet with David Platz. Another up-and-coming songwriter he would run into there was David Jones, whom the world would soon come to know as "David Bowie."

From 1969 to 1970, the careers of Elton John and David Bowie would intersect at several points. Of these several common denominators, music publisher David Platz and competing record producers Tony Visconti and Gus Dudgeon would prove to be amongst the most significant ones.

In 1969 David Bowie met Angela Barnett, and they became an inseparable duo. They were to be married on March 20, 1970. During their highly publicized six-year marriage, David and Angela Bowie became known as rock & roll's "cutting edge" married couple, fashioning their union into the most talked about bi-sexual "open marriage" of the new decade.

On a couple of occasions, Angela Barnett and David Jones ran into Reg Dwight. As Angela explains, "Essex Music and David Platz: they were on Wardour Street, I think, about a block and a half from the turning where you went into the Mews for Trident. They were pretty much around the corner. Trident was tiny. It was a little itty bitty studio, and they did demos there. What David Platz would do, to encourage songwriters—i.e. David Jones, and Reg Dwight—was to pay them on the spot. They would go in and sell him a tune. Sometimes, I guess he didn't have money, or couldn't afford to support them. Every time I would go in with David, which was only three or four times, Platz would give David money for the rights to publish one of his songs. Maybe Platz was looking for music for a movie or a commercial or something that he was thinking this might work for. It wasn't necessarily sung, but sometimes it was just a song, a jingle or something."[100]

Angela fondly remembers the colorful neighborhood that she and Bowie and Elton would frequent, where all of London's music publishers had offices. It was the London equivalent of New York City's famed Tin Pan Alley. "If you walked out on Wardour Street, it wasn't full of junkies, like it was in the '80s or the '90s. It was full of music people. Around the corner was Carnaby Street. You could whip down Carnaby Street and pick up a few little fucking bargains—little fashion bargains."[100]

It was during one of these visits to Essex Music that Angela met Reginald Dwight. Anyone who has ever met Angela Bowie will instantly be impressed to find that there are two sides to her: shy and observant when she wants to be, or gregarious, animated, and outspoken. She found little trouble striking up a conversation with Reggie. Of their first meeting she recalls, "Now Reg, I started talking to him in the waiting room, waiting for David, while he was in talking to David Platz, the door would be open. There was nothing weird going on. Platz would say, 'Yeah, I can get you some money.' It wasn't cash, it wasn't nefarious. An accountant would come toddling along with a check for £50, and you would go down the stairs to the bank, and instantly they would have money. It was the perfect set-up for struggling songwriters."[100]

What did Angela think of Reggie Dwight? "Oh, he was fun to draw out. He was pretty quiet, but when you drew him out, he was witty and friendly. He was one of those people, who, under their breath they would say really funny things. And you say, 'What was that?' And they would say it, and you realized that they were as smart as a whip, and very fabulous. I guess it was because he was gay, that he wasn't trying to seduce me. He was just naturally being funny, and I liked him and warmed to him."[100]

Angela also recalls conversations that took place between David Bowie and Elton John while they were all together at the offices of Essex Music: "They would talk about doing shows, or, 'Are you doing any gigs?' 'Yeah, well come on and see the show.'"[100]

Interestingly enough, it was in 1969 that Bowie and Elton were on the verge of releasing the singular hit songs that were destined to launch both of their careers. In the case of David Bowie, it was the futuristic sound of "Space Oddity." With regard to Elton John, it was the introspective "Your Song."

Not long after he had met Angela, on June 20, 1969, David Bowie went into the aforementioned Trident Studio and recorded "Space Oddity." Like Elton, Bowie had already recorded and released a solo debut album, which also received modest airplay and sales. When it came time for him to do "Space Oddity," he presented the song to his usual music producer, Tony Visconti. Much to his surprise, classically trained Visconti turned his nose up at the song. Instead of Visconti, a producer by the name of Gus Dudgeon was enlisted for the project, a former music engineer, who was to be instrumental in Elton's career as well.

Throughout that year, Elton continued to take odd jobs for extra money. In June of 1969 Elton went into Olympic recording studio in London and recorded a song written by Francis Lai and Hal Sharper, entitled "From Denver to L.A." It was intended for use in a forthcoming film called *The Games*. Although it was briefly released as a single the following year on Viking Records, it quickly disappeared into obscurity.

During this era he also played piano for the television appearance of singer Lou Christie, during his BBC 2 guest spot on the television program *Disco Two*. Television audiences never saw Elton's face; they just saw his back and heard his keyboard work.

In a 1969 issue of *Jackie* magazine, the first feature article on Elton appeared. In it the writer claimed, "Reg is sad and serious-looking, with a sandy moustache and long hair, but in fact he seems cheerful and amusing and gets really enthusiastic about things that interest him. He says he can be unbearably moody and self-pitying, but usually manages to laugh himself out of it."[135] From this era forward, and throughout his career, Elton's self-pitying moods and obnoxious tantrums would often mar—if not eclipse—some of the most significant moments in his life.

While Taupin enjoyed going out for drinks and partying, Elton developed a love of shopping. According to him, "Bernie's a great lover of going out for a drink. I'm not, but I go with him sometimes. We go to the pictures quite a lot, but usually it's a load of rubbish. I like buying clothes."[135] Even at this phase of his life, when his income was small, Elton was clearly born to shop.

Although the *Empty Sky* album wasn't a big hit in any sense of the word, what truly makes it significant is the fact that it was responsible for demonstrating to everyone involved that they were truly "onto something big." Elton's pure performing style and great piano playing teamed beautifully with the engaging songs that he and Bernie were writing at the time. And, while singing on the soundalike budget "hits," didn't make him much money, they helped to build his confidence as a singer in the recording studio. He was coming up with vocals every bit as fiery and impassioned as the original hits.

Dick James himself was impressed enough to put up the money needed to record a follow-up album, which had to take the formula for *Empty Sky* and aurally improve its sound and appeal in every direction. Elton had to assemble his own band for this album, which would enable him to tour and promote the music and ultimately sell copies of the album.

Elton was still showing signs of insecurity. Even he realized that he looked nothing like a rock star, and he was not 100 percent confident about his singing skills. When he looked at his reflection in the mirror, it was still awkward Reggie Dwight of Pinner who looked back at him. As he recalls, "We did the *Empty Sky* album. And we were told we would have to get a band together. And so to get some form of mini-following I had to form a band. Which was the last thing I wanted to do. The last thing I thought I was, was a singer. But they told me I was going to have to do it."[43]

For the time being, Elton had other things on his mind, namely coming up with material strong enough to record on his second album. Music fan that he was, he continued to immerse himself in the music that was making the charts. He would listen to new songs during his job at Musicland, he went to see other performers at local clubs, and he went to every concert he could. Elton saw American folk/rock legend Bob Dylan, who gave a concert on the Isle of Wight in August. In September, he attended a The Who performance in Croydon. Suddenly, new music began to pour out of Elton and Bernie. On Monday, October 27, 1969, Elton sat down at his piano and spent ten minutes composing the music for "Your Song," using a set of lyrics that Bernie Taupin wrote.

While the duo amassed songs for the new album, there was the matter of finding the right producer. Again, Elton John's career intersected David Bowie's. Between June of 1969 and when it came time to produce the Elton John album, Bowie's 'Space Oddity' had become a huge hit. Bowie had recorded it with producer Gus Dudgeon and Paul Buckmaster orchestrating the music. Since the songs that Bernie and Reggie were composing for the new album all tended to be dramatic ballads, the pair figured that they needed someone like Buckmaster directing a full orchestra. They approached him and instantly agreed that they needed him to make certain that this new album was both dynamic and moving. With him in place, they continued to search for the right producer. At first they overlooked Gus Dudgeon, thinking that they needed someone like George Martin—the producer of The Beatles—to assure instant success.

When George Martin didn't work out, thanks to Buckmaster, they revisited the idea of approaching Gus. Elton explains, "We'd heard 'Space Oddity,' which for me was one of the best records of all time and learned that it was produced by Gus Dudgeon, and we knew that we had to get him to produce the second album."[43]

The band that Elton assembled was made up of several of his friends and acquaintances from the music business: Caleb Quaye on guitar, Roger Pope playing drums, and David Glover on bass. In fact, the core band was the group Hookfoot, who were also signed to DJM (Dick James Music). The background vocals included the singing of Tony Burroughs of the group Edison Lighthouse ["Love Grows (Where My Rosemary Goes)"], singer/songwriter Sandy Denny, and the dynamic Madeline Bell of the group Blue Mink. Diana Lewis played the Moog synthesizer on "First Episode at Heinton" and "The Cage." Several other session musicians contributed their talents to the album as well. Gus was the producer, Paul Buckmaster was the musical arranger, Robin Geoffrey Cable was the engineer, and Steve Brown was given the title of "project coordinator."

Gus Dudgeon later proudly recalled, "That first album was planned down to the tiniest detail. Every string note, every drum break, we practically wrote everything down on paper longhand, 'cello comes in here.' That week that we made that album was probably the most exciting week ever, it was just extraordinary for me and I'll be very happy if that ever happens again. I just don't think those sort of things happen very often. There were quite a few people around the studio, only a few of whom Elton actually knew like Caleb Quaye…. Quite a few of those tracks had been laid down live, for instance 'Your Song,' with the exception of the vocal. And when he walked in and saw that orchestra waiting to play his song, he lost about five pounds in five minutes."[30]

The *Elton John* album was the big "make-it"-or-"break-it" project for Reggie and Bernie. It simply had to be a hit, and it had to at least earn back Dick James' initial investment. Elton was to look back on this experience and proclaim, "[It was] the first big budget album I was allowed to make. We're talking about a budget of £7,000—you could get a semi in Pinner for that. I had the very best—Trident Studios, an arranger, Gus Dudgeon, an orchestra. We were going to get George Martin but we already had Paul Buckmaster, a genius who did the strings on 'Space Oddity.' Most of the cash went on the orchestra actually—we had to record three songs per session because they cost so much. Absolutely fucking terrifying! 'I Need You to Turn To' was a really nervous moment. I was playing the harpsichord. While the harpsichord looks very similar to the pianoforte, there's a kind of delay to how its mechanism works so it's very easy to fuck it all up if you're not thinking ahead."[47]

When it came time to record "Border Song," there weren't enough lyrics to get a whole song out of what Bernie had written. Since Bernie wasn't handy, Elton took up his pen and wrote another verse to it. According to Elton, "Lyrically, I wrote the last verse of 'Border Song,' because it was only two verses long, and we thought it really needed another verse. That's why the last verse is very mundane."[63]

Elton found that recording this album was quite a stressful experience. It was true "trial by fire" for him. When he looked up from his piano and saw a group of professional violin players looking at him for a cue, he nearly freaked out. Here he was, 22-year-old Reggie Dwight, school dropout, record collector, and aspiring composer, having his own string section staring at him to see how and what he was going to perform. As he recalls, "Basically, the *Elton John* album was done live—playing with the orchestra.

Just the vocals were overdubbed. I was shitting. There I was, with all these string players who could really read music, and I thought, 'If I make a mistake….' It was a real nightmare week, but it all worked out."[55] Fortunately, the fear galvanized his musical talents, and he delivered performances that impressed everyone present.

How does one turn a rather "geeky" guy from the suburbs into a rock star? First it takes some masterful music, and second it takes an exciting and sexy image to sell it to the public. Still taken to wearing his "Buddy Holly" style eyeglasses, Elton was anything but sexy. He was barely out of his teenage years, and he was already visibly losing his hair. Although he had recently lost a bit of weight, he was still kind of pudgy in the body, and his face was rather plain. To add excitement to his visual appearance, he had taken to wearing progressively louder and more colorful clothes like bright red pants, colorful scarves, and other outlandish things he found in the shops on Carnaby Street.

Nevertheless, Elton's physical look still presented a bit of a challenge when it came to photographing him for the cover of his second album. For the cover of *Empty Sky*, a slightly cheap-looking artist's sketch of him graced the 1969 British release. However, for the *Elton John* album, it was necessary to present the man behind the music in as appealing and sexy a fashion as they could achieve.

The task of coming up with the right photos to sell the album fell upon photographer Stowell Stanford and art director David Larkham. Interestingly enough, the look of the *Elton John* album is oddly similar to the artwork of another popular album of the day: Three Dog Night's *Suitable for Framing*. Since *Suitable for Framing* was the biggest-selling album Elton had ever appeared on—as a songwriter or anything—why not copy the look of it? On the cover of *Suitable for Framing*, Danny Hutton, Cory Wells, and Chuck Negron are dressed in black collarless shirts, against a dark grey background. On the front of *Elton John*, the singer is dressed in black, against a black background, in shadow, with only a sliver of his face showing.

Stuart Epps was Steve Brown's assistant at DJM at the time. He recalls of the *Elton John* cover shot, "Elton wasn't particularly attractive at the time. When we went through the photos, they were all terrible, to be honest. On one photo you could hardly see him because it was so dark, so that was the one we used."[88]

With its Three Dog Night–styled front and back cover, its simple and touching Bernie-written and Bob Dylan–flavored lyrics, its Royal Academy of Music–trained compositions, its John Baldry–like touch of the blues, its occasional flashes of Patti LaBelle and The Bluebelles–influenced R&B ballad singing, and sharing the arranger and producer of David Bowie's "Space Oddity," this album became the synthesis of everything Elton had gone through in the music business in the 1960s. In the spring of 1970, DJM records released the British version of the *Elton John* album. An album's ultimate test is its ability to stand up on its own and emotionally touch or inspire the listener. The bottom line was the music contained on this album, and, happily for everyone, it stood up on its own.

One of the things that the *Elton John* album had going for it was the unifying sound quality due to Buckmaster and Dudgeon. The second aspect to fall perfectly into place was the confidence level of Elton's singing. This was his big chance to become a success in the music business. Since he was forced to record most of the album "live" in the studio, in front of the eyes and ears of several professional musicians and technicians, he was really on the line to deliver the goods. Whether or not he actually understood all of Bernie Taupin's lyrics or not, he made the listener believe he did.

Comprised of ten tracks, the *Elton John* album carried three of the true signature songs of Elton's career: "Your Song," "Take Me to the Pilot," and "Border Song." This makes it one of the most beloved and best-selling albums of his career. Opening with the touchingly personal "Your Song," Elton's heartfelt delivery has the listener's attention at the first line: "It's a little bit funny…" The song sets the somber, heartfelt, and evocative tone of the entire album.

The next song, "I Need You to Turn To" is one of the most beautiful confessions of love Bernie and Elton have ever written. The touching, harpsichord-driven song seems quite clearly to be a song about Elton's love for Bernie. Sung from Bernie's side of the story, it states to someone—very possibly Elton here—that the love is felt, but laments that it is a love that can never be, no matter how many late nights they spend together.

It was years before Bernie publicly admitted that Elton had a mad crush on him and would gladly have been his lover. Taupin never took the offer seriously, instead opting for platonic friendship with Elton. According to Bernie, "He made his affections known. When I started laughing, it sort of broke the ice…he got over it very quickly."[102] Elton was and always has been Bernie's guardian angel, and Taupin needed Reggie to turn to for shelter, friendship, and love.

The other highlights of the *Elton John* album include "Sixty Years On," which is essentially Bernie and Elton's take on The Beatles' "When I'm Sixty-Four." Here the singer wonders where he will be when he is 60 years old. Little did Elton know at the time, but he would be at Madison Square Garden in New York City on the day he turned 60, singing "Your Song" and "Sixty Years On."

"Border Song" is a brilliant mood-changing number, which shows off an impassioned, gospel-flavored mode of singing. It was so soulful in fact, that later that year—The Queen of Soul—Aretha Franklin found it inspiring enough to do a "cover" version on her *Young, Gifted and Black* album. Her 1970 single of "Border Song" made it to Number Five on the American R&B charts later that year, which made it the most successful John/Taupin song of the time.

A fanciful, engaging, and thought-provoking album, *Elton John* was destined to catapult both Elton and Bernie into the forefront of the rock and pop world.

On March 25, 1970, Elton turned 23 years old. It was the year that he finally found himself, in more ways than one. Early that year Elton met a man who was going to greatly help him with his career. John Reid, like Elton, was young and deeply involved in the music business. In 1970, at the age of 19, John Reid became the Manager of the British division of Detroit-based Motown Records, which in Europe was known as Tamla/Motown and was sublicensed to EMI Records. Even though he was just a teenager from Scotland, Reid was bright, innovative, and a real go-getter when it came to his career. One of the first things he did in his new job at Tamla/Motown was to sift through the label's releases to find potential radio hits that were never properly exploited. When he discovered a track on a 1967 Smokey Robinson & The Miracles album that had been overlooked, Reid prepared the song as a British single and instantly took "Tears of a Clown" to Number One. The American Motown office had no other recourse but to release it on the other side of the Atlantic, where it also hit the top of the charts. After that, the British office of Tamla/Motown instantly listened to Reid's suggestions.

Motown Records had been one of the prime hit-making forces of the 1960s, not only in America, but globally as well. Berry Gordy Jr., the president of Motown Records, had taken a dream and turned it into a hit-making machine. It wasn't long before up-and-coming singers like The Four Tops, The Supremes, Martha Reeves and The Vandellas, Marvin Gaye, Smokey Robinson and The Miracles, The Temptations, Stevie Wonder, The Marvelettes, and The Jackson Five were household names. It was this glamorous roster that Reid was suddenly in charge of in England.

John Reid was born on September 9, 1949, at Barstow Hospital, in Paisley, Scotland. The town of Paisley, which is located just west of Glasgow, is known for its textile mills and for being the home of the famed fabric design, also known as a "paisley print." Not surprisingly, John's father and mother lived at 1 Thread Street, and John Sr. worked as a thread reeler at one of the several mills that are located there.

In 1959, some of the mills moved their operation to New Zealand, and the Reid family moved there for two years. Young John was an enterprising lad, and, at the age of 11, he realized that by collecting old newspapers he could sell them to a local greengrocer for a nice profit. The greengrocers would then use the papers to wrap up their produce. Such moxie and business sense were to serve him well later in life, when he began making business decisions for some of the biggest stars in the entertainment business.

After his mother grew homesick, the Reid family moved back to Scotland and into a small house which was located in Gallowhill. John's father took a job on the assembly line of a Chrysler automotive plant in Linwood. In 1964, when all of Britain, and the rest of the world, were going mad for The Beatles and rock & roll music, John too came to fancy going to concerts and cafes featuring music. John also was a boy who was not unaccustomed to schoolyard brawls, and he learned to "hold his own" with his fists, if he needed to defend himself.

A friend told John Reid that he was both aggressive enough and interested enough in music to make a go at becoming a "music plugger" for one of the London music publishers. Reid instantly loved that idea and left Scotland for London. He supported himself for several weeks working in the shirt department of Austin Reed before landing a job with Ardmore and Beechwood, a small publishing branch of EMI Records located on Oxford Street above the HMV record shop.

In a matter of weeks, 17-year-old John Reid went from selling shirts in Knightsbridge to selling songs to singers. One of his first challenges in this new job was convincing singers to record the songs of an aspiring American songwriter by the name of Neil Diamond. At the time, Neil was mainly known as the composer of The Monkees' biggest hit, "I'm a Believer."

In 1969, a job became available at one of EMI's subsidiaries: Tamla/Motown. John applied for the job. Another applicant was a young man by the name of David Crocker. At the time, Crocker worked for a local record store called One Stop. One of Crocker's biggest customers was a chubby local lad by the name of Reggie Dwight.

Although neither Crocker nor Reid immediately landed the job at Tamla/Motown, in 1970 the same job once again opened up. This time 19-year-old Reid was given the position. Meanwhile, Crocker obtained a post at Harvest Records, which was also based within the offices of EMI. Suddenly John Reid found himself helping to successfully launch the 1970s edition of The Supremes (Mary Wilson, Jean Terrell, and Cindy Birdsong), meeting Stevie Wonder at the airport, and promoting The Four Tops.

According to Reid, "All the Motown artists loved the U.K. It gave them a longer career than they would otherwise have had. It was their second home: easy to visit for two or three weeks, to promote the records and make money from gigs. In 1970, Stevie Wonder and The Temptations came to London and cut *Live at The Talk of the Town* albums. Jimmy Ruffin used to live in an apartment on Curson Street; we could never get rid of him. We had three Top Ten hits in one year with Jimmy—more than he had at home. I lent money to Martha & The Vandellas to get their 'uniforms' out of the cleaners; they were always broke. But everyone had real team spirit."[103]

Since Elton was often in the area, it wasn't long before his path crossed that of John Reid. "I had a corner office on the first floor of Manchester Square, to go with the annual salary of £1,650," Reid recalled. "That was bloody good. I was three or four years younger than the other label managers, apart from David Crocker, who had the office next to mine, running Harvest Records. One day, David came in and said, 'This is my friend Reg.' That's how I met Elton. He scrounged some Motown American singles. I can't remember what. He said, 'I made a record,' and gave me a white label [test pressing] of what became the *Elton John* album."[103] Little did Elton know at the time, but John Reid was going to become one of the most significant men in his life, both on a professional and a personal basis.

In March 1970, the initial recording contract that Elton had with Dick James Music was scrapped, and he signed a new agreement. The terms of it called for Elton to record two complete albums—or six album sides worth of music—per year for the next five years. This would provide enough tracks for albums, singles, and "B" sides. At first this seemed like a dream come true for Elton and Bernie, since they had so many songs stockpiled. In fact, there were already enough songs written for his third album, which would ultimately be entitled *Tumbleweed Connection*.

When songs were reviewed for inclusion on the *Elton John* album, Elton and Bernie decided, together with Dick James and Gus Dudgeon, which ones were right for that particular record. The deeply personal ones all went on *Elton John*. Bernie's odes to the Wild West and songs about 1880s pioneers, cowboys, guns, and Americana were saved for *Tumbleweed Connection*. It proved a wise move, as it gave both of those albums a unifying theme and a different sound that set them apart. Recording the first song for *Tumbleweed Connection* took place in March of 1970 at Trident Studios, again with Gus Dudgeon at the helm as producer.

When DJM released the British version of the *Elton John* album on April 10, 1970, it made very little noise. According to Elton, "It sold about 4,000 [copies] and never appeared on the charts. And we had to sit down and say, 'Why?' We came to the conclusion that I would have to go out on the road with a band and promote the record—which I'd fought against tooth and nail for a long time. And I suddenly just decided that was the only answer."[55]

Clearly, what he needed most was a performing band. At first he kept it simple, just his piano playing and two additional instruments. Elton began to go through a list of his musician acquaintances. He recalls, "Nigel Olsson was the drummer with Plastic Penny, and I got him; and Dee Murray, the bass-player, was in a group called The Mirage. So we formed a trio and started doing gigs."[43]

In England, they played fifteen dates including the Krumlin Festival, a couple of Implosions, Leeds University, Mothers, and The Speakeasy. Each time Elton got onstage with Dee and Nigel, his confidence as a performer grew. It was the beginning of a long working relationship with Olsson and Murray.

In April 1970, the middle of the tour, the song "From Denver to L.A.," was released as a single in the United States on the Viking record label. "Actually, that record was withdrawn so if you've got a copy it's worth a small fortune," Elton explains. "It was a 25-quid session I did at Olympic Studios and I just sang this song and it was for the Michael Winner movie *The Games*. And that's it. When the film was released…they thought 'Ahh ha!' and rushed it out but we quickly put an injunction on it and stopped it."[26] DJM certainly wasn't going to let that session track ruin their chances of signing Elton to a major American record company.

As the saying goes, "timing is everything." This was especially true in the case of "breaking" Elton John and his music out in the U.S. market. Fortunately for Elton, American record labels were actively looking for new talent to develop and promote. That year there was a whole raft of new performers and composers on the charts—especially in the United States. Leon Russell, James Taylor, Eric Clapton, Stephen Stills, John Sebastian, and even Paul McCartney all released debut solo albums during 1970. In addition, there was suddenly a huge showcase anxiously awaiting them on the FM radio dials. These radio stations were looking for the kind of introspective, thought provoking, and deeply personal songwriting that Elton and Bernie had so carefully crafted for the *Elton John* album. It became evident that a whole new market awaited the singer and his songs in the United States.

After the original tracks for the *Elton John* album were "in the can," there were talks between Dick James Music and several American record labels. One of the U.S. record company executives contacted was Russ Regan at UNI Records, a division of MCA Records. That was in January of 1970.

Russ Regan recalled his initial conversation with Len Hodes, a representative from DJM. According to Regan, Hodes said to him, "I'll tell you what: If you really like this artist, we're so convinced he's got something that if you really, truthfully feel you can do something with him, we'll give him to you for nothing."[16] This was a deal that was hard for Regan to refuse.

This breakfast meeting took place at the Continental Hyatt House Hotel on Sunset Boulevard in Los Angeles. After Hodes made his pitch to Regan, Regan was presented with a copy of the *Empty Sky* album and Elton's original version of the single "Lady Samantha."

After the meeting, Regan went back to his office and set aside the Elton recordings. He was later to recall, "I just put them off on a shelf somewhere until about five o'clock that afternoon. Then I played the album and found that I really liked Elton as an artist and especially liked the song 'Skyline Pigeon' from the *Empty Sky* album. It was six o'clock by then and I realized, 'My God, they're out shopping this artist. What if he's called some other record company?'"[105]

What he needed to hear now was the new about-to-be-released second album, so he contacted DJM, and they sent him one immediately. Says Regan, "Then I got the *Elton John* album in one day from England. That album totally knocked my lights out. It was such a powerful new thing to find an artist and an album like that."[105]

He instantly knew he was listening to a hit album. According to Regan, "I'd been in the record business 12 years at that time, and I was never more overpowered with an album than I was by that first Elton John album.... The songs were just unbelievable. I shut the office down, shut the phones off, called everybody in, and the entire company listened to the album twice. Everybody was just freaked out by that time, because we knew we had something."[16]

DJM realized that they didn't have an instant to wait. They sensed that releasing *Elton John* in America was the perfect way to recoup their investment and launch Elton's career. When Regan outlined UNI Records' plans to DJM, he was told, "'Just give me your "Russ Regan promise" that you'll put some money behind the kid. We don't want anything in front.' I said 'You've got to be kidding!?!' So frankly, man, I got Elton John for nothing, which is probably one of the best deals ever made."[16]

The first single off of the *Elton John* album, "Border Song," was released therefore on both sides of the Atlantic. In England it came out on DJM Records; in America it was on a division of MCA called Congress Records. The U.S. version briefly made an appearance in *Billboard* magazine, but only made it to Number 93. Although "Border Song" didn't become an instant hit, at least it was a start on the American charts. In England, the single never charted at all, but it did receive some airplay and garnered Elton a guest appearance spot on the television show *Top of the Pops*.

While taping *Top of the Pops*, Elton got one of the biggest thrills of his young life: he met his idol Dusty Springfield while backstage at the Television Centre studios. Dusty had been the pin-up girl of all of Elton's gay adolescent dreams. The walls of his room as a teenager had been covered with her pictures. There she was in the flesh! At the time she had just released her *Brand New Me* album for Atlantic Records, which was produced by Kenny Gamble and Leon Huff, the famed producers of "The Philadelphia Sound." Elton would later work with both of them.

The *Elton John* album officially hit the American record shops on July 22, 1970, with very little fanfare. Meanwhile, Russ Regan was busy working as Elton's biggest champion in America. With *Elton John*, he knew that he had a winning album and a potential superstar artist on his hands. Now all he needed was a gimmick, an event, or a "hook" to introduce his new discovery to the public. Since the lackluster *Empty Sky* was not available in America—except at import record shops—the *Elton John* album was presented to the public as the singer/songwriter's debut disc. "By the time we got it out I think it was July, and in July we had a sales meeting in New York. Everybody loved the album, the presentation, and that's when we planned the August opening of Elton John at The Troubadour," Regan recalls.[16]

Located near the intersection of Santa Monica Boulevard and Doheny since it opened in 1957, The Troubadour has been known in Los Angeles as the primo rock & roll nightclub for showcasing new talent. Late singer/songwriter Jim Croce once claimed, "The Troubadour was one of the most unique and respected places to play. There would be Cadillacs and Porsches parked outside, and inside it was one big wild party. People would be doing drugs and trying to get picked up, while young talent was being revealed onstage. There was no club that was more influential during the '60s and '70s for promoting new talent than The Troubadour. If you were lucky enough to get a gig there then you had a shot at getting discovered and getting signed to a recording contract."[106]

Joni Mitchell, James Taylor, and Kris Kristofferson all looked to The Troubadour to launch their careers. In 1969, Linda Ronstadt performed there with her band who later broke away to start their own group: The Eagles. Jackson Browne was another aspiring musician who first served as an opening act at The Troubadour.

The Troubador owner, Doug Weston, remembered his introduction to the music of Elton John. "We got his album in a group of others from a record company," he recalled. "They were looking for an anchor date on a proposed tour by this new artist, so I listened to about half the record and immediately got very, very excited. I then gave the go-ahead to book him into The Troubadour. There was no record play on him at the time, but we booked him in as a headliner nonetheless."[108]

Elton recalls, "The *Elton John* album was receiving a lot of attention on American radio, and I'd just been signed in America by MCA, so they told me it would be good to play The Troubadour. At one point, the idea had been for me to play The Troubadour with Jeff Beck; I'd met him in London and got along with him fantastically well. But Jeff's manager stepped in and said that because he was already so big in the States, I'd get ten percent and Jeff would get 90. He was telling my manager, Dick [James], that Jeff gets $10,000 a night in some places—and it'd take Elton six years to build up to that. So I'm sitting there, wanting, thinking, '$10,000 a night, wow!' And I hear Dick saying, 'Listen, I guarantee you this boy will be earning that much in six months!' And I say to myself, 'Dick, what a dippy old fart you are! You'd be picked immediately in a Cunt-of-the-Month competition! What a schmuck!' So the Jeff Beck thing fell through and I was sulking. But I ended up going to The Troubadour anyway—Dick paid half, MCA paid half and we came over."[55]

The fact that Elton was so skeptical about The Troubadour gig is actually quite amusing. He looked at it like it was just another tiny nightclub gig, which wouldn't amount to anything. He later told *Phonograph Record* magazine, "The reason I came over to play The Troubadour was because I wanted to go to a record shop. I didn't want to play at The Troubadour. I thought it was going to be a joke. I thought it was going to be a complete hype and I thought it was going to be a disaster, and I just really wanted to go to an American record store and buy some albums."[16] He was about to get much more than just a handful of new LPs for his growing record collection. He was going to leave England as chubby and geeky Reggie Dwight, and when he returned across the Atlantic Ocean, he was coming back an overnight star.

It was Norman Winter's task to make sure everyone in town knew that Elton John had arrived—whoever this "Elton John" character was. "UNI was a small company," explains Winter. "We decided that we had to throw everything we had at the artist, because we believed in the artist, and we didn't realize at the time that the artist himself would ultimately make himself a star or would gain great acceptance based on his appeal as a performer. We decided to do a lot of things that were very 'hypey' at the time, above and beyond the norm. We became so excited it became almost like an orgasm…. We treated him as if an Elvis Presley was opening in Vegas, even though nobody had ever heard of Elton John."[16]

Winter figured that he would do something "very British" to welcome the singer to the United States for the first time. And what could be more English than a big red double-decker bus with Elton's name plastered on the side of it?

When Elton and his band got off the airplane at LAX airport in Los Angeles, there awaited his chariot: the big red British double-decker bus. Elton was simultaneously surprised, horrified, and embarrassed. What was next: some English fish and chips for everyone?

The man behind the publicity stunt, Norman Winter, amusingly recalls, "I thought it would be a nicety to make him feel important, not as a hype to promote or exploit the album, but just to make him and entourage feel welcome. So we got this English bus, and then we thought, 'Well, shit, we might as well go a step farther,' so we put 'ELTON JOHN HAS ARRIVED' on the top. He was in the baggage area when he saw the thing and his eyeballs bugged out. He was very quiet, said 'very nice,' that type of thing. We all rode the bus to Hollywood. Later on he told me that he had expected to be greeted in a big Cadillac limousine."[16]

To get to Sunset Boulevard from Los Angeles Airport (LAX), one must drive up the incline to the Hollywood Hills. There were some doubts whether or not the big red double-decker "Elton" bus would even make it up the hill to their hotel. The hotel to stay in if you were a rock band was the Continental Hyatt House on Sunset. It had such a reputation among rock & rollers that "The Hyatt House" was commonly known as "The Riot House." Fittingly, that's exactly where Elton took up residence for his virgin American adventure.

Although Elton claimed that he was horrified by the sight of the big red bus with his name on it, he had to admit that there seemed to be an awareness of his arrival in town. "Actually, he's worked bloody hard," he said about Norman Winter's efforts. "They really have worked hard. Every store I've seen in Los Angeles has had a window display—that's probably bought, but they really tried, you know? But that bus. I found that extremely embarrassing. Everyone was sort of getting into a crouch and trying to hide below the windows. I don't know, it seemed like a cheap trick. I really couldn't believe it, I didn't think it was happening. I mean, I'm the lover of things that are done with taste…and double-decker busses don't qualify!"[62]

Elton had stayed in touch with Danny Hutton of Three Dog Night. When "Your Song" started getting radio airplay in America, no one was more surprised than Danny Hutton. Here he thought his group's version of the song from their current album was an exclusive. "He didn't tell me—that bugger—that he was releasing it himself," recalls Hutton. "I did not know that he had recorded it. It wasn't like he'd done an album, and we'd done it off his album. We did it off a demo."[101] Nevertheless, Hutton had plans to come to the opening night of Elton's weeklong run of concerts at The Troubadour. "I was really good friends with Doug Westin, and he had The Troubadour," recalls Hutton. "Elton came to Los Angeles. They set up this thing at The Troubadour. I had talked up Elton to Doug, and I think it helped get Elton the gig. He came into town a couple of days before the show—his first show—and that week really broke him at The Troubadour. That first night in town, I ended up with him at about 5:00 or 6:00 in the evening, and I took him to his first restaurant in L.A., called The Black Rabbit. Billy James is the guy who helped find Bob Dylan, and he worked for Columbia Records at the time, and just lived up the street. Anyway, he had this restaurant on Melrose Avenue called The Black Rabbit, and that was Elton's first night. Then he came up to my house, and that Three Dog Night album, *It Ain't Easy*, with the three of us on the cover, with the picture of Christ in the back of us and all that stuff—that's the piano Elton played on that night at my house. He sat there playing, and I phoned up Van Dyke Parks and said, 'You had better come over and check this "cat" out, Van Dyke.' So, Van Dyke came up, and I remember he sat on the floor next to the piano, and then Elton just sat there playing. It was just mind-blowing! That was when he told me, 'Danny, I can't sit and study, and spend days on a song.' He said, 'Bernie gives me a lyric, I put it up on the piano, and just let it all come out. It just comes out at that moment.' That's how he writes."[101]

"Then I took him to Brian Wilson's house," recalls Hutton.[101] As the acknowledged musical genius of The Beach Boys, Brian was also something of a drugged out eccentric. As Elton remembers, "When we hit L.A. [Danny Hutton] took us to meet Brian. I'm this kid from Pinner and Brian's driveway was lined with drum kits and I'm like, 'Uh oh, this is going to be very strange.' We knocked on the door and he says, 'Ah Elton, "I hope you don't mind, I hope you don't mind, I hope you don't mind"'—mimicking the lyric of 'Your Song.' It was very weird but very sweet."[47]

Hutton explains, "This was Brian's house that had been owned by Edgar Rice Burroughs, out in Bel Air. And Brian had painted the house purple. The neighborhood was just freaked out about that! He had this incredible real studio in the house—like a modern complete big-time studio…. So he brought us into the studio, and I said to Brian, 'Can you play "Good Vibrations" for Elton?' So, Brian got the engineer out of bed. I don't know where he lived, but he got up and drove over. Then we were just playing all of the little background parts which were incredible, that you never really hear in the finished product. I could tell that Elton was getting a little intimidated. So, I said to Elton, 'Play Brian some of your stuff.' I remember him playing 'Amoreena.' He started playing 'Amoreena,' and he got about a quarter of way through, or half way through it and Brian interrupted him. He didn't know Brian, and Brian's thing is like, he wants to hear something, then when he 'gets' it, he wants to move on. So Elton was in the middle of singing 'Amoreena,' and Brian says, 'That's good, what else you got?' I remember thinking, 'Oh, God, Elton is gonna think that Brian doesn't like his songs.' Then Elton played another one or two other songs, and each time, in the middle of it Brian said, 'That's good, what else?'"[101]

Elton later recalled, "Seven-thirty in the morning, as I was driving back to the Sunset Hyatt House from Laurel Canyon, going down the hill I was thinking, 'I've never stayed up 'til 7:30 in the morning in my life. I feel really good. I must be excited.' Years later, Danny told me that they'd put cocaine in my food."[184]

Elton, Bernie, Dee, and Nigel spent several days exploring California. It was during these days that Bernie met his first wife. Ray Williams, who had put Elton together with Bernie, was working as a management representative for Dick James Music. On this trip he was basically the road manager and tour manager. When he needed a hairdryer, he phoned an old girlfriend's sister, Janice. When Janice arrived with the hairdryer, she brought a friend, Maxine Fiebelman. When Bernie Taupin met Maxine, he was immediately attracted to her. Maxine became not only Bernie's first wife but also the touring seamstress for the band and the inspiration for Bernie's love song, "Tiny Dancer."

When Janice and Maxine offered to show the British lads Palm Springs, the luxurious desert resort town located two hours east of Los Angeles, Elton showed no interest in this journey and stayed alone in his hotel room. It wasn't long before his indifference turned to boredom, and boredom blossomed into frustration.

That evening, when the rest of the boys returned to the Hyatt House, Elton proceeded to have one of his first true "diva-like" meltdowns. He swore that he was fed up with this nonsense and that he was blowing off The Troubadour gig and going back to London. Ray Williams immediately sensed that Elton had "gone to the dark side" in his mind and did his best to reason with irritated

and irrational Elton. Williams was astonished to see that Elton—
who was not yet a star—was behaving like a spoiled child.

"You've got to do it, you can't spend all this money for
nothing," Ray argued.

"I don't give a fuck, I'm going!" Elton screamed. It was the
first in a career-long stream of "Reggie's Little Moments."

That night, depressed in his hotel room, Elton phoned
Dick James long distance to complain. James had to do his best to
calm him down and assure Elton that he just needed to rest up for
the upcoming gig at The Troubadour.

After much anticipation, on Tuesday, August 25, 1970, the
date of the first Elton John show at the 300-seat Troubadour finally
arrived. When the band pulled up in front of the West Hollywood
nightspot, an amazing sight met them. The marquee placed Elton
John as the headlining act with folk singer David Ackles as the
opening act. Elton and Bernie were big fans of Ackles' records over
in London. They considered Ackles to be the true star. However,
Ackles was virtually unknown in his native America. Seeing Ackles'
name below his added to Elton's opening night jitters. It was to be
just the first of many surprises that evening.

Although the songs and the look of the singer on the cover
of the *Elton John* album might have suggested that the performer
was a shy and slightly withdrawn character, Reggie Dwight was
determined to break out of his shell that fateful night. So that he
was not mistaken for a singing stock broker, he chose an outfit that
would grab West Hollywood's attention. There was an over-the-top
clothing store in London called Mr. Freedom and that's where Elton
went for his costume for the evening: hot pants, a pair of white
boots with green wings on them, and a tee shirt with the words
"Rock & Roll" emblazoned across the front of it.

One of the most mindblowing things that occurred that
evening was the all-star Hollywood audience that showed up to see
him perform. First of all there was fellow UNI Records recording
artist, Neil Diamond, who introduced Elton from the stage. In the
audience that night were Gordon Lightfoot, Mike Love of The
Beach Boys, David Gates of Bread, Danny Hutton of Three Dog
Night, musician and producer Van Dyke Parks, and Odetta. Even
Hollywood film composers like Quincy Jones, Henry Mancini, and
Elmer Bernstein were there to witness this heralded new artist's debut.

By the time Elton finally hit the stage, he started the show off with a couple of his more personal and introspective selections. At first he was a bit stiff and dull. In his review of the performance, Robert Hilburn of the *Los Angeles Times* wrote, "He started going through his songs in a somewhat distant, business-like manner. He looked scared, keeping his eyes on the piano and microphone in front of him."[61] Elton could sense that he was starting to lose the audience's focus. There were sounds of conversations from the bar, and the applause between songs wasn't wildly enthusiastic.

Finally, by the fourth number he became annoyed that some members of the audience weren't paying attention, so he stood up from his spot at the keyboard, kicked the piano stool, and in an irritated tone of voice announced from the stage, "Right! If you won't listen, perhaps you'll bloody well listen to this." He then leapt into his best Jerry Lee Lewis piano playing.

Swinging into high gear, he gave "Take Me to the Pilot" so much extra fire that soulful folk singer Odetta was reportedly up on her feet dancing. As Elton and the band previewed material from the forthcoming *Tumbleweed Connection* album, they lit a musical fire with "Burn Down the Mission," complete with Elton passionately getting down on the floor and playing his piano on his knees. By the time he had finished his set that night, the normally blasé L.A. audience was up on their feet for not one—but two— standing ovations.

Looking back on his opening night at The Troubadour, Elton was later to recount, "I came onstage with a three-piece band and I'm sitting there in hot pants, winged boots, and a Mr. Freedom tee-shirt, and I'm leaping on the piano, standing on it, doing handstands on it, and people went: 'Fuck! What's that?' For the first time in my life I felt released."[171]

When he was finished with his set, he had the crowd eating out of his hands. The stars waiting to see Elton afterward were so numerous that Norman Winter had to organize a receiving line to get everyone backstage and then out of the club.

Russ Regan was completely stunned by the act he had just seen. "It was probably one of the most electrifying evenings ever to happen at The Troubadour," he claims. "We knew, man, within about 45 minutes, that we had a superstar. When they did 'Burn

Down the Mission' you couldn't sit in your seat. It was electrifying. It was a charged evening."[16]

Norm Winter recalled, "The greatest thrill in my life, in the business that is—forget personal things—was that first night at The Troubadour."[16]

"Elton just blew everybody's sox off," Danny Hutton declared.[101]

The crowning achievement was when Robert Hilburn wrote in the *Los Angeles Times*: "Rejoice. Rock music, which has been going through a rather uneventful period lately, has a new star. He's Elton John, a 23-year-old English-man whose United States debut Tuesday night at The Troubadour was, in almost every way, magnificent…. While his voice most often resembles José Feliciano, there are at times touches of Leon Russell and Mick Jagger…. John's songs are co-written by lyricist Bernie Taupin, whose lyrics often capture the same timeless, objective spirit of The Band's Robbie Robertson…a raucous straight ahead rocker…. He's going to be one of rock's biggest and most important stars."[61]

The second night held an even bigger surprise for Elton. In the audience that evening, was his piano-playing, rock & roll idol, Leon Russell. That really knocked him out. "I nearly died!" Elton was later to recall. "He was sitting there, with his beautiful silver hair, looking like Rasputin."[109]

Russell liked Elton instantly, and that evening he invited the British singer/songwriter to his house. Elton was worried that Russell would criticize his piano playing. Instead, he found Russell to be charming and supportive. According to Elton at the time, "He's my idol as far as piano playing, and there he was sitting in the front row. My legs turned to jelly…. I mean, to compare my playing with his is sacrilege. He'd eat me for breakfast. But he said that he wants to record with us, and he told me that he'd written 'Delta Lady' after hearing one of our songs, which was a gas! Really, it's worth five million good reviews if someone you respect as a musician comes up and tells you they like what you're doing."[1]

When Elton was at Russell's house that evening, they talked about the music business and shared their experiences with each other. Russell told him about his secret cure for throat problems. To this day, whenever he has a sore throat, Elton still uses Russell's secret throat-resuscitating concoction.

Jimmy Greenspoon of Three Dog Night came to one of Elton's shows that week at The Troubadour and was just "blown away" by the performance he had witnessed. According to Jimmy, "I hired a limo for the night, because I didn't want to drive, because I knew that I was going to be falling-down, in-the-gutter shit-faced drunk in grand rock & roll style. I got a table in the back in the center of the club so that I could hear everything. Elton took the stage, and the entire crowd went: 'Woah!' He didn't have any of the production values of his later shows—it was pretty stripped-down. Here he was this little geeky guy, who only six months ago was peddling his songs door-to-door, and suddenly here he is onstage with one phenomenal song after another. That night, the 'buzz' in the place about him was unanimous: he was an instant star! It was all about the music. It could just be him and the piano, and it was something special. You could close your eyes and visualize the stories he was singing."[210]

There was no question about it: Elton John had literally taken Los Angeles by storm. Looking back on his career-establishing week at The Troubadour in Los Angeles, Elton proudly proclaimed, "We just played rock & roll and right from the word 'Go,' we've always been a rock & roll band and people were amazed. We played 'Sixty Years On,' 'The King Must Die' and did them better than on the records."[26]

Although he had thrown one of his infantile tantrums at the hotel, the trip to Los Angeles was overall a huge success. Even Elton had to admit, "From the moment we arrived, it was just pandemonium all the way. The first night at the Troubadour was hype night, with all the record company people and the press, and the first set was incredible and it stayed that way. We got unbelievable reviews—I didn't see one bad one."[1]

One of Elton's favorite parts of his Los Angeles sojourn was discovering Tower Records on Sunset Boulevard. It was like being in a supermarket for vinyl. In his eyes, it was the ultimate shopping experience for the obsessive audiophile.

After a bombastic week of concerts at The Troubadour, Elton's mini tour of the United States continued to several more cities. The next stop was San Francisco, where Doug Weston also had an outpost of The Troubadour. He had paid Elton only $500 for his week at the L.A. Troubadour; now Weston generously upped the amount to $750 for a week in San Francisco. Russ Regan continued to convince MCA/UNI Records to pour more money into the cause and bankroll the expense of the tour.

For the engagement in San Francisco, Elton progressively added more rock & roll into his set, since the audiences seemed to respond very favorably to it. He added The Rolling Stones' "Honky Tonk Woman," which remained a staple of his live shows for quite some time.

One of the most notable people to show up for Elton's shows in San Francisco was someone he knew from London: the head of Tamla/Motown, John Reid. By an odd coincidence, Reid was in town on business exactly the same week that Elton was performing there. As Reid later explained, "Motown had its tenth anniversary convention in San Francisco in August 1970. I had become friendly with [Motown's Executive Vice President] Barney Ales and his wife Mitzi. I'm from Scotland, and Barney said I could only come to the convention if I wore a kilt. It was an amazing event, very lavish. They had a party on that island in the middle of the San Francisco Bay, there was a casino, they gave you money to play."[103]

Not only did John Reid come to see Elton's show there in San Francisco, he also allegedly became the first man that Elton went to bed with. The year 1970 was becoming something of a milestone one for Elton, indeed. Not only was this the year that his career came into focus, but this was also the year that he discovered sex with men. He never had been able to relate to women his own age, on a sexual basis, despite his half-hearted attempts at being charming towards them. That one night in San Francisco changed everything. In the next several weeks, John Reid was to become one of the most important men in Elton's life. When they both returned to London, Reid not only became Elton's manager, he also became Elton's live-in lover.

It was only fitting that this would happen. After all, Bernie Taupin had fallen in love with someone during this first trip to America, now it was Elton's turn. According to Elton, his sexual awakening was long overdue: "[I was] about twenty-three [years old]. And then it was like a volcano. Out it came; it was such a relief."[75]

Next Elton and his entourage were off to New York City for a special showcase performance for MCA/UNI Records executives. Unfortunately, following two triumphant engagements—in L.A. and San Francisco—the Manhattan performance was something of a mess. It was part of a private press luncheon that took place at The Playboy Club in midtown. Eric Van Lustbader reported in *Record World* magazine, "Two other new acts were on the bill and, it being a working day, many of the writers left before [Elton] got on [stage]. The sound was so bad that afterwards [Elton] was beside himself, tears of rage in his eyes."[109] Fortunately, this disastrous luncheon was quickly forgotten as things continued to peak for Elton's career.

While they were in New York City, the band stayed at Loew's Midtown hotel on Eighth Avenue, not far from Times Square, which was slighty seedy at the time. Elton and Bernie wanted to go up to Harlem to see the fabled Apollo Theater on 125th Street, just to gaze at the legendary temple of American soul music. It took three cab drivers before they found one that would take them to Harlem. They stood in front of The Apollo in awe before returning to their hotel. They had heard how dangerous New York City was, and it lived up to its reputation when there was a gunfight in Times Square that night.

The next stop on the tour was Philadelphia, Pennsylvania, where Elton headlined The Electric Factory. While this trip was indeed establishing Elton as a major star, it was also costing UNI Records a fortune. Russ Regan recalls having to fight with the company over the money he was spending. "I was questioned on a lot of things that I did," he recalls, "and I was told that I shouldn't have spent the money I spent and that I was spending too much money to support the artist, and, frankly, I resented it. I was in Philadelphia when I got a phone call from the controller of the company. He told me they were calling it 'Regan's Folly' at the Tower because I was spending too much money promoting an artist who wasn't selling any product. Which was true—he wasn't selling millions of albums and millions of singles yet. I think if I was ever going to have a heart attack I would have had it in Philadelphia at the Holiday Inn because I yelled so loud—and I have witnesses to this—telling him to 'fuck off.' I felt we had a superstar and I wasn't going to back off."[16] Fortunately for Elton, Russ Regan fought for what he believed in, and what he believed in was Elton's talent.

One of the most important things that this tour to America had done was to solidify what was to become known as "the Elton John core band." He and Nigel Olsson and Dee Murray had not only bonded as bandmates but as friends as well. According to Elton at the time, "It's a real band now, and the boys have helped me a lot. It's so tight now, but in a year's time it'll be unbelievable. America did our confidence a lot of good, and I don't ever have to tell them what to do, because we all know what we're doing. There are some songs with very broken rhythms, but they just play them without having it explained to them."[1]

After a triumphant several weeks in America, Elton John returned to England feeling both confident and successful. His career had gotten a huge push in the U.S. He had been squired around by Danny Hutton, met and played for Brian Wilson, and been praised by his idol Leon Russell. In addition, he had a new boyfriend. To celebrate it all, he was going to move into a new and luxurious flat with John Reid. Elton had left his motherland uncertain as to what he could expect, and he came back an acknowledged American star.

CHAPTER SIX

Madman Across the Water

In September 1970, when Elton, Bernie, Dee, and Nigel arrived back in England from America, their work was cut out for them. There were live performances to give and albums to be recorded. The prime task at hand was to launch the new *Tumbleweed Connection* album. Like its predecessor, it was to be released in Great Britain before it was to come out in America. Also at hand was Elton's now-blossoming personal life, namely fitting John Reid into the picture. The challenge to this would be working Reid into his life and career, without the public realizing that they were homosexual lovers. In addition, several people from Elton's past were to return to the forefront, including his old pal Long John Baldry.

Everyone in the British music business seemed to know something about Elton John's triumphant first voyage to "The States," and the overnight fame and glowing press clippings that it generated. Something big was clearly happening. No one was more astonished by this news than members of the English press, who had seen him bouncing around from one odd job to another. Only months ago, Elton had been working as a clerk at Musicland, helping customers shop for other people's releases. Now, he was someone whose records were beginning to be sought out by those same patrons.

Amongst the astonished journalists was Richard Cromelin, who wrote of Elton in *Phonograph Record* magazine, "He looked like the last person you'd cast in a rockin' role like that—a small, stubby man, he looked as if he belonged in a physics lab or behind an accountant's desk, but surely not on a concert stage."[16]

However, critics on both sides of the Atlantic were now singing Elton's praises. John Mendelssohn in *Rolling Stone* claimed, "His voice combines the nasal sonority of James Taylor with the rasp of Van Morrison with the slurry intonation of M. Jagger with the exaggerated twang of Leon Russell...he gets off on wearing outrageous costumes, thrashing tambourines, and occasionally impersonating Jerry Lee Lewis…. Elton John really is a gas."[2]

Penny Valentine in Britain's *Disc* and *Music Echo* reported, "It was *Elton John* that set the seal on Reg Dwight's future, and it was *Elton John* that was to start an impetus that almost overtook him. He became the superstar everyone had said we needed for so long, and he did it solely on this album, almost literally overnight."[4]

Everyone was waiting to see what was next for Elton. The answer was: several things. All of a sudden he was all over the place, and Elton had a full schedule in front of him for the next four months. Little did he suspect, but in the next 12 months he would have four separate albums on the charts and still another one that he was about to produce. The first project on the docket was scoring the film *Friends*. This deal had been set up prior to the big smash engagement at The Troubadour, and now it had to be completed instantly.

Elton explained at the time, "It represents what we had to write for the film. The whole story behind the film was they contracted us to do three songs…. They were going to call the movie *The Intimate Game*, and Bernie and I said, 'No, we will not write any songs named for a movie,' and we suggested *Friends*, so [they said,] 'We'll settle for *Friends*.' And we had to write another song, which was 'Michelle's Song.' They wanted another song, which was to last a minute and ten. And for film writing, if they want a song that's a minute and ten seconds long, then you're supposed to write a song that's a minute and ten seconds long. You have to time it, and all this rubbish."[6]

There was the pressure of fulfilling the needs of the film and satisfying their own desire to make sure that the album held together as a musical package. "So we said, right, we're going to do this thing with the 20 and 30 second songs, then we'll write two songs and re-record the whole album. So we recorded the whole album once for the film, and then went back into our own studio which we always use and recorded the whole soundtrack album…so people would at least get a bit of value for their money. They get five songs instead of three and horses galloping…the record company are promoting it as a new Elton John album, and kids will probably think it is a new Elton John album."[6] That was exactly how it was marketed and perceived.

Elton's passion for bizarre clothes was becoming part of his legend as well. His costume choices were now being anticipated in the press. Ray Williams reported in the September 26, 1970, issue of *Melody Maker,* "Despite the sombre quality of many of his recorded works, Elton is nothing if not a raver onstage. He's playing a Royal Albert Hall concert with [the rock group] Fotheringay on October 2, and he's planning to wear a gold lamé tail-suit which was given to him in America."[1]

The former shy Reggie Dwight claimed, "It's from a '30s Busby Berkley musical.... I might sew some sausages on it for the occasion."[1] A simple gold lamé tail-suit would soon seem conservative compared to some of the garish and outlandish costumes that were coming in the very near future.

Elton was always a big fan of Tamla/Motown music, and while John Reid was still at the company he was able to introduce his new "mate" and boyfriend to several of the stars who were on the label. Reid recalls, "I told Elton that Stevie Wonder and Martha and The Vandellas were coming into Britain for a tour. I asked if I could borrow his car to meet them at the airport because mine was out of commission at that time, and Elton wound up coming to the airport with me to meet Stevie. When I introduced them, Stevie asked, 'Are you the Elton John who sings "It's a little bit funny...?"' And, he started singing the song. That started off their relationship."[107]

The Supremes were having an incredible year on Motown Records in 1970. They had hits on both sides of the Atlantic with the songs "Up the Ladder to the Roof," and "River Deep, Mountain High," with The Four Tops. It was Elton John who wrote the liner notes that appeared on the back cover of their next album, 1971's *Touch.* As a true record collector and Supremes fan he wrote: "I am probably their original British fan. I bought their first single 'Where Did Our Love Go' in England in 1964.... Since then, I have gotten every record they have ever made.... When I left London, 'Stoned Love' was still Number One. Imagine my excitement when I not only received an advanced copy of this—their new album—but was also asked by Jean, Mary and Cindy to write the notes. (I felt as if I had really 'made it.').... I like this album very much and am really pleased to hear The Supremes sounding more exciting than ever."[111] Elton's love note to The Supremes was the perfect "touch" for the *Touch* album, especially since Elton and Cindy Birdsong had a friendship dating back when she was a Bluebelle, and he was merely the unknown Bluesology pianist.

The U.K. version of *Tumbleweed Connection* was released on October 30, 1970, and everyone was thrilled with the results. "It came out exactly the way I wanted it, which was incredible," claimed Gus Dudgeon. "Elton and Bernie had already written a number of songs, and we decided that we wouldn't be quite so tight with the format…. We did 'Come Down in Time' with a rhythm section once and decided it wasn't right. We then got Paul Buckmaster to write an entire arrangement for 'Come Down in Time.'… On 'Country Comfort' we used a guy called Pete Robinson, a friend of Paul's, to play the piano while Elton was away in the Netherlands doing a television show. We didn't know that Elton wouldn't be able to make the session until fairly late, and we had already booked a bunch of session musicians to play on it, so rather than cancel it and lose a lot of money, we decided to go ahead and make about three tracks without Elton."[30]

This was to remain a source of irritation for Elton. According to him, "By the time we were making *Tumbleweed* we still hadn't had any success, so we were forced to keep the expenditure down…. I was over in Holland when they recorded that particular track. Pete Robinson played piano and when I came back I dubbed a piano part over Pete's. When I listen to it now, I hate it. When we'd finished the album we took it round to Muff Winwood, who lived just around the corner from Taupin and I, and Muff said, 'The album's good but "Country Comfort" is terrible.' At the time we thought it was great and we were so hurt—but now I realize that Muff was right. Rod [Stewart]'s version is so much more natural and laid-back. But you only realize these things in retrospect."[26]

The *Tumbleweed Connection* album was a whole new concept for Elton. It was not only the most country-flavored album of his career, it was also the first and only one not to have singles released from it. This decision was calculated on his part. Some of the more serious rock musicians wished to be considered "album artists" as opposed to highly-commercial hit-makers producing songs for the singles charts.

The thematic and somewhat somber album did yield some of Elton's favorite in-concert selections like the sensitive "Come Down in Time" and the raucous "Burn Down the Mission." There were also several alternate versions of these songs that were recorded at the same time, which were to remain unreleased for several years, finally coming out as a "bonus track" on the 1995 CD version of the album. One of the songs that was recorded but not included initially was the original version of the song "Madman Across the Water." The eight-minute version of this song featured rock guitarist Mick Ronson and is quite different than the one that ultimately became the title track for Elton's 1971 album of the same name. Ronson would find fame several months later as part of David Bowie's Ziggy Stardust and The Spiders from Mars band.

One of the loveliest songs on this album is Elton's version of Lesley Duncan's "Love Song," which he recorded with her singing background vocals. The vocal choir on several of these tracks also features Duncan's voice. She also had her own solo albums during this era.

Two of the songs on *Tumbleweed Connection*—"Ballad of a Well-Known Gun" and "My Father's Gun"—feature the background vocals of Elton's singing idol from his teenage years, Dusty Springfield. Since he had become chummy with her while taping *Top of the Pops*, he invited her to do a guest spot on the album. She gladly agreed.

Throughout her career, Dusty Springfield was looked upon as being the Queen Mother to the British pop stars of the day. They all worshipped the ground she walked on and longed to breathe the air that touched her trademark beehive hairdo. She was very well respected, and she was also very generous with her time.

Often Dusty lent her talent to other people's albums, including Elton's. Explains longtime Dusty expert Jack Donaghy, "She was someone who had grown up in the music business and was always gracious to other artists she respected. Dusty and Elton were very close friends from the early days of his career. Dusty sang backup for many singers including Madeline Bell and Kiki Dee, so it was perhaps inevitable that she would work with Elton. They also shared an oddball sense of humor: Dusty occasionally performed as 'Gladys Thong' when singing backup, rarely using her professional name. However, for her guest appearances on Elton's albums, she proudly allowed herself to be billed as 'Dusty Springfield,' which thrilled Elton to no end."[185]

According to Angela Bowie, Dusty was always a favorite of the gay boys. Says the outspoken Ms. Bowie, "All of the 'poofs' loved her and wanted to help her. They wanted to say how wonderful she was, and they adored her, because she was gay as well."[100]

The packaging of *Tumbleweed Connection* was quite elaborate for the time. The original LP cover and subsequent CD cover opened up to reveal a double-wide photograph of an old Western town with Elton seated on the ground on the front and Bernie standing several feet away on the back cover, presumably waiting for a steam locomotive. The interior featured a 12-page booklet of lyrics with drawings of 19th-century trains, guns, a paddlewheel riverboat, and various Civil War–era motifs. This same country/Wild West packaging would—in the coming months—be replicated on albums by The Eagles and Loggins & Messina.

Bernie Taupin was to explain, "Everybody thinks that I was influenced by Americana and by seeing America first hand, but we wrote and recorded the album before we'd even been to 'The States.'"[116]

Tumbleweed Connection became the first Elton John album to hit the Top Ten in the U.K., and it remained on the charts for five months. The album's liner notes featured the dedication "For David." It was later revealed that the "David" in question is David Ackles, the folk singer who had been relegated to the position of opening act at The Troubadour in August of that year.

The day before Elton, Bernie, and the band left for another six-week tour of America, DJM threw an album-listening party for *Tumbleweed Connection* at London's Revolution Club. Amidst *hors d'oeuvres* of honeydew melon and chicken wings in a cream sauce, Elton wore a shiny black plastic maxi-coat and red boots. Pinned to the coat's lapel he wore a plastic clown head which lit up when its dangling string was pulled. When he took the microphone, Elton claimed that he was glad he took a new direction on the new recording. "This album, *Tumbleweed Connection*, is the funky one. Wait till you see the clothes I'll be wearing this tour. I'm glad it's out of the way. They wanted me to do another one with an orchestra but I said 'no,' the country one comes first. The next one is going to be more classical and orchestral," he explained.[3]

It was at the party for *Tumbleweed Connection* that Elton announced to the press, "I moved into my new flat yesterday, they want me to live in town now."[3] The apartment was located at 384 Winter Gardens, a modern and luxurious complex that had just been built off of Edgware Road. As Elton took residence, John Reid moved in with him.

Elton's second 1970 visit to the United States was every bit as successful as his first one. On October 31, 1970, Elton kicked off the tour at the Boston Tea Party, a nightclub in Boston, Massachusetts. The tour included concerts in Philadelphia, at The Fillmore West in San Francisco, and at the Fillmore East in New York City.

In Los Angeles, Elton performed at the Santa Monica Civic Auditorium. For part of that particular concert he took the stage in a top hat, a cape, and purple jump suit. The show climaxed with Elton ripping off the jumpsuit to reveal what looked like purple pantyhose underneath. He proceeded to kick his piano stool away and perform some high kicks for the crowd. David Felton, reviewing the concert for *Rolling Stone* magazine reported that, "The crowd, to use Elton's term, 'went mental.'"[113]

Part of the concert was taped and used in an upcoming television special. With regard to the crazy costumes he wore that night, Elton explained, "I never thought the outfits got in the way of the music. I did live my teenage years through my success years in my 20s. I never had the freedom to do that before, so I did it. With me, I'm afraid, I'm very excessive…. I remember doing *The Henry Mancini Show*, which was filmed at the Santa Monica Civic Auditorium, my segment of it anyway. There's a very famous picture of me from that filming where I'm horizontal in the air, and I have on mauve tights and silver boots with stars. I had taken off eight outfits during this song, and the faces on the people in the audience were, like: 'My God!'"[119]

While Elton and John Reid were out in Los Angeles, Elton reconnected with Danny Hutton and went to the studio one night to see him and the rest of the members of Three Dog Night. They were enroute to Roger Vadim and Jane Fonda's house. Hutton recalls, "He and John Reid arrived at American Recording Studio one night. I don't remember what we were doing. They were going to a party at Roger Vadim's house out in Malibu. I remember that Elton had a little Mickey Mouse thing around the zipper on his crotch. And, you pulled the string and it lit up. I said to him, 'I don't know if that's really the right thing to wear.'"[101]

On the 17th of November, Elton gave a radio concert on WABC-FM at A&R Studios in New York City. Elton explains, "During our second tour of The States, which was mostly co-headlining with people like Leon Russell, The Byrds, Poco, The Kinks and so on, we were asked if we'd like to do a live broadcast. This hadn't been done in New York for years, and the radio station said it could be done in a studio, sent out on stereo, and that the sound would be really good. We played in headphones, and it all came out of this little recording studio which had an audience of about a hundred to create the concert hall atmosphere. We didn't know at the time, but afterwards we found that Steve Brown had arranged for an 8-track recording to be made—just to see how it came out—and when we listened to it, we thought it was quite good."[114]

Since that time, there has been confusion about the original radio broadcast. Some sources claim it was on WABC-FM, others list WPLJ-FM. Tom Cuddy, who served as Vice President of Programming at WPLJ clarifies: "WABC-FM and WPLJ-FM are one and the same. About a month after the Elton John concert was aired, WABC-FM changed its call letters to WPLJ-FM."[115]

The original broadcast was a huge hit with New York area listeners. Recalls Cuddy, "The WPLJ-FM broadcast is remembered in such a revered way because it's the first documented live radio broadcast of Elton in America. For our listeners at the time, they were witnessing their introduction to a superstar in the making and they were blown away by the rawness and energy that he delivered."[115]

Indeed, the performances on that particular radio broadcast are so dynamic and energetic that it wasn't long before people started pressing up vinyl albums derived from the concert. At the time, to have "bootleg" copies of Elton's music on the market was a flattering sign. It was proof that he was truly becoming a major star.

That fall, UNI in America and DJM in England both released a new single off *Elton John* with "Border Song" on one side and "Your Song" on the other side. Originally the record companies thought that "Border Song" was the obvious hit. However, radio programmers differed in opinion, flipping the 45 r.p.m. single over and spinning the "B" side on the airwaves. Suddenly it was "Your Song" that was climbing the charts.

So what did UNI Records think of "Russ Regan's Folly" now? Proudly, Regan reported, "Elton started justifying all the expense around November of '70, when he really started coming on and when his album really took off. And he's never taken a backward step since."[16]

After his radio concert on November 17, Elton and his band played Bill Graham's fabled Fillmore East in New York City on November 20 and 21, serving as the opening act for Leon Russell. Following that, they went back to Los Angeles. One of the last things that Elton did in California was to tape another television appearance. This one was a holiday Christmas special starring middle-of-the-road pop singer Andy Williams. Andy played host to several of the day's new stars including Elton, Mama Cass Elliot, and Ray Charles.

One of the things Elton did while in the United States was meet with potential managers, though Elton and his mother also began to try and talk Reid into becoming Elton's manager. After all, he was living with him. Although he didn't have any previous experience in finance, or law, or management, he began to seriously consider it. Elton implored Reid to step up to the plate, but it was Sheila Dwight who was the driving force. Elton had already told her that Reid was his boyfriend, and she accepted it. Not only was she happy for her son, but she also felt that Reid was the perfect person to guide his career as well. They continued to work on him.

Elton and Reid returned from this whirlwind second trip to America in time to catch some of their London friends' Christmas parties. It was at one of those parties that Elton met another musician who would become a lifelong friend: Rod Stewart. Long John Baldry introduced the two and recalled the meeting: "I had introduced Rod to Elton at the 1970 Christmas party at manager Billy Gaff's cellar apartment in Pimlico, the smell of Billy's malodorous cat everywhere. The two had never met and Rod had just signed his deal with Warner Brothers [Records] and

The Faces and somehow or another Rod and Billy mentioned me to Joe Smith, president of Warner Brothers at the time and Joe said he would love to record me but in a rootsy setting, and 'By the way, Rod, would you produce him?' And Rod said straight away, 'Yes of course, Joe, I won't even charge you money for doing so.' True! Can you believe that? Anyway, Rod meets Elton at this party at Billy's and Elton asks what Rod is up to and Rod says, 'I'm having a bit of a problem recording an album with Long John as Warners want it yesterday.' So Elton says quite loudly, 'Ooooh, can I get involved? Can I play piano?' And at the end of the day, Rod produced half the tracks on my two Warner Brothers albums, and Elton produced half the tracks. They were just beginning to get great success themselves; it threw some of the spotlight on my project."[110]

The first album that Elton and Rod and John Baldry collaborated on was 1971's *It Ain't Easy*. Side one of the original disc—tracks 1-6—was produced from January 15 to January 29, and February 4 of 1971, by Stewart. In overlapping sessions, Elton produced side two of the album—tracks 7through 10—at I.B.C. Studios on February 1, 3, 4, 10 and 11. Rod and Elton used different musicians on their subsequent tracks. Elton played piano on all four of the tracks he did, and he was joined by his friends Caleb Quaye, Roger Pope, Dave Glover, and Joshuah M'Bopo. The singers on the album included Madeline Bell, Lesley Duncan, and Doris Troy.

It was from these sessions that Baldry gave his close male friends their female "drag" nicknames. Elton's name was "Sharon," Rod Stewart's was "Phyllis," and John Reid's was "Beryl" in honor of actress Beryl Reid. Their close friend Tony King was "Joy." John Baldry christened himself "Ada." These were names that were to stick forever.

It Ain't Easy was quite eclectic, as it jumped from blues to rock to R&B. Caleb Quaye explained, "You had to adapt to whatever musical paradigm you were given. And that could change. I had worked with Elton since 1967 so I felt comfortable with this and besides it was an honor to have been asked to work with Long John Baldry as he was such a respected man, and deservedly so, in the UK R&B scene."[112]

When Elton and Baldry originally discussed what songs they were going to record together, they clashed on the choice of material. According to Elton, "I hadn't ever done any producing and the idea gave me the horrors but nevertheless I said 'yes,' because I like John. When we started discussing material, Baldry started talking about Della Reese numbers and I said, 'No, John, that's just going back.' The actual sessions were very hard to fit in, 'cause mine were done in five days and Rod's were done in two weeks because he had to fit them in with a tour. One of my favorites on that first album was 'Flying.'"[26]

In addition to the ballad "Flying," Elton produced and played piano on Baldry's rendition of Randy Newman's "Let's Burn Down the Cornfield," Leslie Duncan's "Mr. Rubin," and a soulful blues song that Elton and Bernie wrote called "Rock Me When He's Gone."

Baldry recalls that both of his friends had different ways of working: "Rod loved to record well after midnight and very loosely and I think that's evident on some of the tracks, especially those recorded on my 30th birthday when he showed up with cases of Remy Martin cognac and several measures of good quality champagne! Therefore I had to record 'Don't Try to Lay No Boogie Woogie on the King of Rock & Roll' whilst laying on the floor. Elton's work ethic was to start at eight o'clock in the morning! I was doing two weeks residency up in Manchester so I would do my show 'til 2:00 a.m. and then sleep a few hours, grabbing an early plane to London to do the Elton sessions and then I would fly back in the late afternoon. I was actually quite worn out from all this."[110]

In early 1971, Elton and Sheila continued to pressure John Reid into quitting his job to manage Elton full-time. Finally, Reid agreed. First he had to resign from EMI's Tamla/Motown division. "After two amazing years at EMI, I left in 1971 to manage Elton John for Dick James," Reid recalls. "I was reluctant to go. I had become friendly with EMI's chairman, Sir Joseph Lockwood, and all the senior management. I was terrified of telling them I was leaving. Actually, I was more terrified of telling Barney [Ales]! At first, they talked me out of it. Then Elton's mother talked me back into it."[103]

The Elton machine was off and running in so many directions that John Reid's first task was to try and reel in the upcoming projects and make certain that the current ones were tied up so that they could move forward. As Reid recalls, "When I became involved, *Tumbleweed Connection* and *Friends* had been recorded already. As soon as *Tumbleweed* hit, *Friends* was ganged out and there was a hell of a lot of scrambling to do. There was all of that to contend with within one year, plus touring and trying to move on to new things…. It was like a set of dominoes that all fell almost at once."[107]

John Reid was a 21-year-old streetwise Scotsman with a notorious temper. He was also in love with Elton and prepared to defend him in any way he could. Clearly, Elton was going to be coming into a great deal of money very soon, and someone had to manage it for him. Reid knew he was up for the task, and he provided a barrier between Elton and anyone who could do him any harm in business, in the press, or personally. New contracts were drawn up, and initially Reid was working in cooperation with Dick James.

Chris Chatsworth was a writer for *Melody Maker* magazine in England and during this era he interviewed Elton several times. He also knew John Reid. He instantly recognized Reid's volatile temper. "He was never unfriendly to me, but it seemed like he didn't trust people, or he looked at people with a good deal of suspicion, as if they were trying to get to Elton," Chatsworth recalls. "I don't know if this was gay jealousy, or whether he was worried that Elton might go off and be managed by someone else— although that didn't seem likely as Elton seemed very dependent on him at the time. John Reid was also a very ill tempered man. He could fly off the handle at the slightest thing, and go wild like a little terrier."[88]

Mick Inkpen, Elton's buddy from the original Bluesology, came to visit Elton and Reid at their apartment at Winter Gardens. In his eyes, it just seemed like an economical set-up, a manager sharing a flat with his client. The fact that Reggie and Reid were actually lovers went over his head. "I hadn't realized that their association went beyond the manager/client relationship, but he was exactly what Elton wanted, and Elton was exactly what John needed," says Inkpen. "John was absolutely dedicated. He knew Elton was star material and he knew exactly how to develop him. He was a ruthless man, very tough."[88]

And what did Dick James think about Elton living with and sleeping with his new personal manager? James was certainly used to gay men in show business at this point, notably through his working relationship with the homosexual manager of The Beatles, Brian Epstein. Dick nonchalantly stated, "Oh well. If he's living with his manager, at least he'll have someone to get him up in the morning."[87]

In America, the *Tumbleweed Connection* album was released on January 4, 1971. The sound and sight of Elton John was nearly unavoidable in record shops, on the radio airwaves, and on the charts. Three more brand-new Elton albums would be released before the calendar year was over: the *Friends* soundtrack, the live set *11-17-70*, and eventually *Madman Across the Water* that November. (The live album *11-17-70* uses the American date abbreviation for November 17, 1970, in the United States and the British/European abbreviation there, carrying the title *17-11-70* in those countries. In both cases, the title refers to the date of the recording at the WABC/WPLJ studios.) In January 1971, *Tumbleweed Connection* peaked on the British charts at Number Six. In February the *Elton John* album hit Number Four and *Tumbleweed Connection* crested at Number Five in the U.S.

By early 1971, bootleg copies of Elton's November 17, 1970 concert on WABC/WPLJ were all over the place. It was decided between DJM and UNI that the best answer was to edit the tapes from the live performance to produce an official Elton John "live" album.

As Elton explains, "The *Friends* album, over which we had no control, was about to come out, so we did a quick mix of the live recording at DJM and released an album from the tapes. At the time, I thought it was quite good, and I also wanted it to come out because Dee and Nigel, who had been on very little before, were featured very strongly. It meant that I had four albums in the U.S. Top 40 which hadn't been done since The Beatles."[114]

The *11-17-70* album was actually a great way to stitch together several of Elton's different styles into one album. "Bad Side of the Moon" had been the "B" side of the "Border Song" single; "Take Me to the Pilot" and "Sixty Years On" were from the yet-to-peak *Elton John* album; "Burn Down the Mission" promoted the concurrent *Tumbleweed Connection* album; "Can I Put You On" was from the forthcoming *Friends* soundtrack; and "Honky Tonk Women," "My Baby Left Me," and "Get Back" paid homage to The Rolling Stones, Elvis Presley, and The Beatles respectively.

The *11-17-70* album, which hit Number 11 in the U.S. and Number 20 in the U.K., remains one of Elton John's favorites. Tom Cuddy points out that the singer has always had a fondness for the radio station that was responsible for that concert: "In 2001, during an interview on WPLJ, Elton said, 'I will always have a warm spot in my heart for WPLJ and how they've supported my career.'"[115]

While the *Friends* soundtrack album was originally an experience that Elton had really wanted to enjoy, he found that he was more upset about the results than thrilled. When Paramount Records released the song "Friends," Elton was irritated that it was competing with "Your Song" and "Levon" on the charts. He also felt that it was diluting the sales of the other three albums he had released in the last several months.

The *Friends* soundtrack album was released in America by Paramount Records on March 7, 1971, and the British version came out the following month. Elton later revealed that there had been some problems and conflicts when it was created in the recording studio.

Gus Dudgeon was producing with orchestrations by Paul Buckmaster. The record label that had it, Paramount Pictures Records, had just scored a huge hit with the soundtrack to *Love Story*, one of the top box-office romances to hit the screen. Composed by Francis Lai, the *Love Story* soundtrack spent six weeks at Number Two on the American record charts and was certified Gold. The company was poised to do the same promotional job on the soundtrack album for *Friends*. In the U.S., when the single version of the song "Friends"—on UNI Records— became a Top 40 hit, it received lots of airplay, and the album made it to Number 36.

But Elton was still unhappy with the way the record was packaged. As was to become a frequent occurrence over the years, whenever Elton was irritated, he gladly complained to anyone who would listen. Often he vented to the press. Regarding the *Friends* album in 1971, he whined to *Georgia Straight* magazine. "The guy in London—who's a complete idiot—who runs Paramount Records, said that he wanted a really great sleeve.... And they came up with that strawberry-colored rubbish.... It's not an Elton John album, believe me. The album was Gold within three weeks...it's amusing; I'm knocked out, I'm very glad that it is a Gold record. But it's not an Elton John album."[6]

Elton further complained about the recording experience and took his first swipes at Paul Buckmaster. "If you only knew the circumstances under which *Friends* was made," he was to whine. "Getting that soundtrack album was a real joke because Buckmaster might be brilliant but as a person he's not very together. That album was done for experience and I would never ever do another soundtrack album again."[26]

Elton had been a "star" less than a year, and he was already getting a reputation for being difficult. His once-sparkling association with Paul Buckmaster wasn't destined to last much longer.

Though outspoken about his music, whenever the press asked Elton John about his private life—and particularly his sex life—he would just shrug his shoulders and brush off the question in a blasé fashion. When queried on this subject by *Rolling Stone* magazine in 1971 he defensively claimed, "I've got no time for love affairs. You wake up in the morning—even if you have a day off—and the phone will ring: 'Can you come into the office? There's something I want to talk to you about.' Your solicitor will phone you up, for a start, or your accountant, or your manager, or your publicist—somebody will phone you up. Then you have the day-to-day things to worry about, like your car will go wrong so you have to take it in. Or the stove will blow up. It's amazing how many things go wrong in life."[62] This statement of course made very little sense. What 24-year-old rock & roller in 1971 would believably forego having a sex life simply because his car battery went dead? It made the rock press even more curious about what Elton John really did behind closed doors.

The gay sexual revolution—which some see beginning in 1969's Stonewall Riots in New York City's Greenwich Village—was definitely in full swing by 1971. However, in the rock & roll world, the atmosphere wasn't right for Elton to confidently declare that he was not only homosexual, but that he was also sleeping with his manager.

Meanwhile, when John Baldry's *It Ain't Easy* was released in June 1971, it was heavily publicized as being the album that Elton John and Rod Stewart had co-produced. In America, FM radio stations began playing the distinctive three-minute monologue known as "Conditional Discharge" and the song it leads into— "Don't Try to Lay No Boogie Woogie on the King of Rock & Roll." The album became something of an instant cult classic of the day, made it to Number 83 in *Billboard*, and remained on its LP chart for 18 weeks. Baldry toured North America to support the album on a bill with Fleetwood Mac, Savoy Brown, Delaney & Bonnie, and Tower of Power. Elton and Rod gave their musical mentor the due respect and American launch that they felt he deserved, and he was beginning to reap the results.

Elton gave the John Baldry tracks he produced the kind of country/blues flavor that was similarly featured on his own *Tumbleweed Connection* album, partially due to the track that both LPs shared: "Burn Down the Mission." Right after *It Ain't Easy* was released Rod began recording the album that would catapult him to the top of the charts: *Every Picture Tells a Story*. Baldry himself later pointed out, "You see in many ways *It Ain't Easy* was the blueprint for Rod's *Every Picture Tells a Story*, which was his next project. Many of the same players and singers were asked by him to play on *Every Picture Tells a Story* such as Sam Mitchell, Maggie Bell, Ray Jackson on mandolin, Micky Waller…. It was like a rehearsal for *Every Picture Tells a Story*."[110] In that way, *It Ain't Easy* promoted *Tumbleweed Connection* and helped to begat *Every Picture Tells a Story*. It was a winning situation for everyone involved.

Elton returned to the United States for his next concert tour in late summer 1971. He put everything he could into his performances, to the point where the skin on his fingers would crack and bleed from hitting the piano keys so hard. According to him, "I bang the piano a lot. It's hard work. Like the start of the tour, the first three days, my hands were hell. They bled every night. And my nails broke. Once you've got over the first three or four dates, your hands harden up, the skin just hardens up. My nails split."[62] He continued to wear wild, colorful outfits, often drawing comparisons to Liberace. On the comparisons he said, "I like Liberace very much. He appeals to me. He's just so outrageous. He's like a middle-aged Mick Jagger. It freaks me out!"[6]

September 10, 1971, was Danny Hutton's 25th birthday, and it just so happened that Elton John was in Los Angeles to headline a concert in the Hollywood Hills. The Three Dog Night star had looked forward to seeing Elton but was disappointed by his initial reception. Explains Hutton, "One of the other nights I remember is the night he played The Greek Theater. I went to see him at The Greek, and backstage afterwards he was a little bit distant. And I thought, 'Oh my God, what's this.' I had gone there with a friend, and I drove home and I lived on this little street, so I was a little bummed out. When I got up the street, obviously somebody had been throwing a party, and it was hard to get to my house. So, I got my car in my garage, and I walked in the front door, and Elton is there! It was a surprise party for me! It was great. There was Mama Cass, and a whole bunch of people. She was sitting there in a Karen Black chair from a movie set. That was a wonderful moment, Elton throwing me a surprise birthday party like that!"[101]

After the Greek Theater dates in Los Angeles, Elton and his troupe went on to a series of concerts in Japan and then Australia. Elton was astounded by the pandemonium that his Japanese fans created in Osaka. In Japan they didn't just like Elton John, they loved him. Of the Australian leg of the tour Elton was later to complain, "We played one football stadium, two racetracks and a speedway track—and it was the middle of winter! The stage blew away on one gig, and we literally played in overcoats. It was raining on the piano.... New Zealand was nice, though. It's lovely and green, and the people are great. But Australia...the band had five days off in Adelaide, and they went mad with boredom. If Mary Hopkins can run into trouble there, well, it gives you some idea.... But we'll go back again. Why not?"[87]

Even at this point in his career, Elton was accumulating an odd assortment of fans, both male and female. "Bernie and I do seem to attract weirdos," he said at the time. "I don't know why, because we're not really weird ourselves. People give me pineapples. And some girl gave me her knickers. Yeah, in Scotland, some girl took off her knickers and threw them on stage—along with a bowler hat. Can you get that one together? What upsets me are people who are really spaced out. Like last night there was this guy, as we were driving out he was clinging onto the car, going, 'I must go home with you! Let me be a person!' What can you do, you know? You can't be rude to people. I couldn't say anything nasty to him—we left him sobbing on the ground. That really disturbs me." [62]

In November 1971, Elton's fifth album, *Madman Across the Water*, was released on both sides of the Atlantic. Recording the album had begun months before with the Mick Ronson eight-minute-52-second long version of the title track. However that was shelved for a newer and shorter version of the track with Chris Spedding playing the electric guitar instead of Ronson. Two of the tracks—"Levon" and "Goodbye"—were recorded on February 27, 1971. The rest of the album sessions resumed on August 9 and 14 of that year, with the additions of guitarist Davy Johnstone and Rick Wakeman. A master organ player, Wakeman was about to leave the group The Strawbs. He would later find rock & roll fame as part of the ultimate artful synthesizer band, Yes. Wakeman can be heard on the tracks "Razor Face" and "Madman Across the Water." Another longtime Elton collaborator—percussionist Ray Cooper— made his first appearance on this album as well.

Madman Across the Water reportedly did not have an easy creation process. According to Elton, "That was an album of frustrations for everybody; we were all going through heavy stages. Paul [Buckmaster] was getting…well, he's very strange, Paul, he can't work under pressure, because we had to get that fucking album going. I don't know how that album ever got out. When we were doing the actual track 'Madman Across the Water,' for example, Paul arrived with no score! There were 60 string musicians sitting there and we had to scrap it. There were all those sort of disasters."[63]

When *Madman Across the Water* was finally released, some critics and radio programmers balked at playing the first single, "Levon," because the name "Jesus" was used in the lyrics in a seemingly irreverent fashion. Bernie Taupin explained, "People got their knickers completely in a twist just because Levon called his son 'Jesus,' and he was a balloon salesman. Just because he didn't call his child 'George,' and he wasn't a mechanic or something. I don't know, the story's completely simple; it's just about a guy who wants to get away from his father's hold over him."[63] The song, which was released as a single in America only, made it to Number 24 on the Pop Singles chart in *Billboard* magazine in early 1972.

Madman Across the Water was an album of introspective songs, which made it something of a return to the theme of *Elton John*. However, this time around, rock guitars replaced much of the fully-orchestrated sound of *Elton John*. Furthermore, the lyrics that Bernie wrote for this album were engaging story songs. "Tiny Dancer" is without a doubt the most perfect John/Taupin collaboration at this point in their career. A touching love song, both sensitive and rocking at the same time, it was about Bernie's love, Maxine.

The song "Madman Across the Water" expresses the way that Bernie and Elton thought they were being perceived by their American audiences at the time. But one of the most dramatic tracks on the album is the often overlooked "All the Nasties." The lyrics of this moving song find Bernie and Elton facing their critics, being grilled by the press, and explaining how sudden fame was making them grow up. The gospel-style chorus work of the Ecclesia choir behind Elton on the lengthy choral ending is brilliant and dramatic. Later, Elton revealed that "All the Nasties" was also their first gay-themed song. Elton was being asked about his sexuality by the press more than any other topic. Bernie later explained, "There was one once, 'All the Nasties,' on *Madman Across the Water*, that no one picked up on. That was a song for Elton when the press was really crucifying us. It says something about, 'if asked, maybe I would tell them, then they would understand.'"[118]

Undoubtedly, the fact that Elton remained so evasive about the facts of his sexuality and his personal life only added to his mystique. For the time being, he was content to be a man of mystery, in hot pants and platform shoes no less!

The music critics were mixed about *Madman Across the Water* at the time of its release. In *Rolling Stone* magazine, writer Alec Dubro claimed, "*Madman* won't really crush any John fans, for he sings with the same power and brilliance he's shown since he broke. But, it probably won't draw any either. *Madman* is a difficult, sometimes impossibly dense record. America is worthy of a better story than this record and Elton John needs a better story than this to sing."[117] However, Elton John was already pretty much "critic proof" in the United States. His albums were ideal for FM rock-radio programmers, and his singles had proven to be perfect for pop radio.

Gus Dudgeon had been kept busy producing what seemed like an endless stream of new Elton John projects. Even he had to admit that he was quite amazed at how prolific Elton truly was. Gus claimed, "At this point it looked like Elton was putting out an album once every two months, which is ridiculous, so with *Madman* I decided that we ought to go back to a formula similar to when we did the first album. I wanted to make it clear to the fans that some of the things which had come in between, such as *Friends* and *11-17-70*, were not part of the official situation. I've always liked *Madman*, and I can't understand all the people who knocked it because I think it's a really good album."[30]

Oddly, the reception that Elton received in the U.S. and the U.K. was often totally different. The album *Madman Across the Water* would attest to this. In the U.S., it made it to Number Eight on the charts, while in his own native England, Number 41 was Elton's peak. For that reason, Elton was going to start to spend more and more of his time in America. Another major concern of his was soon to be his tax situation. Since his income had recently spiked upward, he was now in a much steeper tax bracket. He began to entertain the idea of doing all of his recording outside of the British Isles, for tax purposes.

By the time that 1971 came to a close, Elton John had scored three certified Gold albums in the United States. These Gold certifications were awarded by the RIAA (Record Industry Association of America) and signified sales of one million copies sold of a single, or 500,000 copies of an album sold. Later in the 1970s, the RIAA would roll out a further distinction known as Platinum, which meant that an album had sold a million units. Elton soon amassed a vast collection of both Gold and Platinum albums and single certifications for his walls. With John Reid as his new personal manager, the distinction of having simultaneously placed four albums in the American Top 40 and a universal awareness of his music, Elton John was preparing to make 1972 a year of even greater musical milestones.

CHAPTER SEVEN

Rocket Man

When 1972 kicked off, Elton was in high gear for what was going to turn out to be his most successful year yet. Even with all of the previous year's confusion with the dueling Elton John projects, including the *Friends* soundtrack, and the unexpected live radio telecast album, he emerged unscathed, and he succeeded beyond his dreams. Instead of getting sick of the tidal wave of Elton material, the rabid American audience was already clambering for his next release. The press and his fans eagerly wondered what his next album would sound like and what insane outfits he was going to wear to promote it. Elton had positioned himself as rock & roll's favorite court jester, and the former Reggie Dwight of Pinner did his best not to disappoint.

Furthermore, this was the year that Elton really broke through on the record charts, recording two of his all-time greatest and most popularly received albums: *Honky Château* and *Don't Shoot Me I'm Only the Piano Player*. Both of these albums were recorded with diminished help fromPaul Buckmaster. Elton was used to working fast at this point, and he had become increasingly irritated by Buckmaster's much slower pace. On these two albums, only the songs—"Blues For My Baby and Me" and "Have Mercy on the Criminal"—included Buckmaster's full orchestrations.

It was highly publicized that from 1971 to 1972, The Rolling Stones were spending the year in France. Their high income had pushed them into such a steep British tax bracket that they simply left their home country. Elton John found himself in the same situation in 1972. Suddenly, he was done recording his albums at Trident Studios in London.

Elton wanted to remain loyal to England; however, he was becoming a much bigger star in America. He was running an international business, and he had to start looking at his career in "global" financial terms. The idea of recording abroad became much more appealing. Less taxes paid meant more money for shiny new Rolls Royces, gaudy jewelry, garish costumes, and other expensive things.

The idea of recording his next three albums at Château d'Herouville in France was Gus Dudgeon's. Château d'Herouville had recently been used by The Grateful Dead, which intrigued Elton. The studio was located in close proximity to Paris and was actually housed in a 300-year-old château. It had a musical background, as the famous composer Frédéric Chopin once called it home. And in fact, he shared it with his lover, the female writer George Sand. Known also as Strawberry Studio, there are actually two separate studios there, one named "Chopin" and the other "Sand." In addition, there were private sleeping quarters for Elton and John Reid, Gus, Bernie and Maxine, and the three members of Elton's band.

When Elton and party arrived at Château d'Herouville for the first time, he was immediately impressed with the facility. It proved an ideal setting for a much more concentrated series of writing, creating, and recording sessions. Bernie and Maxine occupied quarters upstairs, where Taupin penned his lyrics. Then Maxine ran them downstairs to Elton with the ink barely dry, and he very quickly wrote the music. Then the recording sessions would begin.

It was like they had gone to record the album at sleep-away camp. If a session was going well, it could continue until all hours of the day or night. The Château d'Herouville had its own swimming pool and tennis court, so that the band could unwind. There was no need to go anywhere for food. Everything was catered, and there was plenty of wine, since the Château had its own vineyard as well.

The resulting album, *Honky Château*, was Elton's most rock & roll release to date. The addition of Davey Johnstone and his guitar work instantly took the sessions to another place musically. A fresher, edgier sound is immediately heard on the opening song, "Honky Cat," a New Orleans–flavored song with Elton playing the keyboards as though he was at a Bourbon Street dance hall.

The contentment that Bernie Taupin was feeling in his life is evident on the song "Mellow," with its beautiful and distinctive electric violin playing by Jean-Luc Ponty. "I Think I'm Gonna Kill

Myself" was Elton's most amusing song yet. It not only makes fun of his "head in the oven" routine several years back, it also gave him an arena in which to be a little cheeky. The sounds of tap dancing by "Legs" Larry Smith add to the fun. Smith's association with this album stemmed from Gus Dudgeon's work with Smith, who was the drummer for The Bonzo Dog Doo Dah Band. According to Gus, Smith and Elton hit it off and enjoyed touring together when it came time to promote the album.[12]

The two most dynamic tracks on *Honky Château* are the completely spaced out "Rocket Man" and the character study "Mona Lisas and Mad Hatters." "Mona Lisas and Mad Hatters" was all about Bernie's visions of New York City. Elton and Bernie had always loved David Bowie's "Space Oddity," which Dudgeon had produced. "Rocket Man" was their answer to it.

According to Bernie, "With 'Rocket Man,' the first two lines came to me when I was driving along…and by the time I'd gotten home I'd written the song in my head. I got inside and had to rush and write it all down before I'd forgotten it."[63] One of the lyrics deals with being "high as a kite." Was it really a drug song or merely a metaphor? Confirms Taupin, "It's all because of Elton. Nobody but Elton could have sung that line from 'Rocket Man' about being as high as a kite without getting banned from the radio. It was a drugs song!"[45] Elton was very happy with *Honky Château*. He especially enjoyed the recording sessions. "We were all on the money musically and for me the music always comes first—the music can really express the inexpressible if you let it," he claimed.[47]

According to Gus Dudgeon, "We took so many gambles, and when it turned out the way it turned out I just could not believe it. It was the first album that the whole band played on, as Dee and Nigel had been strictly playing on live dates and only occasionally would play on the records. From then on Elton could go onstage and say, 'This is my band, this is my album, this is what it's about.'"[30]

After the January sessions in France, the group returned to England. On February 5, 1972, Elton headlined a concert at London's Royal Festival Hall accompanied by a full orchestra. The previous year he had done a similar concert with 30 pieces accompanying him, and he rather liked the experience. Now he launched a grandiose plan to do a concert with a full 80-piece orchestra. Unfortunately, it ended up turning into something of a nightmare.

He used Paul Buckmaster as his conductor, but he soon found that the orchestra members were quite elitist, and they looked down on Elton as a mere "pop star" who had no idea what he was doing. Looking back on the concert Elton complained, "But the one we did earlier this year I just didn't enjoy, because I just thought the orchestra were cunts, every single one of them. The one before was with session men, and they're pretty bad, but they really got into it, and freaked out completely. But the Royal Philharmonic—I just thought they gave a quarter of their best, and they didn't take the event seriously, and I was taking it seriously. I felt so tense, because I was uncomfortable playing with them."[10]

Elton paid to have the whole concert filmed, with the idea of making a concert film. Instead of enjoying the experience, he found it to be a fiasco. Elton was still intrigued with the idea of meshing his music with a full orchestra, though, and with a film. This wasn't it, but he was determined to repeat the formula until he got it right.

After recording the tracks for *Honky Château*, and following his frustrating February 5 orchestral concert, Elton started work on another album for Long John Baldry. The *It Ain't Easy* album had been such a hit in America that Warner Brothers Records called for an immediate follow-up project. Both Elton and Rod Stewart again agreed to co-produce the album that would be titled *Everything Stops for Tea*. This time around, Elton would have Side One, and Rod would take Side Two.

The Rod Stewart sessions took place at Morgan Recording Studios from January to February of 1972. Elton neatly did his sessions with Baldry in February at IBC Studios in another part of London. At one point Baldry found himself running back and forth from one session to the other one. Of the two, Elton was much more the task master in the recording studio, and Rod turned his sessions into something of a party atmosphere.

Baldry had recently dropped the "Long" from his stage name. When asked about "Long John" at the time, Elton laughingly pointed out, "No longer 'Long!' I've produced half of two of his albums now. I never really thought I'd want to produce a record, because I'm very impatient in the studio; I like to get things done, and I can't stand wasting studio time."[10]

The songs that Elton produced included Willie Dixon's blues-belter "Seventh Son," the traditional Scottish "Wild Mountain Thyme," the gospel-flavored "Jubilee Cloud," and a perfectly fun version of The Dixie Cups' song "Iko Iko."

For Elton's tracks on the album he brought along three members of his band—Davey Johnstone, Nigel Olsson, and Ray Cooper—as well as Klaus Voormann on the bass. Elton provides vocal accompaniment.

On "You Can't Judge a Book [By Looking at the Cover]," Baldry adlibs some of the lyrics. He sings, "You can't judge Rod Stewart by looking at his nose, you can't judge Elton John by fathering at his clothes, you can't judge Billy Gaff by his lying in the gutter."[120]

Ron Wood was not available at that time to play guitar on the Rod Stewart sessions of the second Baldry album, as he had on the first one, but he created the art for the cover of *Everything Stops for Tea*. A gifted and talented artist, he painted a caricature of Baldry appropriately costumed as the Mad Hatter at the tea party from *Alice in Wonderland*. The drunken dormouse is sleeping in the chair next to him, while Alice and the March Hare are on the back cover of the gatefold package. When it was released in April 1972, *Everything Stops for Tea* made a brief six-week showing on the American charts, making it to Number 180. Although it was a perfect follow-up to *It Ain't Easy*, some of the songs were too eclectic and too far from rock & roll to find the same enthusiastic audience. That was the same year that Elton scored a huge Number One album, and Rod Stewart hit Number 2 with his *Never a Dull Moment* LP. Somehow their chart magic didn't rub off on Baldry's quirky album quite the way that everyone expected. Warner Brothers Records did not renew Baldry's recording deal.

In April 1972, Elton and his band returned to the United States to headline a series of concerts. When they landed at Los Angeles International Airport (LAX), the authorities searched Elton's luggage, looking for drugs. At that point in time, there wasn't a rock star on the planet that didn't seem to be involved in marijuana, cocaine, or something similar. Reportedly, the heels of the insanely high, eight-inch platform shoes that Elton had packed in his suitcase were checked for drugs. With eight inches of hiding space, the drug enforcement employees weren't about to let that flamboyant footwear go unnoticed.

On May 7, 1972, Reginald Kenneth Dwight legally changed his name to "Elton Hercules John." According to British law, it was done "by deed poll." Although he had been using the new name as his show business persona for several years now, at last he was officially known by the moniker he had made up. He was now free to fully blossom as the embodiment of the alter ego that he had created.

The former Reginald Dwight claimed that he thought of several names before coming up with the middle name of "Hercules." According to him, "[I] could have called myself Fiona, I suppose. Elton Fiona John. Or Dalmatian.... No one ever called me Kenneth. I don't know why people bother having middle names anyway. So I thought I'd call myself Hercules. My mother had a fit. Everybody had a fit. They didn't think I was serious until it came through."[58] When it came to being ridiculous, Elton Hercules John was dead serious.

Also in May of 1972, there was an important wedding held within the Elton John family circle. Sheila Dwight finally married Fred Farebrother. Elton signed the wedding certificate as an official witness: "Elton Hercules John." The other witness was John Reid's mother, Elizabeth Reid. To celebrate his success, and his mother and stepfather's wedding, Elton bought Sheila and "Derf" a three-bedroom house in Ickenham, Middlesex. Since he was by profession a designer and painter, Fred Farebrother took it upon himself to redecorate it to their taste. Shelia was able to quit her government job. She began to dress more stylishly, since she was not only Sheila Farebrother, but she was also "mother to the star!" To complete her new look, Elton bought her a flashy white MGB sports car.

With their new income, Elton and John Reid needed a new, more impressive residence as well. In early 1972, Elton found 14 Abbots Drive, located on the exclusive Wentworth Golf Course. A modern, split-level bungalow with a private swimming pool, the house had a lush garden in the back. Elton purchased the new home for £50,000 and promptly christened his new estate "Hercules." If Scarlett O'Hara in *Gone with the Wind* could live in "Tara," and The Who's loony drummer Keith Moon could live in "Minotaur," wasn't it fitting that Elton should live in "Hercules"? It was so pretentious, so queenly, and so Elton all at the same time.

The driveway that led up to Hercules was large and had a slope to it. It was the perfect place to showcase Elton's growing armada of "land yachts" —his flashy car fleet. Now that his income was being measured in the millions, he resumed his addiction: shopping. Cars seemed a natural collectible for a rock star. Elton parked his hardtop Rolls Royce Corniche, his Rolls Phantom VI, his Ferrari Boxer, as well as his Mini GT in the driveway. Inside the new mansion, there was plenty of room for Elton's growing collections. By now his record collection had grown to immense proportions, estimated to be in the tens of thousands—and still all meticulously alphabetized.

The guest list at "Hercules" soon began to read like the Pop Singles page in *Billboard* magazine. Rod Stewart, Keith Moon, David Bowie, Marc Bolan of T-Rex, and Donovan of "Mellow Yellow" fame were among the most frequent guests. Elton told one reporter during this period, "Donovan's having a party [here] next week, and he's invited the whole world. Keith Moon says he doesn't want any Galactic Fairy Dust, he wants a good booze-up. Rod says he's not much into mushrooms and toadstools, but he'll go…. David Bowie was just here. I really liked what Mott the Hoople did with his song ['All the Young Dudes'] so I rang him up and invited him for a meal."[87]

While Elton was collecting and entertaining at his new home, Bernie Taupin had his own project. He released his self-titled debut album—*Taupin*—on DJM Records in the U.K. in 1971 and and then on Elektra Records in the U.S. in 1972. The album remains a little-known rarity. Basically an album of Bernie reciting his poetry—his lyrics—to music, it was produced by Gus Dudgeon. Unfortunately, it was never promoted very well, and it never made the record charts. Since he was making a great living providing his lyrics to Elton's albums and singles, it was a lark for him. It has become somewhat of a collector's item.

Another of Bernie's creative projects away from Elton involved trying his hand at being a music producer. It was Bernie who produced David Ackles 1972 album, *American Gothic*, for Elektra Records. Although Taupin and Ackles had become very good friends, and Bernie believed in the singer's talent, that particular album never made the charts either.

Elton and Bernie were living very different lifestyles at this point. While Elton and John Reid were drinking and partying with Rod Stewart and Keith Moon at "Hercules," Bernie was living a much more quiet and reserved life with Maxine, who had moved to England and married him in 1971. Together they lived in their own stone cottage, which they called "Piglet-In-the-Wilds." There Taupin stored his prized books and Wild West memorabilia. Taupin openly confessed to being a country boy. He stated at the time, "I can't stay in L.A. very long. I could never even live in London. I've just got a little cottage in a village. I don't wish for any more."[7]

In May 1972, *Honky Château* was released on both sides of the Atlantic. In America it became Elton John's first Number One album, sitting on top of the charts for five weeks. Two songs made it into the U.S. Top Ten: "Rocket Man" (Number Six U.S./Number Two U.K.) and "Honky Cat" (Number Eight U.S./Number 31 U.K.). In Britain the album peaked at Number Two. This was the official beginning of Elton's hot streak. He had "the Midas touch," and it seemed that everything he recorded turned to gold.

The critics loved *Honky Château*, and it became the first of seven consecutive new Number One albums in a row for Elton in the United States. In his review of the album in *Creem* magazine, Charles Shaar Murray wrote, "There's a new Elton John album out now…. Elton John is still growing, still playing, still creative and he's still better than James Taylor and Leon Russell put together…. *Honky Château* is going to be a hit album. Make no mistake."[8]

No one was more amazed at Elton's wide-reaching success than Long John Baldry himself. With a good-natured laugh Baldry claimed at that time, "I always knew that Rod was going to become something very, very special. But how could one predict that a boy with an overweight problem…I mean, he is a bit broad across the beam, our Reg…. Who would have thought that this strange boy with his myopic lenses and fat arse…could turn out to be one of the pop sensations of all time?"[124]

In June 1972, Elton and his band went back to France to record their next album under somewhat strained circumstances. According to Elton, "I was in a terrible state with glandular fever.

Before we made the album, I said I didn't want to do it at that time, because it was such a strange situation with *Honky Château* released only a month before, and it was weird to make another album at that time. I wasn't feeling too well, and wanted to chuck it in. Gus said that was O.K., and we could go back and do it in September. I was going on holiday in July for a month to L.A., and I thought it would be great to try one track before I went, so that I could think I'd made a start. So we did the backing track to 'Daniel' and everything worked out fine and we carried on. But I was pretty evil during the sessions, so uptight and shouting at everyone."[10]

Basically, the album took the rock & roll attitude of *Honky Château* and pushed it to another degree. The finished songs from *Don't Shoot Me I'm Only the Piano Player* had more of a 1950s and 1960s classic rock & roll approach. "Teacher I Need You," "Crocodile Rock," "Have Mercy on the Criminal," and "I'm Gonna Be a Teenage Idol" are essentially Elton and Bernie's versions of "To Sir with Love" (Lulu), "The Twist" (Chubby Checker), "Jailhouse Rock" (Elvis Presley), and "Act Naturally" (The Beatles)— respectively. That was part of the key to the success of the album. Elton took old rock formulas and made them all sound new again.

Several of the songs that he recorded for this album found Elton stretching out as a singer and as an interpreter. As he explains, "I started experimenting with my voice on *Don't Shoot Me*. 'High Flying Bird,' for instance was very Van Morrison-ish, and while I was singing 'Teacher I Need You,' I thought of every Bobby Vee record I'd ever heard."[123]

The album's runaway success was the effervescent "Crocodile Rock." According to Elton, "This time I wanted to do something that was a send-up of the early '60s rather than an out-and-out rocker. I wanted it to be a tribute to all those people I used to go and see as a kid. That's why I used the Del Shannon–type vocals and that bit from Pat Boone's 'Speedy Gonzales.' We also tried to get the worst organ sound possible... something like Johnny & The Hurricanes used to manage to produce."[9]

The song "I'm Gonna Be a Teenage Idol" was all about the pop success that Marc Bolan was experiencing at the time. Elton laughingly admitted, "We played it to him and I think he liked it. He didn't hit me anyway."[9]

Marc Bolan had found fame as part of T-Rex with their 1972 hit song "Bang a Gong." He was the latest British teen idol at the time. "I've known Marc ever since that Roundhouse thing we did the first time, and we got all the nasties drained away from the things I said about him before," Elton explained. "I've really got into his music a lot and I really like him, and we've been friends ever since then."[10]

So many songs on *Don't Shoot Me I'm Only the Piano Player* are a synthesis of different albums in Elton's massive record collection. With regard to "Highflying Bird," Elton intended to make it "a cross between Crosby, Stills & Nash and Erma Franklin."[9]

"Daniel" created a sensation and great confusion over the meaning of the song. Was it a song about a man pining for another man? Was Daniel actually being missed by his biological brother? Was it about one of Elton's male lovers who had left him? According to Bernie Taupin, he had read an article in *Newsweek* magazine about a returning Vietnam veteran, who was heading to Spain. There was originally a final verse to the song which speaks about Daniel the G.I. being bid "goodbye" by his actual brother. Elton felt the song was running long, so he cut off the last verse of the song in his recording. In the end, the mystery of Daniel's identity made the song even more popular, and even more riveting.

One of the really interesting outgrowths of the *Don't Shoot Me I'm Only the Piano Player* sessions, was the idea of Elton, Bernie, Gus, and John Reid starting their own record label. Elton's new guitarist, Davey Johnstone, announced that he was recording an album of his own, which he had been shopping around. Elton listened to the tapes that Davey had produced so far and loved them.

According to Elton, "It was while we were making the new album in France, and John Reid and Steve Brown came over and told us that they couldn't get a satisfactory [record] deal on Davey, so we all sat down that night, and got thoroughly drunk, and said, 'Let's start our own label.' You know what those things are like—next morning you get up and it's instantly forgotten, but we remembered, and I came up with the title of Rocket Records."[10]

Supreme record collector that he was, what could be better than having his own record company? Even better, his boyfriend, John Reid, had already been the head of Tamla/Motown in the U.K.

"I always wanted to start my own record company," Elton claimed at the time. "Even as a kid, when I was playing my records, I'd be looking at the label spinning round and dreaming of having my own company."[9]

Elton was determined that he wasn't going to make the same mistakes with Rocket that The Beatles had made with their own Apple Records. According to him, "Everybody has benefited from The Beatles' mistakes. What had looked good on paper for them didn't work out in reality. Everyone has idyllic dreams but not everyone is able to make his dreams work out."[9]

Not long afterwards, Rocket Records set up its offices at 101 Wardour Street, London W1. According to Elton, "Basically, what we're interested in is new talent. There's thousands of me around in small bands—there must be. All I needed, initially, was the encouragement."[9]

Now that he was starting his own record label, what else could he get involved in? Why not films as well? The singer claimed at the time, "I don't want to make a film about Elton John or do a pop music film. I'd like to do a straight role or a comedy role, but it all depends on the script. A couple of years ago I wouldn't have considered it, but I probably would now. I'd like to branch out a bit, but it's very difficult as you're really on the firing range. I know I could make a good one, but it's a question of timing. I'm more interested in the band at the moment."[10]

Since moving into "Hercules," Elton and John Reid had made friends with several of their neighbors in their posh new surroundings. One couple that they became quite chummy with was film director Bryan Forbes and his wife, actress Nanette Newman. In July 1972, they took a vacation to Los Angeles with Bryan and Nanette. The two couples rented a beach house in Malibu and held court there while the beautiful California sunset shone over the waves of the Pacific Ocean.

While ensconced in Malibu, they met and mingled with several members of the Hollywood elite. One of the most important men Elton met was Groucho Marx. At the party where they met, Groucho said to Elton, "They tell me you're number one, but I'd never heard of you until I went into my office this morning and said I was having dinner with Elton John. They all fainted. After that I lost what remaining respect I had for you."[88]

Groucho, who was 81 years old at the time, was still something of a character. Recalls Elton, "Well, he's just awe-inspiring for the first two meetings, because you think you're going down like a lead Zeppelin. He's funny, he just takes the piss out of everybody. First time I ever met him it was in Malibu and it was 95 degrees. We'd been told he likes a fire, so we lit this big log fire. He came in, in an overcoat and beret, which he always wears, arrived an hour before dinner and the first thing he said was, 'When do we eat?' I was petrified."[27]

Elton and Groucho got into a dialogue about the piano player's name. Marx claimed that his name should be "John Elton," and that he had it backwards. As a silly cocktail party retort, Elton said to him, "Don't shoot me, I'm only the piano player." That sentence stuck in Elton's head, and he decided to use it as the title for his forthcoming eighth album.

While Elton was dressing in flashy clothes, cranking out anywhere from two to four albums a year, and becoming an international hit, David Bowie was performing a similar feat. In 1972 alone, Bowie had four separate albums on the charts including *Hunky Dory*, *The Rise and Fall of Ziggy Stardust and The Spiders From Mars*, *Space Oddity* (recorded in 1968), and *The Man Who Sold the World* (recorded in 1970). Furthermore, that same year he produced an album for the group Mott the Hoople and gave them the gender-bending, career-defining hit, "All the Young Dudes."

Elton and Bowie remained good friends during this era, but it wasn't long before they became rivals, and eventually things turned unfriendly. There were several parallels between Elton and Bowie and several ironies that existed as well. While Elton skirted the subjects of "sex" and "sexuality" in the press, David Bowie confronted it head on and teased everyone with his reported bisexuality. His very image and stage act was filled with "gender bending" and outright homosexual eroticism. Onstage, the target of his gay titillation was Mick Ronson, the guitar player Elton had used on the original version of "Madman Across the Water."

Describing Bowie's rock & roll stage act at the time, writer Henry Edwards wrote in gay-oriented *After Dark* magazine, "Mick Ronson, The Spiders from Mars' lead guitarist, a silver-haired giant who glitters under the intense spotlights that are flashing on and off above him, then breaks into an intense electric guitar solo. David disappears in a blaze of throbbing strobe lights and re-appears in a white satin Elvis costume, complete with the long white scarves. A balloon floats across the stage and he crushes it between his thighs. He suddenly grabs Mick Ronson's buttocks. He slides between Ronson's legs. He performs fellatio on Ronson's extended guitar."[53]

The most controversial thing that Bowie did in 1972 occurred during an interview with *Melody Maker* magazine in England, when he proclaimed he was indeed homosexual. Reporter Michael Watts wrote in his article titled "Oh, You Pretty Thing" (January 22, 1972) that "David's present image is to come on like a swishy queen, a gorgeously effeminate boy. He's as camp as a row of tents, with his limp hand and trolling vocabulary. 'I'm gay,' he says, 'and always have been, even when I was David Jones.'"[54]

Here was the dichotomy and the major irony that always existed between Elton and Bowie. David Bowie was a sometimes bisexual but mainly heterosexual man, who was proclaiming that he was gay to help him become a headline-grabbing superstar. At the exact same time, Elton John was a completely homosexual man, who had to pretend that he was straight, so that he wouldn't derail his career. Reportedly, this ironic juxtaposition of Bowie's public sexual stance, and how it magnified his career, irritated Elton to no end. Their long running rivalry had just begun and would continue for years.

In August 1972, John Reid officially handed Dick James Music his resignation. He was severing ties with the company and would henceforth be managing his boyfriend's career from the helm of his own company: John Reid Enterprises. He was all of 23 years old at this point. However, in the short time—less than two years—that he had been working with DJM co-managing Elton, he felt that he had learned all that he could. He had already photocopied all of Elton's contracts with DJM and had been examining every clause in them. Only a year and a half ago, Dick James had generously agreed to share management responsibilities and profits with the young Scotsman. Now here was Reid, poised to hijack DJM's star client. Dick James and his son, Stephen, were horrified, but could do nothing to stop him. John made his father, John Reid Sr., his co-director on the legal papers that were drawn up for John Reid Enterprises.

When asked about John Reid's role in his life and career, Elton explained, "He's always been looking after my affairs. Dick James doesn't know the first thing about managing anybody. John used to run the Motown label in England. It's just that he can handle me very well. He can sort my moods out. I'm inclined to be extremely moody, and he can handle it. He knows what's best for me to do, and he also does extremely good business deals for me— very important, because I wouldn't have a clue. I just need keeping under rein—I tend to go a bit haywire sometimes."[16]

In the fall of 1972, Elton launched a new tour of the United States. Already his stage show was a combination of rock & roll, Broadway, a 1960s "light show," with dashes of Vaudeville and cheap burlesque thrown in for extra measure. "Legs" Larry Smith had been coming out on the road with Elton, so that he could perform his tap dance during "I Think I'm Going To Kill Myself." Not content to have a straight tap-dance number, Elton had Larry wearing a bridal train, the ends of which were carried by two midget courtiers. On Larry's head was a motorcycle crash helmet with a bride and groom wedding cake decoration affixed to the top of it.

Elton's costumes and eyewear continued to reach astonishingly ludicrous heights. His eyeglass frames could be just about anything at this point, from stars to squares encrusted in rhinestones. One pair was heart-shaped, another had more rings around it than Saturn, and still another pair spelled out his name.

While on tour Elton was invited to be one of the acts on *The Royal Variety Show*, which took place at The London Palladium and was televised throughout Britain. In the audience that night were Queen Elizabeth and Prince Philip. Flattered to be asked to play in front of royalty, Elton cancelled a few of his American tour dates to accommodate the request.

When he landed at London's Heathrow airport, Elton noted that there was a crowd of several hundred fans with banners and signs to meet the flight. Elton was instantly impressed. Then the airplane doors opened, and he was horrified to find that the crowd was there to meet The Jackson Five, who were also on the flight.

On the bill for *The Royal Variety Show* was the master flamboyant piano player Liberace, The Jackson Five, The Osmond

Brothers, ballad crooner Jack Jones, and Broadway star Carol Channing. Elton had been asked by the event's organizers to perform his ballads "Rocket Man" and "Your Song." Elton would have no part of that. He instead insisted on performing "Crocodile Rock" and "I Think I'm Going To Kill Myself," complete with dancing "Legs" Larry and the midgets, before the stuffy audience that was gathered there that night.

One reviewer claimed that Liberace blew Elton off of the stage that night, making him "look like the musical dwarf he is." Actually for Elton, the highlight of the show was sharing a dressing room with Liberace and Jack Jones. "He was great," Elton later glowed of Liberace. "He just kept wheeling trunks of clothes in. I just sat there, watching him. He kept calm through the whole thing. All these people were badgering him all the time for autographs and he always did the most ornate autographs, and drew a grand piano around the signature. He was really nice. He was the most professional person on that show."[87]

When *Don't Shoot Me I'm Only the Piano Player* was released in January 1973, it hit Number One in Britain, the United States, and Australia. The cover presented the title on the marquee of a 1950s-style cinema theater, complete with the words "Starring Elton John," and a pair of patrons dressed in Eisenhower-era teenage fashions. There is a poster for Elton starring in a film with the album title on it. Next to it is a poster for The Marx Brothers and their 1940 comedy classic, *Go West*. It was Elton's way of thanking Groucho Marx for the album title.

This was without a doubt the most elaborate and classy Elton John album package yet. It came complete with a full-color, 12-page booklet of photographs and all of the songs' lyrics. There were full-page portraits of Elton and Bernie, Elton and the band, and Bernie playing in the waves of the Pacific Ocean. On the page with the lyrics to the song "Blues for Baby and Me," Elton is shown in a yellow suit, a bizarre black cape, and a stovepipe hat on his head. Pinned to his crotch is one of his light-up clown heads, and naturally his hands are on his crotch pulling the string that lights up the nose. Pinned to his chest is a Donald Duck button. On another page Elton is in a pink satin, double-breasted suit with silver and red eight-inch-tall platform shoes on his feet.

"Crocodile Rock" was the perfect choice for the new album's first single release. It was nostalgic, upbeat, and fun to listen to, all at the same time. It became a huge Number One hit for Elton in America and in Canada, peaking at Number Two in Australia, Number Three in Germany, and Number Five in the U.K.

When it came time to pick the next single from the album, Elton insisted it should be "Daniel." Dick James hated that idea and refused to release it. Elton then went to the press and complained about DJM publicly. Finally James agreed to release the single but refused to put any promotional money behind it. Elton took it upon himself to publicize it. With its beautiful melody and its mysterious subject matter of one man's love for another—whether friend, lover, or brother—"Daniel" was the perfect change of pace from the boisterously appealing "Crocodile Rock." Released in January 1973 in the U.K., and in America in March, the song instantly flooded the airwaves and climbed the charts to Number One in Canada and Number Two in the U.S., becoming Elton's second million-selling Gold single in that country. In England it hit Number Four.

The critics found that Elton's recording in France suited him well. Reviewing *Don't Shoot Me I'm Only the Piano Player* in *Let it Rock* magazine, John Pidgeon declared, "It's not just geography that has affected Elton John's music. There's a full-time guitarist, Davey Johnstone, a band unity coupled with an awareness of instrumentation previously blinkered by Paul Buckmaster's omnipresence, and a set of lyrics from Bernie Taupin that suggests he's finally thrown off his dogged obsession with Old Americana."[11]

With two back-to-back Number One albums to his credit, in 1973 Elton John was in high gear. In a matter of four years he had released eight albums and was one of the most in-demand rock stars. His life couldn't get any more bizarre if he was hit by a tornado and ended up on the Yellow Brick Road that led to Oz. And yet, that was exactly what was about to happen.

CHAPTER EIGHT

Dancing Down the Yellow Brick Road

Did Michelangelo realize when he carved "David" that he was creating his legacy with that one famed piece of marble? Did Shakespeare have a clue that, of all his plays, his tale of the tortured Danish prince in *Hamlet* would be career defining? Did Gloria Swanson realize that by lampooning her silent film career as Norma Desmond in *Sunset Boulevard* that she would create her greatest role? Did Elton John and Bernie Taupin have the slightest inkling that when they recorded *Goodbye Yellow Brick Road* they would be creating their single greatest album? The answer to all of these questions is "No."

By 1973, as Elton and Bernie were plotting out *Goodbye Yellow Brick Road*, they were already dangerously close to spreading themselves too thinly. They were planning on launching their own record label, plotting the most elaborate concert show yet for The Hollywood Bowl, and Elton was contemplating purchasing a controlling interest in the local Watford soccer team that he had once cheered for as a child. Was it any wonder that he was also on the verge of a nervous breakdown?

Furthermore, Dick James was furious with Elton for announcing he was going to launch his own "Rocket Records" recording label. On the heels of that came John Reid's split from DJM. Dick could see the handwriting on the wall. Here he had helped Elton launch the most high-profile recording career of the decade, and now the recording artist wanted his own label.

The grand and elaborate *Goodbye Yellow Brick Road* album was ultimately recorded in France at Château d'Herouville. However, that was not the plan from the beginning. Bernie had already written the lyrics to the songs for the new album in December of 1972. Elton was stunned to find that the Château's studios were not available in January 1973, when he next planned to record. Since The Rolling Stones had just recorded their album, *Goat's Head Soup*, in Jamaica, Elton decided why not give the Caribbean a try?

The Jamaican adventure turned out to be a total disaster from the minute they landed on the ganja-filled Caribbean island. The island was overrun with people who had come to see the championship boxing match between Joe Frazier and George Foreman, which had taken place the night before their arrival. When Elton and his musicians arrived in Kingston, they found that Elton's accommodations were at The Pink Flamingo, while the band was booked to stay across the island in Ocho Rios, miles away from him.

"First of all," Elton recalled, "we couldn't get into our original hotel so we checked into another one feeling totally shattered and went to bed, but at 10 o'clock this great noise started going on which sounded like the rising of The Third World, and we all leapt out of bed and found out that it was [jazz pianist] Les McCann playing outdoors to nobody. So we went and listened to him. The next day, we moved over to the Terra Nova where The Stones stayed and while the group pissed off for three days."[26]

Although spirits had been high for recording in this new tropical island setting, once they got a look at Byron Lee's recording facility, Dynamic Studios, it was a huge disappointment. First of all it was in a rundown part of town, and the property was surrounded by barbed wire and guards bearing machine guns. Elton explained, "If that wasn't enough, there was a strike at Dynamic Sound so every time we drove in there were loads of pickets at the gate."[26]

Gus Dudgeon had asked that the studio be ready for their arrival, and he had sent a request list of musical instruments and recording equipment. None of it was there. Most conspicuously missing was the grand piano that Elton was to use.

Nothing seemed to be going right, so Elton sequestered himself in his hotel suite. "I was afraid to go out of the room, because it was pretty funky in downtown Kingston, and most of those songs were written in two or three days in my hotel room on an electric piano."[132]

Elton at least recalls liking the tropical breezes and the sun. "It was great, the weather was beautiful and the atmosphere really fantastic," he recalls. "The trouble was, everybody at the studio was extremely helpful but the Jamaican philosophy is that anything can wait until tomorrow."[26]

The sessions weren't working, the sound in the studio was horrible, and it wasn't long before Elton sunk into one of his infamous sulking moods. When news came through that his album *Don't Shoot Me I'm Only the Piano Player* had hit Number One in England and America, they threw a celebratory party at The Pink Flamingo. Not even that revelry brought Elton out of his pouting.

The trip was not a complete loss though. Elton later told *New Musical Express*, "Apart from the hassles, and there were a lot, Kingston was still very conducive to songwriting. I loved it because of that, and also because of all the music that I heard blaring out of all those record shacks on the street. The only other bring-down was that I caught crabs after sitting on the toilet seat...publish that if you dare!"[26]

For Elton, the final indignation of the trip was a massive centipede. He recalled, "This centipede, about 14-foot long, had crawled over me! I rushed down into the dining room with just a sheet covering me."[87]

For him, that was the omen that signaled the end of the Jamaican adventure. The troupe decided to pack up and leave. Unfortunately, their exit from Jamaica was not as smooth as they expected. When a dispute arose over the payment for their accommodations, the authorities impounded the troupe's rented automobiles. Taupin would later recall, "We were never so glad to get out of anywhere in our lives."[87]

The one good thing that came about from their stay in Jamaica was the new song "Jamaica Jerk-Off," which Taupin penned with inspiration from their misadventures. The group fled Jamaica and flew to New York City. When they got to New York, they heard that Château d'Herouville was suddenly available to them. Since many of the songs for the new album were written at this point, all they had to do was to dive in and start recording. Plans were instantly set in motion for them to go back to France. To capture the process for posterity, Bryan Forbes came along with his movie camera to film a documentary.

Elton and his party were never so happy to see the sane environment of Château d'Herouville as they were that month. For the most part, once they got to the Château, the songs just flowed out of everyone very naturally. According to Elton, "I'm very private about the way I write and most times I won't do it when there's anyone around, but for this I did it in front of the band. The band set up in the breakfast room at the Château and I'd be in the far corner at the electric piano, and that's how that album took shape. It was a very organic process. We jammed a lot of it until we had complete songs to go with the lyrics. Everyone who was there would join in; it was a very intuitive record."[47] Although they had written enough songs for a single-disc album in Jamaica, by the time they were done recording in France, there was enough material for a double-album set.

However, Elton claims that one of the songs presented a lot of problems. "'Saturday Night's Alright for Fighting' was great live but it was one of those difficult tracks to get onto tape in the studio because of the dynamics and the energy involved. It was a heavy rock song and we'd tried to record it before at a studio in Jamaica and it was really mad and frantic," he explains. "Even though we tried for hours we just couldn't get it down right with just the four of us as a band doing it live in the studio. It kept running away with itself or speeding up or just disintegrating into a unruly mess. In the end I said, 'Right, you three just play the fucker and I'll sing it and we'll do the piano later.' I'd always sung at the piano but this time I did the vocal standing up like most singers do, and it worked. I'm there waving my arms about, really getting into it, just going totally crazy. And this was in my pre-drugs period, too."[47]

Previewing the album during this time period, Elton described his hopes for the new album: "There's a whole set of songs we've already written: 'Candle in the Wind' is one, then 'Goodbye Yellow Brick Road,' and one called 'I've Seen That Movie, Too.' With 'Sweet Painted Ladies,' we have four really classy songs. If we could ever record an album as good as *Abbey Road*, I'd want to retire. Even though it's not my favorite Beatles album, you hear 'Something' and 'Here Comes the Sun,' and you want to fall down. Usually somebody has one good song on an album, but The Beatles had five or six mindblowers. So this is the way I feel about our next one. It's strange, you can compare us against The Beatles: *Revolver* lifted them onto a higher plane, and I think *Honky [Château]* did that for us, and then *Sgt. Pepper* was their most popular and *Don't Shoot Me* was ours, and then they had *The White Album*, and now we'll have a double, too." [63]

In 1973, Elton moved his parents—Sheila and "Derf"—out of their Ickenham house and into a house much closer to him. So close in fact, that their lot touched his property. He also moved his maternal grandmother, Ivy, close by. When Elton appeared at The Empire Theater in Liverpool, his biological father and stepmother, Stanley and Edna, came to see him. Elton sent John Reid out into the audience to find them, which Reid easily did since Elton looked so much like Stanley. There was a reunion backstage that night, but like many of Elton's encounters with Stanley it was nice and friendly, but brief. He did, however, promise to visit with them again.

Elton was also generous with his relatives on his father's side of the family around this era. His cousin Roy, the Dwight soccer star of the 1950s, asked Elton if he could borrow some money to start a clothing boutique. Elton sent the cash, and Roy put it towards the new shop he called Lady Samantha.

When he returned to play a concert in Liverpool in 1973, Elton presented Stanley and Edna with front-row tickets for them and their four young sons. After the show he brought his relatives backstage and presented them with chocolates and gifts.

The following day, Elton and John Reid drove to Stanley and Edna's house for a lunch that she had prepared. They ate chicken and apple pie, and afterward Elton went out in the yard to play soccer with the boys. As they were leaving, Elton gave Edna a check for £ 2,000 and told her that it was for a Peugot 504 he wanted his father to have. Since Elton had originally tried to make the car a gift, and Stanley declined it, he felt that this was the better way to handle it. Stanley purchased the car, but when it became too expensive for him to maintain, he sold it. It wasn't the car that was important; it was the fact that Elton wanted to patch things up with his estranged father.

Meanwhile, in 1973, Elton, John Reid, Bernie, Gus Dudgeon, and their compatriots wasted no time launching Rocket Records. There was no question that their eye was on getting free of DJM Records, moving Elton's records onto his own label, and owning a bigger piece of the pie. There were already disputes arising about the percentage of foreign record sales that DJM was making from Elton's albums. But as it now stood, Elton still had a couple of years left on his existing DJM contract, which was due to lapse in 1975.

The press was comparing Rocket to The Beatles' Apple Records, and they anticipated the same kind of organizational problems that had plagued that label. According to Elton, "That's why Apple ran into so many problems; they tried to do so much at once. But I can see Rocket getting bigger. We've learnt a lot from experiences like Apple. We don't have a lot of money involved."[17]

In its first years of development, Rocket spent a lot of money trying to develop the talents of several other acts, but the majority was destined to fall into obscurity. They included the bands Stackridge, Longdancer, Blue, Solution, The Hudson Brothers, as well as Colin Blunstone, and at one point '60s British rocker Cliff Richard. The Hudson Brothers, who were produced by Bernie Taupin, had a couple of minor hits in 1975 and 1976, the biggest being "Rendezvous" (Number 26 in the U.S.). Another Rocket signing, the duo Brian and Brenda Russell, failed to produce a hit for Rocket, in spite of an appearance by Elton on one of their songs, "A Thing Called Love." Later Brenda would leave Brian and have two solo hits for A&M Records in the 1980s: "So Good, So Right" and "Piano in the Dark."

Kiki Dee was the first artist signed to Rocket and, arguably, the most successful. She had known John Reid from his days at Motown Records. She explains, "I called up John, and he told me that Elton was going to start a record company—and that he was signing. So I went to see John and Elton, and I had a chat with them. And we decided to do the album which became *Loving and Free*. At that point in time, it was very much—for me—a great change. Because before that, I had been doing the cabaret thing, and I had got stuck."[126]

Originally from Bradford, Yorkshire, "Kiki Dee" was born Pauline Matthews. She was only 16 years old when she was discovered in a local dance hall and signed to Fontana Records. From 1963 to 1969 she recorded and released 11 singles including "On a Magic Carpet Ride," which became a minor hit. During this period she also did some background studio work, most notably behind pop superstar Dusty Springfield.

Kiki was thrilled when she became the first British artist on Motown Records. According to her, "Apparently what they do with new artists is to put them out to lots of producers—I worked with four initially—and see who suits the artist best. I ended up working mainly with Frank Wilson, who's done things with The Supremes and The Four Tops. At the time they'd never recorded anybody like me before, and I wasn't aware enough of what I was all about to give them any assistance; so some of the songs I did were totally wrong."[51]

Motown released an album by Kiki in 1970, titled *Great Expectations*. One single was released with "The Day Will Come" on one side and "My Whole World Ended" on the other side. Kiki has always possessed a great voice, but at Motown she was mainly assigned songs that other Motown artists had previously recorded or were later to record. "The Day Will Come" was originally an unreleased song that The Supremes had done, and "My Whole World Ended" had already been a hit for ex-Temptations member David Ruffin. After leaving Motown, and venturing into the cabaret scene, it was in the summer of 1972 that she first phoned John Reid.

At the time Elton fashioned himself as something of a potential "star maker." He felt that whatever the magic was that he possessed, it was going to somehow rub off onto his protégés, and he was going to have this kind of "Berry Gordy creates Motown Records" kind of dream in his head. He always envisioned pulling off a feat like that, and Rocket Records became the focus of this passion. He was determined that he was going to have the successful record label that The Beatles' Apple Records never quite became.

Kiki was a natural choice for John Reid and Elton to focus their energies upon. She had been at Motown when John Reid was the head of Motown's London office. John Reid also thought that Rocket Records would become the vehicle for finally making Kiki Dee into a mainstream superstar, because it was a feat he could not seem to pull off when Kiki was signed to Motown.

Angela Bowie recalls, "She was a big deal in London. Everyone was into Kiki Dee. I think she was a very fine songwriter who had solo albums, and she acted, and everyone was into that. She was always, just ultra-talented and multi-talented. I also think that the people who were into her, all had a gay sensibility. Even

David Bowie, who thought of himself as a big stud, thought the world of Kiki Dee."[100]

Loving and Free was Kiki Dee's first album on Rocket. According to Elton at the time, MCA Records, which distributed Rocket Records in the United States, was quite supportive at first. However, it wasn't long before he was complaining about MCA to anyone who would listen. He told *Phonograph Record* magazine that year, "I think the MCA promotion people have really got to be kicked up the ass, and they're going to be kicked up the ass. The initial ballyhoo was fine, but that doesn't sell records."[16]

One of the people whom Elton had hired was his old friend Tony King. Tony knew Elton from the days when he was still "Reggie Dwight," trying to make money in the music business as a recording session pianist. Since that time, Tony had gone to work for Apple Records. Tony laughingly claimed that he remained at Apple "until at John Reid's insistence, I became Tea-Boy for Rocket Records."[127] Actually, his official title at Rocket was Label Manager.

Meanwhile, in July of 1973, the first single off of the yet-to-be-released *Goodbye Yellow Brick Road* album, "Saturday Night's Alright for Fighting," peaked at Number 12 in the U.K.

On August 15, 1973, Elton kicked off his latest tour of America in Mobile, Alabama. However, the biggest, grandest, most-over-the-top show in the series was the one held at The Hollywood Bowl on September 7, in front of a crowd of 25,000. It was going to be the spectacle to end them all, and Elton wanted everyone to know about it. He said at the time, "The act is going to become a little more Liberaceized, not in a clothes sense, or Busby Berkeleyized—I'd like to have nine pianos on-stage, a cascade of pianos, and make my entrance like that. Just give the audience a really nice sort of show. I don't like to look at groups who come out standing looking like they've just been drowning at Big Sur for five years. I could never go on-stage in denims."[63] It was especially fitting that this mega-event would happen at The Hollywood Bowl, since images of old Hollywood were to play a large part in the show and in the new album. Elton would be previewing four cuts from *Goodbye Yellow Brick Road* during the show.

According to Alice Cooper, it was his own act that was the inspiration for Elton's new show. "When Elton started out playing

L.A., his stage act was just he and the band and his piano. He just sat there and played and sang," recalls Cooper. "Then he came to see our show. I remember he and Bernie Taupin coming to see me in concert at the Hollywood Bowl around 1970. They sat in the front, and I remember the looks on their faces. When he saw the vaudeville, theatrical kind of show we were doing at the time, his eyes lit up. He saw what a rock & roll show could be: with lights and staging and costumes. The next thing I knew, his stage show was theater and he was dressed as Donald Duck!"[290]

The Hollywood Bowl gig was going to be so spectacular that several of the band members had their wives and girlfriends flown in to Los Angeles to see it. Elton flew in his mother to witness it. He commented at the time, "My mum's a veteran—she's been over three or four times including Madison Square Garden."[13]

The afternoon of his show he went to a local hairdresser to have patches of his hair dyed hot pink for the big evening. "They only had to put paint over the faded bits," he explained. "It was just like putting Dulux on the wall really."[13] Elton had truly gone Hollywood!

The concert crowd was first entertained by the tour's opening acts, Sutherland Brothers and Quiver. Once the capacity crowd was sufficiently warmed up, it was time for the main event. Tony King came out onstage into the spotlight to announce the evening's mistress of ceremonies: "And now ladies and gentlemen, this evening's hostess...the star of *Deep Throat*, Miss Linda Lovelace!"[15]

The hardcore porn classic, *Deep Throat* (1972), had made Linda something of a sensation at the time for her cinematic skills at performing fellatio. Lovelace's previous film credit was the highly revered and dignified classic, *Piss Orgy* (1971). Her presence set the perfect tone for the over-the-top glitz and tackiness in store for the evening.

According to Chris Charlesworth of *Melody Maker* magazine, "As the lights dimmed and four arc lights from behind the stage sent their parallel beams up towards the Hollywood Hills, a silence fell. The stage backcloth, which carried the same huge painting of Elton as the one on his Sunset [Boulevard] billboard, was lowered to reveal a set from the swishiest Fred Astaire/Ginger Rogers movie of them all."[14]

Announced Lovelace, "On this spectacular night we hope to revive some of the glamour that's all but disappeared from showbiz."[13]

A huge illuminated staircase came down to the floor of the stage and palm trees were scattered across the stage. Still playing "Mistress of Ceremonies," Linda introduced actors dressed as: the Queen of England, Elvis Presley, Frankenstein, the Pope, The Beatles, Batman and Robin, Groucho Marx, and Mae West.

Continuing her intro, Linda announced, "Here he is, the biggest, largest, most gigantic, and fantastic man, the co-star of my next movie...Elton John!"[15] With that, the "Rocket Man" descended the staircase wearing a white and silver jumpsuit and a wide-brimmed hat.

According to Jerry Gilbert in *Sounds* magazine, "And down the steps he danced in a huge white Maribu feather hat, with a feather boa waistline and an all-white silk boiler suit—white sport coat and pink carnation hair sprouting out from behind his ears. Outrageous!"[13]

On the stage were five grand pianos, each a different color: orange, yellow, blue, purple, and pink. As the lid to each was opened by the actors, the inside of each lid revealed a different letter spelling out: "E-L-T-O-N." The pianos were also filled with white doves, which proceeded to fly dramatically into the air.

With that the band kicked into the song "Elderberry Wine." According to Gilbert, "Judy Garland once walked up the Yellow Brick Road, and Elton certainly wasn't missing out tonight."[13]

From the forthcoming album came "The Young Girls Love Alice," "Funeral for a Friend" leading into "Love Dies Bleeding," and "Crocodile Rock." To bring that song to life, Elton's sound man Clive Franks danced onstage dressed as a crocodile. Elton played a cavalcade of his hits for nearly two hours that night and then exited the stage while the crowd was on its feet cheering.

Sounds reported, "The crowd were in the mood for rock & roll and Elton gave it to them with 'Saturday Night's Alright For Fighting,' which signaled the release of more birds as Elton jumped up on the piano to conduct the massed choir of the Hollywood Bowl Auditorium. He played 'Honky Tonk Woman' which cooked along like crazy."[13]

Afterward there was an elaborate reception at The Roxy on Sunset Boulevard. A virtual Who's Who of Hollywood and rock & roll society attended, including James Taylor and Carly Simon, Britt Ekland, Peggy Lee, Robbie Robertson of The Band, Klaus

Voormann, Carole King, Bruce Johnston and the Wilson brothers from The Beach Boys, Danny Hutton of Three Dog Night, Rod McKuen, Mac Davis, Martha Reeves, Dusty Springfield, Dobie Gray, Henry Mancini, Barry Mann, Johnny Rivers, and Dyan Cannon.

David Rensin, who reviewed the Hollywood Bowl show in *Rolling Stone* pondered, "We've learned to expect different and novel things from Elton John. He is a man, however, whose patently non-outrageous music often clashes with his glam stage show, something that has progressed from mere acrobatics to a full-blown production. But does Elton need all this? His music holds its own."[15]

And what was he doing with Linda Lovelace? According to Elton, "She's a very nice lady, actually. She was far more demure than I thought she'd be. I spoke to her for quite some time and I was very, very impressed. She's been totally misrepresented, like Billie Jean King and John Lennon. I don't give a shit about being misrepresented. If you know down in your conscience that you're all right, you're all right. If you're misrepresented, then you have to fight against it."[27] To Elton, she wasn't just the star of *Piss Orgy* and *Deep Throat*, she was a proper lady.

Elton set out to make a name for himself as a showman, and his Hollywood Bowl concert certainly delivered. According to him, "I think people expect to see a show when I come on stage, and I really enjoy doing the show. I treat my audiences with respect, and they think a lot of that, because so many bands come on and don't treat their audiences with respect."[16]

Two days later, Elton gave John Reid a birthday lunch at The Beverly Hills Hotel, where they were staying. As a present, Elton presented Reid with a wrapped gift box. When the wrapping paper came off, Reid removed a brass sculpture of a man's erect penis and testicles. Instead of being horrified, Elton's mother just laughed hysterically at the off-color humor of it all. For Elton, that particular visit to Hollywood was certainly one of porn stars and penises.

After that, the *Goodbye Yellow Brick Road* tour continued to wind its way through the United States. While he was in Georgia, Elton heard that Iggy Pop was appearing at a small rock club nearby. His publicist, Sharon Lawrence, came up with the idea of Elton making a surprise appearance onstage with Iggy, which he did, dressed in—of all things—a furry gorilla costume.

Iggy was extremely high at the time, and at first he thought that a real gorilla had leapt onstage with him. Pop amusingly recalls, "I was unusually stoned that evening to the point of barely being ambulatory so it scared the hell out of me. I really didn't know what was going on. For all I knew it was a crazed biker on methedrine in that gorilla suit."[291]

Prankster Elton revealed, "Mind you, the gorilla costume stunk, it was about a hundred and ninety degrees in there and I nearly got thrown off for my troubles. I sort of jigged around for a couple of minutes feeling like a prat and then walked off, and then Iggy announced, 'Da guy in da gorilla suit wuz Elton John!' and the audience were going, 'Awww, c'mon.' I mean it coulda been Bob Dylan in there."[20]

On his flight between his New York and Boston concerts, Elton had a surprise waiting for him on his private plane. As he sat down in the front of the plane, Elton was in one of his frequent foul moods. Stevie Wonder was playing the song "Crocodile Rock" on a portable keyboard on the aircraft. Elton was busy sulking and ignored it. Finally Sharon Lawrence had to say to him, "For God's sakes, Stevie Wonder's back there."[87] Elton snapped out of his mood, and went to greet the revered Motown superstar. Wonder had recently survived a car accident that had hospitalized him. That evening in Boston, Stevie was Elton's special guest star onstage.

On September 15, the single "Saturday Night's Alright For Fighting" peaked at Number 12 in America and on October 5, 1973, the double album *Goodbye Yellow Brick Road* was released. The week of October 27 it was Number Six in the U.K., and, by November 10, it was Number One in the U.S., the beginning of an eight-week run at the top of the charts. Assisted by constant promotion and airplay, in December it ascended the charts again to become Number One in the U.K. It made it to Number Five in Norway and Italy, Number 22 in Japan, and Number 41 in Denmark.

According to Elton, he was really happy with *Goodbye Yellow Brick Road.* "I think it's the best thing I've done," he claimed at the time.[17]

The *Goodbye Yellow Brick Road* album succeeded on so many different levels. First of all, as a package, it was certainly Elton's most elaborate one yet. And, with four sides of music, it delivered a quadruple delight of Elton's most varied, most inspired music in his five-year career as a solo performer.

The cover featured an illustration by artist Ian Beck, who portrayed Elton stepping through a poster on a wall, into a different dimension, and onto the fabled Yellow Brick Road of *The Wonderful Wizard of Oz*. He is depicted wearing red glittering platform shoes and a silk tour jacket with his named emblazoned on the back. The two- record-set configuration of the original vinyl album package lent itself to a triple gate-fold cardboard cover. When fully opened up, it revealed photos of Elton and Bernie and the band and all of the lyrics to all of the songs.

The music contained on the album was well thought out musically and lyrically. The theme seemed inarguably to be a cinematic one with which everyone could identify. Cowboys ("Roy Rogers"), naughty ladies ("Dirty Little Girl" and "Sweet Painted Lady"), rock stars ("Bennie & The Jets"), and even Marilyn Monroe ("Candle in the Wind") all shared the space on this ultimate Elton offering. Every song is an imaginative vignette that takes the listener to a different space, from the classical organ masterpiece on "Funeral for a Friend" to the titillating "All the Girls Love Alice" to the beautiful ride-off-into-the-sunset finale on "Harmony." The album wasn't just a bus ride down the Yellow Brick Road, it was a guided tour. The song that sums up the album's contents the most is the telling song, "I've Seen that Movie Too." Even the exercise in island masturbation—"Jamaica Jerk-Off"—hit a fun and irreverent note that was universally embraced. The album was so cinematically inspired that it was nearly entitled *Talking Pictures, Silent Movies*, but John and Taupin changed their minds at the last minute.

When the album came out, Elton and Bernie weren't sure whether or not the critics would praise them or crucify them. According to Elton, he did read what the reviewers had to say about him, and he took their comments to heart. He had been criticized recently in the rock publications *Creem*, *Crawdaddy*, and *Rolling Stone* and was smarting from it. This time around it was different.

Wayne Robins glowingly wrote about the new album in *Creem*, "Elton John and his wordsmith Bernie Taupin, who now have perched a short tier below the 'Beatle/Stones' on the mass pop scale (not enough heterosexual good looks; too many ballads). *Goodbye Yellow Brick Road* confirms it more than ever before: it's their best album (most listenable) to date, and it just might as well be subtitled 'The Americanization of Elton John.'"[18]

Richard Cromelin claimed in *Phonograph Record*, "*Goodbye Yellow Brick Road* contains some of the most beautiful melodies and music Elton has ever made, particularly in 'Harmony,' 'Roy Rogers,' 'Candle in the Wind,' 'Love Lies Bleeding' and the title song."[16]

Record World magazine called it, "A magnificent achievement. Two records of indisputedly brilliant songs and musicianship. Few albums surpass it in spirit and fewer still in intelligence."[138]

Typically, in oft-condescending *Rolling Stone*, reviewer Stephen Davis snidely claimed, "*Goodbye Yellow Brick Road* is a massive double-record exposition of unabashed fantasy, myth, wet dreams and cornball acts, an overproduced array of musical portraits…. This would have made a lovely, if slightly brittle, single LP."[128] But it is funny how time changes everything. In later years the same publication—*Rolling Stone*—heralded the same album as being one of the best rock albums ever. In that publication's 2005 book of *The 500 Greatest Albums of All Time*, they proclaimed, "Everything about *Goodbye Yellow Brick Road* was supersonically huge, from the Wagnerian-opera-like combo of 'Funeral for a Friend' and 'Love Lies Bleeding' to the electric boots and mohair suit of 'Bennie & The Jets.'"[129]

When nerdy teenage Reggie Dwight sat alone in his bedroom in Pinner, he dared to dream of one day composing a rock & roll masterpiece. With *Goodbye Yellow Brick Road*, he had truly created one.

In October 1973, while in Los Angeles, Tony King took Elton to one of John Lennon's recording sessions. According to Tony, "They're both fabulously warm, sympathetic, intelligent people. I felt that they would have a lot in common."[144] Indeed, King was right.

For that particular session, Lennon was working with legendary producer Phil Spector on his 1973 *Mind Games* album. Elton had grown up mesmerized by Spector's trademark "Wall of Sound" formula used to record groups like The Ronettes, Ike & Tina Turner, and The Crystals with Darlene Love and Lala Brooks. Spector and Lennon were close, having worked together on The Beatles' *Let it Be* album. Elton claimed that he was in awe to be in the presence of two such musical legends who had provided so many songs that were a part of his own personal teenage soundtrack.

At the time, John Lennon was in a period of his life that has been entitled "The Lost Weekend." He and Yoko Ono had decided to take a break from their marriage, and Yoko decided that if John was going to have a personal relationship with another woman, it should be one she chose. She suggested her assistant at the time, May Pang. So, off John and May went. The period that John spent away from Yoko lasted nearly two years, and May was with him the entire time.

One of the most notorious events of Lennon's "Lost Weekend" was a night at The Troubadour in Los Angeles spent with May Pang and a group of friends. John was drinking heavily that night. After one trip to the bathroom, he plastered a feminine sanitary napkin to his forehead. When his waitress got surly with him, Lennon said to her, "Do you know who I am?" She replied, "Yeah, you're some asshole with a Kotex on your head."

According to May, while that incident is often portrayed as indicative of all of Lennon's "Lost Weekend," that was just an isolated evening of drunken revelry. This was not only the time when John was doing his *Mind Games* and *Walls & Bridges* albums, it was also an era when he reunited with his estranged son, Julian Lennon, whom he hadn't seen in four years. Into this historic time for Lennon, came Elton John.

"John and I met Elton at exactly the same time," May Pang recalls. "It was in the fall of '73 and it was through Tony King. He introduced us. I don't remember the exact date, but I remember who was there. Elton was there for so many events, like when Tony King was dressed up as the Queen of England, that was done on my birthday, and Elton was there, so that was in October of '73. We thought Elton was really very nice and very talented. I really loved his music, especially 'Your Song,' so I was really thrilled. It was just nice to meet him. He wasn't as outrageous or as outlandish yet. But as the months went on, he continued to change, and I thought, 'Oh, my God!'"[148]

When each of America's top music trade publications tallied up the sales appeal of all of the recording stars on the charts during the entire year of 1973—*Billboard*, *Record World*, and

Cashbox—all unanimously christened Elton the Number One singles artist of the year. He had truly become a hit-making legend.

Amidst all of this activity, the documentary film that Bryan Forbes had been working on was broadcast on December 4, 1973, on the ITV network in England. It was titled *Elton John and Bernie Taupin Say Goodbye Norma Jean and Other Things* and was later broadcast in the United States on ABC-TV, on May 12, 1974.

Elton ended 1973 with a Number One album on the charts and a whole lot of holiday cheer. Inspired by the season, he released his first Christmas single, which became a huge hit in Britain, making it to Number 24 on the charts. Elton gleefully announced, "We just thought it would be nice to do a Christmas single. The Christmas thing is very Spectorish," he proclaimed. "And it's called 'Step Into Christmas' and it sounds like The Ronettes, with everything Christmassy on it, and the 'B' side is called 'Ho Ho Ho—Who'd Be a Turkey at Christmas,' which is slightly lunatic and again is something I've never done before. It's a loon—a jolly *larf*."[17]

In December 1973, Elton fulfilled another longtime dream by presenting a Christmas extravaganza at London's Hammersmith Odeon. It ran for four nights, and—along with the new yuletide-themed single—was his way of wishing his fans a Merry Christmas.

Elton's body started to resemble that of the roly-poly Penguin in the Batman cartoons at this time. Steven Gaines in *Circus* described Elton's weight gain: "His high living, especially in Los Angeles in the fall of 1973, added a good fifty pounds to his frame, and when he returned to England to spend Christmas with good friends Ronnie Lane and Rod Stewart, he spent most of his time eating."[140]

Charles Shaar Murray in *NME* also wrote of Elton's physique: "This balding, bespectacled plumpoid never fails to put on a great show. Young girls adore him, probably because he reminds them of their last teddy bear. What he loses in sinuous attraction/repulsion he makes up in sheer solid lovableness. He's round and cuddly and he sweats a lot…. Unlike David Bowie (who looks convincing whatever he's wearing) Elt achieves his effects by the total contrast between clothes style and physique."[58] Regardless of what the press thought of him physically, this formerly geeky kid from Pinner was now an international sensation, a multimillionaire, and an undeniable superstar. Now that he stood at the absolute zenith of his fame, how was he going to handle it and what would he achieve with his wealth and power? Inquiring minds wanted to know.

CHAPTER NINE

The Bitch Is Back

Starting 1974 with a wildly successful Number One album on the charts should have made Elton John incredibly happy and in many ways it did. But there were new pressures put upon him as well. The press proclaimed that at present, Elton was rivaling his Number One idols: The Beatles. He was already friends with Ringo Starr, and later that year he would become extremely friendly with John Lennon, the most elusive member of The Beatles. It was to be a year of extremes for Elton, yielding two more Number One albums and more "standing room only" global touring. Those were completely believable goals for him to attain. The truly unbelievable one was that he was about to purchase a controlling interest in a sports team. Who could have predicted that this man dressed in hot pants and platform shoes, with pink hair and light-up eyeglasses, would throw his hat into the sports ring and become the superstar director of a soccer club?

When asked by one journalist what the key to his success was, he wryly replied, "Vitamin E. Quaaludes. Heroin. Plus sexual intercourse with sheep."[20] If that was indeed the secret to his success, it seemed to be working.

However, the pressures of fame pushed him into seclusion when he was in England. According to Elton at the time, "You can't be famous and be available to the public. I don't mean that in a snobbish sense at all, but if I walked about in London all the time people would say. 'Hmmm, he shouldn't do that.' They don't want to see you in Camden Town buying vegetables, they want to see you on the fuckin' stage wearing your whatever you wear. They don't associate you with going to the toilet or buying fruit or having troubles with your plumbing at home—they don't. You wouldn't expect the Royal Family to go out and buy budgie seed. 'Oh yes, saw her yesterday walking the corgis.'"[58]

Yet, he knew that he couldn't spend his life as a recluse. After all, he was only 25 years old at the time. That was a little young for him to pull off an "I *vant* to be alone" Greta Garbo routine.

Although he was sitting on top of the musical world, still Elton found things in his life that pissed him off and threw him into dark moody depressions. He was very aware of the pressures of his current recording contract with Dick James, and the fact that he had to release two new albums during 1974. He had hoped that he could make *Goodbye Yellow Brick Road*, a two-record set, contractually count as two albums. It did not.

Meanwhile, he was also pursuing a passion that dated back to his childhood. He used to go with his father, Stanley, to root for the local Watford soccer team. It was an interest that had not died in him.

In the latter part of 1973, when he was interviewed for *New Musical Express*, writer Julie Webb confessed she was a Watford fan. Elton and Julie spoke of their mutual love of the team. During their conversation, Julie mentioned to him that Watford was in financial trouble, as well as suffering a losing streak on the playing field. She suggested to him that perhaps he could do some sort of a benefit concert for the team to raise both funds and the spirits of the players.

Once this idea was planted in his head, Elton started to ponder how he could help. The big question was: "Would a soccer team accept the assistance and the cash of a flamboyant rock star, who regularly dressed as the gayest creature on the planet?" The answer was "Yes." Not only would they accept his high-profile presence, but they would also gladly welcome his money.

While he considered a possible role in the world of sports, there were other more pressing matters on his mind. He had a stretch of ten days in January 1974 when he could record his next album. Right afterwards he had a scheduled concert tour of the Far East, and the months that followed were to be occupied with already-booked British and European tours. Somehow he had to come up with the new songs and new recordings to complete what was to become his tenth album.

After recording a consecutive trio of albums at Château d'Herouville in France, it was time for a new setting. His live *11-*

17-70 album had been recorded in The United States. Why not give "the colonies" a try this time around?

Out in the middle of the woods of Colorado sat the perfect setting for recording: a forest retreat called Caribou Ranch. It was a totally modern recording facility located about thirty miles between Denver and Boulder in a tiny town called Nederland. Nederland had a population of less than 500 people. *Caribou* was owned by the management team of James William Guercio and Larry Fitzgerald. Among the major artists they were managing at the time was the highly successful group, Chicago. Guercio was also the director of the popular 1973 Robert Blake police film *Electra Glide in Blue.*

Elton had high hopes for the whole recording experience in the Rocky Mountains. They were on a tight schedule to finish the album in less than a fortnight, so the pressure was on. Unfortunately, Elton instantly fell into one of his dark moods, causing the first three days to be wasted.

Although Gus Dudgeon and Elton would later whine and complain about the recording process and finished product on the *Caribou* album, in fact, it yielded two of Elton John's all-time, career-defining, top-twenty hits: "Don't Let the Sun Go Down on Me" and "The Bitch Is Back."

Elton was later to explain, "*Caribou* was a disaster period for us, because I was in such a state. We'd been working nonstop and we had to go and make this album just after Christmas, and then go to Japan and Australia. The album was cut in ten days, two days of which were lost because of the studio going wrong. In the end, we more or less cut 14 tracks in three or four days."[26]

According to Dudgeon, the biggest nightmare was getting a decent performance out of Elton for the song "Don't Let the Sun Go Down on Me." "When Elton sang the vocal track, he was in a filthy mood," Gus claimed. "On some takes, he'd scream it, on others he'd mumble it. Or he'd just stand there, staring at the control room. Eventually, he flung off the cans [headphones] and said, 'O.K., let's hear what we got.' When I played it to him, he said, 'That's a load of fucking crap. You can send it to Engelbert Humperdinck and if he doesn't like it, you can give it to Lulu as a demo.'"[87]

After the *Caribou* recording sessions were finished, Elton, Bernie, and the band took off for Los Angeles, and then it was on to his concert dates in Asia and Australia. While the stressed "Rocket Man" and his crew were on tour, Gus Dudgeon was left with all of the tapes, which he had to mix and try and make some sense of in Elton's absence. He felt that the songs needed some more instruments to bring them to life, and he brought in the horn group, The Tower of Power Horns. He also felt that they needed some more vocal strength and some dynamic background singing on the tracks. So he brought in the very best: The Beach Boys, Dusty Springfield, and Toni Tennille of The Captain & Tennille.

As Elton explained it, "I wasn't at all happy with the vocal when we did it at the Caribou Studios, but once we got to L.A. it didn't sound too bad and by the time we'd got back to London it sounded all right. It was all very strange, 'cause Gus was telling The Beach Boys not to take any notice of the vocals because they're rubbish and The Beach Boys were saying, 'It doesn't sound too bad to us.' So finally, I think, they brought Gus around to kind of liking it. To be honest, for a time I thought I was going to have to redo all the vocals on *Caribou*.... I did redo one, 'Dixie Lily'.... Making *Caribou* was a very trying experience."[26]

When the album was completed with Gus Dudgeon's new musical touches added, it really had a brilliance all its own. However, the producer was not completely happy with the result. After it was recorded, released, and became a huge hit, no one was more amazed than he. "*Caribou* is a piece of crap," Dudgeon complained. "The sound is the worst, the songs are nowhere, the sleeve came out wrong, the lyrics weren't that good, the singing wasn't all there, the playing wasn't great, the production is just plain lousy. When I got nominated for 'Best Produced Single/Album of the Year' I couldn't stop laughing, I thought it was ridiculous that I could be nominated for an award for the worst thing I'd ever done."[30]

Perhaps, in his quest to make the original and mediocre tapes sound great, he over compensated and delivered exactly what the fans wanted. Furthermore, The Elton John Band all sounded great on *Caribou*. This was the first album to feature Ray Cooper's percussion work. Together with Dee Murray and Davey Johnstone, they were becoming established as a key part of Elton's stage show, and they were also an integral part of creating the sound and character of his albums from this era.

According to Elton, *Caribou* was just Cooper's initiation project as part of the team: "It was just a feeler for him. He did a couple of vibes things and some percussion. The next time we record, he'll be playing drums, he'll be playing keyboards. He'd only just joined the band. Now we're getting him organized with ARPs and things like that."[20]

While all of this was going on, the album *Goodbye Yellow Brick Road* continued to be a huge hit on the international charts. There was so much good music on it that the public could not seem to get enough. In America the song "Goodbye Yellow Brick Road" hit Number Two, while in England the song "Candle in the Wind" climbed to Number 11.

They didn't anticipate releasing any more singles off of the album; however, American radio stations had a different idea. "Bennie & The Jets" was suddenly getting airplay on R&B stations. In fact, Elton was still at Caribou Ranch when he got the phone call that CKLW, the Windsor, Ontario, radio station that reached all of the Detroit area, had been playing "Bennie & The Jets" constantly. The Motor City's black radio station, WJLB, was playing it as well and was taking credit for breaking Elton to a whole new audience. The song went on to become his first hit on the "soul" stations in America, and it hit Number One on the Pop Chart. "Bennie & The Jets" also sold nearly three million copies and became one of the year's biggest smashes on the airwaves.

Meanwhile, Elton's concert tour of Asia and Australia started out well but featured some unfortunate events along the way. It was also a tour that found Elton stretching out even further in his flamboyant stage costuming. Never afraid of looking too much like a drag queen, this tour featured a costume that paid homage to Josephine Baker, the Roaring Twenties showgirl who took Paris by storm. Covered in puffs of feathers, it included pants and a jacket which were red on the left side and green on the right. Another of his outfits included a green net veil, dripping from a wide-rimmed hat all decorated in brownish-red pheasant feathers. For some of the shows he was clad in a black jumpsuit with fluorescent pom-poms all over it. Although he was acknowledged as the "King of the Pop Charts," he was dressing like "The Mad Queen of Rock & Roll."

Since his 1971 Australian concert tour, Elton had complained to the press that his trip to "The Land Down Under," was something of a disaster. This did not sit well with his Australian fans. One of the people who took offense was television personality Ian "Molly" Meldrum. In an Australian magazine, Meldrum wrote an "Open Letter to Elton John," defending his country and the sincerity of the singer's fans. According to the letter, "Everywhere throughout your Australian tour you had almost capacity houses and...the audiences time and time again gave you incredible receptions. Well, we'd love to have you back because if you judge popularity on record sales then you are one of the most popular artists in this country."[136]

In time, "Molly" Meldrum would become one of Elton's best and dearest friends. He was also gay, and, throughout the years, he introduced Elton to Australian society, as well as to a countless supply of handsome, gay Australian men.

True to what Meldrum had promised, Elton's 1974 tour of Australia was a huge smash. His opening night in Perth drew a record-setting crowd of 14,500. He went on to surpass that audience when he performed in Melbourne before 19,000 people. Then in Sydney, at Randwick Racecourse, he drew 25,000, setting a record at that venue for ticket grosses. During this same month, teen star David Cassidy was also in Australia touring. Although he was the heartthrob of the moment, at that same facility, Cassidy had drawn a crowd of only 12,500.

Elton's final concert on this tour was to be his February 28 show at Auckland, New Zealand. He arrived in Auckland a couple of days before that final show. On February 26, Elton not only attended Cassidy's concert, he made a surprise onstage guest appearance in the middle of it.

For some reason, John Reid seemed to be involved in one dispute after another during the Australian tour. After the first gig in Perth, he accused the concert promoter of not giving him his fair share of the box-office take, causing a huge controversy.

The day after the David Cassidy show, Elton and John Reid were scheduled to attend two parties. The first one was given by the local distributor of his albums and singles, Festival Records. When the wine and liquor ran out before the party was over, Reid got into a snit and started a heated argument with Kevin Williams, one of the company's representatives. One of Williams' friends there was Judith Anne Baragwanath, a well-known model and journalist. According to Reid's later account, when Judith ran to Williams' defense, she called Reid and Elton "a couple of poofs." According to Judith's later testimony, she didn't call them "poofs," she only called John Reid "a rotten little bastard."

Although he was now 24 years old, inside Reid still had the instincts of the scruffy Scottish schoolboy. He hauled off and—allegedly—socked Judith square in the face. Elton had missed the incident, but, upon Reid's insistence, they promptly left. They had another party to go to that evening. Held in another part of town at the Auckland Town Hall, this one was for David Cassidy. The news that Elton's manager had just slugged Judith traveled quickly from one party to the next. When Reid came up to Elton at the Cassidy party and told him that they had to leave immediately, Elton asked, "Why?" Reid informed him of what had happened and that he had just gotten wind of the fact that there were a couple of men who were there to "even the score" for the previous party's incident.

Reid suspected the source of the threats was coming from journalist David Wheeler. Elton marched over to Wheeler and asked what the problem was. When an ugly dialogue ensued, Reid came to his lover's defense and allegedly slugged Wheeler, knocking him down and kicking the reporter while he was writhing on the floor. Reid and Elton promptly exited the party right afterward.

The following day, John Reid was arrested on two separate charges of assault and was put in jail. Ultimately, he was incarcerated for the next 28 days. Actually, most of his "incarceration" was spent under house arrest, residing in the home of a prison warden and his wife. Having Reid arrested only further distressed Elton's mental state.

With a full schedule of European concerts ahead of him, Elton went back to England without his boyfriend/manager. Depressed, embarrassed, and exhausted, Elton made the decision to cancel his upcoming tour. It wasn't long, though, before he had a new project.

Elton's acting debut would be in The Who's *Tommy*. His path to portraying "The Pinball Wizard" in the outlandish film is a twisted one indeed. He explains, "The story with *Tommy* was that the role was originally offered to Rod Stewart, and he said to me, 'What do you think?' I said, 'Oh, don't do that! It's not a good thing for you to do.' Rod and I are friends and kind of rivals. Then they romanced me so much that in the end I did it because Pete Townshend rang me up…. So, I told Rod not to do it, and I ended up doing it. He was really furious and rightly so."[137]

Gus, Elton, and the band went into a London recording studio and did a new version of the song "Pinball Wizard" that emphasized the piano work at the beginning. Elton then filmed his one scene—with a huge pinball machine, wearing a wool lumberjack's cap and a pair of enormous three-foot-tall Doc Marten boots. He had to be put in them with the assistance of several stagehands.

Elton filmed his segment in three days, and when he was done, he talked director Ken Russell into letting him have the boots as a souvenir. When Reggie Dwight was a young boy he always wanted to stand above the masses. In his three-foot-tall boots in *Tommy*, grown-up Reg got to do exactly that.

Back in rural England, Bernie decided that he was too isolated in the middle of nowhere with Maxine at Piglet-In-The-Wilds, so he sold the cottage and purchased a huge house in Elton's neighborhood on the Wentworth Golf Course. Bernie and Maxine quickly became an integral part of Elton's social scene. Bernie had also purchased a home in Los Angeles located on Doheny Drive, next door to legendary Hollywood director George Cukor.

Elton was still enjoying his home, "Hercules." It was stuffed with his ever-growing collection of toys. It seemed that he was filling it up with new possessions by the day. "It would look like the British Museum, except that I've got Gold records on the ceiling," Elton said at the time.[140]

Realizing that he was looking a bit rotund of late, in 1974, Elton packed his bags and went to Gardiner's Tennis Clinic in Arizona. The plan was to throw himself into tennis and lose weight. Having successfully dropped a couple of inches off his waistline, Elton was recharged by the experience. "I went to a tennis ranch in

Arizona for two weeks because I had to get away from everything," he claimed. "I was screaming.... I just couldn't loon. Very depressed, very overweight—I was really blimpish at Watford—so I went away and lost about 28 pounds. It's all discipline. I just played tennis for seven hours a day and dieted a lot."[20]

Meeting tennis pro Billie Jean King and becoming friends with her was one of the highlights of going to Arizona. King had a tennis team, The Philadelphia Freedoms, and she casually asked Elton to write a theme song for them. The obvious result was the song "Philadelphia Freedom," which Elton recorded during studio sessions in Los Angeles in June and July of 1974.

Meanwhile, Elton hadn't forgotten his old passion for the Watford football team. On May 5, 1974, he staged a benefit concert for the team with Rod Stewart. Together they drew a crowd of 40,000 people at the Vicarage Road facility. Since his team was called The Hornets, Elton let his stage costume reflect his reverence and respect for the team. He dressed as an actual hornet, wings and all. One of the songs that Elton performed at that concert was The Beatles' psychedelic classic "Lucy in the Sky with Diamonds." The crowd's reaction was so good that he considered recording his own version.

Elton took his job as the director of a soccer team very seriously. According to him, part of his role became that of the team's cheerleader. He recalled, "With Watford I never sat in the stand until I became a director. I used to stand on the terraces. So it was the same as before: I couldn't believe it was happening. But if it was happening, my approach to it was to be totally committed and professional."[43]

On May 18, Elton gave another benefit concert in England. This one was for The Invalid Children's Aid Society and was held at Royal Festival Hall. In the audience was Her Royal Highness, Princess Margaret. She was a big fan of Elton and his music, and it was at her request that he performed.

Since it was more of a staid and formal audience, the songs that Elton selected for that concert borrowed heavily from his first couple of "less rock & roll" albums. He played "Love Song," "Your Song," "Border Song," and two selections from the pre-hits days, "Skyline Pigeon" and "Bad Side of the Moon." For "Love Song," Elton's friend Lesley Duncan sang harmony.

Meanwhile, as the *Caribou* album was being prepared for release, Elton became quite enthusiastic about the results. In spite of the fact that he had originally thought that the *Caribou* album sessions were a disaster, by the time Gus Dudgeon was done fiddling with them, Elton loved the songs they had produced. He revealed, "I haven't mixed any of my own stuff for four or five albums. Gus does two or three different kinds of mixes and plays them for me. I just pick out the one I like best and make suggestions on how to improve the most superior of the lot."[140]

He was also happy recording at the Colorado ranch facility. Elton explained, "I could not do an album where you have to take a cab to the studio in the morning. I like to write all the songs there and rehearse them there too."[140]

After he narrowed down the 14 original tracks recorded to his ten favorites, Elton loved the results. "'The Bitch Is Back' is a real raunchy rock & roll number that has the Tower of Power horn people playing on it. That's one of my favorite tracks on the album. It's one of the best rock & roll things we've ever done. We were even going to call the album *The Bitch Is Back,* but we thought it was a bit too passé to call it that. It doesn't really sum up what the album is about. Then there's 'Pinky,' which is a very traditional Elton John–type of ballad. The words are really nice on this one. It's very influenced by the cold winter in Caribou."[140]

The *Caribou* album was released in America on June 24 and in England on June 28. In both countries it hit Number One within weeks, as well as in Australia. In America it debuted at Number Five, becoming only the fifth album to achieve such a feat in *Billboard* magazine. The previous albums to debut that high on the chart had been *All Things Must Pass* by George Harrison, the soundtrack from *Woodstock, Hey Jude,* and *Led Zeppelin III.* Elton was setting and breaking records on the charts and as a concert performer.

The first single off of the *Caribou* album was "Don't Let the Sun Go Down on Me," which peaked at Number 16 in the U.K. and Number Two in the U.S., where it was certified Gold. The second single, "The Bitch Is Back" made it to Number 15 in the U.K. and Number Four in America. In Australia, both songs hit Number One.

"The Bitch Is Back" was one of the most brilliant songs on the *Caribou* album, along with the dramatically sweeping "Don't Let the Sun Go Down on Me" and the absolutely engrossing seven-minute-long story song "Ticking." When "The Bitch Is Back" was released as a single, radio programmers constantly wondered who was the "bitch"? They assumed it was a woman. For anyone who ever knew Elton, there was never any doubt that in this case the "bitch" was truly Elton himself.

The inspiration for the song came during one of Elton's tirades. This one occurred in Bernie and Maxine's presence. Upon hearing Elton's foul-mooded complaining one day, Maxine rolled her eyes and said to her husband, "The bitch is back." That was all it took, and lyricist Taupin was at work. To complete the sound of this exciting tongue-in-cheek rock song, Dusty Springfield is heard singing in the background.

Speaking of dynamic backgrounds, the vocal accompaniment on "Don't Let the Sun Go Down on Me" was nothing short of incredible. This was the official beginning of superstar guest spots on Elton John albums. Singing behind him on this song are The Beach Boys, and their original beach girl: Toni Tennille. Toni and her husband Daryl Dragon would soon find pop music stardom as The Captain & Tennille in 1975 with their first hit "Love Will Keep Us Together." Before that, they were part of the Beach Boys stage show.

One of the most dramatic songs on *Caribou* is the song "Ticking," about a deranged man who takes a group of hostages. It was essentially the same story later filmed in *Dog Day Afternoon*. One of the most exciting aspects of the song is that it is just Elton and his piano, telling the story of a desperate life on the line.

The press was mixed on *Caribou*. Since the album followed the blockbuster *Goodbye Yellow Brick Road*, expectations were high. Charles Shaar Murray in *NME* claimed, "*Caribou* had 'product' stamped all over it: it came on thin and forced, with only 'The Bitch Is Back' displaying the full tilt rock & roll naiveté that has characterized most of Elton's best work."[32]

"Is it as good as *Yellow Brick Road?*" asked Chris Welch in *Melody Maker*. He quickly answered: "Well, it's different. An entertaining selection of hot ditties…. There seems to have been a conscious effort to break away from the doomier aspects of Elton's last winner, but that doesn't mean Bernie Taupin has relaxed in the lyric department…most of the lyrics have that bitter-sweet Martini quality…. Overall, an excellent compilation."[19]

Bud Scoppa in *Phonograph Record* loved it. "For an artist with distinct limitations—vocal, compositional, and stylistic—Elton John makes awfully good records," he declared. "One of the reasons is his avowed love of rock & roll records and parallel need to make recordings that fall naturally into the historical stream of classic rock & roll."[21]

On the cover of the *Caribou* album, Elton was photographed wearing a faux fur, tiger-striped jacket that looked like someone had skinned Tony the Tiger from the Kellogg's Frosted Flakes cereal box. His eyeglasses were enormous with rose-colored lenses and little pink roses painted on the clear plastic frames. Discussing his famous passion for goofy eyeglasses, Elton claimed, "I don't think people buy my records because of my spectacles—or because of my testicles!"[20]

Obviously the album's title was a salute to the recording studio in which it had been recorded, though Elton once mentioned that other titles had been considered: "Bette Midler said my new album should be called *Fat Reg from Pinner*."[20]

True to form, when *Caribou* was released, Elton was already thinking about what was next for the group. Ultimately, Elton and Bernie chose an autobiographical theme. It was something of a risk. Would the critics find it conceited and self-indulgent? The finished product was eventually titled *Captain Fantastic & The Brown Dirt Cowboy*. According to Taupin, it was a unique writing experience: "It's possibly one of the least commercial albums we've ever done, because we went out to make a concept album. I'd written the songs chronologically, so we had to put them in that order."[146]

In addition, Elton got this idea in his head that he should compose the music for this new album while on a trans-Atlantic cruise ship, as though he was Noel Coward and this was 1932. If it were the plot of a '30s film, he would be Fred Astaire, and he would run into Ginger Rogers on the boat. Instead, he ran into a large female opera singer, who was also a hearty eater.

In June 1974, Elton and Tony King boarded the S.S. *France* in Southampton, England, on a five-day cruise bound for New York

City. Elton had tried to book the one room with a piano, but found that an opera singer had reserved it for herself. When she stepped away to eat, Elton swept in and quickly wrote the melodies that would become his next studio album.

When the ship docked in Manhattan, John Lennon was at the Record Plant recording studio, and Tony brought Elton to the session. John was recording tracks for his *Walls & Bridges* album, which was to become—along with *Imagine*—the only other Number One solo album he had while he was alive. That night he was in the middle of the song "Whatever Gets You Through the Night."

Lennon described that session: "I was fiddling about one night and Elton John walked in with Tony King of Apple—you know, we're all good friends—and the next minute Elton said, 'Say, can I put a bit of piano on that?' I said, 'Sure—love it!' He zapped in. I was amazed at his ability.... I knew him, but I'd never seen him play. A fine musician, great piano player. I was really pleasantly surprised at the way he could get in on such a souse track and add to it and keep up with the rhythm changes—obviously, 'cause it doesn't keep the same rhythm...and then he sang with me. We had a great time."[143] Elton also sang backing vocals on Lennon's song "Surprise, Surprise (Sweet Bird of Paradox)."

Lennon fan that he was, Elton was thrilled to be in the studio with his idol. The way he described it was: "A fucking dream! I really did think I'd died and gone to heaven."[47]

Since, at this point in time, Elton's recording contract with MCA in the United States was due to lapse, John Reid made the rounds of potential bidders for Elton. Not wanting to lose their superstar artist, MCA offered him a substantially better contract than his previous deal. He was to be paid eight million dollars for five albums. At the time, it was the most lucrative deal in recording history. On June 13, 1974, he signed a new deal with MCA. To make a splash, John Reid took out huge one-page advertisements in both the *New York Times* and the *Los Angeles Times* to let the world know that Elton was back and that MCA had him. "I was endeavoring to make a lot of statements in one simple way. It made a statement to the public, to the financial community, to the record industry, and for myself."[147]

The end of June and the beginning of July 1974 were set aside for the recording of Elton's next album, *Captain Fantastic & The Brown Dirt Cowboy*, as well as the singles "Philadelphia Freedom" and "Lucy in the Sky with Diamonds." Elton invited John Lennon to sing as a guest on his version of "Lucy in the Sky with Diamonds."

According to May Pang, Lennon loved the idea: "He said, 'Oh, great!' So, we went to Caribou and had a great time up there. Caribou is all open space and everything is built log cabin style, everything there is built like that. There is a mess hall, then there are several houses. The elevation there is 9,000 feet high; they are definitely not on sea level…. Elton said that we should come a week ahead of time to adjust to the altitude and acclimate ourselves, so we did. Everyone had a great time. You can go and ride horses, and you were in the country atmosphere of a ranch. I remember seeing Jim Guercio riding by on his horse."[148] While May and Lennon were there, Lennon and Elton also recorded a John Lennon–composed song, "One Day at a Time," with Lennon providing harmony vocals.

During this era, Elton was pleased to lend his songwriting talents to other artists. He commented that now that Bernie and he owned their own music, they would like "to collaborate more and try and write songs for other people. We've just written one for Roderick [Rod Stewart] on his new album and we've just written a couple for Kiki, and we want to write one for Etta James or Ray Charles, people we idolize, like Dusty Springfield and get the good singers back in the chart again…"[17] Rod Stewart's recording of the Elton John song "Let Me Be Your Car" was included on Stewart's *Smiler* album, which was released in October 1974.

Elton also wrote the song "Snookeroo" for Ringo Starr, who by now was one of Elton's closest friends. The song appeared on Ringo's top-ten *Goodnight Vienna* album, which was released later that year.

Elton was also looking to expand his own sound musically by adding another keyboard player to his touring and recording band. He wanted someone who could play: "Electric piano, Moog and Mellotron, just to fill the sound out. When we were in the States, Gregg Allman played one number with us, and it was amazing, the effect one extra instrument made."[17]

But it was Rocket Records that was really on Elton's mind. Rocket had yet to yield a strong hit. In fact, they had just dropped everyone from the label, except for Maldwyn Pop and Kiki Dee. Elton was actively looking for new talent to sign. "We've listened to so many tapes—that's how we found a lot of people," Elton explained.[58] "We turned down Queen and Cockney Rebel, so we're pretty good judges of character," he laughed. According to him, "They wanted a lot of money and we just couldn't afford it."[20]

Thus far, the only significant artist on the Rocket label was Kiki Dee, and her records weren't exactly blockbusters yet. Elton and Reid were determined to produce a hit for Kiki Dee, though. She was so obviously talented and lovely, and she had instantly become a part of their social circle. Kiki also toured with Elton singing background vocals. Her second album for Rocket Records was to be entitled *I've Got the Music in Me*. They were recording at the New York City studio that Jimi Hendrix had started: Electric Ladyland. When it came time to do the album's title track, somehow Kiki just froze. This was a song that she was supposed to really let loose and belt out, and she couldn't seem to get in the right frame of mind. Part of the problem could have been that she was feeling a bit intimidated. Here she was in Hendrix's former studio, singing with the great soul singer Cissy Houston, being produced by Gus Dudgeon and Clive Franks, with Elton John looking on. It was enough to make anyone freeze in their tracks.

Recalled Kiki, "Cissy was there doing the backing vocals with these two black women. They were absolutely fantastic singers. And I just bottled it. I lost confidence."[88]

Elton decided to completely break the mood and the tension. He stripped off all of his clothes and ran naked through the studio. Kiki was laughing so hard that whatever tension had previously existed was instantly dissipated. After that Kiki delivered one of the most exciting solo performances of her career.

When the song "I've Got the Music in Me" was released late in the summer of 1974, it became her biggest selling and highest charting single in the U.S., peaking at Number 12. The album of the same name, made it to Number 38 in *Billboard*. That same year, Neil Sedaka made his debut on Rocket Records. Neil had been a singing star in the late 1950s and early 1960s with a string of top ten hits, including "Oh! Carol" (1959), "Stairway to Heaven" (1960), "Calendar Girl" (1960), "Happy Birthday, Sweet Sixteen" (1961), "Next Door to an Angel" (1963), and his Number One hit "Breaking Up is Hard to Do" (1962).

In the summer of 1974 Elton met Sedaka, who had a British hit with his new recording "Laughter in the Rain." When Elton asked him if it was going to be released in America, Sedaka laughingly told him, "Don't ask! Over there, they think I'm a ghost."[87]

When Elton heard that Sedaka's new recordings weren't even available in the States, he offered the former teen idol a deal with Rocket Records. This was exactly the kind of challenge that Elton was looking for: the chance to revive the career of someone he had always admired.

Within a matter of weeks, the best tracks of the three recent British albums by Neil Sedaka were compiled onto one new Rocket Record entitled *Sedaka's Back* and blasted off to America. Twelve weeks later Neil's recording of "Laughter in the Rain" was Number One in the U.S. Who would have ever dreamed that it was Neil who was to give Rocket Records their very first chart-topping hit.

While Elton was on his American tour in the fall of 1974, he gave an interview with the *Chicago Tribune* and spoke of his hobbies at the time. "Rod [Stewart] and I go to the football games a lot, or to dinner, or a club, or sometimes a movie. Bernie's really more into films than I am, but I liked *Blazing Saddles* and *Death in Venice*.... The only thing I can't stand is musicals. The idea of someone getting up and dancing in the middle of a movie— it's atrocious."[70]

While he was feeding the press innocent stories about going to the movies with Bernie or catching a soccer match with Rod, he left out another hobby. By this time, both Elton and Reid had begun to dabble in cocaine. It was the perfect drug for those in search of a boost of energy. Unfortunately, it can also enhance mood swings to new extremes. Considering the moodiness of both Reid and Elton, it often led to fights and tantrums from the most famous closeted gay couple of the rock & roll set.

When he was asked by the press about his drug habits, Elton pleaded pharmaceutical ignorance. "What's a 'J?'" he lamely asked. "Oh, one of them. I don't smoke at all. I once tried puffing on a cigarette to the great delight of the band and almost choked myself to death. I've never touched anything...pot or LSD, though a lotta people think I'm into cocaine."[26]

John Reid was later to look back at this era and say, "I joined the record industry and I got a desk and a drink cabinet. I ended up on two or three grams of cocaine a day. It was always there."[88]

Mary Wilson of The Supremes recalls the way in which cocaine was offered to members of the Hollywood show business elite in the early 1970s: "The best parties were usually given by movie producers, and a group of elite partygoers would be invited to indulge. [Cocaine] was served with the formality of having champagne in a champagne bucket. When I first started attending Hollywood parties I wasn't aware of what went on behind closed doors. There was always a general party and then a more exclusive 'private' party going on in another room.... It was the crème de la crème of Hollywood indulging in its own opulence, and most of us didn't realize the danger that it would hold in the future because of the glamour that surrounded the scene."[142]

In October 1974, Elton embarked on a 44-date concert tour of North America. Although it seemed from the outside that everything was charming and lovely and friendly in the Elton John camp, in fact, there were several private conflicts that the general public was not privy to, nor heard about, due in part to the escalating cocaine use.

Elton recalls getting high with John Lennon in a suite at The Sherry-Netherland Hotel in New York City. When Andy Warhol showed up at the door of the suite, knocking to be let in, Elton and Lennon were completely "coked out of our heads...so paranoid." Elton remembers Warhol's persistent knocking and Lennon's reaction: "John's going: 'Fuck off! Don't let him in!'"[184]

One of the most memorable concerts on the 1974 tour also involves Lennon. On November 28, which was the evening of the Thanksgiving holiday, Elton performed at Madison Square Garden. He had made a bet with John Lennon, regarding the song "Whatever Gets You Through the Night."

"We saw Elton on-and-off all the time," explains May Pang. "One of those times Elton said, 'Listen, if this becomes Number One, which I think it's gonna be, you are going to have to come up and play it on stage with me, because I have this tour coming up.' And John said, 'Sure.' And he turned to me and he said,

'It ain't gonna be Number One.' So that was the only reason he took the bet. And then when it did become Number One, it was like: 'Oh God! It did become Number One! What am I going to do here? Elton expects me to play it on stage with him!' But Elton was gracious and said to him, 'Look, if you don't want to do it, you're not obligated.' And John said, 'No, a bet is a bet.'"[148]

May was at The Garden that night. "I was standing on the stage.... Yoko knew that John was going to perform. Granted, we didn't know what time she came waltzing in the door and sat down, and John did not know when she was going to sit in her seat, but backstage she had already sent both Elton and John gardenias, to wish them well.... So, in the end Tony King organized it, because Yoko said that she didn't want to sit too close, or too far back, over here, over there; she had a perimeter of where she wanted to sit. So they worked it out."[148]

So many accounts of that historical rock & roll evening claim that John Lennon was actually quite nervous before the show because he hadn't performed in front of a live audience in quite some time. May confirms, "Because he wasn't actively doing it at the time. But that was John. Even before a recording session he was pacing, he was like a cat wandering."[148]

May Pang recalls having actually been on the stage at Madison Square Garden, watching Lennon and Elton perform the songs "Whatever Gets You Through the Night," "Lucy in the Sky with Diamonds," and "I Saw Her Standing There." Explaining how she found herself onstage that evening, she says, "It was because someone needed to be on stage with him, and I stood next to Elton's piano.... It was amazing because Elton is right here, and I'm right there next to him, looking out at the audience like I was one of the players. Standing there I could actually feel the room go up and down because the floor of The Garden has some 'give' to it, and when people were on their feet stomping and screaming I could feel the stage move. It was unbelievable. Unbelievable."[148] For May, the night became an indelible memory.

Elton John was mesmerized by the events of that magical evening. Speaking of his dear friend John Lennon, he claimed, "He hadn't played live onstage for a long time and he was almost ordinary again, at least as a person. So when he came onstage with us at Madison Square Garden I watched him go, 'Oh Christ, what the hell is this?' because he'd forgotten what it was like. The applause went on for 10 whole minutes, the band members were crying and it really was just the most emotional experience. The amount of love from people just happy to see him on a stage was overwhelming and very different from the kind of response I was used to getting."[47]

Even Elton's mother, Sheila, was flown in to witness her son performing in concert with John Lennon. When Elton started crying towards the end of the show, one journalist claimed that it was because Sheila was there. Elton claims that it had nothing to do with his mother's presence.

"That was ridiculous!" he recalled. "I was so knocked out by Lennon—everyone was just standing there in amazement. I was halfway through 'Don't Let the Sun Go Down on Me'—which I always do with my eyes closed—and suddenly there were all these lighted matches in the audience. Usually they do that at the end, when you come back for an encore, but this time it was right in the middle of the song. And I just started to cry. As far as getting emotional over my mother—oh, bullshit! The rush I felt came from the audience—and from Lennon, who really stole the show. It was magic."[55]

That particular evening became John Lennon's final concert appearance anywhere. History was being made, and Elton was part of it.

That night there was a huge party held at the Ballroom at The Hotel Pierre for Elton and his guests, including several record company insiders and journalists. John Lennon, May Pang, Elliott Gould, Angela Lansbury, Neil Sedaka, Andy Warhol, and the trio of divas who were now known as LaBelle—Sarah Dash, Nona Hendryx, and Patti LaBelle—were also there. While people drank, partied, and carried on, The Larry Elgart Orchestra played music in the lushly appointed room decorated in shades of blue and white, complete with gilded cherubs flying overhead.

In a first hand account of the party, a writer from *The New Yorker* magazine reported, "All of the tables in the room, including Elton John's table, had anemones on them, and glasses full of cigarettes.... Elton John was sitting at a table, and the crowd was watching him eat. He was dressed in white, and he had short blond hair. John Lennon was trying to elbow his way through the crowd to get to Elton John's table, and that did not accord with our idea of reality. Our idea of reality would be Elton John trying to elbow his way to get to John Lennon's table."[151]

While Elton was holding court at his party, Yoko Ono made her entrance. According to May Pang, "John saw her—we all did—at the party afterwards, which was at The Pierre, and she said 'Hello,' but that was it."[148] Part of Elton's entourage that evening was Jim Morris, a handsome, muscular, black, bearded bodybuilder who concurrently held the title of "Mr. America." For this tour, Morris was officially described as Elton John's "bodyguard." For the encore at the concert that night, Elton had arrived onstage seated on top of Jim Morris' massive masculine shoulders. It was just one of many not-so-thinly veiled "gay" moments in Elton's show.

Elton's sexuality soon became an issue later that night. The party was going along very nicely, and everyone seemed to be having a great time. Then things suddenly turned ugly. When the wife of a New York City disc jockey called Elton John "a fag" to his face, Reid leapt up to come to his boyfriend's defense, shouting, "This is my party and I am ordering you and your slag wife to get the fuck out right now!"

Elton bitterly screamed, "I never want to see you again—you or *yer* fucking slag! You're both lucky to be getting out of here without a scratch on ya."[150]

In an article that appeared in *Rolling Stone* magazine, writer Ed McCormack described the scene: "With the D.J. taking his adamant wife by the arm and pulling her across the room...John Reid trotting along behind to make damned sure they really were leaving, with people spilling out into the corridor behind them, hoping to witness whatever bloodshed might goose an otherwise anticlimactic party; with Elton John suddenly appearing on the fringe of the crowd, waving a finger like Truman Capote playing *The Godfather*."[150]

As the loud woman's husband led her out of the party, she shouted at the red-faced singer, "Elton, you just don't know what American fun is!" Elton shouted back at her in retaliation, "Do me a favor: Drop fucking dead."[150] What's a Manhattan cocktail party without a little added drama? Elton was very quickly acquiring a reputation as being rock & roll's Number One "drama queen."

Rolling Stone magazine, renowned for its vendettas—Billy Joel, Joni Mitchell…the list goes on-and-on—had been on a not-so-secret mission to "out" Elton as a homosexual. In retaliation, Elton and John Reid had done their best to block all *Rolling Stone* staff members from attending the party at The Hotel Pierre that night. This juicy story further fanned the flames of a brewing scandal.

In spite of the comments from the drunken woman, Elton reportedly had a great time that evening. He told Henry Edwards, a reporter for gay-oriented *After Dark* magazine, "It was a touching night."[152] Not even that confrontation could dampen the overall joy that Elton felt about John Lennon having appeared onstage with him. It was a dream come true.

Elton loved the time that he spent with John Lennon. According to him, "John was just the nicest man deep down; genuinely a great and quite humble person. The time we spent together—what I remember of it—is just one laugh after another. John was the kind of man who would walk into a room full of people and instead of going up to the biggest celeb, he'd go round the room talking to everyone one by one. A real man of the people. He took my parents out to dinner once; John got up to go to the toilet and when he came back my dad had taken his false teeth out and put them in the water glass. Lennon just pissed himself laughing."[47]

One of May Pang's favorite memories of her time spent with John Lennon and Elton John was one occasion when Lennon and she went through Elton's steamer trunks and tried on some of his insane clothes, hats, and gear. "He did his show at The Troubadour and he was very subdued. But, by the time he did The Garden the following year he was wild!" she recalls. "I remember John and I were trying on these different lassos and things like that of Elton's, in 1974 at his hotel room, and he had these anvil cases— like heavy duty luggage for touring—that were heavy duty steel and aluminum. And we opened them up, there were about three cases on the floor, and they were filled with these outrageous outfits, and John and I were just trying them on. It was like Halloween, and there were John and I dressed up in Elton's colorful assortment of clothes, and insane accessories. It was a very funny scene to witness!"[148]

It was six years since the first British Elton John album, *Empty Sky*, had been released, and five years since he was first successful on the record charts. Finally, it was time for a greatest hits album. *Elton John: Greatest Hits* very quickly shot up to the top of the charts in the U.S., the U.K., and Australia. From the week of November 30, 1974, to the week of February 1, 1975, Elton's *Greatest Hits* collection was Number One in America. It was the "must-have" vinyl album, cassette, or 8-track tape of the season.

Included on the album was Elton's version of "Lucy in the Sky with Diamonds." It had been a truly inspired idea for Elton to record "Lucy in the Sky with Diamonds." When he had performed it at the Watford benefit the previous spring, he had been amazed at the favorable crowd reaction. Then, when he went into the studio at Caribou to record it with John Lennon singing vocal harmonies, it became a magical musical creation.

The song hit Number One in both America and Canada, Number Three in Australia, and Number Ten in the U.K. Said a stunned Elton, "It didn't surprise me in England, but it surprised me over here. *Sgt. Pepper* is a revered album in England—it's the most acclaimed album ever released. It's like the *Bible*. So all the kids knew it, anyway—even the very young kids that I attract to concerts. They all knew it. But over here, it was a different ball game. People went nuts when I did 'Lucy' from that album. Some kids hadn't even heard it. And that really floored me. I thought, 'Oh, my God, there's a new generation coming up somewhere!'"[55] Aided by the success of "Lucy in the Sky With Diamonds," the album *Elton John: Greatest Hits* proceeded to sell over 12 million copies worldwide.

Elton had had so much fun doing his Christmas concerts in London the previous year, that he repeated the event in December 1974. This time around the concert was broadcast as a holiday episode of the British television series *Old Grey Whistle Test.* This year's holiday shows began with a surprise entrance from Elton. A mannequin dressed as Elton, complete with platform shoes, eyeglasses, and a hat, was suspended from a cable. The mannequin slid down from the balcony and landed stage left. As it disappeared into the wings, the real Elton John emerged wearing an identical costume, giving the illusion that the singer had miraculously flown down from the balcony. The trick worked smoothly until one night the mannequin's pants somehow got caught up in the rigging and were down around the faux Elton's ankles by the time it hit the stage.

In *Melody Maker*, Chris Welch had nothing but praise for Elton's Christmas show. "Elton's band are now a wonderfully tight organization, and the months of touring America has honed them to a peak of professionalism…. There are few singers in rock who could sustain interest in this fashion, or cope with such demanding material, without cracking up or resorting to vocal gimmicks."[24]

The show was every bit the extravaganza that Elton had hoped for. Furthermore, he and his band were at a highpoint of interaction onstage and in the studio. Elton's band was treated like an integral part of his entourage, and their names and images were now regularly plastered all over the interior pages of his record albums. A new year was about to begin, and Elton claimed, as 1974 came to an end, that he was ready for a new image. He was afraid of becoming too predictable. And how did he propose to do that? According to him, "I'm gonna give up playing piano. I'm gonna become a rock & roll suicide, take my nasty [penis] out and piddle all over the front row, just to get rid of my staid old image."[20] Well, if that didn't do it, nothing would!

CHAPTER TEN

Captain Fantastic &
The Pinball Wizard

In Greek mythology Daedalus dreamed that men could fly. He constructed a pair of human-sized wings for himself and his son, Icarus. On their debut flight, Icarus found flying so exhilarating that he ignored his father's warning and flew too close to the sun. The sun's heat melted the wax that held the wings together, and Icarus fell into the sea. Like Icarus, at the start of 1975, Elton had been flying so high and so fast, his head was spinning. He was beginning to lose his perspective and was flying too close to the sun.

In the past year, Elton had placed two consecutive albums in the Number One spot, had recorded a new album that was awaiting release, had signed a new recording deal in the U.S., and had become the highest-paid rock star in the world. He had multiple houses, collected Rembrandts, drove Rolls Royces, and traveled in his own private plane. In the last five years, he had generated an estimated $75 million worth of business. And, he had just headlined Madison Square Garden with John Lennon as his special guest star.

On the downside, Elton was in the public spotlight day and night, he was doing a lot of cocaine, and he was gay—two things he denied publicly. Furthermore his personal relationship with John Reid was starting to fray, he was getting bored playing with his current band, and, in spite of his Herculean accomplishments, he just didn't seem to be having as much fun as he thought he should.

Somewhere inside the big, glitzy, day-glow, sequin-encrusted rock star the world knew as Elton John, chubby little Reggie Dwight was having some major growing pains. This was going to be a year of even bigger feats, higher and grander career peaks, and new challenges. However, Elton started out the year depressed, wrapped up in self-doubts, and having a self-destructive emotional meltdown.

"All of a sudden I became deflated," he claimed. "In January I sat brooding for two weeks. I couldn't understand why I was feeling so depressed. In the end I just had to own up that it was because I wanted a change."[29]

Elton took to using members of the British press as his psychologists, confessing his problems in interviews. "Oh, but I am self-destructive," he told Caroline Coon in the pages of *Melody Maker.* "I get terribly, stubbornly depressed. It's my desperate craving for affection coming out. I'll get in a mood and I'll sit at home for two days in bed, getting more and more depressed, wondering if it's all worth it, and all those silly thoughts. But I have friends who are very good for me. My manager [John Reid] can't help me when I'm depressed because, since he's my manager, I fight him. But Muff Winwood or Tony King will ring up and say, 'Well, run out of Pledge [furniture polish] have we?' You know, I [vacuum] and dust. Things like that are really good for my mind. I used to love ironing. It soothed me out. I'm one of those people who go around emptying ashtrays, washing them and putting them back. And so, as soon as I'm in a bad mood, one of my friends has only got to ring up and send me up a bit and I'll come out of it."[29]

He confessed his self-doubts to Charles Shaar Murray of *New Musical Express* in its March 8, 1975, issue. The forthcoming *Captain Fantastic* album was a departure for him, as far as subject matter and in sound. Elton pondered, "I worry every time a record's released. I only had one Top Ten single in England last year, and that was 'Lucy' and that didn't worry me because the albums did all right. I don't worry about self-doubt, because if something's bad I know it is and I'll own up to it."[27]

Explaining his modest lifestyle to Caroline Coon, he claimed, "I know I've got a reputation for being a jetsetter, but really I only have two and a half friends in show business. Ringo, John Lennon, and Rod. I don't know anybody else. The only other friends I have are Watford FC and the people I've known in the business for years. I detest the Hollywood syndrome."[29] He hangs out with two of The Beatles and party animal Rod Stewart, and that's his version of "living the simple life?" No wonder he started to lose his perspective!

Elton was also becoming jaded by his success. He bragged in 1975, "In America for the next three or four years I could get a Gold [record] on my name alone. As Pete Townshend said, 'I could shit bricks and people would rush out and buy them.'"[29]

He proceeded to prove the point by unleashing his lackluster 1969 *Empty Sky* album on the American market in January 1975. It instantly shot up the charts, hit Number Six in the U.S. and was certified Gold. So, where did this depression come from? "I don't know," he claimed. "I can never figure it out. And that does worry me a bit, because I do consider myself very fortunate. I can be very happy and then, all of a sudden, I'm on a comedown…. I consider myself slightly insane in a funny way."[29]

Was he still hurt and mad that he wasn't closer to his dad? According to him, "Funnily enough, no. I was terribly bitter at the time but I see my Dad now, sometimes. And I feel really sorry that we didn't get closer. He has four kids now who he loves, but I don't feel that he's a shit. I just wish he could have loved me like that, too…. I had an awful inferiority complex as a kid. My father wasn't the slightest bit interested in me, and he was a snob, which I hated."[29]

One of Elton's first matters of business in 1975 was to tape a high-profile television appearance for American network television. While Elton had been burning up the record charts, Cher had been dominating the tabloid magazines as one half of the hugely successful husband and wife team, Sonny & Cher. After having been together for a decade, Cher dumped Sonny.

When the couple split up, so did their hit television show, *The Sonny and Cher Comedy Hour.* ABC-TV picked up Sonny's television series *The Sonny Comedy Revue*, and CBS-TV signed Cher. Sonny's show debuted on September 22, 1974, and it was an instant disaster without Cher. On December 29, 1974, the thirteenth and last episode of Sonny's show aired. Now, several weeks later, all eyes were on Cher and her brand-new program: *The Cher Show.*

Cher and her producers realized that the first episode of her series was strictly "sink or swim" time. It had to be big and splashy, and it had to feature glamorous guest stars who would be an unbeatable draw. To accomplish this they booked Bette Midler, Flip Wilson, and Elton John. To further bolster her ratings, Cher continued to work with her dramatic costume designer, Bob Mackie.

Despite being in the middle of a personal meltdown, Elton delivered on the show. It was great exposure for him and incredible for Cher's ratings when it was broadcast on February 16, 1975. At the time, Elton's recordings were selling like hotcakes. The week of January 29, 1975, the R.I.A.A. certified Elton's single version of "Lucy in the Sky with Diamonds" Gold. On February 1, both *Elton John: Greatest Hits* and *Goodbye Yellow Brick Road* were certified Platinum by the B.P.I. His appearance on the show certainly added to those tallies.

Furthermore, Elton got to know Bob Mackie while there and to wear clothes personally designed by Mackie on the show. According to Mackie, "Depending on the number of costumes, Cher's clothes bill for her weekly show runs between $3,000 and $10,000. And for the special she did with Elton John and Bette Midler, the bill hit $30,000."[155] Cher was thrilled with the results. Prior to the show's airing she proclaimed, "The look is really hot! It's not quiet. It doesn't lay back. It's just hot. It comes out and punches your brains out."[154] Mackie was to be responsible for some of the most outrageous costumes of Elton's future.

On the show Elton performed "Lucy in the Sky with Diamonds," solo. He was wearing a bizarre sort of space-age Robin Hood hat made of embroidered silver lamé. His outfit had a huge collar. He looked like *The Sorcerer's Apprentice* meets LaBelle on Mars. At one point he is seen through a fish-eye lens, with five separate Elton Johns rotating around the main center image, in a kaleidoscope effect.

Later, in another segment, attired in more standard garb, Elton sang a great duet version of "Bennie & The Jets" with Cher. The show also included a truly elaborate production number featuring Elton, Bette, Cher, and Flip doing a medley of some of the current chart hits of the era including: "Mockingbird," "Proud Mary," "Ain't No Mountain High Enough," and "Never Can Say Goodbye." Elton sat at the keyboard of a mirror-tile-covered grand piano, wearing a white tuxedo covered in silver glitter balls. On his head he wore an oversized top hat that was festooned with silver. Bette was in a white dress with a low-cut top and a white-and-silver skirt slit up the middle—nearly to her crotch. Cher had her trademark waist-length hair, cascading down her left side, and a tight-fitting dress with an ample leg-exposing slit up the side. Flip, in a white suit embroidered in silver, waltzed out onto the set to do the spoken-word part of "Ain't No Mountain High Enough."

When the show was reviewed, *Newsweek* magazine claimed, "Television hasn't seen so much glitter and flash since NBC did a special on Liberace's closet."[156] Indeed, Bob Mackie's costumes were as much a part of the show as any other element. Elton was in his element.

The show was such a hit, in fact, and Elton was so convincing as a musical comedy performer, that Las Vegas became an obvious outlet for his theatrical and musical performances. But Elton wasn't interested. "People are always saying to me, 'Obviously the next step for you is Vegas.' And I think 'God, don't you get it? The whole point of me is that I hate all that.' All the sparkle bit is tongue-in-cheek, it's humorous. I hate Vegas."[29]

Even with all the attention for his career, the press still asked about Elton's personal life. When he was pressured to speak of his love life in *Melody Maker,* he skirted the issue of his sexuality by stating, "Women fascinate me because they are harder to get to know than men. They are so confused, and that fascinates me.... Ladies are so messed up. You get the wrong person behind a lady and it ruins them.... I can't think of a female artist I've met who seems at all secure or confident. There is so much more to find out about women than men."[29]

When asked point blank if he wanted a woman in his life, he replied, "Oh yeah, of course. I find it far easier to get to know ladies in America, though. English ladies put up so many fronts. American ladies are very bold, and that breaks the ice for me. I can never say 'boo' to a goose to anybody. I'm very shy and I need somebody to help me out."[29]

The media watched Elton's progress with Rocket Records as well. Rocket had its first original bona fide hit album and singles at this time. In 1975, Neil Sedaka recorded and released *The Hungry Years,* a new album for Rocket. It hit Number 16 and went Gold in the U.S. The single "Bad Blood," which was written by Neil Sedaka, featured Elton very conspicuously behind Neil's lead voice. When the song hit Number One in the U.S., it put both Sedaka and Rocket on a winning streak.

When a newly recorded version of Sedaka's "Breaking Up is Hard to Do"—from *The Hungry Years*—was released as a single in 1975, it made it to Number Eight in America, making Neil the first artist ever to place two versions of the same song in the Top Ten.

In March 1974, the rock & roll extravaganza of a film, *Tommy*, had been released. In addition to Elton, the film also starred Ann-Margret, Jack Nicholson, Oliver Reed, Tina Turner, Eric Clapton, Arthur Brown, and of course The Who—Pete Townshend, John Entwistle, Keith Moon, and Roger Daltrey in the title role of the deaf, dumb, and blind boy. Director Ken Russell had a reputation for making over-the-top films, and this loopy tale of a handicapped kid named Tommy was certainly over the top.

In the film, Eric Clapton played the rock guru in the church scene. Everyone was worshipping a statue of Marilyn Monroe. For the final sequence, the part of Clapton's character is suddenly portrayed by Arthur Brown. According to Brown, "On the day they were going to film the final sequence of that scene in *Tommy*, Eric was too strung out on drugs to report to the set, so they got me to do it. If you look closely at that scene you will see me in it instead of Eric."[158]

Elton's scene as "The Pinball Wizard" was essentially an elaborate music video. However, it was a great part for him. Dressed in his white pants, red suspenders, a spangling blue shirt, and his trademark oversized eyeglasses, Elton perfectly portrayed his brat-like character in the film.

The gala premiere party that was held for *Tommy* was something unique as well. Elton, Tina, Pete Townshend, and Ann-Margret were all there, in addition to Andy Warhol, Anthony Perkins, and an elite crowd of 700. They gathered on the mezzanine level of New York City's 57th Street subway station. It was a truly unique event. As partygoers entered the roped off area, they were greeted by an eight-foot-long sculpture of the name "Tommy," fashioned out of vegetables, including broccoli, cauliflower, radishes, and over 3,000 red tomatoes.

The catering was something else, too, with a potpourri of exotic seafood including 50-dozen oysters from Virginia, five thirty-pound Nova Scotia Lobsters, fifty pounds of octopus from the Bahamas, and a twenty-pound Alaskan king crab. For the carnivores there were one hundred pounds of Omaha roast beef. It wasn't the food that impressed Elton the most, it was the fact that he was in a Manhattan subway station. According to him, "I've never been so frightened in my life."[159] However, he managed to energetically dance with Ann-Margret, and he signed several autographs for fans while there.

Tommy was the crazy rock & roll hit film of the season, and it was a great career move for Elton to have been in it. To this day it still stands up as one of the wildest and most over-the-top rock movies ever produced. Although it was never officially released as an American single, Elton's version of the song "The Pinball Wizard" from the film was played all over the radio internationally in 1975.

Elton received great notices for his brief but magical film debut. According to film critic Leonard Maltin, *Tommy* was an "energetic rendering of The Who's best-selling rock opera, with standout musical performances by Clapton, John (who sings 'Pinball Wizard'), and Turner."[160]

Amid the success, relationships were changing for Elton in 1975. Elton and John Reid were growing apart on a personal basis, and they were each pursuing the attention of different people in their sex lives. Bernie's marriage to Maxine was also falling apart, and she began an affair with Elton's new bass guitar player, Kenny Passarelli.

Since LaBelle—Patti LaBelle, Sarah Dash, and Nona Hendryx— had scored a huge 1975 hit with the song "Lady Marmalade," their *Nightbirds* album had been certified Gold, and they were on tour in Europe, including performances in Paris, London, and Madrid. Like Elton, they had also appeared on Cher's network television show that year, and they were now the hottest female group in the business. They came to England, and Elton went to see them in concert.

Kenneth Reynolds was working as the road manager for LaBelle during that tour in England. As Reynolds explains, "I was introduced to Elton backstage when he came to see Patti, Nona and Sarah. We chatted, and I found him to be extremely friendly—so friendly in fact—that he invited me to go home with him. I was quite impressed, because he had a Mercedes Benz limousine, and I had never seen a Mercedes limo, let alone rode in it. We got up the next morning, and he had the limo take me back to my hotel. As the LaBelle tour continued on to the United States, he came to the Philadelphia concert, the Detroit concert, and the Chicago concert. He and I got together in each of those cities. We had a great time together, and then I never saw him again."[89] Kenneth was just one of several handsome young men whom Elton would sexually pursue during this era.

In April 1975, it seemed that Elton was everywhere. His newest hit single, "Philadelphia Freedom," which was released under the name "The Elton John Band," hit Number 12 in England, and hit Number One in America, where it became his second single to chart as an R&B single in *Billboard*. It peaked at Number 32 and became his sixth Gold single in the United States. At the same time, Ringo Starr's two-sided single, with "No No Song" on one side and "Snookeroo" on the other side, made it to Number Three in the U.S. Elton not only wrote "Snookeroo," he sang background and played piano for Ringo.

At this time, for some reason, Elton began to take public swipes at his own success. "In America I've got 'Philadelphia Freedom' going up the charts again. I wish the bloody thing would piss off. And 'Pinball Wizard' is being played to death. I can see why people get sick and tired of me. In America I get sick and tired of hearing myself on AM radio. It's embarrassing. The success constantly amazes me."[29] He had constructed this giant monolith of a career, and now he was throwing stones at it by whining to the press, as though anyone should feel sorry for him.

From the outside, it looked like pop superstar Elton John had nothing in his life that could make him unhappy. At twenty-eight years old, he was literally sitting on top of the world. He was a singing star, a television star, a movie star, and one of the biggest concert draws on the planet. Yet, in his mind there was something very wrong. The first manifestation of his unrest came in April 1975.

Just prior to his birthday that year, Elton gave an interview with *New Musical Express* and told them that his musicians were now officially called "The Elton John Band." He claimed, "I feel that over the last year we've become more of a unit. We're happier, we enjoy doing live gigs." [26]

But did the band resent that he was their employer? According to Elton, "The others resented it in the early days when there was just the three of us—Nigel, Dee and me—because I got all the press interviews.... After playing together for four or five years, it's much more like a band, and it's become a very close and spiritual relationship, therefore I feel that it's only right that we should now call ourselves 'The Elton John Band.' It's not just me. Okay, I write the songs, and Taupin writes the lyrics, but when we come to record, it's very much an equal thing." [26]

From those flowery statements, one would have thought that Nigel, Dee, Ray, and Davey were his best friends. Then, suddenly and without warning, he fired two of them. Here he was on the verge of releasing the *Captain Fantastic & The Brown Dirt Cowboy* album, which heavily featured that quartet on the cover and in all of the art, not to mention on all of the music. Furthermore, he also was on the verge of launching his next concert tour. Wouldn't it make more sense to showcase in concert the musicians who helped create the album? Apparently, Elton had other thoughts.

Elton telephoned Dee and Nigel and told them that their services were no longer needed on "Team Elton." And how did they feel about being canned? According to Elton, "I don't think Nigel or Dee would have liked that very much. But I didn't discuss it with them, because you can never be totally honest about a thing like that. I wanted a complete break. It was difficult and sad but it's been quite amicable." [29]

What was Elton's rationale for bragging about "The Elton John Band," and then pulling a Donald Trump–style "You're fired!" routine on them? According to him, he wanted to "rock out" more. "It's fulfilling one of my lifelong ambitions," he said. "I've always wanted to be part of a good driving rock & roll band. The old band never used to drive—we used to rattle on." [29] After all the "hearts and roses" bullshit he had pontificated only weeks previous, suddenly temperamental Elton had a new band.

Elton hired Roger Pope away from The Kiki Dee Band to be his new drummer. Kenny Passarelli became the unit's new bass player. For this tour he hired his old friend from his music publishing days in London, Caleb Quaye, as his lead guitar player. As a second keyboard player Elton added James Newton Howard to the lineup. And for select dates, guitarist Jeff "Skunk" Baxter from The Doobie Brothers joined the Elton band.

Bragging about his newly reconfigured band, Elton explained, "But I was going to steal Roger anyway. Kiki's band was successful to a degree, but Roger and Caleb deserve so much success. They're both amazing musicians. Technically, Caleb and David [Davy Johnstone], and to a certain extent Ray, can play anything and, what with Kenny and James, it's worked out that I'm, literally, the worst musician in the band. I've got to work hard to keep up with them, which is going to make me play harder and better."[29] He also added three new backup singers to the band, Brian and Brenda Russell, and Donny Gerrard.

As the *Captain Fantastic* album was about to be released, there was a huge listening party in North Hollywood at the Universal lot for sixty executives and press members. It was held at one of the screening rooms, and it included a visual slide show of the album's artwork. The plan was to play the first side of the album, take a slight break, and then play the second half of the album. While listening to the first side, the sound quality of the playback was seriously off.

The house lights were turned up, and John Reid proceeded to have a meltdown. He grabbed the man who was running the audio equipment and started fighting with him. Stephen James, Dick James' son, recalls, "John screamed at this guy, something like 'The sound's a fucking shambles!' The guy turned to John and said, 'Sorry, it's the best I can do.' John kept screaming at him, really violent: 'The whole fucking album's being ruined, and it's your fault!'"[87] Then Reid hauled off and slugged the sound engineer in the face with his fists. Members of the staff had to pull them apart, and the sound engineer emerged with blood dripping from his mouth. It was just the beginning of serious problems with this album and showed off the fact that the once-invincible armor surrounding the Elton John camp was starting to seriously crack.

Elton had grand plans for introducing *Captain Fantastic & The Brown Dirt Cowboy* to the masses. Little did he suspect, but his elaborate world-debut concert scheme was going to be a disaster as well.

On June 21, 1975, Elton John was booked at a mammoth all-day event at Wembley Stadium. The crowd was a massive horde of 72,000 people, and there was an all-star series of opening acts. The show was started in late morning by the group Stackridge, who were concurrently signed to Rocket Records. They were followed by Rufus and their incredibly appealing powerhouse of a lead singer, Chaka Kahn. That afternoon came country rocker Joe Walsh, who had originally found fame as part of the popular group The James Gang, then began a solo career. Walsh was followed by a brand-new band he would later join: The Eagles. Late that afternoon, Elton's buddies The Beach Boys performed a long, appealing set.

The crowd was still going strong, and Wembley was filled with more enthusiastic spectators than populate many British towns.The crowd was star-studded, drawing actress Candice Bergen, tennis champions Jimmy Connors, Martina Navratilova and Billie Jean King, plus Elton's rock star buddies Ringo Starr, Paul and Linda McCartney, and Harry Nilsson.

Elton's grand plan was to open his act at sunset and instantly play every song from the *Captain Fantastic & The Brown Dirt Cowboy* back-to-back, then follow it up with an assortment of his hits.

Although some people love that album, for others it is a bitter, whiny album that is sheer torture. It is comprised of slow, personal, egotistical songs about how Elton and Bernie were once poor and struggling friends who loved each other, and then became famous. While Elton thought it was the height of creativity, others found it to be musical masturbation that only pleased its creators.

All-day rock festivals are tricky affairs. On one hand it seems like a brilliant step to have round-the-clock music, drinking, and partying on a Saturday afternoon in the summer. However, there is a certain burnout factor. This was an element that Elton apparently didn't anticipate when he put together the day-long extravaganza.

The Beach Boys were the perfect afternoon act for a summer's day melting into evening. After their set was over, many of the once enthusiastic patrons were growing tired, sunburned, and restless. In between The Beach Boys and the beginning of Elton's set, there was a long intermission, while the stage was set and instruments were changed. Already, hundreds of members of the restless crowd were starting to leave the stadium.

The stage set Elton had that day included a huge neon sign with the word "Fantastic" as a backdrop, and the stage floor was covered with a small forest of tall potted plants. Not even the jungle of plants, nor the glowing neon, nor Elton's enthusiasm, could add electricity to the proceedings. As the band plodded along through the dreary *Captain Fantastic* selections, the crowds continued to stream out the exits. Although the crescendo at the end of "Someone Saved My Life Tonight" was enthusiastic, the album was only half over, and the exodus of the audience accelerated. At this point mere hundreds weren't leaving the stadium, thousands were. Although Elton kept his spirits high onstage, the only real excitement from what was left of the audience came for the final numbers—"Pinball Wizard" and "Saturday Night's Alright for Fighting." Ultimately, the event was a huge disappointment for Elton and for the bored crowd.

Clearly, Elton's English success was flagging. The British press was nothing short of brutal when they published their reviews of the Wembley "Midsummer Music" event. *Melody Maker* headlined their story: "Beach Boys' Cup Runneth Over. Elton Left to Pick Up the Empties."

However, Elton was such a huge star at this point, and his fans—especially his American fans—all anticipated the release of this album so greatly that when it was released, it became an instant sales success. In fact, *Captain Fantastic & The Brown Dirt Cowboy* was so highly successful on the charts that it became the first album in the history of the record business to enter the charts in *Billboard*, *Record World*, and *Cash Box* at Number One! It also went to Number One in Australia, and Number Two in England and Norway.

In spite of the fact that both of his latest singles—"Lucy in the Sky With Diamonds" and "Philadelphia Freedom"—had both hit Number One in the U.S., he had yet to have a chart-topping hit in England. When "Someone Saved My Life Tonight" was released as the only single from the new album, it made it to Number Four in America. But it stalled at Number 22 in the U.K. As the album was released, Elton did his best to explain its theme. According to him, "The new album that we've done is all about ourselves and it's very open and very honest about our personal relationship and also, it's very honest about all the business things we went through. That's why I probably think that the songs are better and so, too, is my singing because I could relate to everything on the album."[26]

One of the things that Elton could not deny was the fact that *Captain Fantastic & The Brown Dirt Cowboy* was also something of a mean-spirited album, filled with ambition, pain, and disappointment. "Yes, it's quite a bitter album because everybody has to pay their dues," he had to admit.[29]

The song "Bitter Fingers" is about being forced to write "commercial" music instead of following one's heart. According to Elton, "Well, at the time we were having to write trash. We were desperate. We were trying anything and any combination. We were completely destroying ourselves for a long period of time, obeying those people's commands: 'You have to write this, you have to write that.'"[29]

He channeled his sense of envy into the song "Meal Ticket." Elton claimed, "That's a song about jealousy and envy and about seeing people being successful while you're not. I was always desperate to become a success, and I was envious and very bitter and very narrow-minded about anybody who was successful."[29]

Undoubtedly, the most personal song was "We All Fall in Love Sometimes," the one where Elton expressed his love for Bernie Taupin. "Well, I knew I was going to be asked about that, and, well, I'm glad," he said, when the press pressured him for an explanation. "Yes. Bernie and I were very close. We were like brothers and I loved him very dearly. I desperately wanted, as a kid, to have brothers and sisters…. I love him dearly."[29]

The only truly memorable song from this awkward album is "Someone Saved My Life Tonight," its one hit single. The song was about the night that Long John Baldry—that tall "Sugar Bear"—figuratively pulled Elton's head out of Linda Woodrow's oven back in the 1960s.

The bizarre artwork on the cover of *Captain Fantastic & The Brown Dirt Cowboy* was dark and eye-popping. In addition to cartoon versions of Elton, Bernie, and his former four-piece band, it is densely populated with slimy-looking fish and toads, crocodiles, and futuristic beasties. They are all darkly sinister-looking creatures, like a rat with flames as eyelashes, and a frog wearing far too many rings on his fingers. The cover only further enhanced the bizarreness of this often thematically cold album.

Naturally, Elton was depicted as "Captain Fantastic," some sort of keyboard hero in boots and a top hat. Bernie is depicted on the back cover in a glass bubble surrounded by the kind of cute forest animals he preferred in his realm. He was dubbed "The Brown Dirt Cowboy" for his love of the American West and the types of songs that had dominated *Tumbleweed Connection*.

The album came packaged with all sorts of printed goodies in it. There was a booklet with the lyrics to the songs. It was filled with early photos of Elton and Bernie, separately and together. They also included a snapshot of Elton's mother and "Derf." There was a separate scrapbook of press clippings and photos of Elton, with Bernie, with his mom, with his band members, and even a shot with Patti LaBelle and Cindy Birdsong, taken in one of those old coin-operated photo booths. It included a photo of the Musicland record shop at 44 Berwick Street, where Elton once worked as a clerk.

Gus Dudgeon, who had produced all of Elton's big hit albums, thought that this was one of Elton's true masterpieces. "First of all, it's the best that they've ever played, it's the best that he's ever played, and it's the best collection of songs," he declared.[30]

The press, however, was mixed in their reaction. Some loved it. Others hated it. Charles Shaar Murray in *New Musical Express* gave it a "thumbs down." He claimed, "*Captain Fantastic* seemed like an album that Elton actually deeply wanted to make; it was somewhat excruciating to listen to."[32]

Greg Shaw wrote in *Phonograph Record*, "Elton and Bernie seem to be standing at a new plateau, secure enough in their success to attempt expunging certain memories and settling a few old scores…. This is 'The Year of Elton John,' and this is the album that, in retrospect, may prove to be the focal point of his career."[28]

John Tobler pondered in *ZigZag*, "If I could turn to the conceptual aspect of the album, it would be surprising if the more recent episodes in the story of Elton and Bernie would evoke any particularly violent emotions, and the second half of the record is much less urgent and more relaxed. If you were successful, wouldn't you lose some venom?"[33] Shouldn't Elton and Bernie be happy with their success instead of being bitchy and complaining? Apparently not.

Jon Landau in *Rolling Stone* was surprisingly kind, announcing, "This is one of Elton John's best albums.... It isn't weighted down with the over-arranging and over-production that marred so much of *Goodbye Yellow Brick Road*. It sounds more relaxed than *Caribou*. His voice sounds rough, hoarse, almost weary. But that only helps make him sound more personal and intimate than in the past."[153]

Wayne Robins glowingly wrote in *Creem*, "In this thoroughly autobiographical album, The Captain (Elton) and the Cowboy (Bernie Taupin) achieve a unity as a songwriting team that they've been striving for.... For the first time, Elton does not seem to be speaking someone else's words."[31]

Ben Edmonds in *Phonograph Record* strongly disliked both *Caribou* and *Captain Fantastic*. According to him, "The platinum-shipped *Captain Fantastic* was the first album that sounded like he was doing it for himself rather than for the radio, and though it contained a Number One single, it required you to care as much about Elton John as you did about the music to make it completely work."[34]

When he was branded by several press members as being an egomaniac, Elton argued, "I've always had a lot of confidence in this album, and I can't understand the critics who say that Bernie and I must be egomaniacs. The album wasn't meant to say, 'Here we are, we're wonderful!' The reviews did make me feel that maybe we'd been a bit self-indulgent. But for me it's a completely honest album. I've laid myself on the line."[29]

That summer Elton John appeared on the cover of the July 7, 1975, issue of *Time* magazine in America. The cover of *Time* most often features the President of the United States, major news stories, world disasters, or the Pope. A colorful cartoon of bespectacled Elton on *Time*'s cover signaled the fact that he had truly arrived. With his $40,000 eyeglass collection and his ever-evolving wardrobe spotlighted in the magazine, he was now a bona fide household name in the U.S. and in the world.

According to that particular issue of *Time*, "[To date] John has sold 42 million albums and 18 million singles worldwide, nine of his 12 albums are over the million mark in the U.S. alone."[176] The article painted a picture of a rock star in all of his fun-loving glory. What the story missed was the emotional minefield that lay only millimeters beneath the surface. When the cover story's reporters observed Elton parading in and out of London's most fashionable stores—including Cartier—dropping tens of thousands of dollars in minutes, they depicted him as a gleeful kid in a candy store. What they failed to report was that he was also secretly snorting line after line of cocaine, was a flamboyant closeted homosexual, and that he was teetering on the edge of a nervous breakdown. It seemed Elton had become a rock & roll master of disguise.

During June and July of 1975, Elton returned to Caribou ranch to record his next album with his new band. When he was in Colorado, The Rolling Stones were on tour. When they played Denver, Elton made a guest appearance in the middle of their set.

When he took to the stage, he was introduced as "Reg from Watford." It pissed him off to be introduced as anything but "Elton John," and The Stones knew it. To the members of The Rolling Stones that is who Elton would always be, chubby "Reg" and nothing more. To this day, whenever Bill Wyman of The Rolling Stones is asked to comment on Elton John, he still replies, "You mean 'Reg Dwight of Watford?'"[175]

Describing Elton's appearance that evening, Keith Richards made some snide comments about him to *Rolling Stone* magazine, and Mick Jagger complained, "We should have kicked him off the stage, but we didn't." Elton was reportedly livid to be publicly snubbed by The Stones.[175]

Apparently, for the recording of *Rock of the Westies* at Caribou that summer, the cocaine and alcohol were flowing freely. "That period of time is a little foggy because we were all at a highpoint of abusing ourselves to the max," Bernie Taupin later explained with amazement. "It was Jack Daniels and lines [of cocaine] on the [recording] console, and for some reason we got it done. I don't remember anything about the sessions and I don't think anybody in that band will remember them either."[162]

On August 9, Elton John and Diana Ross hosted the telecast of *The Rock Music Awards* at the Santa Monica Civic Auditorium. One of the nominees was the group LaBelle, Elton's friends. That night their song "Lady Marmalade" was nominated in four categories, and Sarah, Nona, and Patti took home the trophy for Best R&B Single.

Sarah Dash recalls Elton was quite warm towards them during this era. "It's been really nice over the years to know someone like Elton. He is always really, really cool as a person. There are several artists I can see after many years, and they seem to have changed, but Elton is always nice…and fun to run into. Because— let me tell you—some of us do: 'Go to Hollywood!' Elton is not one of them. He is always the same charming guy who was our piano player back in the '60s."[98]

In what seemed like an inspired move, on August 25, 1975, Elton John returned to The Troubadour in Los Angeles to do a special six-show "Five Year Anniversary" engagement at the place where it all started. Well, it seemed like a great idea at the time. It would have probably been a better idea to have him reunite with Nigel and Dee onstage. Instead he put his newer, bigger, and louder band onstage at a club that was tiny at best.

On one hand, it was a very successful evening. He sold out at $250 a ticket and raised $150,000 for the Jules Stein Eye Institute at UCLA. Also, he drew capacity crowds that included stars like Cher, Tony Curtis, and even Mae West.

However, the critic who had blown the trumpet to herald Elton's arrival on the scene in August of 1970, suddenly changed his tune. In the *Los Angeles Times*, Robert Hilburn wrote, "There'd been so much excitement at the thought of seeing Elton back at The Troubadour, and fighting for tickets, that when he finally walked onstage, it was almost anticlimax. He had that big band, which sounded deafening in a small place; people were pressed tight up against the stage; the whole effect, with all those celebrities and VIPs, was overpowering. But not so magical any more."[163]

Although Elton was a British citizen, he was also earning a great deal of money in the United States, millions of dollars in fact. This money had to be taxed by the country in which it was earned. However, if he were to move this money into his British bank account, England could legally tax him as well. There were different strategies for Elton to retain more of his money. One of them was to spend more time as a "resident alien" of the U.S. So, John Reid helped devise a plan whereby Elton would remain in Los Angeles for several months, rent a residence, and spend his American dollars there.

While it would have made just as much sense for Elton to lease or rent a house, he decided to buy one. The house he purchased was located on Benedict Canyon in Beverly Hills. It was a million-dollar home of a Moorish design. Although it had a glittering past, the house had a darkly secluded look to it, and the walls were lined in very staid wooden paneling.

Describing the house, Elton revealed at the time, "Originally, it was owned by John Gilbert, the silent-screen actor. Then Greta Garbo moved in. There's a little gazebo in the garden she had built to sleep in when it rained. Also, she had a waterfall put in, so she could hear the sound of running water. After that, Jennifer Jones and David O. Selznick owned it. It became the orgy house. In the bath, there used to be a trap door where Gilbert used to get rid of all his ladies by catapulting them down into the bedroom below."[55]

Elton moved into the house alone because John Reid had business in London. Like The Four Tops song "Seven Rooms of Gloom," before long he started to go a bit stir-crazy in his solitude.

In addition to the solitude and sudden inactivity for several weeks from August to October, things happened which made Elton feel paranoid and threatened. His new house was located in the vicinity of the Sharon Tate murders several years earlier. Hollywood had yet to fully recover from that shocking event. In addition to this, Elton's yard backed up onto Alice Cooper's property, and Alice's presence occasionally drew some menacing-looking fans to the neighborhood. Then, in the middle of one night, Elton woke up to discover a strange girl sitting on his bed. She nearly scared him to death. It seemed that she very easily slipped past Elton's security system and entered the house unnoticed. Although the girl was just a harmless fan, who was easily removed, Elton began to worry what would happen if a genuinely crazy person suddenly broke in and wanted to do him harm.

Although he was freaked out by this incident, he at least had a sense of humor about his paranoia. "Good old L.A.," he said at the time. "There are a bunch of weirdos around this town, like Charles Manson. I never got that feeling from any other town, even New York. There the weirdness is different."[55]

If he felt that way about Los Angeles, what was he doing living there? According to him, "First, it's convenient; it's the center of the record business and I'm one hour from tennis in Phoenix or from San Francisco. Anyway, it was the first place I came to in America, so I regard it as a sentimental 'home' sort of thing. I like playing other places in the States, but I prefer to live here."[55]

Alice Cooper has several amusing memories of Elton as a next door neighbor. "Elton lived in the house next door to me in Benedict Canyon. I remember he had a garage sale at his house one day. Now imagine an Elton John garage sale! He was selling things like pairs of his platform shoes. There were normal platform shoes, and then there were Elton's platform shoes, which had five inch heels on them. They weren't my size, but I was with my father who's a preacher, and they were his size. He bought a pair of Elton's shoes, and I said to him, 'What are you going to do with those?' He said, 'I'm not quite sure, but I am going to work them into a sermon, and announce the fact that I am wearing Elton John's shoes!'"[290]

At the time, Sharon Lawrence worked for Rocket Records in their Los Angeles office. At 3:00 a.m. she received a frantic phone call from Elton. John Reid was out of town, and Elton was begging her to come over and talk to him. She promised to come visit him during the day. When she arrived, she was startled to see a slightly disheveled Elton, behaving like a neurotic wreck. Elton insisted that he give Sharon a preview of the *Rock of the Westies* album, which was due in stores that October. According to Lawrence, "He seemed most panicked about it. He put it on at full volume and sat there staring at me, waiting for me to say it was brilliant. I didn't think so, but I said it was because he seemed to need that so desperately. While I was still at the house, John Reid came back. I realized that

Elton had been in a real snit because John had gone away, and had got me over there so to prove he could get along without him. It was like, 'There you are—other people care about me, too.'"[87]

Lawrence recalls, "Part of him adored and treasured his success, but another part seemed to want to do its utmost to destroy it. I've seen it with other big stars who start to take risks, knowing they have everything to lose. It's like they're consciously saying, 'If people love me, then how much do they love me? How far can I go and still get away with it?' Elton and John Reid were alike in that respect. There was something in both of them that liked walking on the very edge."[87] Elton's behavior was a classic case of manic/depressive behavior, and the excessive cocaine use only magnified it.

Elton's relationship with his boyfriend, already on the rocks, didn't seem to make him happy either. According to Elton, "Even though I was in a relationship with John Reid, I felt lonely. There was an incredible drive and passion. But all I had in my life was my music. Not a bad thing to have, but there was a loneliness."[184]

By October 1975 his career was back in high gear, and Elton was not left alone for long periods of time. That month he had a new album coming out, a sold-out pair of concert dates at L.A.'s Dodger Stadium, and he was about to get his star on Hollywood Boulevard. Furthermore, he had already completed the *Rock of the Westies* album, which was supposed to be his final studio album for DJM Music.

With the exception of a live-concert album and a second greatest-hits package, he would no longer be obligated to crank out two full albums a year. Elton should have been ecstatically happy. However, his sense of depression, the pressure he was under, and his escalated cocaine use gave way to a deeply-rooted unhappiness. Nobody would have predicted his next suicide attempt, though.

First came the October release of the new *Rock of the Westies* album. In America it became the second Elton John album to enter the *Billboard, Record World* and *Cash Box* charts at Number One. It also hit Number Six in both Norway and Sweden. The first single from the album, "Island Girl," hit Number One in the U.S. and Number 14 in the U.K.

If *Captain Fantastic & The Brown Dirt Cowboy* was the height of a concept album, with a story and continuity, than *Rock of the Westies* was the direct opposite. *Rock of the Westies* is a patchwork quilt of past Elton John successes and songwriting formulas. It contains Calypso rock ("Island Girl"), progressive jazz/rock ("Feed Me"), and more of Bernie Taupin's songs of the Old West ("I Feel Like the Bullet [In the Gun of Robert Ford]").

One of the most intriguing songs on *Rock of the Westies* is the opening track, "Medley (Yell Help/Wednesday Night/Ugly)." It features the background vocals of LaBelle. Here Elton had once been their piano player on those tours of England back in the 1960s, and that very year they each scored huge Number One hit singles. It was a truly inspired move to have them on this album.

Another musical appearance of note on this album is the credited background singer Ann Orson, who appears on several tracks. Critics and rock journalists wondered who was this unknown girl and mentioned her in their reviews. She was in fact Elton, in just another of his several famous pseudonyms. This was one of "Sharon's" female personas.

The reviews for *Rock of the Westies* were highly varied. Elton had set the bar so high for himself with *Goodbye Yellow Brick Road* that every album he would subsequently release during the 1970s would be compared to it.

Ben Edmonds, in *Phonograph Record*, warned rock fans, "If [you]'re looking for another *Goodbye Yellow Brick Road*, [you]'ll probably feel a similar dissatisfaction with *Rock of the Westies.* The single from it, 'Island Girl,' is one of the least-effective radio songs he's ever released."[34]

Charles Shaar Murray in *New Musical Express* literally hated the album. Critiquing it he pointed out, "Elton has been making an awful lot of records recently.... The last couple have shown severe signs of strain, and *Rock of the Westies*...is so rickety it'd collapse if you breathed heavy on it."[32]

The two sold-out concerts that Elton John gave at Dodger Stadium on October 25 and October 26, 1975, were not only massively successful in their own right, but they were the first rock concerts held at that venue since The Beatles in 1966. The Beatles' crowds had gotten unruly, and rock concerts had been banned from

Dodger Stadium for years. The owners of the stadium were promised that Elton John's typical audience was anything but unruly and that it would be two shows that contained several slow ballads, during which his fans typically sat still and listened, instead of tearing up the stadium.

The concerts at Dodger Stadium were the final appearances of a short American concert tour with the new band, which had also included concerts in Oakland, California, and Las Vegas, Nevada. That way the mini-tour could climax with his triumphant week of activities in L.A.

Reviewing the Vegas show, Ben Edmonds of *Rolling Stone* found that for a change, Elton was letting the music take the front seat in his show. There was a lack of typical theatrics and more emphasis on the songs. According to Edmonds, "For the first time in recent memory, an Elton John concert wasn't as much a glittering extravaganza. Elton and band performed…without the neon signs, spangled keyboards and peacock costumes of recent tours…on this night, Elton gave his people everything they wanted."[165]

To intensify the importance of the Los Angeles events, that same week Elton was booked to come into Hollywood to officially unveil his star embedded in the sidewalk on Hollywood Boulevard, in front of historic Grauman's Chinese Theater. It was going to be such an exciting week that Elton chartered a Boeing 707 jet to fly over an elite party of guests. His guests included the entire London office of Rocket Records, Sheila and Fred, John Reid's parents, sports star Rodney Marsh, talk-show host Russell Harty, and an entire film crew from *London Weekend Television*. To top it all off, he also flew in his beloved Grandma Ivy.

Elton's dear friends Bryan Forbes and Nannette Newman were also on the plane. Bryan was having a great year, as he had just directed the 1975 original film of Ira Levin's creepy novel, *The Stepford Wives*.

The Elton John party was put up at the Westwood Holiday Inn, and they had an open tab for whatever they wanted during their stay. There was an organized excursion to Disneyland, as well as a party on John Reid's 65-foot yacht. The luxury boat had been his birthday present from Elton that year and was appropriately christened *Madman*.

The main events all went without a hitch. The October 21 ceremony in front of Grauman's Chinese Theater was a big treat for Elton's parents, and a crowd of nearly 6,000 spectators had gathered to see Captain Fantastic in all his glory. There was such a throng of fans that Hollywood Boulevard had to be temporarily closed.

In an effort to control the multitudes, a Chamber of Commerce official took to a microphone and commanded, "Boys and girls, if we kept the noise down, we'd all hear what Mr. John says when he arrives." Elton did not disappoint the adoring crowd. He arrived exactly at noon as planned, donning a green satin suit decorated with film-star badges all over it. He made his entrance on a gold golf cart that had a bowtie as its headlights. "I declare this supermarket open," he proclaimed to the throngs of cheering fans as his own square of sidewalk was exposed.[166]

Next on the Rocket Man's agenda was the incredible pair of L.A. concerts. For them Elton had Bob Mackie create a sequin-and-bead-covered replica of a Los Angeles Dodgers outfit, complete with his last name and the number "1" on the back. He wore a Dodgers' baseball cap, which was also covered in bangles and beads. Those two amazing shows found Elton John in front of a cumulative number of more than 100,000 people.

After the two shows, Bryan Forbes saw Elton's hands and noted that there was actually blood dripping from them, as the performer had played his keyboards so hard he broke the skin. Apparently the stress of it all turned up the emotional pressure a further degree.

Following the duo of triumphant shows, as family and friends lounged around the swimming pool of his Beverly Hills house, Elton came out to the pool dressed in a terrycloth bathrobe. He suddenly announced, "I have taken 85 Valiums. I shall die within the hour." With that he hurled himself into his swimming pool while his family and friends looked on in horror. Caleb Quaye recalls the medics coming to pump Elton's stomach. Following his suicidal nosedive into the swimming pool, Elton's Grandma Ivy nonchalantly remarked, "I suppose we've all got to go home now."[136]

According to Elton's mother, "It was a terrible, terrible time, those days. I wouldn't want to go through them again. It's an awful thing to see someone you love unhappy…. There were the drugs, which he denied frantically, but I'm not daft. I knew he was taking the drugs."[161] Elton was truly one sick parrot, and his friends and family knew it. Obviously, Elton was crying out for help.

The real miracle was that somehow this latest suicide attempt by Elton was kept out of the press. It would have caused a huge scandal. After two days in a coma and some rest and rehabilitation, Elton was back on his feet and continued to work in late 1975 as though the suicide attempt had never happened. Back in London, he picked up where he left off with his activities and social obligations.

Since the previous year when John Lennon and he had appeared at Madison Square Garden, Lennon had reunited with Yoko Ono and parted ways with May Pang. The result was John and Yoko's son, Sean Lennon. When the boy was born, John asked Elton to become Sean's godfather, and he gladly accepted.

Elton finished 1975 with another series of Christmas concerts at The Hammersmith Odeon in London. The shows were as wildly popular as they had been the two previous holiday seasons.

For the very first time, Elton also began to entertain the idea of recording with other lyricists. "Oh yeah, probably," he pondered. "I don't really want to, because the occasion hasn't really arisen. It might do. Taupin doesn't want to write with anybody else. I keep telling him to write with other people occasionally."[27]

It had been quite a year for Elton John. He had made recording business history by becoming the first artist in music history to debut not one—but two—albums at Number One in America. He was now immortalized with his very own star on the sidewalk of the Hollywood Walk of Fame. He became a movie star that year, thanks to *Tommy*. And he was even a godfather. One could only imagine what his next role would be.

On the pages of *Phonograph Record* in 1975, writer Greg Shaw innocently proclaimed of Elton, "He has nine Platinum albums; this one had sold a million before it was even released. And all without fuss, without controversy."[28] All that career, all those deep dark secrets about his personal life, and so far no fuss, no controversy, and no scandal? Hopefully, Elton was enjoying his concurrent fast-paced life through the "Scandal-Free Zone" because that was all about to change forever.

CHAPTER ELEVEN

Sorry Seems to Be the Hardest Word

While he was recuperating from his depression, exhaustion, and attempted suicide at the end of 1975, Elton's fame and legend continued to rise. As they did, so did the demands and expectations on his time and creativity. In terms of record sales, concert ticket grosses, and songwriting income, 1975 had been a true highpoint for Elton. He would never quite match that success again. Elton had been riding a fast-paced roller coaster for the last five years, and he had just come to the top of the highest hill. It seemed like the only way he could go from here was down. Ultimately, the year 1976 was to be one of many changes and challenges for him. It was also to be one of breakups, great controversy, and some disappointment.

Elton kicked off the year by giving a deeply personal interview to *Playboy* magazine for their January 1976 issue. They found the Rocket Man to be a tantrum-prone, sad, and moody person who spent more time with his record albums than with his true friends. It was like they weren't interviewing the fun party animal, "Elton John," so much as they were interviewing whiny and spoiled Reggie Dwight of Pinner.

One of the topics he talked of extensively was feeling unloved by his father. He claimed, "My father was so stupid with me…. You know, he never saw me for two years. I mean, I was two years old when he came home from the Air Force. He'd never seen me. And it got off to a really bad start, 'cause Mother said, 'Do you want to go upstairs and see him?' He said, 'No, I'll wait 'til morning.'"[55]

According to Stanley, that was sheer nonsense. Not only had he been there, but he had been around until little Reggie was eighteen months old. Back home in England, reading Elton's interview in *Playboy* deeply hurt his biological father's feelings.

Elton's time of being in touch with Stanley Dwight and taking interest in the lives of his half-brothers suddenly ended. From this point forward, whenever Elton talked about his father to the press, it was done with bitter resentment and hurt.

Wealthy beyond his wildest dreams, Elton continued spending a fortune on his wild costumes and bizarre eyeglasses. According to him, these colorful clothes and Halloween-array of spectacles unleashed him when he was onstage and when he was offstage as well. "The clothes were important," he claimed. "And I developed all those glasses I wore, and people developed glasses for me, and they became funnier and funnier and wilder and wilder at a time when glasses were really boring, I hasten to add. It was kind of like: 'Listen, I'm not David Bowie. I'm not Mick Jagger, and I'm not Rod Stewart. I'm not sexy.... ' When I put my costume on, that's when I know I'm ready to go onstage. It's such a necessary thing for me. I'm putting on a show for people and I not only want to give them something to listen to, I want to give them something to look at, too."[171]

He was not yet even 30 years old, and already he was feeling jaded and "world weary." What would it take to impress Elton, circa 1976? "Very few people can enter a room and make me gasp. 'Oh, my God!'" he claimed. "Jagger, Sinatra, Elvis, probably. Also people like Noel Coward, Edith Piaf, and Katharine Hepburn. They could do it to me. Dietrich. Uh, Mae West. No, maybe not. She's been seen at too many functions recently. Judy Garland had it. That was an awful mystique she had. She just wanted to destroy herself."[55]

He also began to ponder the meaning of his fame and what his critics were saying. According to him, "Well, if I took notice of all the bad things that were said about me, I'd be in a loony bin by now. If somebody has written something shitty about me in the past, I don't rush up to them and say, 'You cunt!' I just shrug it off."[55]

On the up side of Elton's life, in February 1976, it was announced in the press that Elton John was now the highest earning person in pop music history. In a story run by The Associated Press, it was estimated that since January of the previous year, the public had paid more than $60 million for Elton concert tickets and recordings. He was not only a musical legend; he was an industry unto himself.

It was to be a year of career ups and downs, though. He may have been an industry unto himself, but when the second single was released from his *Rock of the Westies* album it never made the charts at all in the U.K. The second single was the two-sided "Grow Some Funk of Your Own" backed with "I Feel Like a Bullet in the Gun (of Robert Ford)." However, it was found to be so unappealing by radio programmers that it never even hit the Top Ten, peaking at Number 14 in America.

When Rick Sklar, who was the Program Director at WABC in New York City, refused to add the "A" side—the song "I Feel Like a Bullet in the Gun (of Robert Ford)"—to his station's playlist, Elton tried to charm him into it. He sent Sklar a cake with the message, "Give Elton a Shot, 'Feel Like a Bullet' is a hit." Sklar refused to be moved. The following week Elton sent him another cake with the message reading: "Disregard first cake. 'Grow Some Funk' is a hit!"[144]

The Elton John roller coaster soared up again on March 7, 1976, when Elton became the first rock & roll star—since The Beatles—to have his likeness reproduced at Madame Tussauds Wax Museum in London. The following month, the single version of "Pinball Wizard" hit Number Seven in Great Britain. To promote it, on April 29, 1976, Elton kicked off a 29-date tour of the U.K.

The tour coincided with the release of Elton's fifteenth album, *Here and There*. His first live album since *11-17-70* (U.S.)/*17-11-70* (U.K.), *Here and There* was something of a disaster. In fact it was his first major fumble in quite some time. Though previous albums and songs had not always lived up to expectations, none had bombed as this one did. This was the album that was going to finish off his recording obligation to DJM Records. Unfortunately, it looked and sounded like a contractual obligation and marked his first real slip downward on the album charts. It peaked at Number Six in the U.K., Number Four in the U.S., Number 19 in Norway, and Number 30 in Sweden.

The album was a mistake, and Elton knew it. Originally comprised of five tracks on each side, it was pieced together from the London concert he performed in front of Princess Margaret on May 5, 1974, and his historic Madison Square Garden performance, featuring John Lennon on November, 28, 1974. (Though the album did not contain any tracks with Lennon himself.) It was a hollow album of divergent styles, neither special nor memorable. Furthermore, the sound quality seemed muddy.

This was an era when "live" albums were both dynamic and crisp sounding. That was especially evident in the revolutionary *Frampton Comes Alive!* by ex-Humble Pie star Peter Frampton. In contrast, *Here and There* had little going for it and seemed forced. Behind the scenes at the Elton John camp, the album was a painful point of contention for all involved.

Elton already had his next album, *Blue Moves*, in the can, and he didn't want Dick James to have it as his final DJM release, so he forced *Here and There* on James. It would have been much more significant had the John Lennon songs been on the second side, since they were recorded on that same concert tape. According to Elton, "I wasn't going to let them use any of that on *Here and There*. No way. It would have been taking advantage of John who did the gig as a favor."[177]

He knew it was a "grade C" album at best, but he was glad to finally put an end to his dealings with DJM. In spite of poor reviews, *Here and There* was certified Gold in the United States in June 1976. Interestingly, when *Here and There* was updated in 1995 to become a two-compact disc set, sixteen new tracks were added, including John Lennon's songs with Elton. The update created a time capsule of what Elton and his band sounded like back then. However the sound quality is still muddy at best.

In spite of the incredible recording career that Elton had, and a string of five Number One hits on the U.S. charts, Elton had still not scored a chart-topping hit in his native England. It was an ongoing sore point with him. When Elton played The Grand Theater in Leeds, England, *Sounds* magazine sent writer Vivien Goldman to review it. She found him uncomfortable and trying too hard to impress the crowd. England was still skeptical about "Reg of Watford." Vivian claimed, "Elton John was nervous, in a bad way.... It was his first British live show since the Wembley fiasco of last year, and his last before forsaking the concert-hall venues for stadiums (in my guess). Although he's the biggest selling artist in the world, earns more money than all The Beatles put together ever did, or so they say, he still hasn't cracked this country open the way he yearns to."[35] Then Elton suddenly had an idea for a hit single that he could record with Kiki Dee.

Explaining the genesis of "Don't Go Breaking My Heart," Elton states, "That song was done in the studio when I was making the new album [*Blue Moves*]. That isn't on the album but, like so many of the songs, I just came up with a chord sequence on electric piano and thought up a title. Then I rang up Bernie and asked him to write lyrics to the title. I've wanted to do a duet with Kiki for a long time."[36] Bernie and Elton wrote the song under the pen names of "Ann Orson" and "Carte Blanche."

The Elton John/Kiki Dee duet of "Don't Go Breaking My Heart" was recorded in May 1976, in Toronto, Canada. By July it was Number One in the U.K., and in August it topped the American charts, where it would remain at Number One for four weeks. It was the perfect song for Elton and his female protégée, and to this day it remains one of his most beloved hits.

Speaking of the British success of "Don't Go Breaking My Heart," Elton claimed, "I've had about three Number Twos, but never a Number One before. When I heard it was Number One, I rang everybody I knew to tell them. They were pretty annoyed, but hell, it got me excited again. It really did."[36] The roller coaster was back up again. Although he had finally scored a chart-topping hit in England, the glory of this song made him want to hit Number One with a solo song. He was going to have a long wait to accomplish this goal.

From this point forward, everything that Elton John did made headlines, especially in the tabloids in England, Australia, and America. According to Elton, "There's one guy who writes for *The Daily Express*; he's got a gossip column. He's printed a couple of things about me—they've not been nasty or anything, they've just been absolute rubbish. When Evel Knievel was supposed to jump that canyon in the rocket, I was supposedly by his side, singing the national anthem…. *The National Star* wrote that I'd become an egomaniac when I broke up the band and said I believed after my role in *Tommy* that I was the world's biggest film star. At that time, I was hiding behind the walls of my Hollywood mansion. Not even my servants knew where I was."[55]

According to Elton, he wasn't going to quit living his life just because he was under the scrutiny of the press. "I refuse to become a recluse," he claimed.[55]

Bernie was in a decidedly "down" mood when they were recording the sessions for *Blue Moves*. On the other side of "Don't Go Breaking My Heart" was a song titled "Snow Queen." It was Bernie Taupin's way of writing about Cher.

A beautiful guitar and conga-led, medium-tempo ballad, "Snow Queen" is actually a lovely song. The combination of Elton's lead vocals, teamed with Kiki Dee's clear and beautiful harmony vocal, makes this a forgotten gem. In the lyrics of the song, Cher, who is the so-called "Snow Queen," lives in a perfect house "in the hills"—obviously the Hollywood Hills in this case. She resides behind the "cold black gates," and she is as delicate as "bone china." However, in the lyrics of the song, Bernie accuses Cher of wasting her time on "men with no taste." Presumably that was a dig towards Cher's boyfriend at the time, rock star Gregg Allman.

"You know even the B-side of 'Don't Go Breaking My Heart' was really hateful," Elton admitted. "'Snow Queen' it's called and it's about somebody. I didn't realize who until I'd started to record the vocal. 'Allo, allo,' I thought. 'It's Cher!' It was so cutting I had to tell her in advance and apologize in advance. She was okay about it."[40] Obviously, Cher had weathered worse storms than this and took it in her stride.

While he was recording *Blue Moves*, Elton found himself desperately seeking a new love in his life. Unfortunately, it was a case of him looking for love in all the wrong places. "I've fallen in love with the wrong people so many times," he explained. "I used to go to clubs and I'd see people at the bar, and by the time I managed to get to talk to them I had already planned our entire lives together."[47] With everything in his life whirling around him at a breakneck pace, Elton found himself suffering from self-doubts and deep depression. Reviewers were dogging him about his latest album, his public was demanding more and more of him, and he increasingly was turning to drugs just to cope with it all. In addition, the press—especially *Rolling Stone* magazine—wanted him to "come out of the closet." Much of Elton's sadness and frustration seemed to stem from the fact that he was, in reality, a gay man but couldn't tell anyone. And so, his downward cycle of depression continued to spin out of control.

On June 29, 1976, Elton was to start his new thirty-one-date U.S. concert tour in Landover, Maryland. It would run until the show on August 21, in Seattle, Washington. According to Elton, after this tour, he was retiring from the stage, at least the big arenas, for an indefinite period of time. He was beginning to feel too drained emotionally and creatively.

One of the monumental events on this tour came when Elton John and Bernie Taupin attended an Elvis Presley concert with Elton's parents, Sheila and "Derf." After the show they were ushered backstage to meet the King of Rock & Roll himself. By all accounts, it was a bizarre and slightly surreal event for all parties concerned.

By 1976 Elvis Presley was only 41 years old, but he was at the end of his life. His dependence on prescription drugs, combined with his poor diet and ballooning weight turned him into a caricature of himself. In his last two years, he was constantly surrounded by his tight circle of friends known as The Memphis Mafia. Furthermore, that year he was employing two of his teenage stepbrothers, David and Ricky Stanley, as additions to his staff of personal bodyguards. He thought it was a great way to get them involved in the Presley family business.

"We were on tour in 1976," recalls David Stanley. "We were listening to a lot of the *Captain Fantastic & The Brown Dirt Cowboy* album and *Caribou*. We were listening to a lot of stuff on those albums when we were in Vail, Colorado. I was living with Elvis, but I was listening to everything but Elvis. I was carrying a Sony 'Jam Box' and it was cassette, and I just wore it out—I played it all the time. And Elvis would always come in and say, 'Who's that?...Who's that, Elton John?' 'Yes, Elvis,' I said to him, 'he wrote a song called "Don't Let the Sun Go Down on Me."' And he said, 'Yeah, I know that song. I'm familiar with that song.' That was all of the conversation with me that he had about Elton John. I told him that I was a big fan of Elton's. But, he didn't say anything about that."[149]

When Elvis' tour came to Washington, D.C., arrangements were already underway for Elton and Bernie to come backstage and meet their favorite singing idol from the 1950s. As David Stanley recalls, "We were out on tour and we were in D.C., and Jerry Shilling came backstage and said, 'Elton John's here.' Now, we knew when we were flying in that Elton was going to be here. Jerry was kind of the 'go-between,' and of course Concerts West handled Elton John: Jerry Weintraub and Tom Hewett, they also did the Elton John tour. We were backstage and I was talking to Elvis about Elton John. I said, 'Elton John's here.' And Elvis said, 'Yeah, he's that guy that wrote "Don't Let the Sun Go Down on Me."' I said, 'Yeah, that's him. I'm a big fan of his.' He said, 'That's the stuff you listen to all the time?' And I said, 'Yes.' So Elton walks up, and Elton acted like everybody did with Elvis—he was in total awe. Elton was dressed flamboyantly, because this was his 1976 attire. And, the same guy who made Elvis' glasses—Dennis Roberts who had a company called Optique Boutique—and so Elvis had his glasses made by Dennis, and Elton had on a custom-made pair of glasses. So, Elton said to Elvis, 'We have the same optician.' Elvis said, 'Yeah that's right,' and then he said, 'Well, listen, didn't you write that song, "Don't Let YOUR SON Go Down on Me?"' Elton just looked at him. Elton didn't know how to take it anyway, he just looked at him and had a little grin on his face, like he knew that Elvis was just 'busting his balls.' My brother Ricky and I just busted out laughing; we were laughing our asses off. Elvis said, 'What?' I said, 'Elvis it's: "Don't Let THE SUN Go Down on Me."' And he goes, 'Oh, yeah, O.K.' Elton never moved; he just stood there in awe. Elvis reached out to shake his hand, and Elton says, 'Elvis, well it's real nice to meet you, I admire your music.' Then Elton moved forward and suddenly threw his arms around Elvis, hugging him. As bodyguards, we knew that Elton wasn't going to do anything to Elvis, but nobody ever got that close to Elvis. Elton had moved towards him and just put his arms around Elvis, like he was giving him a big bear hug. As he did, I watched as Elton put his head on Elvis' chest. Then Elton unwrapped himself from Elvis, and he just turned around and walked away. It was a moment I will never forget."[149]

   According to David Stanley, although it was unspoken of in Elton's presence, Elvis' entourage all presumed that Elton was homosexual. Says Stanley, "Elvis would make derogatory statements about gay people from time-to-time. He would say about someone: 'He wouldn't suck on it, but he'd hold it in his mouth.' That was

As a performer, Elton emulated his piano-playing idols: Liberace, Jerry Lee Lewis, and Little Richard. He became famous as one of the most flamboyant and colorful pianists in history. (Photo © Retna Ltd./Michael Putland)

The Rocket Man has often said that without Bernie Taupin writing the lyrics, there might never have been an Elton John. By 1973, everything they touched turned to "Gold."
(Photo© Retna Ltd./Michael Putland)

One of the keys to Elton's success was his ability to mount elaborate concert tours and mesmerize crowds with his incredible songbook of hits.
(Photo© Retna Ltd./Michael Putland)

By 1975, Elton had sold 42 million albums and 18 million singles worldwide. However, with the release of his *Blue Moves* album the following year, he felt that he was losing his direction. (Photo© Retna Ltd./G. Hanekroot)

In 1970, when Elton John's recording of "Your Song" first hit the radio airwaves, it was clear that a new star had been born. (Photo© Retna Ltd./Peter Mazel/Sunshine)

As time went on, the costumes and wigs just became more and more outrageous. It seemed like there was nothing that Elton wouldn't wear to grab everyone's attention.
(Photo© Retna Ltd./Adrian Boot)

Elton is known for his insane costumes onstage, including dressing as clown Ronald McDonald. Performing with George Michael at Wembly Stadium on June 28, 1986.
(Photo© Retna Ltd./Steve Rapport)

In the 1990s Elton John started touring with Billy Joel. Their duet concerts have been so successful that they continued performing together in 2009.
(Photo© Retna Photos/Brian Snyder/Camera Press)

Tina Turner and Elton John planned to do a concert tour together in 1999, but Elton threw one of his famed tantrums, and that was the end of that. (Photo© Retna Ltd./Michael Putland)

Elton John longed to come out of his shell and become a performer who was bigger than life. He has certainly achieved that. (Photo© Retna Ltd./Robb D. Cohen)

Elton is famous for his feuds with fellow performers, including Madonna. Here's the duo, comparing their breasts. (Photo© Retna Ltd./D. Raban/allactiondigital.com)

In his career Elton has had many duet partners, but his most famous one is Kiki Dee, who helped him make the song "Don't Go Breaking My Heart" a Number One hit. (Photo© Retna Ltd./Michael Putland)

After seven hectic years in the spotlight, in 1977 Elton stripped down his stage show to himself at the piano and his percussionist Ray Cooper. (Photo© Charles Moniz)

For his 1980 Central Park concert in New York City, Elton had designer Bob Mackie create a Donald Duck costume for the grand finale. (Photo© Charles Moniz)

The entire world was in shock when Elton suddenly married a woman: sound engineer Renate Blauel. It was a "masquerade" marriage at best. (Photo© Retna Ltd./Monitor Picture Library)

On April 25, 2006, Elton John and Bernie Taupin appeared on TV's *The Today Show* to promote their first Broadway show together, *Lestat*. The vampire musical, however, was a huge flop. (Photo© Retna Ltd./David Atlas)

Elton and David Furnish made certain that everything was bigger than life at the singer's 50th birthday in 1997. The duo had to arrive at the event in a truck, since Elton couldn't fit his wig into an automobile. (Photo© Retna Ltd./Davies/Peters/allactiondigital.com)

One of the most traumatic events in Elton's life was the death of Princess Diana in 1997. He performed a rewritten version of "Candle in the Wind" at her funeral, as the entire world looked on. (Photo© Retna Ltd./ROTA/Camera Press Digital)

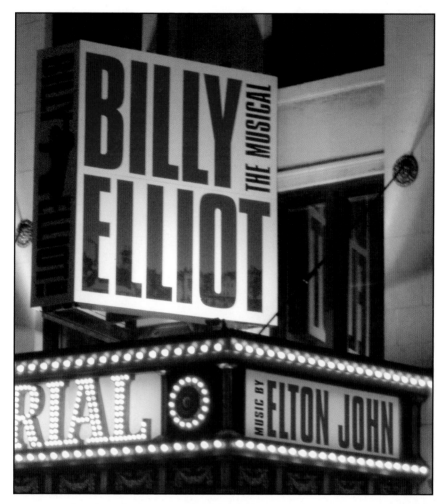

In November of 2008 Elton John debuted his fourth Broadway show, his musical version of the film *Billy Elliot*, at the Imperial Theater in New York City. (Photo© Mark Bego)

In the mid-1980s Elton started wearing straw hats, which he made one of his trademarks after he wore one in his video for the autobiographical song "I'm Still Standing." (Photo© Retna Ltd./Gary Gershoff)

just how Elvis talked. So, when he saw Elton, I don't think that Elvis was intimidated by the obvious fact that Elton was gay. Elvis was not 'Politically Correct,' so when he purposely said, 'Don't Let YOUR SON Go Down on Me,' he did that as kind of a joke to let Elton know that he knew what was going on. I thought that Elton handled it well. The entire time he was in Elvis' dressing room, Elton was lit up; and he looked just like a younger version of Liberace. In fact, Elvis said something about that: 'I haven't seen a guy like that since Liberace!' Elton didn't do a lot of talking. He was just star-struck at the sight of Elvis. He did say, 'I love your music.' The Elvis shows in '76 weren't all that great. I don't know what Elton was thinking, but when he got backstage it wasn't the Elvis he had seen before. Regardless, I could certainly tell that Elton was overwhelmed by Elvis Presley."[149]

However, what Elton and Bernie recognized was that Elvis was undeniably bloated and addled by all of the prescription drugs he had been taking.

Bernie Taupin was later to recall, "We went to see him do a show, but it was absolutely pitiful. He was so drugged, he could hardly sing—he just stood there, handing out scarves. Then we were taken backstage to see him. There was this dressing room, full of Memphis Mafia, with Elvis in the middle of them on the stool, wrapped in towels. He looked awful, and he was sweating, with the dye from his hair running down his face. And all these guys in suits around him in a kind of huddle. I don't think he even knew who we were. As we walked away afterwards, Elton said, 'He's not long for this world.'"[87]

Indeed, Elton was correct. Elvis died at the age of forty-two the following year. However, that meeting left a lasting impression on both Taupin and Elton. In Elton's case, it underscored the urgency of his plan of taking a long break from concert touring. Bernie, on the other hand, put his thoughts onto paper, to pen one of the most poignant and haunting songs for the forthcoming *Blue Moves* album: "Idol."

Meeting Elvis had a profound effect on Elton John. He saw, in a dramatic way, what can happen if you let the show business machinery devour you, pushing you towards an early grave. Elvis Presley was only eleven years older than Elton, yet he appeared to be a battered and bloated wreck decades older than his forty-one years.

Seeing Elvis that evening, it was even easier for Elton to decide to take a break from touring. In an interview at the time, he said, "Yes, I feel like stopping for a time. I've done it for six years and I'm fed up with it. I'm not so much fed up with playing, but I'm fed up with having no base and constantly roaming around. I just want to spend time doing things, other things, that I want to do…. I'm not retiring. I just want to lay off for a bit."[36]

In the United States, Elton John was currently the biggest performer on the planet. In the 1940s there was Frank Sinatra. Elvis Presley was the phenomenon of the 1950s, and The Beatles reigned supreme in the 1960s. Now, in the 1970s, everything was about Elton John. This was to be Elton's tenth concert tour of the United States. It was estimated that by the time the thirty-one shows were finished, he would have played in front of 750,000 people that summer alone. The tour also included a week-long booking at Madison Square Garden in New York City. The show and the stage sets were so elaborate that a team of fifty-seven traveled with him to assemble it, make it run, and tear it down every night. Elton had his own private jet called *The Starship*.

Bernie was on this tour as well, with a prime view of the shows from the soundboard. He claimed at the time, "I feel like a member of the road crew. But I dig touring, and with this band it's like a big family. I don't want to miss anything that happens. I know it sounds corny, but I really get high listening to the words and watching Elton."[36]

Since his career had started, in the span of seven years, Elton had released sixteen albums and a countless string of singles. According to Elton, "Not bad going for a podgy, balding fellow with atrocious eyesight, who never really wanted to sing in the first place."[36]

The arenas and the crowds in America just seemed to be getting larger and larger. In the Detroit area's Pontiac Silverdome, he and his band played in front of an astonishing audience of more than 80,000 people. It was all starting to get insane. According to Elton, "Sometimes I get a bit depressed playing big places, especially when we did Pontiac stadium on this tour. It's like seeing animals in a cage when you look out towards the audience. I thought…'Oh God. This has really got to stop.'"[36]

As he had before, Elton continued to wear his crazy costumes. His American audiences had come to anticipate some sort of outrageousness from Elton, and he did his best not to disappoint them. His outfits that summer included a matador jacket decorated with black and white piano keys; a stars and stripes, Uncle Sam outfit complete with a stovepipe hat; and crazy stuffed vegetables. On July 4, 1976, America was celebrating its Bicentennial. At Foxborough, Massachusetts's Schaeffer Stadium, Elton John was performing in front of a sold-out crowd. He dressed as the Statue of Liberty. The United States was marking their independence from the King of England, and here there were tens of thousands of American countrymen and countrywomen on their feet cheering a vocalizing English "queen" in Lady Liberty drag!

For some of the shows Elton wore a huge stuffed banana around his neck, frequently sticking it in his pants so that it resembled a big yellow dildo. For additional flair, he carried with him a suitcase containing thirty-two pairs of eyeglasses in a rainbow of colors.

Elton was the crazy, over-the-top, British clown. He may have been overweight, balding, and insecure, yet through his evocative music, he had the innate ability to crystallize the thoughts and emotions of everyone.

Although he burned up a lot of calories onstage, Elton's weight continued to grow while he was in America. This was partially due to the fact that his favorite on-the-road food was calorie-laden Kentucky Fried Chicken. When the entourage pulled into a new city, he sent crew members out to get cardboard buckets full of it.

With regard to his weight, he claimed, "I fluctuate. But I'll never be really skinny, because I have a big frame. I do like garbage food, I must admit…. I'd love to be like Mick Jagger, all lithe and slim, and come out looking great. But I'm never going to be like that, so—let's have a laugh."[55]

To compensate for his lack of a sexy body, there were the outlandish outfits he wore onstage. But what was the movtivation behind his fascination with all of the costumes? According to Elton, "Oh, I just like to get up and have a lark. I do it tongue-in-cheek with an 'up yours' attitude. I love people who expect me to wear great, feathery costumes—and I do it…. I might have a hair transplant. It's just a matter of going down there with the courage to say, 'I want some more hair, please.'"[55]

However, not everyone found Elton John amusing that summer. Condemning his August 10, 1976, concert at Madison Square Garden, *Rolling Stone* writer Ken Tucker claimed, "Elton's a garish, tuneless shuck and decidedly out of fashion since about the time of *Rock of the Westies*…. He was ultimately a tedious concert: cold-bloodedly entertaining, artless, and other than hopping off the piano, no chances were taken."[179]

Critics aside, the cheering crowds that greeted him every night onstage loved him. They expected him to act crazy and sing all of their favorite songs, and he did them proud. In his fans' eyes he seemed unstoppable.

Furthermore, while in New York City that summer, he made certain that he had a "gay old time." The final night of his engagement at Madison Square Garden he had an all-star lineup onstage including surprise guests Alice Cooper, Billie Jean King, Kiki Dee, and colorfully overweight drag queen Divine.

According to Charles Moniz, who worked on Divine's show as the drag performer's personal assistant, "Elton came to see *Women Behind Bars*, and he was in town to do his upcoming concerts at Madison Square Garden. He wanted Divine to make an appearance in the middle of his shows. He wanted the producers to close *Women Behind Bars* for the days that Divine was going to appear with Elton. The house capacity of The Truck & Warehouse Theater in the East Village was only 300 seats, so the producers wanted Elton to pay full price for all 300 seats. Obviously, Elton wasn't going to do that. There was one day that Elton was performing when *Women Behind Bars* was 'dark,' and Divine was available, so Divine agreed to do it. Divine told me that it was 'a very confusing evening.' It culminated with Divine joining Elton on stage, and the two of them throwing bananas to the crowd."[281]

That night after the show, Elton went out bar-hopping with Divine, and they hit all the "male-only" gay clubs in town. Along the way, Elton pitched one of his fits. "Divine took me to Crisco Disco," Elton explained. "We went in and they looked at us. Everyone in New York wears jeans or fatigues and I had on a striped jacket and the guys [at the door] said, 'What the fuck is this, Halloween?' We couldn't get in so I was a bit high and really pissed off, and I threw an ashtray. Anyway it was printed in the *London Daily Mail* that I was pushed against a wall and got beaten up and caused a fuss."[57]

One of the other men-only gay clubs they hit in Manhattan was 12 West. Located at West 12th Street and the West Side Highway in the Meatpacking District, 12 West was the hottest gay disco in the city. Since it was technically a private club, it was not uncommon for dancers to snort, smoke or inhale any number of mood-enhancing substances. Recalled Elton, "I went dancing one night at 12 West and that was great fun. Everyone left me alone. They were so into their disco records and passing their 'poppers.' If the Queen of England had been standing in the middle of the floor with a tiara on her head, nobody would have paid any attention."[57]

His drug use was continuing as well. If he had trouble sleeping, he simply popped a pill. He had also escalated his alcohol consumption. "When I'm making an album at Caribou," he explained at the time, "I drink a lot of wine. And I started drinking 100-proof liquor and getting really out of it—for no reason whatsoever. It was a habit. I'd get up feeling all grumpy and go through spasms of drinking."[55]

During this period Elton received some of the all-time worst reviews of his career. When *New York Times* critic John Rockwell wrote that his recent concert was "Smooth...wallpaper music of the most banal sort," Elton had a fit. He was booked that week to make an appearance on Manhattan radio station WNEW-FM as a guest disc jockey, and he did so after drinking two bottles of Dom Perignon champagne. As part of his embarrassing diatribe, Elton scolded the critic on the air. "I bet he is four-foot three.... I bet he's got boogies up his nose.... I bet his feet smell."[167] Elton made a complete fool of himself, sounding more like a petulant thirteen-year-old boy than the wealthiest superstar in the rock world.

At the time, Elton was in the middle of several fights with his other rock star rivals. Apparently, "Sharon" and "Phyllis" were feeling bitchy towards each other. Elton claimed, "I used to be on very good terms with Rod and we're still speaking to each other. But in an interview with *SOUNDS* [magazine] he said: 'I went down the pub the other day. You'd never see Bowie or Elton down the pub. I'm one of the lads.' And I felt like sending him a telegram saying, 'Oh "well done," Rod. You've been down the pub. Maybe next week you'll go on a tube or a bus.' One of the lads! I'm not, but I feel I'm closer to the public than he'll ever fucking be."[40]

Then Mick Jagger had his turn at Elton, continuing to refer to him in the press as "Fat Reg." Likewise, David Bowie gave an interview with *Playboy* magazine and called Elton "the Liberace, the token queen of rock." Bowie further proclaimed, "I consider myself responsible for a whole new school of pretensions—they know who they are. Don't you, Elton?"[57]

Elton retaliated by explaining, "I first met David when I took him out to dinner when he was 'Ziggy Stardust.' We had a nice time, y'know? He was with Angie and I was with Tony King, who's now with Rocket Records.... He was out of it completely. I don't think I've seen him since. We really can't say we have a feud going, although he obviously doesn't like me very much. I'm not being bitchy."[57]

While all this was going on, Elton's relationships with his biological mother and father were taking two separate paths. He was closer than ever with his mother. On the other hand, the icy and uncomfortable rapport between Stanley and Elton continued to go from bad to worse.

Especially perturbed by Elton's dismissal of him in *Playboy* magazine earlier that year, Stanley Dwight was coerced into giving an interview with Britain's *The Daily Mail*. According to Stanley, "He doesn't seem very happy to me. Last time we saw him I asked him who his friends were, and he said, 'Elvis Presley and Billie Jean King.' But when he was a child, they were his idols. How can someone you've only just met be described as a friend? There are friends, and 'friends.' And I think Reggie has to buy his friendships."[164] The "cold war" between Elton and his biological father continued to drop several degrees from this point forward.

On the other side of the coin, Elton's relationship with his mother was so strong that she not only approved of his gay lifestyle, but she screened his potential mates as well. When asked how he got along with his mother, Elton claimed, "Oh, good. She lives two doors away now. We've always had a good relationship. My father was an ogre to her, but she was always great to me. She's just straight about everything and can smell a rat for a mile. She'll say, 'Don't bloody well trust him! He'll run off with all your money.' She's always been right."[55]

When he returned to England, Elton had only one more concert appearance planned. It was in Scotland at the Edinburgh Cultural Festival on September 17. He was due to put the final touches on *Blue Moves* and then go into the recording studio to produce a new album for Kiki Dee. There was also talk about a feature-length cartoon film of *Captain Fantastic and The Brown Dirt Cowboy*, and there was a rumor about Elton playing the title role in a projected film version of the 1956 Broadway musical, *Candide*. It would have been an interesting vehicle for him, since the most famous number from *Candide* is the song "Glitter and Be Gay." He also had his role as the director of the Watford Football Club to keep him busy.

While he was in New York City that summer, Elton gave one of the most important press interviews of his career. It was to appear in the November 7, 1976, issue of *Rolling Stone* magazine. In a frank conversation with writer Cliff Jahr, Elton finally opened the closet door to his sex life. However, that did not mean that he didn't layer his admission with vagueness and subterfuge as well. First of all, he didn't admit that he was exclusively "gay." Instead he chose to admit to being "bisexual," which at least found him admitting he slept with men.

Dismissing the fact that he had lived for several years with his lover, John Reid, Elton replied, "I go home and fall in love with my vinyl.... I suppose I have a certain amount of love and affection as far as 'affection' goes. From friends and stuff. My sexual life? Um, I haven't met anybody I would like to have any big scenes with. It's strange that I haven't. I know everyone should have a certain amount of sex, and I do, but that's it, and I desperately would like to have an affair. I crave to be loved. That's the part of my life I want to have come together in the next two or three years and it's partly why I'm quitting the road. My life in the last six years has been a Disney film and now I have to have a person in my life. I have to—

let me be brutally honest about myself: I get depressed easily. Very bad moods. I don't think anyone knows the real me. I don't even think I do."[57]

He alluded to relationships with women, which did not exist. "I don't know what I want to be exactly," he claimed. "I'm just going through a stage where any sign of affection would be welcome on a sexual level. I'd rather fall in love with a woman eventually because I think a woman probably lasts much longer than a man. But I really don't know. I've never talked about this before. Ha, ha. But I'm not going to turn off the tape. I haven't met anybody that I would like to settle down with—of either sex."[57]

When asked point-blank by Jahr if he was "bisexual," Elton side-steppingly replied, "There's nothing wrong with going to bed with somebody of your own sex. I think everybody's bisexual to a certain degree. I don't think it's just me. It's not a bad thing to be. I think you're bisexual. I think everybody is."[57]

When Jahr pointed out that Elton had never come this close to admitting his "bisexuality" before, the singer laughed, "Probably not. It's going to be terrible with my football club. It's so hetero, it's unbelievable. But I mean, who cares! I just think people should be very free with sex—they should draw the line at goats."[57]

Asked if he and Bernie Taupin were lovers, Elton replied, "No, absolutely not. Everybody thinks we were, but if we had been, I don't think we would have lasted for so long. We're more like brothers than anything else. The press probably thought John Reid and I were an affair, but there's never been a serious person the whole time. Nobody really. And it's very dangerous to have relationships within the circle you work in. It's too close for comfort. Bernie's whole situation is up in the air as well."[57]

For *Rolling Stone*, the article was the true home run they had been looking for. They got the scoop that all of the British tabloids had wanted. News spread like wildfire that Elton had publicly confirmed that indeed he had sex with men. For Elton, this revelation was to become a two-edged sword.

He had just completed the most successful American tour of his career. He had drawn crowds that included hundreds of thousands of teenage girls and their parents. As unlikely as it seemed, Elton was something of a "teenage idol." Now, in the form of this interview in America's most widely circulated rock magazine, he essentially announced to all of these teenagers and their parents: "I have sex with boys."

America was especially homophobic in 1976. In several states it was still against the law to have sex with a member of one's own sex in any shape or form.

As he was on the eve of releasing his *Blue Moves* album, Elton John had suddenly divided his audience in half: those who accepted his homosexuality, and those who did not. This separation also extended to media outlets. Several radio stations, which had gladly played all of the latest Elton John singles, were suddenly passing on adding his recordings to their play lists.

As if the backlash from Elton's sexual revelations were not enough to shake the foundation of his public appeal, the *Blue Moves* album certainly worked against it, from the cover to the music.

Blue Moves was intended to be a change in direction for Elton. It was his first album to be released on his own Rocket Records label. For a cover image, Elton chose to use one of his favorite paintings. It was a piece of art from his private collection, and it was the depiction of several people seated on a blue-colored lawn. Some of them are lying down and relaxing on the grass, some are seated upright, and several of them have their shirts off. They are all men. The painting was done by openly gay artist Patrick Procktor, and it was called *The Guardian Readers*.

The album's official debut took place in a posh London art gallery. As part of a promotion, the British newspaper *The Sun* was going to have a contest and give away copies of the album to their readers. That was before they saw the cover, however. When they found out that it was all men on the cover, and that it apparently depicted a gay park scene, they instantly backed out of the *Blue Moves* contest.

Elton commented on why he chose the painting: "The Patrick Procktor painting on the front of *Blue Moves* is mine," he claimed. "I bought it without realizing it was all blokes. It fitted the mood of the album exactly. People said I should have a picture of me on the front but I've had enough of those. I put me little foot down. And then *The Sun* were going to use the album as contest prizes and they rang us to say they couldn't do it because of the painting. Silly, isn't it?"[40]

The other thing that *Blue Moves* had going against it was the gloomy material it contained. Meant to be a personal and well-thought-out concept album, it was mainly filled with doom and gloom. It did directly reflect what was going on in the lives of Elton and Bernie.

Not only were there major changes going on in the middle of Elton John Land, but the entire music marketplace was changing as well. In New York City, Los Angeles, London, Sydney, and Paris there was a massively growing audience for disco records, and it seemed that the entire record industry had jumped on the disco bandwagon. Eight of the Number One singles of 1976 were disco songs. Not only was disco creating new careers, but it was reviving old ones as well, as witnessed by The Miracles' "Love Machine," Diana Ross' "Love Hangover," The Supremes' "I'm Gonna Let My Heart Do the Walking," and The Bee Gees' "You Should be Dancing." There was also an explosion of European disco music at the hands of fresh new producers like Georgio Moroder and Pete Bellotte.

A new wave of teen idols was on the scene as well: 1976 had begun with Scottish heartthrobs The Bay City Rollers at Number One with "Saturday Night." In a way it was a teenage version of the Elton John song "Saturday Night's Alright for Fighting." The year's big new teenage family act was The Sylvers and their Number One hit "Boogie Fever."

Blue Moves did not fit this disco mood. Upon first listening to *Blue Moves*, there is no question that it was flawlessly recorded. However, the songs weren't all as engaging as some of Elton's past work. It is much less upbeat and fun than his hit with Kiki Dee, "Don't Go Breaking My Heart." The song "Tonight" is without a doubt one of Elton's finest touching ballads. "Sorry Seems to Be the Hardest Word" was obviously about the demise of Elton's love affair with John Reid and Bernie Taupin's marriage to Maxine. Elton later explained that it was one of his most personal songs because the emotions were all his own, "Most of the lyrics on 'Sorry' are mine," he revealed. "I was sitting out there in Los Angeles and out it came: 'What have I got to do to make you love me?'"[88] It became one of Elton's signature songs.

One of the songs on *Blue Moves* is a bittersweet look at the life of one of the music industry's most tragic legends: Edith Piaf.

The song "Cage the Songbird" features beautiful harmonies provided by David Crosby and Graham Nash. This "Crosby, Elton & Nash" song is a beautifully sung ballad about forcing a broken heart to sing.

However, it is the song "Idol" which is the most haunting blue move of all. With Elton playing and singing like he is a jazz performer in a smoky Greenwich Village club, he sadly sings the tale of a former 1950s heartthrob now trapped in a nightmare of his own design. It was clear that this was the duo's homage to Elvis.

It seemed that Elton was pointing to the sad endings that both Piaf and Presley met, or would meet, as a way of saying that he feared a similar fate for himself. Elvis and Edith were both heavy substance abusers who completely lost themselves in their careers, and they were both doomed to die at an early age. In spite of Elton's own failed suicide attempt the previous year, he didn't want to meet a similar end. He didn't want his career to devour him.

There are some incredible songs contained on this two-record set, but there is also some boring filler as well. "Between Seventeen and Twenty" sounds like a leftover from the *Captain Fantastic* album, and the two instrumental numbers—"Your Starter For" and "Theme from a Non-Existent TV Series"—are a sheer waste of space. Elton would have been better served putting "Don't Go Breaking My Heart" on this album to buoy up the proceedings. The album ends with Elton's first foray into the disco realm with "Bite Your Lip (Get Up and Dance)." While that song creates some heat, it never blossomed into the kind of infectious dance number it should have become.

To create more of an ensemble feel on the album, several guest singers and top musicians were included on *Blue Moves*. In addition to Crosby and Nash on the Piaf song and "The Wide Eyed and Laughing," the voices of Bruce Johnston of The Beach Boys and Toni Tennille can be heard on the lamenting "Someone's Final Song" and "Chameleon."

The reviews for *Blue Moves* ranged from "awful" to praising. *Rolling Stone* magazine absolutely hated it. Writer Ariel Swartley claimed, "*Blue Moves* is one of the most desperately pretentious albums around. It's a two-record catalog of musical excess."[180]

Mick Brown of *Sounds* basically gave it a "thumbs up." According to him, "Even before I'd heard one note of *Blue Moves* I had divined that this album was going to be the Big One...*Blue Moves*...a disappointment in some areas; a triumph in others."[37]

Bud Scoppa in *Phonograph Record* declared, "Elton has given us a more-than-generous supply of often-breath-taking, often-moving rock & roll to sing along with and ride our ponies to."[38]

John Tobler in *ZigZag* was a fan of the disc. "*Blue Moves* is absolutely essential listening," he proclaimed. "A very high class record...it's the best record I've heard this year."[39]

The release of the *Blue Moves* album was the end of an era for Elton. It was the last of his really classic albums, and everything was about to drastically change for him. On the record charts *Blue Moves* made it to Number Three in the U.S., Number Three in the U.K., and Number Five in Norway. Not making it to Number One on the charts, and not containing any upbeat fun hits, it unfortunately sold less well than its predecessors.

As he played the last night of the summer 1976 American tour, Elton was aware that this was to be his last concert for the foreseeable future. He had to admit, "It was a pretty weird night, a very sad occasion, I must say. It came to the point where I sang 'Yellow Brick Road' and I thought, 'I don't have to sing this anymore,' and it made me quite happy inside. Yeah, it could be the last gig forever...who wants to be a forty-five-year-old entertainer in Las Vegas like Elvis?"[57] This is an oddly ironic statement coming from a man who was going to end up a sixty-year-old performer in Las Vegas!

After *Blue Moves* was released, Elton wanted to start with a clean slate. He and Bernie Taupin split up professionally. Elton fired his band. John Reid was no longer his lover, although he was still his manager. And, as a final blow, he had a parting of the ways with Gus Dudgeon as well. Actually, it was a dispute about Rocket Records that lit the fuse of that upset. Suddenly, Elton John was single in just about every way possible.

Following the depressing tunes that Taupin turned in for *Blue Moves*, it was clearly time to try a new formula. According to Elton, "We sometimes saw too much of each other back then, but now I don't see him as much as I'd like."[55] Elton told Bernie that he should be working with some different singers, and so ended the first golden phase of the John and Taupin songwriting team.

According to Bernie Taupin, "*Blue Moves* was our Mount Everest. We'd gone to the top. I'm sure drugs, alcohol, the geographical thing, it all contributed. But the base core of it was I don't know if we knew what we wanted to do next. Or if we could do it. But we never argued about it."[184]

Recalls Elton of his hiatus from working with Bernie, "Never had an argument with him. We're not those kind of people. I could never shout and scream at Bernie, 'cause I love him too much. Which is kind of extraordinary when you think of some of the great partnerships that have fallen foul of each other because of jealousies and egos. And it's never been the case with him and I."[184]

Elton also revealed at the time, "You know I've never rejected one of his lyrics before but some of the stuff he did for *Blue Moves* I said, 'Taupin, for Christ's sake, I can't sing that.' They were just plain hateful three or four of them. His lyrics have always been a bit down-in-the-mouth.... His life's been going through a strange turmoil.... I've told him time and again to write for someone else. Now he's doing it, with Alice Cooper, and really enjoying it."[40]

Thus 1976 was the end of an era for Elton John. In 1975 he had released two huge Number One albums. A year later he released two more albums, and they both completely missed the mark. How quickly the fickle finger of fate moves. In a business where you are "red hot" one day and "ice cold" the next, what did this all mean for Elton John? Now that the world officially knew he was homosexual, how would that affect his career? Was that the reason for the relative "failure" of *Blue Moves* on the charts? Would his disclosure on the pages of *Rolling Stone* erode his once-strong fan base? He described it as, "the anti-climax of the year. More people wave at me than before that's all. Nobody seems to harbor a grudge against me [because of the *Rolling Stone* interview], especially within the football club. Though there's a bit of shouting from the terraces—'You big poofter' and such. It really was the first time I'd ever been asked about it [his sex life] and I'm glad nobody had done it before because I don't think I'd have coped very well. It would have been 'Er, yes, well, good morning.' The guy from *Rolling Stone* was very good. When I answered the question he offered to rub it out on the spot but I said it was okay. The only bitchy thing I've had was in *The Gay News*. It was all: 'Well dear, he's stepped out of the closet at last.' Them of all people."[40]

Would Elton John find happiness in his latest decisions? For the first time in a long time, Elton John was a gay man who was all alone with his vast riches and his extensive record collection. He was free to choose his own path from this point forward.

But what path would he choose? It remained to be seen.

CHAPTER TWELVE

A Singular Man

Elton John began the year 1977 with his new self-imposed solo lifestyle. In his mind he was finished with concert touring and recording for awhile. Elton was convinced that he was going to throw himself into his job as the director of the Watford Football Club, and that was to be his salvation. In a way, it was to be exactly that. However, was it really going to be a "centering" return to the "normal" life for Elton? Or was it just another one of his follies and a further arena for his outrageous behavior? It was to become a bit of both.

On both sides of the Atlantic, the news of his sexual disclosure in *Rolling Stone* traveled like wildfire. And—just like *Blue Moves*—it drew decidedly mixed reactions from his adoring public. The minute that the controversial interview appeared in print, the British tabloids jumped on the bandwagon. *The Mirror*, *The Mail*, and *The Express* all carried quotes from the article. *News of the World* headlined their story "Elton: My Love Life Isn't So Strange."

"When the news broke in England," Elton recalls, "I remember I'd just played a solo concert in Edinburgh, one of the few things I did. And I was due to fly down to Manchester to go to the game at Rochdale—we [the Watford team] were still in the Fourth Division. And my mother was up with me, and she came into the hotel bedroom with all the Saturday papers: 'Bi-sexual Elton says'…. She said, 'Ave a look at this then!' I thought, 'Oh, my God, thank you'…. I'd expected it to come out, but on a Saturday morning when I'm going to meet the [soccer] team. And I walked into the hotel in Manchester, and the then manager Mike King came out and said, 'Listen, we've seen the papers: what you do with your life is your own business.'… It was something I never flaunted at the club. It wasn't exactly common knowledge. But this was like a confirmation of it. But they handled it superbly. British people do."[43]

In America, *The Village Voice* converted the story into a singular cartoon by artist Sorel. In it Elton was depicted standing at a light post speaking into a police call box, verbally reporting a man having sex with a goat several paces behind him. The cartoon's headline dubbed Elton "Prude of the Week," and reprinted several lines of his *Rolling Stone* interview, including: "There's nothing wrong with going to bed with somebody of your own sex…people should be free with sex—they should draw the line at goats."[181]

Additionally, *Rolling Stone* magazine itself became a battlefield between the tolerant readers and the bigots. The "Correspondence, Love Letters, and Advice" section of a subsequent issue of *Rolling Stone* was a very telling microcosm of the way people felt.

There is no question that this disclosure changed a lot of things for Elton. From this point forward, it was no longer guaranteed that all of his singles would be added to radio playlists. In America especially, admitting that he was a practicing bisexual closed doors for him. He was to look back at this era and recall, "A few radio stations were a bit upset and people burnt my records. But you know what? It was a very small price to pay for the freedom that it gave me."[184]

The way that a segment of the U.S. now perceived him had suddenly changed. Commenting on the dichotomy that is the United States and comparing it to England, Elton claimed, "That did it. I didn't realize it was going to. It didn't harm me at all in England. In fact, I think it did me good. 'Out' in America, 'Land of the Free,' it did me a lot of damage."[43]

Elton only performed eight concerts in 1977, all of them charities. Six of the shows were held at London's The Rainbow nightclub in May of 1977. It was just Elton at the piano and Ray Cooper providing percussion. On June 17, he played one of the most unlikely gigs of all. At the last minute, a little-known party band had backed out of playing the Valedictory Ball at Shoreditch College Chapel in Egham, South London. Someone phoned Elton, who lived nearby, and he came over and did a six-song concert as the evening's entertainment. On November 3, 1977, Elton performed at a soccer charity benefiting The Royal Variety Club and a sports organization called The Goaldiggers.

For Elton, sports were his new game, and he intended to throw himself into them, most specifically soccer. According to him at the time of his "retirement" from touring, "That [Watford Football Club] will take a lot of my time up next year because I have got a lot to learn in that department. I'm really going to give that a shot because it's something I really enjoy doing. I guess I'll miss performing a little bit, but over the last six years I've missed not having a home life."[36]

In light of the potential career disaster that his "bisexuality" disclosure had caused, his involvement with Watford could have been the perfect balancing act for his over-the-top career. However, when he showed up at a Watford game against Rochdale, Lancashire, he wore a checkered suit with bright orange trimmings and a pair of pink-framed eyeglasses. He looked more like a gay clown than a sports fan.

This was not a fact missed by the spectators at Watford games—especially from supporters of the opposing teams. They would chant the phrase "Elton John's a homosexual" to the tune of "Glory, Glory, Hallelujah" or shout out the words "poof" and "queer." He did his best to ignore the jeers, while standing there in one of his crazy multi-colored outfits.

In an attempt to make super-rich superstar Elton John look more like "one of the guys" with his Watford team members, he posed for several press photos with the soccer team in the locker rooms. An *Elton* fan magazine from that era showed an undressed Elton soaking in a Watford locker room bathtub. In other photos, team members Billy Jennings, Duncan Welbourne, Pat Morrisey, and Dave Buller, clad only in towels, are pulling the Rocket Man out of the tub. In another shot, he was captured in his soccer jersey, face down on the lawn, wearing a pair of his outrageously large eyeglasses. In *People* magazine Elton was photographed clothed and looking down into bathtubs filled with naked soccer players with the caption: "Their primitive locker room aside, owner John has sunk a fortune in the Watford Hornets and hopes to make them British champs within a decade."[183] Instead of looking like a serious sports chairman, he appeared to be a gay man excited to be amongst his towel-clad male players. He was definitely sending out conflicting sexual signals to his fans.

One of Elton's first matters of business was appointing Graham Taylor to the position of the Watford team's manager. Three years older than Elton, he was levelheaded and could put up with the singer's outlandishness. Graham was also the perfect appointment, as he actually knew how to run a soccer club.

The Watford team was in big financial trouble, and they were in need of the kind of money and attention that a star like Elton John could lavish on them. In June 1977, he was officially elected Chairman of the Watford Football Team. It was the perfect ending to a lifelong dream. As a boy, Reggie Dwight had cheered for the home team, now he was their Chairman. Not bad for a non-sports-savvy lad who dyed his hair hot pink for attention, answered to the name "Sharon," and wore outlandishly gay outfits to their games!

For television show comedians and the general press, Elton's public disclosure on his sex life tipped off an endless tide of "gay" jokes about him. Instead of letting the comments roll off his back, he sunk into a deep depression. Without a new album to record or a concert tour to mount, Elton found himself at Woodside, left to tend to the demands of his already fragile ego.

At this time, rock music was changing yet again. Richard Branson had launched his new discovery, The Sex Pistols. They were—almost single-handedly—destined to change the London music scene, as they became the first break-through act of the late-seventies Punk movement. With their spiked hair, torn-up blue jeans, and street looks, they were the exact opposite of the pop art colorfulness of Elton John and Kiki Dee's images. The Sex Pistols looked like they were more likely to urinate on the Yellow Brick Road than take a charming stroll down it. Throughout 1977 the punk movement continued to gain popularity.

While Elton was hanging out with his towel-clad soccer players, his domestic and foreign record companies continued to crank out singles from *Blue Moves* throughout 1977. The single "Bite Your Lip (Get Up and Dance)" peaked at Number 28 on both sides of the Atlantic, while in the U.K. "Crazy Water" was also released and charted at Number 27.

In America, 1977 saw only six Number One albums the entire year. Two live in-concert albums hit the top of the charts for one week apiece: *Wings Over America* and *Barry Manilow Live.*

The soundtrack for Barbra Streisand's film *A Star is Born* stayed at Number One for six weeks, and Linda Ronstadt's *Simple Dreams* repeated that feat for five weeks. However, the winners that year were The Eagles' *Hotel California* at Number One for eight weeks and Fleetwood Mac's *Rumours*, monopolizing the zenith of the chart for a record-shattering thirty-one weeks. *Blue Moves* was still selling, but clearly Elton had lost the once-tight grip on his winning streak.

Amid some legal wrangling, Dick James insisted that he was owed one more album from Elton. This begat 1977's *Elton John's Greatest Hits, Volume II*. It was released in England in October by DJM and in November in America on MCA. The album reflected Elton's cooling off on the charts, peaking at Number 21 in the U.S. and Number Six in the U.K. He was all done hitting Number One on the album charts for a long time.

Something else that was upsetting Elton at the time was his hair, or lack of it. He had just turned thirty in March 1977, and he was almost fully bald on the top of his head. There was a big "pin-up" sized portrait of him on the inside of the *Blue Moves* album, where he is mugging for camera with an awful comb-over. Medical hair transplants at the time were mainly of the "doll's hair" variety, where concentric circles of hair "plugs" would attempt to replicate a youthful hairline. Elton decided that he was going to try and recover his hair, no matter how much money it cost. Unfortunately, it was to be a painful, expensive, and ultimately losing battle.

When Elton appeared at the November 3, 1977, soccer benefit at the Empire Pool, Wembley, it was anticipated that this would mark his triumphant return to the concert stage and to touring in general. It was an exciting evening and even featured a couple of impressive guest stars: Kiki Dee was there for a duet of "Don't Go Breaking My Heart," and Stevie Wonder performed "Bite Your Lip (Get Up and Dance)" with Elton. However, Ray Cooper recalls that Elton was in one of his foulest moods. Nothing seemed to make him happy that evening.

Elton got up and addressed the crowd, claiming, "I'd like to say something. It's very hard to put into words. I haven't been touring for a long time and it's been a painful decision whether to come back on the road or not. I've really enjoyed tonight, thank you very much. But I've made a decision that this is going to be my last show. All right? There's a lot more than playing on the road. And this is the last one I'm going to do."[88]

According to Ray Cooper, "I could see John Reid saying, 'Stop him! Grab him!' It was totally out of the blue."[88]

Looking back on this era, Elton claimed, "I did try and come back too early. That Wembley gig…when I announced that I was retiring, was a charity gig that I'd got talked into, and I promised to do it. And I suddenly saw all the machinery and all the reasons that I wanted to stop, and I was doing it again…. I felt like something out of Las Vegas."[43]

Without his former band, his contract with Dick James, his former producer, or his former full-time songwriting partner, Elton began to explore some new musical options. He had a clean slate, and he was in the mood to experiment. His first new musical foray found him venturing off into a lifelong dream. He had always been a fan of the "Philadelphia Soul" sound of groups like The Spinners, The Three Degrees, Harold Melvin & The Blue Notes, Teddy Pendergrass, and The Stylistics. They were all part of a Motown-like group of performers, primarily produced by Thom Bell, or the duo of Kenny Gamble and Leon Huff, mainly recording for Philadelphia Records.

In November 1977, Elton flew out to Seattle, Washington, and at Kay Smith Studio there, he recorded six tracks with Thom Bell, which he held onto for several months. This was the first time since *Empty Sky* that Elton had worked with anyone other than Gus Dudgeon in the role of producer. He and Bell got along well.

According to Elton, "I'm a big soul fanatic, and that led me to Thom Bell, because I was a big fan of The Stylistics and The Spinners. I just loved the way his records sounded. Very dry sounding records. He was the first person that ever taught me about my voice. He said, 'Listen, you're not using your voice correctly. You write too high for yourself.' Which I actually do; he was right. I wasn't very pleased with him telling me at the time."[78]

One of the biggest thrills for Elton was that he was not only going to be recorded by the producer of some of The Spinners' biggest hits, he was going to have The Spinners as his background singers. One of the six songs he recorded with Thom Bell used lyrics from Bernie Taupin ("Nice and Slow"); however, several of the best songs were from Bell's stable of writers, including "Mama Can't Buy You Love," "Are You Ready For Love," and "Three-Way Love Affair."

When Elton performed The Royal Variety Club/ Goaldiggers benefit on November 3, he performed with Davey Johnstone's new band, China. One of the background vocalists was singer/songwriter Gary Osborne. Elton had known Gary for a while, since Osborne had written the Kiki Dee song "Amoureuse." When Elton asked Osborne for some lyrics for his upcoming Thom Bell sessions, Osborne gave him the lyrics for "Shine on Through."

After the Thom Bell sessions were "in the can," Elton was not certain as to what to do with them. Should he record a whole album with Bell? He wasn't sure. He was not finished experimenting with some other new musical directions. With a lot of time on his hands, Elton reportedly indulged in heavy drinking and cocaine use. This did not help his infamous mood swings or the frightening sense that he had lost his way musically.

On March 10, 1978, Elton went into a recording studio in Cookham, England, and recorded a song which he had hoped would be a frank and revealing new hit single. It was appropriately called "Ego," and it was another one of the leftover songs from his partnership with Bernie. An ambitiously paced song, "Ego" was dark, self-absorbed, and slightly hostile in nature. While singing about placating his own "Ego," it is a song that clearly wallows in Elton's own self-pity. A one-off single release, it was viewed as a strange curiosity when it peaked at Number 34 on the charts in the U.K. and the U.S. The flip-side of "Ego" featured a slow and amusing song called "Flintstone Boy." Apparently, the song is about a boyfriend of Elton's who is thought to be about as bright as a caveman out of *The Flintstones* cartoon show. Now that he had unburdened himself with the secrets of his sexual orientation, from this point forward Elton would release several songs which made it even clearer that he was indeed a gay man. Once he teamed up with his new lyricist Gary Osborne, he started to write music again, and soon the creative juices started flowing.

In October 1978, Elton's first recorded album without Bernie Taupin and Gus Dudgeon, *A Single Man*, was released.

Although it was a downward step for Elton, it was still a million-selling Platinum album reaching Number Four in Norway, Number Eight in England, Number 12 in Germany, Number 15 in *Billboard* in the U.S., and Number 17 in Australia.

Gary Osborne specifically wanted to put more of Elton in the tracks on this album, and what could be more natural than to do a totally gay song? The end result is the ribald song "Big Dipper." Like Rainer Werner Fassbinder's outlandish "sailors-in-love" film *Querelle*, here we find Elton singing about a friend, cruising a cute sailor boy who has a "Big Dipper." He then proclaims that the sailor has his eye on his friend's own "Big Dipper."

Osborne explains, "The song 'Big Dipper,' which was a bit of fun, was very definitely a gay song. What happens in that song is that Elton meets a young lad, goes up on a Big Dipper, and is given 'head.' It had to be slightly disguised because, firstly, it was 1978, and secondly we wanted the Watford football team to sing on it and we couldn't have them singing words that were…too puffy. I was trying to put a bit of Elton's wicked sense of humor into his songs. Elton had said that it was about time that he wrote a gay song, so that was what that was about. Graham Taylor and the whole team and whoever else was in the studio sang on the track."[88]

The album's one big hit was the song about casual sex: "Part Time Love." "Part Time Love" made it to Number 22 in the U.S. and Number 12 in the U.K. The other notable single from the album was the slow almost-classical-sounding instrumental "Song for Guy," which made it to Number Four in the U.K.

"Song for Guy" has something of a unique story of its own. Guy Burchett was working as a bike messenger for Rocket Records while Elton was working on the album tracks for *A Single Man*. In an unfortunate turn of events, Guy died in a motorcycle accident in the rain. Elton had been working on a delicate piano piece the week of Guy's death, and he decided to record it as an instrumental and dedicate it to the memory of Guy Burchett. Although it is an instrumental selection on the album and as a single, at one point under the track you can hear Elton repeating the mantra "Life isn't everything," and "Everything isn't life."

On the paper sleeve for the single version of "Song for Guy," Elton wrote: "As I was writing this song one Sunday, I imagined myself floating into space and looking down at my own body. I was imagining myself dying. Morbidly obsessed with these thoughts, I wrote this song about death. The next day I was told that Guy, our seventeen-year-old messenger boy, had been tragically killed on his motorcycle the day before. Guy died on the day I was writing this song."[195]

Without Gus Dudgeon around to bounce ideas around, Elton wasn't sure which tracks were going to be included ultimately on *A Single Man*, and which ones were going to be shelved. He invited people into the studio, played them all eighteen proposed tracks, and let them vote on which ones should be included. The result, along with Elton's experimentation on the songs themselves, is a "collage" of different parts instead of a well-devised, unified album.

Instead of enlisting an all-star cast of musicians to support these songs, Elton utilized Davey Johnstone and Ray Cooper from his former bands and augmented them with studio musicians. He dedicated the album to his new soccer buddy, Graham Taylor.

On the cover of the album, Elton is photographed in the driveway of Windsor Castle, dressed like a 1970s Oscar Wilde, in a black stovepipe hat, below-the-knee black overcoat, and knee-high, high-heeled boots.

A Single Man is Elton John's most misunderstood album. Musically, it was an interesting collection of songs which truly command a listening. However, the "Elton goes to a funeral" cover, paired with the lack of a sure-fire rock & roll hit, doomed this album from the start.

The critics unanimously hated it. In *Rolling Stone* magazine, Stephen Holden ripped it apart, from the artwork on the cover, to the music, to the new lyricist. He claimed Elton had achieved a brand-new low point in his career: "John's coproduced himself and used studio musicians to turn out his sparest LP since *Honky Château*. But this move towards simplicity is a step into emptiness, since *A Single Man* is nothing more than a collection of trivial hooks performed about as perfunctorily as possible."[59]

Gary Osborne is perhaps the most misunderstood of all of Elton John's collaborators. The lack of success that *A Single Man* had was not due to his songs, because they were strong and took a fresh approach. However, replacing Bernie Taupin in the eyes of Elton's fans was a thankless task.

According to Gary, "Actually the first assumption was that I was gay and I was his new boyfriend. The fact that I lived with a woman and I was just about to have a kid, and the fact that Elton never fancied me—which of course is quite hurtful—were all overlooked."[88]

One of the most fascinating aspects of *A Single Man* was that it became the first of Elton's albums to be openly distributed in Russia. The old guard of the U.S.S.R. was loosening up trade with the West, and *A Single Man* was the debut Elton John album to find its way into Moscow record shops. It was quite a unique accomplishment for Elton. He truly had become a global superstar.

While Elton was on his vacation from touring, how was he spending his time? He was busy playing with his expensive toys, drinking, and indulging in cocaine. He now had more time to indulge in his lust for automobiles.

His other passions included toys, electronic gadgets, and artwork. "I like gadgets," he confessed. "Ringo and I are gadget fanatics. I like pinball machines…. But I spend most of my money on things like art."[55]

It was his record collection that was his longest hobby. During this era he claimed, "I own 25,000 singles—and I don't know how many albums I've got. I go through *Cashbox, Record World* and *Billboard* and write down all the records I want. I put them in alphabetical order and then just go to a record store…. I keep Tower Records alive. I mean, when I first saw Tower Records, I died. I didn't know where to start…. You must understand that if it all ended tomorrow, the job I would most plug for would be to work in a record shop—work at Tower Records or open my own shop."[55]

The big question was whether or not Elton's income would continue while he was on this expensive sojourn from mainstream recording and touring. It remained to be seen what would happen. The Beatles had overplayed their hand with Apple Records, and their fashion store, and their half-baked business deals. Wasn't Elton taking the same path with Rocket Records and a soccer team that seemed to be bleeding money by the moment?

Like his recent hit "Part Time Love," in his personal life, it seemed that Elton was jumping from one obsessive love affair to another, with none of them working out very well. He would focus his attention on one young boy after another. However, Elton always proved to be an overwhelming force, and none of his affairs would last very long.

Not long after *A Single Man* was released, Elton was at his home, Woodside, and he suddenly collapsed. He was rushed to the coronary unit of London's Harley Street Clinic. He was diagnosed as suffering from exhaustion. It seemed that at the ripe old age of 31, Elton John was already falling apart both physically and emotionally. Lying around the house doing cocaine and feeling sorry for himself was doing him no good at all.

Like Elton John, Alice Cooper had also flown too high in the mid-1970s. From October to December of 1977, Alice checked himself into a New York mental hospital to treat his alcoholism. Cooper had been working with Bernie Taupin on the album *From the Inside*. *From the Inside* and *A Single Man* were released around the same time.

Bernie brought along several of the key players from Elton's band to provide the music for *From the Inside*. Behind Alice, on this album you can hear Kenny Passarelli, Davey Johnstone, Dee Murray, and even the background vocals of Kiki Dee.

While all of this was going on, in 1978, DJM licensed several of Elton's recordings to budget labels. St. Michael Records released a compilation album of album tracks and live recordings called *Candle in the Wind*. Pickwick Records then released *Elton John Live 17-11-70* and *London & New York Live!*, which were repackages of his two previously released live LPs. In 1979, DJM Records assembled a five-disc Elton John boxed set.

The fact that these albums were released at all totally pissed off John Reid and Elton. DJM was diluting Elton's British marketplace by slicing and dicing the singer's old tracks onto new LPs. Elton and Reid were especially unhappy with Dick James, whom they felt should be satisfied with marketing the original albums in their original format and owning a piece of them. Reid especially felt that Dick James was trying to milk every cent out of the catalogue by giving the songs away for a discounted royalty rate, thus cheapening the product. Reid was already auditing the books, from which he would begin to build a legal case against DJM.

Finally, in early 1979, Elton got tired of not performing in public. However, he was leery of going back into huge arenas. His first official return to the concert stage took place on February 5, 1979, in Sweden at the Stockholm Concerthaus. For a European tour that would last until April 21, 1979, Elton chose not to tour with his full band. Instead he played an entire set alone at the piano. Then, for the second act, he was joined onstage by Ray Cooper playing various percussion instruments.

The tour was entitled *Elton John: A Single Man Concert with Ray Cooper*, and it took them to Copenhagen, Denmark; Antwerp, Belgium; Lucerne, Switzerland; Munich, Cologne, Weisbaden, Berlin, Manheim, Dusseldorf, and Hamburg, Germany; Madrid, Spain; Glasgow, Scotland; and Paris and Nice, France. It was a low-impact tour in smaller houses in cities he had never played.

The final test was in Edinburgh, Scotland. His concert there was broadcast live. Had Elton gotten his self-confidence back to the point where he and the audience were both happy with the performance? Fortunately, the concert was a big success, and Elton was in "top form." According to him, the stripped-down two-man formula tore away the glitter and glitz and made the focus the music.

During this era the boy-band, The Bay City Rollers, continued to produce hit after hit. In 1977, they placed three singles on the charts, including "Dedication," "The Way I Feel Tonight," and the Top Ten song "You Make Me Believe in Magic." When Les McKeown dropped out of the group in 1978, he was replaced by Duncan Faure, who was originally from South Africa, and they released several albums after shortening their name to "The Rollers."

They attended Elton's Edinburgh concert. "I met him at The Gibson Theater," recalls Duncan of Elton. "We went to the Gibson Theater in Edinburgh, which was home ground for The Bay City Rollers, because they'd played there many times. So, in two seconds we were whisked backstage, and there he was. It was like a cartoon character coming to life. He reminded me so much of my late brother Bill, the same sort of mannerisms. Elton is extremely funny. He made us laugh, first you laugh because it's Elton. Once you get over the hurdle of thinking: 'He's Elton John!' He is just so funny."[212]

One of The Bay City Rollers' publicists in New York City was Beth Wernick. She became a close friend of Duncan Faure's and knew that Elton really liked Duncan. According to her, on another occasion, Elton made his feelings known while onstage at a concert that The Rollers attended. She laughingly recalls, "So they went back out into the audience and sat down in their seats. Then Elton came out on stage and in the middle of his concert he says into the microphone, 'And this one is dedicated to Duncan.' He then proceeds to go into the song that begins, 'What do I have to do to make you love me…?'"[209]

Clearly, Elton fancied Duncan. Faure has nothing but fond memories of his many times with Elton and was highly flattered when Elton invited him to Woodside one night for dinner at his mansion. Faure was also impressed when Elton sent a car and driver to come and get him. "In those days, Bob Halley would drive for Elton," he explained. "Bob picked me up for that long drive to Windsor. At Windsor, it's just a huge house. I remember waking up in the morning, and I couldn't find the kitchen. I was led to The Rod Stewart Suite, as he called it. That was where Rod Stewart usually stayed."[212]

Duncan recalls the grandeur of Elton's opulent mansion as being breathtaking, and filled with treasures: "At his house there was Marilyn Monroe memorabilia all around, and pinball machines. He also has Gold records imbedded in the floors, so you are walking around on them. It looks beautiful. He has so many Gold records that he has made floorboards out of them! It's just too beautiful."[212]

And, what else was on the menu that evening? How did he end up in "The Rod Stewart Suite?" Duncan explains, "There was never anything sexual. I actually stayed at his house, but there were always people around. It wasn't just me and him. There was kind of an entourage around him."[212] For several years to come, Duncan Faure was to remain one of Elton's close friends whom he would see from time to time in odd places around the world. Since his new, stripped-down *Single Man* tour was a success and a centering experience for him, Elton now needed a new set of challenges. He decided to play some concerts in Israel and Russia. From May 1 to May 6, 1979, Elton and Ray gave five concerts in Tel Aviv and Jerusalem. Even more revolutionary were the May 21-28 concerts, which found them performing four shows in Leningrad and four in Moscow. For Elton, the shows in Russia proved a huge triumph. *The New York Times* reported, "The first concert in the Soviet Union by the British rock star Elton John erupted into a frenzy last night, with nearly 4,000 Russian fans dancing on their seats and in the aisles. Uniformed policemen and other Soviet officials were helpless to control the screaming, clapping mob in the Oktyabrsky Concert Hall here."[194]

There was a lot of red tape that had to be ironed out before these East-meets-West concerts could even be booked. However the political climate seemed right for this kind of cultural exchange. Elton agreed to not kick his piano bench over mid-show—which he was famous for—and he was forbidden from singing The Beatles' song "Back in the U.S.S.R." Well, he didn't kick over the piano bench, but he did manage to squeeze "Back in the U.S.S.R." into a medley with The Beatles' "Get Back," just to "push the envelope" a bit. According to him, "It just came to me, and I was singing it before I realized I didn't know any of the words. So, I just sang 'Back in the U.S.S.R.' over and over again."[196]

John Rockwell in the *New York Times* pointed out, "The irony of Elton John's triumphant reception in Leningrad is that it comes after two years of artistic and commercial eclipse in the West. But he is the best-known rock star ever to be allowed to perform in the Soviet Union. Thus the fanatic enthusiasm of the Russians may be as much an attestation of his symbolic status and a sign of their longing for Western popular music as it is a response to his considerable performing talents."[193]

Many people were asking why Elton John was to be the first allowed to perform in Russia. Elton explained, "We discovered that they wanted people like The Who and Led Zeppelin. They just didn't know how to go about it. They didn't trust American promoters. When I came back I understood the political situation between the two countries much more."[43]

This was just the kind of excitement to really make Elton feel alive again in front of concert audiences. "It was an amazing experience," he proclaimed. "I'd love to go back. Only ten per cent of the tickets for those shows went on sale to the public, which I didn't know about. Only at the time it was terrifying going out to play to eight rows of Politburo housewives with beehives. We had one confrontation on the tour. I played 'Benny & The Jets' and kicked the stool away, which upset them. And the first night as an encore I did 'Back in the U.S.S.R.' And they went ape shit. It was like playing 'Philadelphia Freedom' in Philadelphia."[43]

After that, a full-fledged "Elton John rebirth" was underway. According to him, touring solo—with Ray Cooper—was how he got his "mojo" back. "I'd lost my edge completely," he admitted. "It was too comfortable, I could've gone onstage and read poetry for an hour and they'd have applauded. In '79, when I did come back, Ray Cooper and I did the most dangerous thing and the best thing I've ever done. It was three hours of just piano and percussion. I wanted to sit there and just play and we didn't do any dramatics. I wanted to prove that you could play all the slow and romantic stuff and also play rock & roll with just two people. And we did it. And that got my confidence back."[43]

From September 19 to November 11, Elton traveled across the United States for what he called the *Back in the U.S.S.A.* tour. To add fresh material to the tour, Elton released not one—but two new albums. Actually, the first one was a three-track EP (extended play) album called *The Thom Bell Sessions*. It was released in June 1979, and one of the three tracks—"Mama Can't Buy You Love"— was released as a single. The other two tracks on the EP are the songs "Are You Ready for Love" and "Three Way Love Affair." A decade later the three missing tracks from Elton's 1977 recording session with Bell were added to the EP, which was now known as *The Complete Thom Bell Sessions*. The missing tracks were the songs "Nice and Slow," "Country Love Song," and the first unreleased version of the song "Shine on Through."

Oddly enough, it was one of the tracks from *The Thom Bell Sessions* which signified Elton's 1979 return to the American Top Ten, for the first time in three years. The song "Mama Can't Buy You Love" made it to Number Nine in the U.S. and Australia and Number Ten in Canada. "Are You Ready for Love," in its original release, hit Number 18 in the U.K.

While he was on the U.S. tour, Elton released his twentieth album, *Victim of Love*. In his post-Bernie Taupin experimentation, in 1979, he tried his hand at putting out a disco album. So many of Elton's contemporaries had scored huge hits by recording disco music, most notably Cher ("Take Me Home") Diana Ross ("Love Hangover") and Rod Stewart ("Da Ya Think I'm Sexy?"). Elton went into the recording studio with European disco master Pete Bellotte. What they created was a seven-track album which melded a rock sound with a disco beat, a strange sort of rock/disco hybrid. The title song, "Victim of Love," which featured background vocals by Michael McDonald and Patrick Simmons of The Doobie Brothers, was released as a single in the U.S. and made it to Number 31. A second single, a remake of Chuck Berry's "Johnny B. Goode," was also released as a single but failed to chart.

Critics universally hated *Victim of Love*. In *US* magazine, reviewer Martha Hume claimed, "*Victim of Love* is the title of the first album Elton John has made since he retired four years ago; he should have called it *Victim of Boredom*.... If *Victim of Love* is the best Elton John has to offer these days, he ought to retire."[192]

According to Stephen Holden in *Rolling Stone*, "Elton John's entry into the rock-disco sweepstakes comes a year too late to make much of an impact.... Munich pop disco with no climaxes...*Victim of Love* hasn't a breath of life."[204]

This was an era of musical experimentation for Elton. It also seemed like one long party that would never end. A million-copy-selling rock musician, who attended several of Elton's "boys only" house parties at Woodside during this era, recalls being amazed at the volume of cocaine he saw consumed. The "Anonymous Source" claims they weren't doing just a little of the drug: "They were doing heaps of coke!"[213]

In August 1979, Elton was in Grasse on the Cote d'Azur in the south of France. While there he wrote all of the music for his next album release: *21 at 33*. This time around Elton relied on the lyric-writing skills of four different collaborators. His new writing partner Gary Osborne contributed the songs "Little Jeannie," "Dear God," and "Take Me Back." Singer/songwriter Judie Tzuke also contributed. She was a singer and songwriter signed to Rocket Records at the time, and she contributed the lyrics to the song "Give Me Love." Controversial recording artist Tom Robinson was Elton's third collaborator. In 1978, Robinson became famous overnight for the song "Glad to be Gay," which he recorded with his group, The Tom Robinson Band. Being gay himself, Robinson became instant friends with Elton John. On the *21 at 33* album, Robinson contributed the lyrics to two songs: "Sartorial Eloquence" and "Never Gonna Fall in Love Again."

However, the really big news was the fact that three of the songs on *21 at 33* marked a return to Elton's partnership with Bernie Taupin. For this album, Bernie contributed a trio of the most unique and personal songs on the nine-song disc. "Chasing the Crown" was about Elton's lust for fame, in light of the fact that his crown as the "King of Rock Ballads" had been tarnished lately. The next Taupin offering on this album was "White Lady White Powder," which was an obvious homage to Elton's lust for cocaine. And the third Taupin song was to become something of a classic. Entitled "Two Rooms at the End of the World," it is actually about Bernie's conquering his alcohol problems. However, it was later thought to be a song about Bernie's relationship with Elton as well.

Unlike Elton, who was moody and unhappy during this era, Bernie Taupin was putting his life back together again and was quite happy. After the *Blue Moves* album, Bernie went to Mexico to quit drinking alcohol. He came back to the United States clean and sober.

Looking back at his drinking binges in the mid-70s, Taupin claimed, "I have very little recollection of those years. They all passed by in a blur.... There's nothing heroic in being a fall-down drunk. It's pathetic."[45]

In the late 1970s, Bernie had been romantically involved with Loree Rodkin, but in 1978 that affair ended. A year later Taupin met a model by the name of Toni Russo, the sister of actress René Russo. He fell in love with Toni, and they later married. Happily, Taupin now had a new muse in his life.

As he was recording *21 at 33*, an interesting thought occurred to Elton. On March 25, 1980, he turned 33 years old. And, if he counted his album releases the way that Elton chose to count

them, this was to be his twenty-first legitimate album. To come up
with this figure, the British *Empty Sky* (1969) and the American
Empty Sky (1975) each had to be counted separately, and *The
Thom Bell Sessions* mini-LP had to be counted as a full album as
well. Hence, the new album was titled: *21 at 33*.

Most of the basic tracks to the *21 at 33* album were
recorded in August 1979 at Superbear Studios in Nice, France.
However, the song "White Lady White Powder" and all of the
overdubs on the vocals and instrumentals were done from January
to March of 1980 in Los Angeles. The album included several guest
vocalists and high-profile musicians. Background vocalists featured
included Don Henley, Glenn Frey, and Timothy B. Schmidt of The
Eagles; Toni Tennille; and Peter Noone, lead singer of Herman's
Hermits. The choir arrangements were done by Bruce Johnston of
The Beach Boys. One of the alto saxophone players featured on
these tracks was Richie Cannata, who is best known as the sax man
on several of Billy Joel's greatest hits.

Richie Cannata's musical presence on the *21 at 33* album
is just one of many parallels and coincidences between Billy Joel
and Elton John. Billy recorded album tracks using Elton's band
back in the 1970s; the pair toured together in the 21st Century.

Throughout the 1970s, Richie was an integral part of Billy
Joel's band, and he was featured on albums like *The Stranger* (1977)
and *52nd Street* (1978). As the 1970s were coming to an end, Richie
felt that it was time to try something new, and he left Joel's band to
become an in-demand session musician. As he recalls, "Things and
events had happened. It was time to move on. People thought that
it was a money issue, and it really wasn't.[191] He had other dreams
that he wanted to pursue, like one day playing on one of Elton
John's albums. According to Cannata, playing saxophone on Elton's
21 at 33 album was one of the highlights of his career.

While Elton was in Los Angeles working on the final
touches on *21 at 33*, movie producer Allan Carr threw him a
birthday party. At the time Carr was working in post-production
on the Village People's disco feature film: *Can't Stop the Music*.
One of the guests at Elton's 1980 birthday party was Angela Bowie.
She had divorced David Bowie and was in Hollywood pursuing her
own music and acting career.

As Angela recalls, "I was invited to his party in Malibu, for his birthday. That was wild...! I was quite happy that he came over to say 'hello' to me, and I recall thinking that he was quite stoned. He was just being hospitable and wonderful to everyone. But I do think he was 'stoned as a bat.'"[100]

Angela also remembers that he had a certain look of sadness to him that night. "He complained to me that night that he felt that he had to entertain everyone at the party. I said to him, 'You've got a whole party full of people who love you. You will be fine dear.' He thanked me, and then he turned and wandered back to the party." [100]

According to Micky Dolenz of The Monkees, he was invited to an Elton John party in Hollywood during this period as well. Micky wanted to look especially sharp, and he went out and bought a new shirt for the event. When he arrived at the party in his colorful new outfit, there stood Elton in the exact same shirt. Instead of finding it humorous, Elton was horrified. He purposely stayed on the opposite side of the room—away from Dolenz—so that they didn't look as if they had dressed as twins. Elton was unquestionably one of the biggest superstars of 1970s and 1980s, and here he was still dealing with such silly insecurity issues.

In early 1980, Elton found himself involved in a French recording project, which yielded his most unpredictable hit single. When French singer France Gall released her album Paris, France, it contained a song called "Il Jourait du Piano Debout," which means: "He plays the piano standing up." It was a tribute to Elton John. The next thing he knew, Elton was in a recording studio recording the songs "Les Aveux" ("Avowals") and "Donner Pour Donner" ("Giving for Giving") as duets with France Gall. When the songs were released in France, "Donner Pour Donner" became a big hit, giving Elton the first foreign language hit of his career.

When *21 at 33* was released in May 1980, *Rolling Stone* magazine reviewed it in a way that seemed to be more intent on reviewing Elton's flagging career than the album. Writer and critic Ken Tucker began his piece by stating: "We're now into the fifth year of the Elton John crisis, and frankly some of us here on the Elton watch are getting worried. Ever since 1975, when the anti-John backlash set in and the piano pumper's finest album, *Rock of the Westies*, only went umpteen-Platinum instead of his usual quadrabillion, Elton has sounded confused, bitter, exhausted. Efforts to re-enter John into the mainstream of things failed…the record is just slow, dull and blatant."[60]

Actually, *21 at 33* became quite a successful album. It hit Number Six in Norway, Number Ten in France, Number 12 in the U.K., and Number 13 in the U.S. Even better than that, was that the single "Little Jeannie" hit Number Three in America, making it Elton's first U.S. Top Three song since "Don't Go Breaking My Heart" in 1976. Furthermore, "Little Jeannie" hit Number One in Canada and Number Nine in Australia.

Starting with the *21 at 33* album, and continuing through 1984's *Breaking Hearts*, in the liner notes of his albums Elton identifies his managers as being Frank Presland, Derek MacKillop, and Keith Bradley at Twenty-First Artists. For this interim, Elton took the reins of his career away from his former boyfriend, John Reid.

The next single, "Sartorial Eloquence," made it to Number 44 in England when it was released. In the United States, the title of the Tom Robinson-penned song was changed to "Don't Ya Wanna Play This Game No More?" and it made it to Number 39 on the charts.

In 1980, the disco group Village People was sitting on top of the world. On the music charts, they were in the same position that Elton John had held four years earlier. While the disco craze was on in the late 1970s, everything they touched or recorded went to the top of the charts. They had just completed their feature film *Can't Stop the Music*, which Allan Carr produced. When they were in London for the premiere of *Can't Stop the Music*, Elton attended it and was fascinated with the group of—primarily—gay men.

Randy Jones, the Village People cowboy, soon found himself on the receiving end of Elton's legendary generosity. "Elton does have a proven history of sharing with up-and-coming new-to-the-scene talent," Jones explains. "During the week we were in London, Elton planned and hosted an elaborate dinner party at one of his favorite restaurants with several of his closer friends…. The dinner party was lavish, tasteful and tasty!" Randy recalls. "After the meal, some of us were invited to accompany Elton back to his home in Windsor. It was an invitation I simply could not refuse."[206]

That night the "bumps" of cocaine and the glasses of alcohol all flowed freely. Randy recalls, "He still had most of his over-the-top jewelry on. I remember being at the base of the stairway as he came down and casually yakking with him as he went to the room which had been converted from a butler's pantry into a walk-in size safe where he carefully placed each piece of outlandish and very expensive jewelry in its exact resting place. I was struck by the thought that this must be what it's like when the Queen removes the Royal Jewels and puts them away after a day doing all her queenly things. It was simply impressive…! Of course we were fueled by the top shelf booze and substances of the times. As dawn broke, those needing to get back to London were shuttled back in style, with sunglasses of course, to our hotels. I will never forget that glorious evening in the company of one of the true titans of pop music and pop culture: the great and the talented Elton John."[206]

Elton had changed everything else in his career of late; next on his schedule was a change of American record companies. One of the reasons that Elton was anxious to leave MCA Records was that he had had several disputes with them over which of his songs would or would not be released as singles. In particular, they had fought over releasing "A Song for Guy." Ultimately, Elton won that battle and retaliated by shopping for a new deal.

In the second half of 1980, it was announced that Elton John had signed a lucrative new recording deal with a brand-new record label: Geffen Records. Geffen was to be the new home for Elton's recordings for seven years, and seven new albums. David Geffen had created several superstars in the 1970s with his own label, Asylum Records. He courted Elton openly. Once signed to Geffen, Elton soon found himself in a roster filled with several other "A" list music stars including Donna Summer, Joni Mitchell, Neil Young, and even John Lennon and Yoko Ono.

At the time, Elton was very optimistic that he was going to be recording for a company owned by another gay man. Unfortunately, by the time the seven years—and seven albums— were over, the two men would be at each other's throats.

The next major landmark in Elton John's career was a record-breaking concert in New York City's Central Park. Four-hundred-thousand people were drawn to hear Elton that day, the highest attendance of his career. Held on September 13, 1980, with free admission, the event was sponsored by Calvin Klein jeans. The New York City Parks & Recreation department sold souvenirs to raise money to maintain the famous public park. The event was also carried live on WNEW-FM radio.

Prior to his Central Park engagement, Elton appeared on WNEW as the star disc jockey of the day to promote the concert. In the process, he caused a minor scandal with the censors at the FCC [Federal Communications Commission]. Amongst his "guest DJ" tasks on the radio was the reading of local advertisements. When he came to one for a Greenwich Village sex shop called The Pink Pussycat, he did a bit of on-air adlibbing as he read from the script. Elton entreated the station's listeners to contact The Pink Pussycat and "send for our catalogue, so you can sit home and masturbate at your own free will."[41]

September 13 was a beautiful day in Manhattan, and Elton's "free" concert had a very Woodstock-like feeling to it. As anyone who was at that concert will attest, it was not only helping to make Central Park "green" again by financing a new lawn, it was also an event where a lot of "green" things were being smoked.

The show began on The Great Lawn, right off Fifth Avenue, at 3:00 p.m. with opening act Judie Tzuke. Promptly at 4:00 p.m., Elton took to the stage dressed in a white cowboy hat and a custom-made shirt complete with lights sewn in.

Among the 400,000 screaming fans were several celebrities including Carly Simon, actor Dudley Moore, television personality Susan Anton, and tennis star John McEnroe. Elton gave the crowd an incredible show, a full three hours in length. He pulled out all of the stops that afternoon and gave a concert filled with passion, humor, excitement, and great fun.

When he introduced the John Lennon song "Imagine," he did so by stating, "We're going to do a song written by a friend of mine who I haven't seen for a long time. He only lives just over the road." He was referring to Lennon's apartment in the Gothic landmark building, The Dakota.

Just to make certain that every one of the 400,000 gathered spectators remembered the evening, Elton planned a special costume change for the concert's finale. Leaving the stage amidst the applause for "Someone Saved My Life Tonight," he frantically squeezed himself into the most insane costume of his career to date.

As he returned to the stage, there was Elton John dressed as the Walt Disney cartoon character, Donald Duck—complete with a big yellow bill and a huge pointed duck's tail. Launching into his first encore song—"Your Song"—he was much more than "just a little bit funny," he was full-out ludicrous. For the final song, the jubilant "Bite Your Lip (Get Up and Dance)" he played the piano standing up, while wiggling his duck tail to the music. The outfit had been Elton's brainstorm, and he had Bob Mackie custom-design it for him, including big yellow flippers for feet.

Robert Palmer in the *New York Times* was knocked out by Elton that warm summer afternoon. According to him, "Mr. John's Saturday afternoon performance in Central Park, his first New York show with a full band in several years, emphasized his strengths from the very first…the sound was crisp and bracing, and even Mr. John's garish suit recalled the shows he gave when he was at his commercial zenith."[197]

In *Musician* magazine, writer Roy Trakin heralded Elton's Central Park triumph: "The hits kept coming as if E.J. were some human jukebox programmed for three hours non-stop…. The bitch was, indeed, back."[41]

Elton continued his 1980 tour, zig-zagging across the United States, into November of that year. It concluded with a series of four concerts at The Forum in Los Angeles and then a series of concerts in Hawaii. For the L.A. shows Elton had Bob Mackie go a step further than he had with the now-famous Donald Duck costume. For the Forum dates, Elton performed the encores dressed in drag as Minnie Mouse. Even he was later to admit that Minnie Mouse was perhaps the most insane costume of his entire career— which is really saying something.

What was Taupin's reaction to Elton standing onstage, singing his delicate song lyrics while dressed as a gigantic cartoon female rodent in a bright red dress with a bow in his hair? Admits Elton, "Bernie fucking loathed it all."[184]

Despite the rapturous reviews and enthusiastic reception at his concerts, Elton's sadness and sense of despair was overwhelming to him at the time. He seemed to be on a perpetual quest for a boyfriend who could be his emotional anchor. Several boyfriends floated in and out of Elton's life. Often they served as a muse for his musical creations. There was a lover by the name of Charles, whom Elton gave the drag nickname "Chloe." Elton wrote the song "Chloe" about Charles (on *The Fox* album). The song "Blue Eyes" was written for another boyfriend, by the name of Vance (on the *Jump Up!* album). Then came Gary Clarke, whom Elton would nickname "Crystal." The song "Crystal" is naturally written about him (on the *Too Low for Zero* album).

It was actually in December of 1980 that Elton first met Gary Clarke. He had been introduced to the young man by Molly Meldrum during a trip to Australia. In the world of Australian mainstream pop music, Molly was a key figure. He had his own top-rated television show called *Countdown*, his own regular column in *TV Week*, and he wrote for a pop-culture newspaper called *Go-Set*. When Elton John began coming to Australia on a regular basis in the 1980s, he deepened his friendship with Molly.

Ian "Molly" Meldrum got his nickname from Australian slang for a "groupie," or a "band moll." He was so tied into the music business that the name "Molly" seemed like a perfect fit. Becoming close friends with Elton yielded not only the exciting glare of media attention, but a circle of handsome boys as well. Needless to say, he and Elton shared a lot of common interests.

Molly went into an ice cream parlor one day and met a cute young boy by the name of Gary Clarke, who was working behind the counter. When Molly met Clarke, there was an immediate connection. Molly began taking Gary to several high-profile events, including tea with Sheena Easton and a luncheon with Bette Midler. Clarke was thrilled to suddenly find himself in the middle of all of this activity. When Elton came to Australia to perform on an episode of *Countdown* in Brisbane on December 5, 1980, Molly took Gary and introduced the young man to Elton both at the taping and at the next night's concert. According to Gary, who was twenty-one years old at the time, there was an immediate attraction between Elton and him. By the time Elton departed Australia, he had left a lasting impression on Clarke. Little did the attractive, blond boy know, but he was destined to become one of Elton's main lovers. Their affair continued in an on-and-off fashion throughout the 1980s.

While Elton was in Australia, one of the most tragic events of his life took place. On December 8, 1980, in front of the famed Dakota apartment building where he resided, John Lennon was shot and killed by a deranged fan. It was every rock star's biggest nightmare. For Elton, because of his close friendship with Lennon, the news was especially devastating.

When he took the stage in Melbourne on December 11, 1980, he announced, "This week, the worst thing in the world happened. This is a song written by an incredible man." He launched into Lennon's signature song "Imagine." After singing the impassioned number, Elton had to go backstage where stagehands consoled him.

There were many moments of great despair for Elton. His depressions came on without warning, and he desperately sought out the company of friends whenever his blue moods would come over him. Having returned to England from Australia, during Christmas week of 1980, he suffered one of his worst depressions. When his current boyfriend, Charles, failed to show up at Woodside for the holidays as planned, Elton was reduced to tears. Desperate not to be alone for Christmas, he phoned Gary Osborne. Crying on the phone, he begged Gary to come down with his wife, Jenny, and their baby son Luke. They immediately came to his rescue.

After the holidays were over, Elton rented a sumptuous apartment in France. The plan was to resume recording for his next couple of albums: *The Fox* and *Jump Up!* Suddenly, another one of his dark moods came over him, and he refused to leave the apartment. Osborne recalls, "We were in a fantastic flat overlooking the Seine in Paris and Elton refused to come out for a month.... He wouldn't go to the studio; he wouldn't even get dressed. So I was there in the flat with Elton, his [personal assistant] Bob Halley, and Vance, and we had this sweet girl called Faith cooking for us. We just played poker and we took drugs for a month."[88]

The Fox was to be the first album in Elton's new deal with Geffen Records. When he turned in several tracks for David Geffen's approval, many of them were rejected. This upset Elton even further. Ultimately, *The Fox* used many of the same songwriting sources as *21 at 33*. Gary Osborne was responsible for "Breaking Down Barriers," "Heart in the Right Place," "Nobody Wins," and "Chloe." Bernie Taupin provided the lyrics for "Just Like Belgium," "Fascist Faces," "Heels of the Wind," and "The Fox." Elton composed two instrumentals: "Carla/Etude" and "Fanfare" (with James Newton Howard).

Tom Robinson provided the album with "Elton's Song." In the lyrics the singer rhapsodizes about being in love with another man and how he longs to be with him. Leave it to socially-conscious and envelope-pushing Robinson to give the album its edgiest track. Here we specifically find Elton performing the part of a schoolboy in love with one of his male classmates.

One of the most satisfying tracks on the album is "Nobody Wins." Originally, it was a song sung in French by Janic Prevost called "J'Veix d'la Tendresse." Elton discovered it while on the Riviera in the summer of 1980. According to Elton, "[It's] a record I heard driving out of town in St. Tropez in a traffic jam and it just suddenly came on.... [It] just sent shivers up and down my spine even though it was sung in French."[200]

Elton handed the song over to Gary Osborne, to see what he could do about writing some English lyrics. Using writer Jean-Paul Dreau's music, Osborne took the song about seeking happiness and recrafted it into an ode to a crumbling marriage. Elton immediately thought of the demise of his own parents' marriage when he sang it, and he turned in a heartfelt vocal performance.

On the surface, *The Fox* seems like a haphazard collection of songs from different sources. And it is. However, there were several deeply personal themes dear to Elton's heart explored on the album. He sang of his parents' doomed marriage, of his love for another boy, and secretly, of one of his current boyfriends. He made a political statement; he even sings about deception on "Heart in the Right Place." The album was produced by Chris Thomas, whom Elton had known for years as part of the London music scene.

Generally, the critics hated *The Fox*. Steve Pond in the *Los Angeles Times* claimed that Elton had reduced himself from "Captain Fantastic" to a much more dismal "Corporal Pretty

Good."[201] Robert Palmer from the *New York Times* wrote it off as being "flawed but uneven…with some potential hit singles that are more finely crafted than much of today's AM radio fodder."[202]

Stephen Holden in *Rolling Stone* wrote, "Lyrically, *The Fox*'s high point is a first-person remembrance of a homoerotic boyhood crush, 'Elton's Song'…. *The Fox* sounds less like a comeback than a graceful, mature coda to pop's banquet years."[203]

When it was released in May of 1981, *The Fox* made it to Number Five in Norway, Number Ten in France, Number 12 in the U.K., Number 21 in the U.S., Number 25 in Sweden, and Number 34 in Germany. The first single, "Nobody Wins," peaked at Number 21 in the U.S. and Number 42 in the U.K. The song "Chloe" made it to Number 34 on the American and Canadian charts. And, the song "Just Like Belgium" was also released as a single, but failed to chart.

While all of this was going on, there was a behind-the-scenes battle between Elton's former record label, MCA, and his new one, Geffen. When *The Fox* was released on Geffen Records, MCA claimed that they were owed one more album to fulfill their contract with Elton. In response, Elton delivered to MCA all six of the original sessions he had done with Thom Bell in 1977, and claimed that these six tracks complied with his obligation to the label. MCA was not amused and refused to accept the six tracks (three previously released and three previously unreleased ones) as "an album." After much legal wrangling, MCA held on to the six complete Thom Bell–produced songs, and the time limits of the original contract lapsed, leaving Elton free to continue to record for Geffen.

Between the death of his friend John Lennon, his relationship problems, his paranoia, the fact that his hair transplants were not all that successful, and his escalated cocaine use, in 1981 Elton John was not having a good time. He decided not to tour or perform in concert at all. However, there was one gig too irresistible to miss. Elton was invited to play in a concert for Prince Andrew's twenty-first birthday celebration at Windsor Castle on June 20, 1981.

In spite of Elton's mental state and his self-imposed exile in his mansion, when the royal family requested his presence, it certainly got his attention. He accepted the invitation. It became one of the most surreal experiences of his life. According to him, "When I arrived there was no one there but the dance band and Princess Diana. We danced the Charleston alone on the floor for twenty minutes. Then Princess Anne came up to me and said, 'Would you like to dance?' What am I going to say? 'No—fuck off?' We went into this disco where the music was so quiet you could hardly hear it. As we're bobbing up and down, the Queen comes up with an equerry and says, 'Do you mind if we join you?' Just at that moment, the music segues into Bill Haley's 'Rock Around the Clock.' So I'm dancing to 'Rock Around the Clock' with the Queen of England!"[207]

This was the beginning of his close association with the Royal Family of England. Although he felt like a bit of an outsider at first, it wasn't long before he was part of their social circle. He was especially impressed with young Diana Spencer, who was engaged to Prince Charles. They would be married only weeks later in the fairy-tale wedding of the decade. Elton was so impressed with Diana that he and Bernie wrote the song "Princess" about her and included it on his next album.

In late 1981, Elton began recording tracks for *Jump Up!*, his twenty-third album and second one for Geffen. He intended on recording in Paris, but when that didn't work out, the project was moved to Air Studios in Montserrat in the Caribbean.

The album *Jump Up!* had several significant tracks on it, but like *The Fox* and *21 at 33* it was another patchwork quilt of divergent styles. Elton expanded his repertoire of collaborators, recording his first song with Tim Rice. Together with Andrew Lloyd Webber, Rice had scored a string of brilliant and successful Broadway musicals, including *Jesus Christ Superstar*, *Evita*, and *Joseph and the Amazing Technicolor Dream Coat.*

When Rice wrote the song "Legal Boys," it was about a messy divorce, and it was meant to be for an Andrew Lloyd Webber project. However, when Webber changed his mind, Rice gave "Legal Boys" to Elton.

Bernie Taupin contributed five compositions, including "Spiteful Child," "I am Your Robot," "Where Have All the Good Times Gone," "All Quiet on the Western Front," and "Empty

Garden (Hey Hey Johnny)." Gary Osborne contributed four songs: "Dear John," "Ball and Chain," "Princess," and "Blue Eyes."

The two most significant songs on *Jump Up!* are its pair of hit singles. The uplifting and biggest hit was "Blue Eyes," which was about Elton's current lover. As Gary Osborne explains, "Elton was seeing a lovely guy called Vance, who tragically later died of AIDS. He was a humongous fan of Bowie, which was always a big bone of contention between them! Vance had blue eyes."[88]

The somber classic on the album is the tribute song for John Lennon, "Empty Garden (Hey Hey Johnny)." According to Elton, "When John died, it really did affect me a lot. I still can't believe sometimes that he's actually not there. I was living in Paris at the time, and not going through a particularly good period of my life. I was very depressed, and I wrote an instrumental called 'The Man Who Never Died.' I really like it a lot. And Taupin wrote 'Empty Garden.' I didn't think anyone would be able to say anything [about John] without being clumsy or cheesy."[78]

On the other side of the coin, the album also contained the joyous song, "Where Have All the Good Times Gone." In the song Elton wonders why he now lacks the fun that he used to have in life, and in one recurring chorus line he asks where "all of those" Four Tops songs have gone. It was a great tribute to the famous Motown quartet that made songs like "Reach Out I'll Be There" and "Standing in the Shadows of Love" into international hits.

The year 1981 was one of the lowest emotional points that Elton had ever visited. In addition to doing a ton of cocaine, he was drinking heavily. Although he thought that being the Chairman of the Watford Football Club was grounding him, in reality it was not. He had taken to showing up at Watford games reeking of booze. Finally on December 26, 1981, Graham Taylor, the Manager of Watford, had a talk with him. According to Elton, "I used to drink a whole bottle of Yukon Jack bourbon every day.... Anyway, I was drinking a hell of a lot of brandy then. And Graham Taylor said that he wanted to see me for lunch. And I knew everybody was thinking, 'Oh God, he's drinking a lot.' And you can't hide from yourself: when you're like that you're very unhappy. So I went round to his house for lunch a couple of days later and he said, 'Here you are: here's your lunch'—a bottle of fuckin' brandy. 'What the fuck is wrong with you? What is the matter, man? Why are you doing this to yourself?' And I was so relieved somebody had actually come out and said it…. Graham said, 'Listen, for fuck's sake: Stop!' And I did." [43] At least for a while he did.

When *Jump Up!* was released in the spring of 1982, it hit the Top 20 on both sides of the Atlantic, peaking at Number Five in Norway, Number 12 in France, Number 13 in the U.K., Number 17 in the U.S., Number 25 in Sweden, and Number 47 in Germany. The beautiful ballad, "Blue Eyes," made it to Number Five in Canada, Number Eight in the U.K., Number 12 in the U.S., and Number 13 in Australia. "Empty Garden" did much better in America, hitting Number 13, while in England it stalled at Number 51. Like *21 at 33* before it, *Jump Up!* was also certified Gold in the U.S.

This time around, the critics were on Elton's side. According to Parke Puterbaugh in *Rolling Stone*, "*Jump Up!* is the album that redeems Elton John from his famine years as a fallen superstar…a tour de force of a record that says he knows he's worth it." [208]

Gene Sculatti in *Creem* loved *Jump Up!* According to him, "Whether this means Elton's 'back' or on top again, is for someone else to figure out…. *Jump Up!*'s an exceptional record. In today's devalued pop economy, that's not small change." [42]

Meanwhile, in the two years since his initial meeting with Elton, Gary Clarke had thought of the gay Rocket Man several times. When Elton came to Australia in March of 1982 for a series of concerts, Molly Meldrum phoned Gary and announced, "Elton's back in town, and he wants you to come to dinner." [167]

The next thing Gary knew, he was seated at an Indian restaurant with Elton, Elton's devoted assistant Bob Halley, his publicist Patty Mostyn, and Molly, listening to everything from charming tales of dancing with the Queen at Prince Andrew's 21st birthday celebration to gossip that David Bowie had always wanted to be Judy Garland.

One of Elton's favorite stories to tell about the Royal Family was that the Queen Mother once told him her secret for keeping her diamonds clean and gleaming. She soaked them in her favorite beverage: gin. According to Clarke, he was mesmerized by Elton and his tales.

Two days after the Indian dinner, Elton had Patty Mostyn phone Gary. When Gary answered the telephone, Patty put Elton on the line, and he proceeded to invite the young man to attend that night's concert. Clarke agreed and was given instructions as to where and when he was to arrive at the venue. He was admitted to the backstage area and into the star's dressing room. Clarke arrived in time to see Elton strip down to his underpants, and he later commented, "It was something else to see a star strip down to his underwear. Elton was as unlikely a sex symbol as you could ever find—and he would agree. He was pudgy, and I was fascinated by the amount of hair on his body."[167]

That night, after the concert, Gary was invited back to Elton's dressing room, where he was present for a small after-the-show party. As the other guests began to leave, Elton asked Clarke to remain. When they were alone, Elton invited Gary to go on the rest of the tour with him and then to move into his house in England with him. This was all without having consummated their affair. Although he declined at first, Clarke inevitably agreed to both offers. Later that week, Gary found himself in Elton John's bed, and so began their intense love affair.

Elton has admitted several times in interviews that he had the habit of meeting men he was attracted to, and in a matter of hours, planning his entire life together with that person. Gary Clarke was to fall into that category. Within days, Gary had quit his job and was preparing to spend the rest of his life as Elton John's boyfriend. By April 1982, Gary found himself ensconced in the pop icon's twenty-seven acre Woodside estate.

As Elton's new love object, Clarke was moved into the main house, while there were two other structures on the property. One of them, known as The Orangerie, was the home of Elton's Grandma Ivy, and the other one was used by Sheila and "Derf" when they came to visit from their home which was located an hour and a half away.

Rubbing elbows with royalty was affecting Elton. It is official protocol that when Queen Elizabeth is in residence at her estate, the Union Jack is flown at full mast to indicate her presence. When Elton was at Woodside, it became his habit to fly a Watford football team flag at full mast, to signify that the neighborhood's other queen was in residence.

When Gary moved into Woodside, Elton showed him to what was to be the young lad's own personal room. Clarke later confessed that he was miffed by this. Should he be flattered or insulted? If he was going to be Elton's lover, should he not share the star's bedroom? Apparently it was a blessing. Soon Gary was initiated into Elton's frequent foul moods, tantrums, and drug-induced bad behavior. The separate bedroom was to become a sanctuary of sanity more than anything.

Clarke later wrote a searing memoir of the pop star, *Elton, My Elton*. In it he claimed, "Those closest to him would probably also argue that a lot of the loneliness was brought upon him by his own immaturity, his willful refusal to take responsibility. If he wasn't hiding behind his lackeys or his cocaine, he would still manage to avoid confronting a crisis...the drugs made him insensitive to those around him."[167]

Days after returning to England, on April 30, 1982, Elton and Gary and the entire entourage were in Stockholm, Sweden, for the opening night of Elton's latest European concert tour. Apparently, the sound quality at the venue, The Johanneseshovs Isstadion, that evening was less than perfect. That was all it took for one of "Reggie's little moments" to manifest itself. That night Clarke witnessed his first of the singer's pouting snits. John Reid knew the routine all too well and took Gary aside to tell him not to leave Elton's side, as it was now the young man's job to placate the often childish singer.

Clarke also found Elton vascillated between being either distant and withdrawn, or incredibly needy and clinging. When Gary went off to explore a bit of Helsinki, Finland, on his own, he returned to find a tearful Elton, commanding him to never leave him again like that. It seemed that Elton liked to treat his "boy toys" like poodles on a leash. Whenever he wanted their attention, he wanted them right next to him to attend to his every need.

Amongst the activities on this particular trip was attending a drag show in Gothenburg, Sweden, and an elaborately drunken dinner in Nice, France. The dinner in Nice was for ten people and cost Elton a stunning £5,000. He thought nothing of such expense. Clarke recalls, afterward, as their private car passed the chic Negresco Hotel in Nice, Elton pulled his pants down and "mooned" the well-dressed patrons.

Much to his surprise, Gary Clarke found that a rock & roll concert tour with Elton was not quite the exotic sightseeing tour that he had expected. He and Elton seemed to spend all their time either in a concert hall, a plane, or locked in a hotel suite. When he complained to Elton that he wanted to go home to Australia, his host/boyfriend promised that the forthcoming visit to America would be different. Elton enticed Gary to stay by promising trips to Disneyland and more fun activities.

But Elton wasn't necessarily pleased with Gary's complaints. To protest Gary's displeasure, Elton decided to shave off his eyebrows. Horrified, Clarke told the singer that he looked like a drag queen with his eyebrows suddenly missing. Clarke was also shocked to find that although he had only been living as Elton's boyfriend for less than two months, already the singer was bringing other young men into his bed, expecting three-way sex of all sorts. At his Frankfurt, Germany, concert, Elton invited three British soldiers onstage mid-show, then he invited all of them back to his suite after the show. Gary watched with displeasure when the evening ended with Elton bedding one of them.

Although Clarke had met Elton during one of the lulls in Elton's cocaine usage, by the Paris engagement, the white powder abounded like a sudden blizzard. On this trip, Elton was visited by his close friend Rod Stewart. One night in Elton's suite at the Plaza Athénée Hotel, Gary decided to go to bed at 12:30 a.m., leaving "Sharon" and "Phyllis" to catch up with each other. The following morning when Clarke emerged from the bedroom, he recalls, "I was amazed to find the two stars doing lines of coke through crisp £50 notes, chattering like gibbons. After about half an hour Rod said his goodbyes and staggered off."[167]

After the thirty-two day European concert tour, Elton and Clarke were off to Los Angeles. They would be spending several days in California, complete the promised tour of Disneyland, and have several days off. Elton had even encouraged Gary to invite one of his friends, Cameron, to visit from Australia. However, Gary reported that Elton's cocaine consumption escalated that week, and so did his mood swings.

When Gary and his friend, Cameron, started having too much fun together, suddenly Elton decided that he was done with

Gary Clarke, and he was sending him back to Australia. The love affair was over. John Reid took Gary to LAX airport, gave him his ticket, and Elton promised to phone him soon. It was months before Elton was to pick up the telephone. Gary returned to Australia after a whirlwind affair that lasted only three months.

Gary moved back into the Melbourne home of his parents, who were just getting ready for a trip to England. The Clarkes were going to visit an aunt there, and Gary asked if they could stop by Woodside to retrieve some of his belongings. He phoned Elton's mother in England to tell her that his parents would be there soon, and could he send them by for his things. Sheila couldn't have been nicer and told Gary she looked forward to meeting his parents.

He was surprised when he received a phone call from his dad, telling him that not only had they met up with Sheila and "Derf," they were now staying with them at Woodside. Elton and Gary were no longer speaking, but their respective parents were now hitting it off like old friends in England.

Then in the middle of the year, Gary received a phone call from Elton. He was going to be in Sydney to make a television appearance, and "Why don't we get together then?"[167] He agreed.

Before that rendevous, in 1982, a court case came about that was of great interest to Elton John and John Reid. The folk singer Gilbert O'Sullivan won back the rights to his 1970s catalogue of songs from the man who had signed him to a substandard contract when Gilbert was an unknown young kid. That was all that Elton and Reid had to hear. They decided to sue Dick James for all of the pre-*Blue Moves* publishing rights that he still owned. They were determined to win back their rights to the songs, and to—hopefully—recoup millions of British Pounds in royalties. The court case was to be a long and dragged out one, lasting for the next four years. This was all going on when Elton made his next visit to Australia.

When Gary arrived in Sydney for his reunion with Elton, he was not certain what to expect this time around. Would he just have a two-day visit, or would the affair resume?

Elton was thrilled to see Gary. However, he had a bombshell of an announcement to make: "If you want a relationship, you have to agree to having other people included. I'm talking about three-way sex. If you don't agree, then you'd better go back to Melbourne now!" For fear of losing Elton again, Clarke agreed to give it a try.[167]

After a lovely time together in Australia, Gary again moved back to Woodside. At least this time he knew what to expect.

One of the things that characterized Gary's second trip to England was another of Elton's self-loathing depressions. Sick of seeing the pudgy, overweight image of himself in his mirror, he had taken to stuffing himself with food and then puking it up. For Clarke, this "binge and purge" form of bulimia was quite upsetting to witness. Gary later recalled, "I knew what was going on for I could smell the vomit on his fingers and in the toilet, and although he attempted to conceal his problems from me, the smell was a big turn-off."[167]

To further curb his appetite, Elton continued to indulge in heavier cocaine use. Clarke claimed that in Elton's case, the cocaine would also unleash some of the superstar's most obnoxious and evil rants. But wanting to make his relationship as Elton's boyfriend work this time around, Gary agreed to give cocaine a try. Although he initially liked the feelings of exhilaration, he was not happy with the downside of the drug. As it wore off, he got a taste of the listless drug hangover it also induced.

Elton made good on his promise of a ménage a trois. On one occasion Elton fancied a chef and invited him to Woodside. When Gary declined to participate, he wondered what the repercussions would be. Fortunately for Gary, though, Elton went through with the fling with the chef and allowed Gary to pass on the ménage a trois.

As the time came close for Elton to record his next album, *Too Low for Zero*, he curbed his cocaine usage. Clarke claims that the singer wanted to be at his best when he arrived on the tropical island of Montserrat in the British West Indies. While the other musicians took their wives, Elton brought Gary. Although this was something of a "reunion" album for Elton, Nigel, Dee, and Bernie, instead of using Gus Dudgeon as the producer, they chose Chris Thomas, who had worked with Pink Floyd, Pete Townshend, Badfinger, and The Sex Pistols. It was from these sessions that came some of the most memorable recordings of Elton's '80s career, including "I'm Still Standing" and "I Guess That's Why They Call it the Blues."

Elton had toned down his cocaine usage during the recording of the album, and Bernie had gotten his excessive drinking under control. For both of them, the song "I'm Still Standing" wasn't just a cheerful tune, it was a deeply personal anthem of survival.

According to Clarke, his time in Montserrat with Elton definitely had its rewards, including having the song "Crystal" written about him. As part of Elton's inner circle of boys, he had been given the female nickname of "Crystal." According to Clarke, "Sharon" had given Gary the name of "Crystal" in honor of country singer Crystal Gayle.

Gary Clarke was convinced that his relationship with Elton was stronger than ever, especially when the Rocket Man told him in bed one night that he wanted them to be together forever. When, after four weeks at Montserrat, Elton asked Gary to go back to England to sort out some business regarding a new car that was being purchased, Gary didn't feel that there was any possible threat to their relationship. However, when he later discovered some of Bob Halley's photos from Montserrat, he went berserk. There were snapshots of Elton in bed with a couple of cute young men, obviously taken after Clarke returned to England.

When he confronted Elton with this evidence of the singer's inability to be faithful, it caused a huge rift. As per usual, Elton had Bob Halley handle anything unpleasant. Bob came into Gary's room and told him that he was being sent back to Australia immediately—that very night. When Gary confided his problems to his best friend in England, Sheila Farebrother, Elton's mother insisted that Elton not send him away empty-handed. Bob handed him £3,000 and took him to the airport that evening. For the second time, Gary Clarke was banished from Elton's life.

When he returned to Australia, it was just in time to be mentioned on the cover of a lurid tabloid story. Apparently the press had gotten wind of Gary's role in Elton's life and headlined an article: "ELTON'S MELBOURNE MAN."

No sooner had Gary been sent back to Australia, than Elton moved his next "boy toy" into Woodside. His name was Tommy

Williams, a young lad Elton had met while on tour in the U.S. That affair was about as short-lived as the affair with Gary Clarke.

For Elton, most of 1982—from April to December—was spent touring the world in concert. He ended the tour on December 24, back in London, at the Hammersmith Odeon Theater, doing that year's version of his Christmas show. Each show in the fourteen-date engagement ended with duet performances of five songs with Kiki Dee. Together they sang, "Don't Go Breaking My Heart," "Whole Lot of Shakin' Going On," "Jingle Bells," "I Saw Her Standing There," and "Twist and Shout."

Meanwhile, in addition to contributing songs to Elton's *Jump Up!* album, Bernie Taupin was happy in Los Angeles, collaborating with other people. In 1982, he worked with Melissa Manchester, contributing his writing to the title song "Hey Ricky (You're a Lowdown Heel)" on her *Hey Ricky* album.

By early 1983 a new scandal was brewing in Elton's life. This one was investigated by the police. There was a robbery at Woodside. A diamond and sapphire ring valued at £50,000, a £6,000 watch, and an additional £100 in cash were missing. It was something of a mysterious robbery, since the tight security system at Woodside included alarms and dogs.

Come to find out, it was not a case of Elton's home being broken into at all. When the police traced the stolen merchandise to twenty-one-year-old Cornelius Culwick, they asked him where the "hot" goods came from. The cheeky young lad replied, "I'll give you a clue: 'The Pinball Wizard.' You work it out."[167]

A trial was held, and the story came out in the press. Apparently, Elton had returned to Woodside with Tommy Williams, Cornelius, and another young man for a sex party. When Cornelius left Woodside hours later, he did so with the watch, ring, and cash that Elton had left on the night stand. There was a court trial, and when it all came to light that Elton had invited Cornelius for sex, the charge of "theft" was changed to a lesser offense of "dishonest handling." Cornelius was later acquitted and allowed to keep the watch as a souvenir of his night in the pop star's bedroom.

This was just the beginning of the tabloid stories that Elton's sex life was to garner in the 1980s. Some of Elton's greatest adventures and his most lurid episodes were still yet to come.

CHAPTER THIRTEEN

I'm Still Standing

In 1982 and 1983, Elton John was looking for some answers in his life. He knew that things had to change and that he somehow had to get everything back on track both in his personal life and in his career. In many ways, putting his career together was going to be a much easier task than fixing his emotionally-damaged personal life.

One of the first things that had to be accomplished was to record a great new album. He was always the happiest when his musical creativity was in full blossom. Looking back at his body of music, there were certain formulas that worked for him. As a lyricist, he was always at his best working with Bernie Taupin. After working for the last seven years with "session musicians," he longed for his old bandmates. So for *Too Low for Zero*, Elton invited back his former musicians: drummer Nigel Olsson, guitarist Davey Johnstone, and bass player Dee Murray.

The biggest news, though, was the fact that Elton John and Bernie Taupin were working together on a whole album's worth of music for the first time since the ill-fated and much-misunderstood *Blue Moves* album. According to Bernie at the time, "We both realized how much we wanted to do this album. Before, we'd taken each other for granted and hadn't allowed each other to grow."[211]

This meant that Gary Osborne had to be "fired." Osborne recalls, "What happened was that *The Fox* had been disappointing sales-wise, and although *Jump Up!* did quite well, Geffen Records wanted the old team back."[88]

Whenever Elton fired someone or decided to sever his ties with him, he either cut them out of the picture, or he'd simply let someone else do the dirty work. Elton didn't bother to tell Gary Osborne that he was no longer working with him, instead he let the lyricist read it in the newspaper. How could Osborne not be deeply hurt? "Remember, we were just coming off a worldwide hit in 'Blue Eyes,'" Gary recalls, "and I was not expecting to be dumped. I learned from reading it in the papers."[88]

With regard to his full-time reunion with Bernie, Elton felt compelled to state: "Let's clear up this misconception. I was living in England, Bernie was living in the US, but we never at any time in our lives fell out with each other or had arguments; it was never, ever, a split, it was just a healthy time apart. If we hadn't had that break, we might never have survived."[214]

The work on the *Too Low for Zero* album started in June 1982, when Elton spent ten days with Bernie, putting together the new band and figuring out a game plan for the album. Recording and writing the ten songs for the album took place in September 1982 at Air Studios in Montserrat. Rough tapes were made with a rhythm machine, and producer Chris Thomas took those tapes to Los Angeles. It was in L.A. that a week of "overdubs" took place, building from the bottom upward.

While in the Caribbean paradise of Montserrat, Chris Thomas was again at the helm of the project as the album's producer. It was there that Elton made one of his most significant—and unexpected—alliances of the decade. Renate Blauel was a tape operator at Air Studios, while Elton was there. She was in her mid-twenties, and she was always casually dressed in tee shirts and jeans. She wore very little makeup and had a pleasant and warm personality. Who would have guessed that she eventually would become Elton's wife? When the *Too Low for Zero* album was released in May 1983 in the U.S., and June 1983 in the U.K., it immediately made an impact on the British charts, hitting Number Seven. However, it wasn't until the next year, by which time several hit singles had been released from it, that *Too Low for Zero* finally hit its American peak at Number 25. It also peaked at Number Five in Germany, Number Six in Norway and Switzerland, and Number 11 in France.

The singles that this album yielded were among Elton's most significant songs of the decade. "I'm Still Standing" is without a doubt the most frankly autobiographical Elton had recorded since "The Bitch Is Back." It precisely stated the way Elton looked at himself and how the world viewed him. In spite of the scandals, the tantrums, and his public meltdowns, somehow "Uncle Reg" was still cranking out memorable tunes.

"I'm Still Standing," hit Number One in Canada, Number Three in Australia, Number Four in the U.K., Number Ten in

Germany, and Number 12 in the U.S. Then the song "I Guess That's Why They Call it the Blues," featuring Elton's old friend Stevie Wonder on the harmonica, became another big international hit, making it to Number Four in Australia and the U.S., Number Five in the U.K., and Number Nine in Canada. In addition, "Kiss the Bride"—with vocals by George Michael—was a Top 40 hit in the U.K., Australia, the U.S., and in Canada. When Christmas of 1983 rolled around, the song "Cold as Christmas (In the Middle of the Year)" was released as a single. It became a Number 33 hit in the U.K. and made it to Number 52 in Australia.

Unfortunately the critics were not thrilled with the *Too Low for Zero* album. Don Shewey in *Rolling Stone* claimed, "Elton John and Bernie Taupin have written some great hit singles, but since the early *Elton John* LP, they have never produced an album of consistently first-rate material. And although *Too Low for Zero* is a big step up from losers like *Blue Moves* and *A Single Man*, it doesn't hang together either."[215] In spite of what the critics said, *Too Low for Zero* stayed on the album charts for months, and the song "I'm Still Standing" has gone on to become one of the true signature songs of Elton's career.

One of the reasons for the great success of "I'm Still Standing" was the brilliant video that was filmed to accompany it. The early 1980s saw a new phenomenon in rock & roll: the video revolution. It spread around the globe like wildfire. Stations that played music videos twenty-four hours a day were suddenly the rage, including MTV and VH1 in America and MuchMusic in Canada.

The "I'm Still Standing" video was produced by Australian filmmaker Russell Mulcahy. Working mainly in television and videos, Mulcahy has since gone on to direct dozens and dozens of episodes of television shows, including *Queer as Folk* and *Tales from the Crypt* and the film *Scorpion King 2* (2008). In a way working with Elton prepared him for these projects: Elton was certainly "queer as folk," and when he drank he was truly a "tale from the crypt."

The video was primarily filmed at the promenade located outside the Carlton Hotel in Cannes, with a cast of beautiful boys and girls in tights and bathing suits. In the video Elton solidified one of his signature looks of the 1980s. He had taken to covering his failed hair transplants with a 1920s straw hat known as "a boater." It was the type of hat that one would expect to see a young Maurice Chevalier wearing. Elton fashioned himself as a Jazz Age balladeer with a 1980s flair.

After a long day of filming, Elton decided to unwind with his buddies in the band Duran Duran, who were also in Cannes that week. Elton then proceeded to drink eight vodka martinis in a half hour, and then he went crazy. Apparently the camera crew filmed him going into a striptease, which ended up with him rolling around on the floor stark naked. Again and again he changed colorful outfits and then stripped them off in front of the camera. Simon Le Bon of Duran Duran took the heat for getting Elton drunk and turning him loose on unsuspecting Cannes. When John Reid tried to get Elton to calm down, Elton wrestled Reid to the floor, punched him in the face and broke his nose. Cocktail hour with Elton: charmingly priceless.

Elton was later to admit, "I can't really remember the rest of the video. I woke up the next morning and I had all these cuts and bruises all over me. I had destroyed one of the rooms and completely blacked out. Thank you, Duran, Duran."[88]

Throughout 1983, Elton John's social calendar took up as much time as his music career demanded, if not more. From February 26 to March 7, Queen Elizabeth II and Prince Philip came to the United States for an official visit to the West Coast, including stops in San Diego, Los Angeles, San Francisco, Santa Barbara, and Seattle. When President Ronald Reagan and First Lady Nancy Reagan hosted a dinner for the Queen in Hollywood, the guest list included James Stewart, Fred Astaire, Bette Davis, and Gene Kelly. There were several British subjects from the show business world invited as well, including Michael Caine, Julie Andrews, Jane Seymour, and Elton John.

In true Elton fashion, he complained about the dinner to the Los Angeles correspondent from the London newspaper *The Sun*. He called the dinner "boring," and he whined that the event was so stiff he nearly fell asleep. Not even entertainment provided by Dionne Warwick, Frank Sinatra, and Perry Como had held his attention.

That April, Elton was invited to participate in an elaborate press and celebrity junket to launch a new line of Cartier 22-carat gold sunglasses. In addition to Elton and John Reid, and an assortment of journalists, the guest list included actor Christopher Cazenove, singers Hazel O'Connor and Lynsey de Paul, and Royal Family members Lady Elizabeth Shakerley, who is a cousin of the Queen, and the Countess of Lichfield. The festivities called for the party to be flown to Monastir, a Tunisian resort. With bad timing, the event was perfectly planned to coincide with local typhoon season. When Elton and the glittering party of Cartier devotees deplaned in Tunisia, they were greeted by gale-force winds and driving rain. Then there was some sort of screw-up with the room accommodations at the Hannibal Palace Hotel, and some of the guests found that there were no rooms for them. The deluxe first night banquet dinner that was to be served at 9:30 p.m. didn't commence until right before midnight. Then, when the food was served, everyone was disappointed. It could have been an even bigger disaster if Elton had one of "Reggie's little moments." Instead he took to the piano and gave the Cartier party an impromptu concert.

According to *Daily Express* columnist Christopher Wilson, "I've never seen anyone turn a room full of people around so totally. In about twenty minutes, he had everyone clapping, singing, standing on tables. It was an incredible performance that seemed to come from absolutely nowhere. And once he got going, there was no stopping him. As a finale, he led all these quite starchy jet set types, in their evening dress and jewelry, in a Pied Piper line out of the hotel and down to the beach, where the remains of this marquee were still standing. He grabbed his trousers and wiggled his bare arse. Which, everyone felt, summed the whole thing up perfectly."[219]

Still looking for a new direction, Elton was also exploring a couple of possible new acting projects. Among the proposed ideas was a film starring Elton and Rod Stewart which would be a rock & roll version of the classic Marilyn Monroe film *Some Like it Hot*. In that movie, actors Tony Curtis and Jack Lemmon dress in drag to escape Jazz Age Chicago after being eyewitnesses to The St. Valentine's Day Massacre. Naturally, Elton and Rod would play the drag characters. This project never got off the ground. It could have been perfect for "Sharon" and "Phyllis," but it was never to be.

There was also a proposed Elton John and Rod Stewart concert tour that would take place in 1984. The pair went so far as to try out the "duo" concert idea at Sun City in South Africa in 1983. However, they ultimately decided not to pursue it.

Another film was announced in the press. To be called *Hang Ups*, it was to star Elton and Liza Minnelli. Blake Edwards, the director of all of the great Peter Sellers "Inspector Clouseau" films, was set to take the helm of the movie. When it came time for Elton to do a screen test, it was a bust. He later proclaimed, "It's a dual part—an English guy who works in New York and adopts an American alter ego. I had to go to Hollywood to do a screen test for it and I was absolutely petrified. I threw up and everything."[218]

In May and June of 1983, Elton went along with the Watford Football Club to China. The team was set to play three exhibition games, and Elton wanted to go along and see China. He stood on The Great Wall and visited several sites. Happily, Watford won all of its three games against the National China team.

In 1983, Elton reconnected with Duncan Faure of The Bay City Rollers. At this point, Duncan had gone back to his homeland of South Africa, and his bandmate, Stuart "Woody" Wood, came along with him. According to Duncan, "Elton called the house, and my mother answered the phone. She didn't believe it was him, and of course it was. The next thing we were invited to Sun City, and that's when Rod Stewart was performing there, so Elton was just hanging out. I couldn't believe that I was standing in the wings with Elton on one side of me, and Rod Stewart on the other. It was a moment I will never forget."[212]

Several months passed, and Elton came back to Sun City for his own gig at the concert facility. According to Duncan, Elton telephoned him to invite him to come along to the gig and bring some of his buddies along with him.

Before the show, Duncan went up to Elton's suite to see the singer. Elton had the habit of answering the door wearing very little. Duncan recalls, "It was in Sun City. He was getting ready for a show, and he invited me up. I knocked on the door, and Elton was in a bathrobe."[212]

After the show was over, Elton invited Duncan to stay with him in his private suite. He also made it clear that this was to be a party for two, only. As Faure explains, "I remember one of my friends, Johann, came to Elton's rooms with me. Elton opened the door to his suite, and Elton let me into the suite and said, 'O.K., Johann, good to see you,' and he shut the door on him. He never forgave me that he never got into the room with Elton. I explained to him, 'Hey, it's Elton.' I stayed in the suite!"[212]

However, Duncan is quick to clarify that it was a platonic evening. "There was never anything sexual done," he explains. "Maybe it could have gone that way. It didn't bother me. My brother was gay, and I grew up with that, so it was fine."[212]

So, what happened? "He was very cool," Duncan insists. "He accepted me as a friend. Going back to our first meeting: he understood that since I had just joined The Bay City Rollers. If we'd have done anything, it would have been 'Roller news.' It would have reverberated through The Rollers for the next three years. We just became great friends. I know that I loved him, and I know that he had a thing for me, too. I think he went for anybody. He's a musician, you know? We liked each other; we got on."[212]

Seeing Elton in Sun City in 1983, Duncan felt that the star was feeling a bit sad and lost. Duncan recalls, "He did say to me, that he would give up all his success for true love. But I don't know if he knows what it's like to be on the other side, when there is no money. I don't know if he'd say that if he actually had to live it. But he did say, during that period, that he would give up his success to find true love."[212]

In the middle of 1983, Elton began phoning his former boyfriend, Gary Clarke, in Australia to gossip and chat, as though banishing Clarke a second time the previous year had never happened. Since that time Gary had taken a job in computers and had gotten his life back together. However, he still had a crush on Elton, in spite of the fact that they had broken up twice before.

When the album *Too Low for Zero* came out earlier that year, with the song "Crystal" on it, Gary found himself haunted by memories of his brief time as "boyfriend" to the Rocket Man. According to Clarke, "Playing 'Crystal' constantly, I could envision an excited, emotional Elton composing lovingly for me on the piano."[167] It made him long for another chance at making his affair with the mood-swing-prone pop star work.

In one of their phone conversations late that year, Elton mentioned to Gary the possibility of spending Christmas at Woodside. That was all it took to revive the spark of love, and Clarke told Elton he would love to spend Christmas there with him. Elton agreed, but this time around, Gary purchased his own plane ticket, so that he had more control over his return to Australia.

When Gary arrived back in England, Elton was thrilled to see him. It was like old times. That first night they attended a star-studded party at the home of Billy Gaff, Rod Stewart's manager. On the way back to Woodside late that night, while Bob Halley drove the car home, Elton said to Gary, "Let's get back together again. Let's give it another chance." According to him, "As the Bentley raced through the night I could feel Elton's fingers fumbling around my zip. Next minute he was giving me head."[167]

Although it proved to be a romantic reunion, there was a new drama brewing in Eltonland, and Gary again found himself in the middle. Since it was the Christmas holidays, Elton's parents were in residence at The Orangerie on Elton's property. While at Woodside, Gary overhead one of Elton's servants, Gladys, complaining about Sheila. Since Gary was quite devoted to Sheila, he told her what had been said. Much to his horror, Sheila marched up to the main house and barged into Elton's bedroom. Since Elton was in the middle of an all-night cocaine binge, he was in an irritable mood to begin with.

Sheila lit into Elton, and he told her to get out of his room immediately. She told him he was not to talk to her like that, but Elton insisted. A loud argument ensued, and when Sheila stormed out of the house, Elton told Gary, "I just told Mum to 'get the fuck out of here.'" The next thing he knew, "Derf" came storming into the kitchen where Elton, Bob, and Gary were and proceeded to give his stepson a piece of his mind. The heated argument that ensued peaked with "Derf" telling Elton, "If you ever speak to her again like that, I'll tell the police what you bleedin' well keep shoving up your nose."[167]

Overcome with emotion, and full of drugs, Elton fainted on the spot. When he was revived, he explained to Gary that he had been having these similar spells, but that they were nothing to be alarmed about. Clearly, Elton was ruining his health with his cocaine habit. Now it was beginning to affect not only his body but his relationship with his parents as well.

Elton took Gary with him after Christmas, for a return to Montserrat in the Caribbean, where work was commencing on his new album, *Breaking Hearts*. According to Gary, this particular trip to the British West Indies was one of gay sex and drugs. While there, Elton had a fling with a young man he flew in for sex. Both he and Gary made a play for a handsome young tape operator at the studio. However, the lad was straight and uninterested in their advances.

Renate Blauel reentered Elton's life at this time. A tape operator on *Too Low for Zero*, she became an engineer on *Breaking Hearts*. According to Gary Clarke, Renate had "zero" fashion sense and dressed in a frumpy tee-shirt and jeans. Most of Elton's party suspected that she was a lesbian, simply because of her mannish style of dressing. Although she was something of an introvert, she had a good sense of humor, and Clarke found her to have a pleasant personality.

The plan was for the entire entourage to proceed to Sydney, Australia, following the Montserrat sessions and continue to work on the album. Both Gary and Renate were going along as well. Gary was going as Elton's companion, but Renate's role was in an official capacity. The mixing sessions for *Breaking Hearts* were to take place at EMI Studios in Sydney.

Although Elton and Gary were getting along well, Elton's constant mood swings continued in Australia. When they arrived in Sydney and checked into the Sebel Town House Hotel there, Elton was to occupy the Presidential Suite, and Gary was to have a room of his own, several floors below—much to Gary's surprise.

Using one of his nicknames for Gary, Elton presented this plan with the lame excuse: "Chook, I forgot to tell you. I've booked us into different rooms. There'll be so much activity going on in my room…meetings and interviews. It'll be easier for you not to have to put up with it."[167] Clarke was crushed by this insult, though he could not have predicted what came next. When Gary looked at his hotel key and reservation, he found that he was not registered under his own name, but as "A. N. Other." It was as though he was not even considered a real person: he was just "another" member of the Elton party. Already Gary was becoming suspicious that Elton had brought him back to his native Australia just to dump him again. At least this time Gary was in his home country.

Clearly, Gary would be entertaining himself for much of his stay in Sydney, so he set about to do just that. When a friend of his—a hunk of a bodybuilder and a part-time male hustler— phoned him, Gary invited him to spend the night in his room. According to Clarke, "It was Mr. Gay Sydney himself, Sean Roney, the young, blond and beautiful rent boy who'd successfully stalked the 'red light' area of King's Cross, Australia's center for sex hire."[167]

After spending the night in Gary's bed, the following morning Sean came downstairs to the lobby with him. There was Elton, whose eyes popped at the sight of Sean. When asked to introduce him to Elton, Gary presented Sean to his superstar part-time lover.

Elton took Gary aside and told him to invite Sean to the Presidential Suite that evening for a night of cocaine, champagne, and sex. Clarke complied, and they had a drug- and alcohol-filled *ménage a trois.*

On Friday night of that week, Gary Clarke had dinner with record producer Chris Thomas at a Japanese restaurant and then returned to the Sebel Town House. When he entered the lounge of the hotel, there was Elton and his entourage. Gary instantly noted that there was an odd air in the room.

Elton stood up and whispered in his ear, "Don't be upset, Chook, I have asked Renate to marry me." Clarke recalled, "It was nightmareish, like a drawn out death in a horror movie." Then Renate entered the room and said to the shocked Gary, "I can understand how you feel." After that, John Reid put his arm around Gary and sympathetically whispered the word "Unbelievable!" in his ear.[167]

Gary felt betrayed and an air of sheer disbelief. That same week Elton had been snorting cocaine and having three-way gay sex with himself and a male hustler. Now he was suddenly marrying a woman? Who did Elton think he was fooling?

The wedding was to take place four days later, on Tuesday, February 14, 1984, which was Valentine's Day. In New South Wales, the law required that a marriage license had to be applied for thirty days prior to a wedding. Because Elton was a media star, and a wealthy one at that, some legal wrangling took place, and the details were ironed out for the ceremony to take place as planned just four days later.

Renate needed a wedding dress. Elton turned to someone whom he could trust for this task: Gary Clarke. All in the same week he had Clarke lining up a rent boy for sex, and now Elton was giving his male lover the task of picking out a dress for his bride. According to Gary, "Not one of Elton's closest friends would believe he'd take that plunge into hetero marriage. 'It must be a stunt' was the common opinion…it is not often that a homosexual man gets his ex- to choose a wedding dress for his female bride."[167]

Here was John Reid ironing out legal details, and Gary Clarke picking out a wedding dress for the bride. Even Elton had to later concede, "It was basically dishonest…I was so unhappy, I thought that any sort of change…when you take a lot of drugs, and you're out to lunch half the time, you think a change of scenery…. I'll get another house, I'll move to another country."[168] Or, in Elton's case, he just decided to see if he could "switch teams" in the middle of the game. Such is the sheer disillusionment of cocaine.

When news of Elton's impending wedding hit the media, there was a sudden feeding frenzy. The world was in disbelief at this latest development. Messages of shocked congratulations came in from his friends and associates. The British tabloids—especially—had a field day with their coverage. *The Sunday Mirror* even tracked down Linda Woodrow [Sawford] who warned Renate, "I really hope he makes a success of marriage…. If Renate is expecting romance, though, she's picked the wrong guy. He was lousy in bed."[169]

The Daily Express claimed, "Probably none is more startled than his personal assistant and live-in companion of more than eight years, Bob Halley…. Halley who started life with Elton as his chauffeur, has faithfully followed him almost everywhere to the collapse of his own marriage in the 1970s, when he split from his wife, Pearl…. He and his boss even wear 'His and His' earrings, one each of a pair of diamond solitaires."[170]

It was the rock & roll wedding of the year. The bride was dressed in white lace and had tiny blossoms of Baby's Breath in her hair. The groom was in lavender, black, and mauve. He had an orchid pinned to his lapel, and atop his head was one of his 1920s-style boater hats. For him, it was just another show, and for all who observed it the event seemed like more of a publicity stunt than a real wedding.

In the photos taken at the ceremony, Elton flashed smiles, while Renate looked out of her element. Guests at the ceremony included Olivia Newton-John, Bernie Taupin, Molly Meldrum, and drag queen Barry Humphries whose female persona is "Dame Edna Everage." Former lover, John Reid, served as Elton's best man.

Gary was never officially invited to the ceremony at St. Mark's Church in Darling Point and did not attend. He was too shocked and hurt. How could he not have felt utterly betrayed as a friend and as Elton's lover? He felt utterly left out in the cold.

A huge crowd had gathered at the church to catch a glimpse of Elton as a groom. One astonished onlooker shouted out, "Good on you sport, you old poof!"[167] Clarke opted to sit in his hotel suite and soak in his bathtub, hoping to wash away some of his pain. While in the water-filled tub, he heard the front door of his hotel room open and in burst Molly. It seemed that Meldrum was worried that Gary had done something drastic. Meldrum was directly followed by the bride herself, still in her wedding dress and holding her bouquet of wedding flowers. Renate placed her bouquet on the television set and told Gary that the flowers were for him. It wasn't until 10:30 that evening, in the middle of the reception, that Elton realized that Clarke was missing. He phoned him, imploring him to come down to the hotel ballroom.

Gary arrived in time to hear the groom make a speech, including reading aloud the congratulatory telegram that Michael Jackson had sent. Imitating Jackson's oddly Mickey Mouse–high voice, Elton read: "I had to set my hair on fire to make the front pages but you only had to go and get married!"[167]

However, one of the funniest telegrams sent was from Billy Gaff who wrote, "You may still be standing but we're all on the fucking floor!"[88]

At midnight Elton announced that he and his new bride were on their way up to their Honeymoon suite. That was his way of clearing out the crowd, but a select group—including Gary Clarke—was invited up to Elton's room for an after party. Most grooms would like to have been left alone with their new bride at this point. Not this one. The party full of gay boys and ex-boyfriends went on until sunup. According to Clarke's autobiography, one of the party activities included snorting lines of coke.

Molly Meldrum passed out at 4:00 a.m., and Gary took him downstairs to sleep in his room and then retuned to the party. By the time he left, at 6:00 a.m., it appeared that the bride and groom were not yet ready to end the party.

It had been a shocking week of bizarre events for Gary Clarke. The next morning, when Gary ventured out into the hotel lobby, he ran into Elton, who told him that he was no longer invited to join the entourage on the upcoming New Zealand tour. It was Elton's tactless way of telling Clarke to "piss off."

Clarke understandably felt hurt and dejected, though he was coming to expect such treatment from Elton, the petulantly spoiled superstar. The one consolation was that Gary was allowed to retain the rental car Elton had ready for him for an extra week. With that, Clarke made the 1,000 kilometer drive from Sydney to Melbourne. "Round Three" of Gary's love affair with Elton John was officially over.

Less than two weeks later, Renate came to Melbourne to see Gary before she flew off to England—alone. It seemed that the marriage was already on the rocks. As Clarke was to describe the situation, "Elton was panicking and Renate had fled to England." On the way to the British Isles, she stopped in Melbourne to see Gary. Renate told Gary, "We'll sort out our problems at Woodside. We'll have a lot more time to ourselves to talk...I guess...no interruptions."[167]

While Renate was confiding in Clarke that the marriage was already an impossible mess, a press release was sent out claiming that she was going to Woodside to redecorate it as the new "lady of the house."

Although John Reid tried to talk Elton into getting Renate to sign a prenuptial agreement prior to the wedding, he wouldn't think of it. The roses from the bridal bouquet were barely dead, and already it seemed that this was a huge mistake. It wasn't a matter of: "Will this marriage fall apart?" It was a matter of: "How long until this marriage falls apart?"

When Renate got to Woodside, the staff was instructed to do all they could to make her happy. Ultimately, the only things she changed at Elton's mansion were some renovations in the kitchen and setting up her own bedroom, since the pop star had instructed her that she should have her own room.

He already realized that this marriage was a huge mistake. In retrospect he explained, "The reason I got married is because I met a wonderful girl who I thought was the most incredible human being, and when I was an addict I would do anything to change my situation. I thought getting married would make me more responsible. Nothing changed, because the real problem was, I was a drug addict…. I was totally irrational."[171]

After Renate went to England, and Elton was finished with his New Zealand engagements, he returned to Australia. Elton flew Gary to Sydney, but he did not resume his sexual relationship with Clarke. At least not yet.

On April 17, 1984, Elton launched a 44-date concert tour of Europe. It started in Sarajevo, Yugoslavia, and finished up in London at Wembley Stadium on June 30. In the middle of the tour, Elton flew back to England from Copenhagen, Denmark, to attend the Watford Football Club's very first FA Cup Final. The event was held in Wembley Stadium, and they lost to Everton with a score of 2-0.

With Renate on his arm, Elton hoped that he would gain respectability in the eyes of the Watford soccer club fans. Claimed Clarke, "Elton craved acceptance from Watford's board members and supporters who he thought considered their patron 'a big fat poof with too much money and no brains.'"[167]

Back on tour, when he played Gdansk, Poland, Elton's show was attended by Lech Walesa, who was the Nobel Peace Prize winner and leader of Poland's Solidarity trade union. Elton visited Walesa's apartment for over an hour while a pack of press photographers paced outside the building to get a shot of the world-peace advocate and the Rocket Man. What did Elton John talk to Walesa about for an hour in his residence? What else? Soccer!

According to Elton, "Lech Walesa's a fantastic bloke. I went 'round to his house in Gdansk, and we just talked about football for an hour-and-a-half. He was wonderful. He came to the gig that evening. I said, 'Why did you want to meet me?' He said, 'It's the only way I can get any media coverage.'"[43]

In June 1984, Elton's twenty-fifth album, *Breaking Hearts* was released in America and in July in Europe. Recording with his longtime band—including Davey Johnstone, Dee Murray, and Nigel Olsson—it was another attempt to recapture the classic Elton magic of the mid-1970s. Produced by Chris Thomas with lyrics by Bernie Taupin, *Breaking Hearts* peaked at Number One in Australia and Switzerland. In addition, it hit Number Two in the U.K., Number Five in Germany, Number Seven in Norway, and Number 20 in the U.S. It was also certified Gold in both the U.S. and the U.K.

Elton tried a lot of different musical styles on *Breaking Hearts*. One of the most winning tracks is the beautiful ballad about regrets, "Breaking Hearts (Ain't What It Used to Be)". It has the flawless sound of a song that might have become a hit standard in the 1950s for the likes of Peggy Lee or Perry Como.

However, *Breaking Hearts* is best remembered for the huge international Top Ten hit: "Sad Songs (Say So Much)." That single hit Number Four in Australia and Canada, Number Five in America, Number Seven in England, and Number 22 in Germany. The anti-Apartheid inspired song "Passengers" hit Number Five in the U.K. and Number Nine in Australia. "Who Wears These Shoes" made it to Number 16 in the U.S. and Number 50 in the U.K. And, "In Neon" hit Number 38 in the U.S. And, the song "Breaking Hearts (Ain't What They Used to Be)" made it to Number 59 in the U.K.

In America, it was on the Adult Contemporary chart where Elton was scoring the strongest. On that chart in *Billboard*, Elton's "Sad Songs" hit Number Two and "In Neon" and "Who Wears These Shoes" both hit Number 11.

Interestingly enough, the song "Breaking Hearts (Ain't What They Used to Be)" was released on February 14, 1985, to commemorate the one year anniversary of the wedding of Elton and Renate. It seemed that Elton's fans had even less interest in his marriage than even he did, if that was possible.

The press reviews for the *Breaking Hearts* album were lukewarm at best. According to Peter Puterbaugh in *Rolling Stone*,

"Elton John's latest single, 'Sad Songs (Say So Much)' sounds like an oldie-but-goodie the first time you hear it. Besides being alliteratively catchy, it sinks into the subconscious like some vapidly inveigling ad jingle."[216]

Mary Ann Cassata, in *The Elton John Scrap Book*, points out, "Musically, *Breaking Hearts* suffered from being the first in a long line of albums released throughout the '80s and into the '90s that took the emphasis away from the most important sound, Elton's piano."[221]

Meanwhile in Australia, Gary Clarke still considered Renate to be a dear friend of his, and he often talked to her on the telephone. She told him about her marriage, "The two of us spend hours watching video movies together, and he's been buying heaps of movies, so I told him, 'I'm going to catalog them.'… I thought I loved chocolates but Elton's just as bad. When we're watching movies, we go through mountains of them."[167]

Bernie Taupin had used this image in a new song for the forthcoming *Ice on Fire* album. It was a song called "Candy by the Pound." Essentially, the song heralded the fact that being in love with Renate was as sweet as eating candies by the pound.

In late 1984, Sheila and "Derf" flew to Australia to vacation with Gary Clarke's parents, with whom they had remained quite friendly. While there, Sheila confided in Gary that she was still stung by the public insult of not having the chance to attend Elton's wedding to Renate. Furthermore, she was not happy with her son's new bride. Sheila found her to be pleasant, but not overly warm. She also told him that she and "Derf" were not the frequent guests at Woodside that they had once been, before Renate's arrival.

Furthermore, the staff and everyone in the Elton entourage knew that the marriage was a disaster from the words "I do." However, Elton kept chirping to the press that everything was wonderful with his new bride. It was like the marriage was a fairy tale story that he had dreamt up. He gushed to the media about how in love they were, and how he longed to have children. In reality, it was sheer nonsense.

Elton was having more fun gallivanting around with his new pal, George Michael. They shared so much in common. They both complained about growing up with distant fathers and doting mothers. They had both become pop stars and millionaires at a very young age, and they were both gay men who—at the time—were holding up a façade of being heterosexual.

In March 1985, it was Elton who publicly presented George Michael with an Ivor Novello Award as the year's Best Songwriter. The award was for penning the song "Careless Whisper." Elton told the audience that George was "the Paul McCartney of his generation." The sentiment brought the honoree to tears.

George Michael was honored to appear on two of the most important and memorable songs on Elton's *Ice on Fire* album: "Wrap Her Up" and "Nikita." When Elton met him, George was about to leave his singing partner in the group Wham!, Andrew Ridgeley. George was also about to embark on an extremely successful solo recording career.

Elton gave George Michael a huge boost to his solo career by asking the young singer to do a duet version of his song "Don't Let the Sun Go Down on Me" at the televised *Live Aid* concert, held on July 15, 1985. At the event, Ridgeley and Kiki Dee provided the background vocals.

Live Aid was a huge event, simulcast from London's Wembley Stadium, RFK Stadium in Washington D.C., and from Luna Park in Sydney, Australia. While Elton and George sang their duet at Wembley, Gary Clarke was at Luna Park as the guest of Molly Meldrum. Whenever Meldrum introduced Clarke to the VIPs there, he did so by announcing, "This is Crystal. He used to be with Elton."[167]

Ice on Fire was one of those albums you either loved or hated. Some people find it to be the most consistently effervescent of Elton's '80s albums. The joyful pop confection "Candy By the Pound," the diva fest with George Michael on "Wrap Her Up," and even the confessional "Tell Me What the Papers Say," all have a lot of life and excitement. *Ice on Fire* had Gus Dudgeon back on board as Elton's producer. For that reason, the sound quality sparkled with some of the audible glamour and sharpness that Elton's albums possessed during his heyday in the 1970s. The opening number, "This Town," features background vocals by the disco quartet Sister Sledge. Roger Taylor and John Deacon from the rock group Queen can be heard on the song "Too Young," which has long been suspected to be about Elton's relationship with Gary Clarke.

When the album was released, the critics didn't exactly love it. In fact, Rob Hoerburger in *Rolling Stone* was especially chilly towards *Ice on Fire*. According to his review of the album, "It's too much to expect a substantial album from Elton John at this point, but with the return of his longtime producer, Gus Dudgeon, for *Ice on Fire*, there was hope that he might at least whip up a few frothy singles.... Elton John is now an old cartoon."[217]

In England, *Ice on Fire* hit Number Three on the charts. But in America, it peaked at a dismal Number 48. It is best remembered for its biggest chart hit, the song "Nikita." The song became as controversial as "Daniel" had been in the 1970s. In Russian the name "Nikita" is a man's name and the song is a love song. To camouflage this gender-bending, the video that acompanied the song on MTV featured a woman in a Russian military coat as the elusive "Nikita." Regardless of whether he was singing about his love of a man or a woman, the song hit Number One in Germany, Number Two in Canada, Number Three in the U.K., and in America the song hit Number Seven. Two additional singles from the album also scored well on the charts: "Wrap Her Up" and "Cry to Heaven."

Two of the biggest singles Elton had in 1985 and 1986 found him sharing the microphone with other singers. Although it was never officially released on any of Elton's 1980s albums, the aggressive rock & roll song "Act of War," with soul singer Millie Jackson, is truly one of the most dynamic recordings of Elton's career.

Originally, Elton had conceived "Act of War" as a duet to record with Tina Turner. However, when he sent her the song, Tina turned him down. Not about to scrap his song, he invited Millie Jackson to record it with him. Millie is the voice of such '70s R&B hits as "Ask Me What You Want," "Hurts So Good," and "If You're Not in Love By Monday." She also had a bawdy reputation with her stage acts and her recordings. One of her most famous albums depicted her on the cover on a toilet, and her other albums included *Get It Out'cha System* and *Back to the Shit*. The slightly off-color Ms. Jackson proved the perfect foil for Elton on this song.

When Elton learned that Millie Jackson was scheduled to come to England for a series of concert performances, he got a demo tape of "Act of War" to her immediately. According to Millie, she leapt at the opportunity to record with Elton, declaring, "I'll do it no matter what key it's in!"[220]

In this song, Elton plays the part of the henpecked man whose woman—Millie Jackson—considers it an "Act of War" that he is running around town drinking and carrying on scandalously. In the colorful and fun-to-watch music video, both Elton and Millie look like they are having a blast hurling verbal bombs at each other. Elton is dressed in one of the most bizarre outfits of the decade: an overly long waistcoat, tuxedo pants, and yards of military braid. On his head is an odd sort of pillbox hat decorated with feathers. The video ends with Elton and Millie covered with dust after blowing a hole in a brick wall.

"Act of War" appeared as a bonus track on the original versions of the *Ice on Fire* CDs and cassettes. It was also released as a 12" single and a standard 7" single as well. It later became one of the highlights of Elton's 1990 boxed set *To Be Continued*. It made it to Number 32 in the U.K., Number 39 in Germany, Number 50 in Australia, and Number 94 in America.

In January 1986, the quartet of Dionne Warwick, Stevie Wonder, Gladys Knight, and Elton John took the song "That's What Friends Are For" all the way to Number One in the U.S. and Canada, and Number 16 in England. The Dionne Warwick album that featured the song, *Friends*, hit Number 12 in America and was certified Gold. In the U.S., this was to be the highest charting single and album Elton appeared on in the 1980s.

"That's What Friends Are For" was significant for many reasons. First of all, it was Elton's first American Number One single since "Don't Go Breaking My Heart" with Kiki Dee in 1976. It was also the big reunion of Dionne Warwick and her '60s hit-making composer Burt Bacharach. To top it all off, the sales of the single became the first and biggest hit song to give some of its proceeds to AIDS research.

It was very fitting that Elton should be part of this record-breaking single, which sat in the Number One spot in America for four weeks. The video that was filmed for the song depicted each of the stars in their prime, raising funds for a worthy cause.

At the time, it was controversial to speak out about AIDS. In the early 1980s, when AIDS spread around the world, it was labeled "the gay plague." Even in usually liberal show business, many gay people experienced extreme prejudice during this era. Finally, several people in show business—starting with Elizabeth Taylor and Dionne Warwick—stood up and supported victims. Elton was proudly part of this movement.

In January 1986, Elton John and Bernie Taupin were awarded £5 million in their lawsuit against Dick James Music. However, subsequent appeals brought the awarded monies down to six figures, substantially less than £1 million. It had been a long and drawn out court case that ended up costing Elton millions of dollars. What he was awarded barely recouped the court costs.

On February 1, 1986, Dick James had a massive heart attack, from which he would not recover. The pressure of being hauled into court week after week to testify in his defense had taken a great toll on him. According to his son, Stephen James, "I'm sure that if it hadn't been for the strain of the court case and the impugning of his reputation, which hurt him so much, he would never have had the attack, and might still be alive today. I still feel so furious that something so unimportant by comparison with my father's life should have caused that."[87]

For Elton, the guilt of possibly hastening Dick James' death weighed heavily on him. When it was suggested that maybe he should contest the court's decision, Elton claimed, "I didn't really want to go to Court. I don't really want to talk about it much, because Dick's dead now. It was unfortunate. It means a soured relationship between the James family and myself. Which I didn't have before. Before we went to court I tried to have lunch with Dick. I tried to say, 'Let's settle this,' and he wouldn't."[43]

That same year, the British tabloids began to run stories about how the Elton/Renate marriage was hitting the rocks. It seemed that the only time they were together was at high-profile events, including Watford games, an occasional awards show, or at the 1986 royal wedding of Prince Andrew and Sarah Ferguson.

Whenever he could, Elton tried to deflect questions about his marriage. That year he appeared on a French television show called *The Truth Game*. In the context of the show, callers on the phone would get to ask celebrity guest stars embarrassing questions, in the hope of getting some sort of "scoop." One caller said to Elton, "I remember seeing you on a beach in St. Tropez, you were surrounded by beautiful boys." Very quick on his feet, Elton volleyed back the reply, "Before the caller saw me with a beautiful boy, and now I'm with a beautiful woman."[174]

In 1986, Elton was still making grand statements about how his marriage to Renate was wonderful. Was Elton trying to convince himself that the marriage was sound, or was he trying to convince others? That year he told Chris Salewicz of Britain's Q magazine, "I'd never ruled out the possibility of getting married if I met the right person. And when I met Renate, it was quite clear that I was going to marry her, even though I'd never been out with her. I wasn't really surprised, I suppose. I think a lot of other people were.... But I'm sure there were quite a few bitchy remarks going about around the world."[43]

Much of Elton's 1986 schedule was filled with what was being billed as the *Elton John World Tour*. On January 3, 1986, Elton was performing in Glasgow, Scotland, part of a "British Isles" tour leg that would encompass shows in Newcastle and Belfast. The final Belfast concert was on January 11. The touring resumed March 1 in Barcelona, Spain, and Elton and entourage traveled their way through France, Switzerland, Germany, Austria, and the Netherlands, before finishing in Belgium on April 26.

On June 20, Elton performed as part of the all-star charity concert, *The 10th Anniversary of The Prince's Trust*, before a sold-out crowd at Wembley Stadium that included Prince Charles and Princess Diana. The other acts on the bill that night included Paul McCartney, Tina Turner, Big Country, Paul Young, Phil Collins, Eric Clapton, Joan Armatrading, Rod Stewart, George Michael, and more. Elton performed "I'm Still Standing" and played piano for Paul McCartney's set of songs, including "Long Tall Sally," "Get Back," and "I Saw Her Standing There."

The American leg of Elton John's 1986 World Tour was a huge success. Reviewing his opening night concert in *USA Today*, Jim McFarlin reported from Pine Knob, the famed outdoor auditorium in suburban Detroit, "John lit up the night all by himself, in floor-length capes of glitter and multi-colored spangles, designed by Hollywood's Bob Mackie, and topped off at first by a foot-high wig."[224]

The thirty-eight dates in the American tour were taking their toll, though. There were reports from the road that Elton was suffering from laryngitis, and by the time he got to many of his encores, he was raspy and had no vocal power at all. Suddenly, and without warning, things started to spin dangerously out of Elton John's control again.

CHAPTER FOURTEEN

I Fall Apart and Go It Alone

It was in late 1986 that things started to crumble for Elton John. His marriage, his recording career, and his personal life all began to unravel. His latest album, *Leather Jackets*, was released that fall, and it had the sad distinction of being labeled the worst album of his entire career. Furthermore, his marriage to Renate was crumbling, he was depressed, and his personal substance abuses only magnified the problems.

Yet, from the outside it seemed like business was as usual. While he was on his world tour that year, on September 13, 1986, I personally met Elton John for the first time. My publicist, David Salidor, had gotten us tickets to see the Rocket Man in concert at Madison Square Garden. In addition to a great pair of tickets, we also had backstage passes so that we could meet Elton before the show. This was all arranged by Elton's close friend Tony King. I had known Tony for years at that point, through David, and if Elton was around, Tony usually was not far away.

When we got backstage at The Garden, David and I were shown to Elton's dressing room. Actually he had a waiting room outside his main dressing room, and when we got there, who else should be waiting for an audience with Elton but Andy Warhol. I had known Andy for a couple of years, having met him at several parties and media events.

"Andy, how are you doing?" I asked as I extended my hand to shake his.

"Good, how are you?" he asked. Shaking hands with Andy Warhol was always an odd experience because he was one of those people who would present his hand like he had just handed you a dead chicken. He never moved his hand, you would shake it, and then let go of it to have it instantly retracted.

David and I chatted with Tony King for a few minutes, and then Tony glanced towards the door that led to the rock star's inner-sanctum. "There's Elton," Tony announced as The Pinball Wizard himself emerged from the dressing room.

Sure enough, when Elton walked into the room, there was a certain "star quality" that he instantly exuded. "Hi, Andy," Elton said, walking over to Warhol. Andy mumbled a greeting to Elton, as Tony said, "And, I want you to meet my friend David Salidor, and his friend the writer, Mark Bego."

Elton warmly greeted us and said, "Nice to meet you, thanks for coming to the show." Obviously, Elton had a lot of things on his mind that night. It was a fast exchange without a lot of small talk, and Elton excused himself saying, "Well, we have a show to do here."

David, Andy Warhol, his guest, and I left the dressing room. Although it was not a long visit, at least I got to say "Hello" and find out firsthand what the Rocket Man was like face-to-face. When David and I got to our seats, we witnessed a phenomenal show. It was kind of hard to believe that the "Elton John" we saw onstage, jumping around and singing his heart out, was the same unassuming man whom we had just met backstage.

But that was the dichotomy that was Elton John. On one hand he could be a shy and modest person, and only minutes later he was onstage pounding on the piano keys like there was no tomorrow. One of the most memorable and outlandish things that happened that night was the concert's encore: Elton John came out onstage dressed in full drag as Tina Turner, complete with leather mini-skirt, makeup, and a huge "What's Love Got to Do With It?" wig on his head.

The evening inspired Andy Warhol to write in his famed *Andy Warhol Diaries*, "September 16, 1986.... Left at 8:00 to go to see Elton John (tickets $40). He came out like an angel in a halo with a red wig, plus a tommy-hawk wig. And, oh God, is he fat. He had on a silver-lame caftan, but tight—a skintight caftan—and the audience loved him.... At 10:00 Elton was still going strong but I had to leave."[234] It was quite a memorable evening for everyone involved, even if Andy did miss the Tina Turner dress.

One of the things that Elton had on his mind at this time was his next album. With a rougher, more stripped-down sound, *Leather Jackets* should have been a huge success for Elton, but it missed the mark and failed to find an audience. It contained several songs about what was going on in his life at that time: "Don't Trust that Woman" sounds suspiciously like the end of his wedded state. "I Fall Apart" and "Go It Alone" find Elton in a fragile and somber mode. Although the album's songs were mainly written with Bernie, a couple of other notable writers were involved as well. The song "Memory of Love" reunites Elton with lyricist Gary Osborne. Having gone through all of the lyrics that Bernie had given him, Elton turned to old files and found this leftover gem from his work with Osborne.

The cover of the *Leather Jackets* album is a very Andy Warhol-style, nine-image montage of Elton in a leather jacket, screened in various colors on a background of hot pink. On the back of the CD booklet, Elton and his band were photographed in leather, as though they were members of a tough motorcycle gang. Elton appears more appropriately dressed for a night at West Village gay discotheque 12 West than he does for a stint in a motorcycle gang.

Leather Jackets had a nice array of guest stars on it from Cher (songwriter), to John Deacon (bass) and Roger Taylor (drums) of Queen, and Kiki Dee (background vocals). Gus Dudgeon was back to produce this album, and John Reid was once again credited as Elton's manager. Whatever problems "Sharon" and "Beryl" had been having, they managed to patch them up. According to Duncan Faure, Elton would laughingly refer to John Reid as "My manager moll," as though Reid was his female sidekick.

It was also during this era that Elton first publicly admitted that he and John Reid were once live-in boyfriends as well as client and manager. "Yeah, for five years," Elton told *Q* magazine. "Yet we still work together, and are still as close as we ever were. That was quite incredible: the fact that we got through that."[43]

According to Elton, "There are some records where I was not together at all. *Leather Jackets* comes to mind, with its biker cover. Very butch, but a total disaster. I was not a well budgie: I was married and it was just one bag of coke after another."[47]

One of the songs on *Leather Jackets* is called "Don't Trust That Woman," and it is credited to the songwriters "Lady Choc Ice" and Cher. Elton had already called himself "Lord Choc Ice," now who was this lady? It is actually Elton himself, under another one of his female names.

When Cher wrote the song "Don't Trust That Woman" with Elton, she was looking forward to her songwriting credit on a song with Elton with her name appearing first, since it was in alphabetical order that way. To completely piss Cher off, Elton decided to credit himself as "Lady Choc Ice," so she wouldn't be credited on an "Elton John" song after all.

Like all of Elton's albums, *Leather Jackets* does have some flashes of brilliance. The song "Paris" is a beautiful and completely overlooked ballad. In 1985 Elton and Renate had temporarily separated. He took up residence in London's Mayfair Hotel. He wrote the song "Paris" while there. According to Elton, "The melody was written practically all the way through without a break."[223]

The song "Angeline" has a gritty rock & roll sound that Elton's albums had been lacking for quite some time. When "Heartache All Over the World" was released as a single, it made it to Number Seven in Australia, Number 45 in the U.K., Number 55 in the U.S., and Number 58 in Canada.

Looking back on *Leather Jackets*, Elton John considers it the worst album of his career. "Gus Dudgeon did his best, but you can't work with a loony."[184]

The Philadelphia Inquirer reviewer Ken Tucker hated the album—a lot. He wrote, "This is the worst album he's ever recorded, the first time he hasn't even written a melody that can redeem the banalities of songwriting Bernie Taupin."[222]

Leather Jackets peaked at Number 12 in Norway, Number 13 in Switzerland, Number 21 in Germany, Number 24 in the U.K., and an astonishing low Number 91 in the U.S. "Slow Rivers," a song which Elton recorded as a duet with his friend Cliff Richard, made it to Number 44 in the U.K. and Number 82 in Australia in 1986.

In February 1986, Elton was given a joint award along with Andrew Ridgeley and George Michael of Wham! by the British Phonographic Industry. They received the BPI Awards for "Outstanding Contribution to British Music." After accepting the award, Elton complained continuously to the London music media. According to pissed-off Elton, "I wanted to go on holiday with my wife, and I curtailed my holiday because they said they were going to give me an award for, basically, being old. And the day of the actual thing I was told, 'This is going to be the biggest event of your life: the biggest tribute you'll ever receive.' And I go up there, and there's Wham! up there and it was suddenly apparent this was all bullshit. And I'd fallen for it. I knew all along that it was bullshit."[43]

Whenever Elton is upset with something or someone, it isn't long before he makes his opinion made. He never has been much for suffering in silence.

According to Elton, he was very happy with the way he had put his career back together in the 1980s. "I worked my way back," he proclaimed in 1986. "It's been nice work. In Europe, for example, that happened. Previously my success had been in Britain, America and Australia, but in Europe I didn't sell a thing. But in America I'd lost my acceptance: I used to be the darling of FM…"[43] Oh well, no use crying over spilt milk. It was a whole new period of creativity, growth, and experimentation for Elton's music. It was also an era when Elton wore some of his craziest stage outfits. In addition to dressing as Ronald McDonald and Tina Turner, he was not afraid to play the part of rock & roll's Court Jester.

Although it was anything but stable, Elton continued to claim to the press that his marriage to Renate was on solid ground. According to him in 1986, "We've been married three years next February, which is longer, I'm sure, than most people thought it would last."[43] Much longer!

Since Renate remained in England during the majority of 1986, she and Elton were essentially living separate lives at this point. When Elton was in Australia from November 5 to December 1986, doing a series of twenty-seven concerts, including the one which was captured on the album *Live in Australia*, he was free to do what he pleased. He got hold of Gary Clarke and asked him if he could arrange for a ménage a trois with another guy. Still hopelessly in love with Elton, Gary complied.

Living near Melbourne's red-light district, Gary had become friendly with a pair of eighteen-year-old male hustlers, Stephen and Mick. Clarke took the duo to the first of Elton's Melbourne shows. Elton didn't like Stephen, as he looked a bit rough, but he was attracted to Mick. As Elton told Gary that he fancied Mick, he licked his lips with approval.

When Gary and Mick arrived at Elton's suite, an hour after the show, there was the Rocket Man wearing nothing but a bathrobe. After preparatory cocaine and champagne, the festivities began. The encounter was over before long, and Gary was handed a wad of cash to pay for Mick's services. Elton suggested they leave immediately.

Here was Elton still feeding the press stories about how he and Renate were so happily married, yet the reality was something quite different. Cocaine and boys still reigned supreme in Eltonland.

When he returned to Sydney later that year, Elton had a local blond surfer boy in tow. According to Clarke, the members of Elton John's entourage referred to the boy as "ELF." The letters stood for: "Elton's Latest Fuck." As a token of Elton's appreciation for the boy, the singer bought the surfer a new surf board.

In November and December of 1986, Elton launched his 27-date tour of Australia, which was formally dubbed *Tour De Force*. His concerts with the Melbourne Symphony Orchestra on this tour were brilliant high points in a very muddled year for Elton. They yielded a television special, a Top 40 album, and huge Top Ten single. However, they did not come without a high degree of drama and extreme trauma attached.

One of the most exciting aspects of his trip to Australia in late 1986 was his return to one of his old gimmicks for several of the concerts. He was going to perform some of his greatest hits with a full orchestra, utilizing Paul Buckmaster's arrangements. In this case, it was the Melbourne Symphony Orchestra. The grand scheme was that the final show of the tour was not only to be a huge live event but it was also going to be an Australian live television telecast and a new live album as well.

Just as in the 1970s, again Elton had problems with some of the members of the Melbourne Symphony Orchestra, getting them enthused about playing with a "mere" rock star. Some of the musicians refused to participate in the concerts. Elton recalls, "I came out to meet them and let them know they weren't dealing with Ozzy Osbourne."[235]

The shows were set up so that Elton would first present a rock & roll set with his rock musicians, and then for the second half of the show, he would return to the stage dressed as Amadeus Mozart, complete with wig. While dressed as Mozart, he would then go into a set of his songs with the Melbourne Symphony Orchestra.

The earliest songs from his career, which appeared on the *Elton John* album, fared especially well, particularly "Sixty Years On," "I Need You to Turn To," and "The Greatest Discovery."

However, it was not all smooth sailing. In the middle of the tour came another of Elton's love dramas. It seemed that Elton had fallen madly in love with the first violin player with the Melbourne Symphony Orchestra, a man by the name of Robert. When the violin player invited Elton to his house for Christmas Day dinner, the pop superstar expected something under the mistletoe. Imagine his surprise when the violin player opened the front door only to introduce Elton to his wife and kids.

Elton was crushed when Robert wouldn't have sex with him, and he bitterly complained to ex-boyfriend Gary Clarke about his unrequited love for Robert. When Clarke asked Elton if Robert knew of his feelings, Elton replied, "I told him I loved him, and I wanted him. Can I get any more direct than that?"[167] He was frustrated that sometimes even his star stature could not garner him sex with people he wanted.

More worrisome, while he was on the Australian leg of the tour, Elton had progressively suffered from throat problems. Gus Dudgeon was to recall, "He did two concerts in Perth that went fine, then on the third night, he was sitting in his dressing room beforehand, and suddenly found he couldn't speak at all. The concert had to be cancelled, and Elton was told by a doctor not to speak at all for four days. He had to go around with a little blackboard, writing down everything he wanted to say."[87]

For three consecutive nights in Sydney, Elton had severe throat problems and would go off in coughing fits in the middle of the show. Finally, he went to see a real throat specialist. As Dudgeon recalled, "We were all at the bar at the Sebel Town House when he came in. He said, 'They think it might be throat cancer.'"[87]

The tour finished with eight consecutive dates in Melbourne. There was talk about Elton pulling the plug on the tour right then and there, but somehow the shows did go on. And, miraculously, he made it to the climactic night in front of the live television cameras on December 14, 1986. However, clearly something was very wrong with Elton's throat. When doctors discovered nodules on his vocal cords, surgery became the only answer. There were two important medical issues at hand. First of all, were the nodules cancerous or not? Only a biopsy would determine that. And the second issue concerned what lasting effects that throat surgery would have on Elton's singing voice.

On January 6, 1987, Elton John had throat surgery, at the hands of John Tonkin at a private clinic in Sydney, Australia. Fortunately for Elton, the growths on his vocal cords were benign, and he was expected to make a full recovery. As he recuperated in Australia, he was flooded with get-well cards, flowers, and telegrams, including notes from Sarah Ferguson, Duchess of York, and Diana, Princess of Wales. The one person who was conspicuously missing from the sick bed was his wife, the estranged Renate. Instead of coming to Sydney, she decided to remain in Los Angeles.

Clearly, there was major trouble in paradise. Reportedly, Elton had routinely left Renate out of his life for most of the past year. Then when it came time for his surgery in Australia, he demanded that she come rushing to his side, for the sake of what the press might think. When she refused to come, Elton went into one of his rage-filled tantrums.

Sure enough, Renate's absence did not go unnoticed. Elton had yet to recover from his throat surgery, when he found himself in the middle of his latest battle with the British press. The January 11, 1987, issue of the London tabloid, *Sunday People*, reported "Superstar Elton John's marriage is on the rocks because of his bisexual lifestyle. Friends say he is now determined to get a divorce after spending just three days with his wife Renate in the past four months."[236]

Quoting a mysterious "Graham X," *The Sun* also published several lurid allegations about Elton's personal involvement with "rent boys" and activities at coke-laden brawls. "[Elton] loved his boys to be tattooed skin-heads or punks with spiky hair, snorted cocaine, throughout the orgies, which lasted up to four days, and begged the teenagers to indulge in his bondage fantasies."[237]

Although Elton immediately denied these allegations and issued a libel writ against *The Sun*, he soon found that such issues had to be taken into court and took a long time to resolve. Although he professed his innocence, a case had to be built and then resolved legally. In the interim, the press continued to spin their tales of debauchery about Elton, gambling on the fact that their main source—"Graham X" [a/k/a Stephen Hardy]—was telling the truth.

Rather than ignoring the story and just letting it disappear, Elton chose the very expensive route of suing *The Sun*. *The Sun* was owned by one of the richest men in the media world, Rupert Murdoch. Elton was not going to back down, though. After all, he was one of the richest men in Britain, so he could afford a team of top-notch solicitors to argue his case. However, he was opening a huge can of worms by taking this action.

According to Elton, "As soon as I announced I was going to sue, Mick Jagger rang me up. He said, 'Listen, I've been through this kind of scandal—just leave it for two or three days and it'll be forgotten. In the long run it's not worth fighting because they'll try to rake up so much muck.' I said, 'No, I'm going ahead. They can say I'm "a fat old sod," they can call me "a poof," but they musn't lie about me because then I'm going to fight."[44]

The case of "Elton vs. The Tabloids" became a regular soap opera throughout 1987. Suddenly, whatever Elton did, he was front-page news, and he found he was now living his life under a microscope. Wherever he went, he was tailed by reporters. According to him, "It became James Bond.... I was looking over my shoulder the whole time, I didn't know who to trust. You see, I hadn't lived my personal life in public before. I've always been very discreet. But now my private life was on the front page...it did me in."[44]

When it ran out of "rent boy" stories, *The Sun* turned its focus to Elton's treatment of his dogs. *The Sun* alleged that Elton had the voice boxes of his Rottweiler dogs removed, starting an investigation by the RSPCA. Elton's denials merely served as further stories in *The Sun*. As lust for this "Elton-Gate" was swelling, a man claiming to be Elton's former lover suddenly surfaced with Polaroid snapshots of their trysts. It literally became insane. Before this was all resolved, Elton's legal team had issued more than ten writs of protest against *The Sun*'s actions.

Elton spent his 40th birthday at a gala party in his honor, held at John Reid's ten-bedroom opulent Georgian mansion, near Ricmansworth, Hertfordshire. The guest list included George

Harrison, Ringo Starr, Bob Geldof, Lionel Richie, Eric Clapton, Phil Collins, Britt Ekland, and film director Ken Russell. Not long before midnight, in a chauffeur-driven Jaguar, accompanied by Secret Service agents, the Duke and Duchess of York arrived to pay their respects to the birthday boy. Conspicuously absent from the event was Elton's wife, Renate.

While he was in the middle of his battle with *The Sun*, Elton went into one of his deepest blue moods. For several weeks he became a prisoner in his own house, afraid to leave the secure walls of Woodside.

In spite of what all was brewing in the British headlines, Renate remained legally married to Elton. However, there were already rumors claiming that Elton was ready to buy Renate out of the marriage for a settlement of £5 million and a luxury West End flat.

On April 1, 1987, Elton made his first concert performance post-throat surgery at the AIDS benefit show billed as *Stand by Me* at Wembley Stadium. He sang the Carole King classic, "Will You Still Love Me Tomorrow" and his own recent hit "I Guess That's Why They Call it the Blues."

In July 1987, *Elton John Live in Australia* was released in the United States, where it peaked on the charts at Number 24. In September of that year it was released in Europe, hitting Number Nine in Switzerland and Number 43 in the U.K. Three singles were released from this album. The live version of "Your Song" hit Number 85 in the U.K. and Number 90 in Australia. And "Take Me to the Pilot" charted at Number 37 on the American "Adult Contemporary" chart. However, it was the live remake of "Candle in the Wind" that became the album's biggest hit. That song peaked at Number Five in the U.K. and Canada, Number Six in the U.S., Number 55 in Germany, and Number 92 in Australia.

The press was mixed on the *Live in Australia* album. According to Brian Chin in the *New York Post*, "The idea of recording this live album was a strange one. Elton's voice is stretched to a painful breaking point.... But the quality of the songs—some not performed live in a decade—is undiminished."[246]

In *The All Music Guide*, Stephen Thomas Erlewine writes, "It's easy to think of this as a fairly standard live album…it's far more interesting, even vital, than you might think."[96]

Speaking of *Live in Australia*, Elton stated, "It was a very special album to me. It was me falling to bits, I couldn't sing. I sang, but I don't know how I sang. Most of that album was taken from the last night of the tour, and on things like 'Don't Let the Sun Go Down on Me,' I was crying when I was doing that."[78]

This was an era in which Elton had a lot of time on his hands to reassess his life. One of the things that Elton was most known for was his generosity. When he had done the concerts in Australia in November and December, he went overboard with lavish gifts. He went so far as to give all 88 members of the Melbourne Symphony Orchestra £500 watches from Cartier. "I still am generous," Elton admitted. "That's part and parcel of me. That's part of my nature. And I hope I never change that."[43]

By now his tantrums had taken on legendary status. According to Elton, "I've thrown my fair share of rock star tantrums. Always over totally unreasonable things. *Spinal Tap* stuff, like the bread won't fit the cheese. I used to have a very explosive temper like that. I think it's much better now. Suddenly I used to snap. I don't do that so much anymore. But if I do, people think, 'Oh, fuck off!'"[43]

Depression was still a factor with Elton. But what the hell was he doing being depressed? Elton could afford to do anything he wanted. "Usually it's personal stuff," he explained. "If I was involved with somebody and it wasn't going right."[43]

He still claimed that it was his involvement in Watford that kept him centered. It was obvious that Elton's "deep pockets" were an enticement for Watford Football Club to put up with the rock star's shenanigans. Exactly how much money had Watford cost Elton, circa 1986-1987? "Up to this point I've put in over two and a half million," Elton admitted.[43]

Earlier that year, Elton had resigned his recording contract with MCA Records, making the ill-fated *Leather Jackets* his final studio album for Geffen Records. It was in September 1987 that Geffen Records released *Elton John: Greatest Hits Volume III* in the United States. The album compiled the best of Elton's six 1980s

Geffen albums, including: "I'm Still Standing," "Blue Eyes," and "Nikita" and teamed them with "Mama Can't Buy You Love." The album fulfilled the final obligations of the Geffen contract, and peaked at Number 84 in the U.S.

Although Elton was in the headlines of *The Sun* himself, there were other headlines which caught his attention and snapped him back to reality. When he read the details about the November 8, 1987, bomb placed by the Provisional Irish Republican Army (IRA), at the town war memorial in Enniskillen, County Fermanagh, Northern Ireland, he realized that others were showing great courage, while he was sitting at home whining. According to him, "It was the Enniskillen bombing that did it. That man, Gordon Wilson, whose daughter died beside him under the rubble, was burning inside but he was so forgiving, so gracious. I thought, 'Christ, this is what courage is about—Elton, just shut up will you. Shut up immediately and get back to work! After all, once you've been exposed naked on the front page of *The Sun* you ought to be able to face anything.'"[44] Finally, he had gotten his perspective back.

Elton decided that it was time for him to clean out his closets and to say "goodbye" to so many of his possessions and his costumes from the past. In 1988 he put souvenirs of his opulent past on the auction block. As he explained it at the time, "I've got this huge house in Windsor and we couldn't move for things. It wasn't a home, it was more like a museum or a warehouse. It suffocates you after a while. I wanted to divorce myself from Elton John for a while. Not come home to constant reminders."[44]

The 1988 Sotheby's auction of "The Elton John Collection" was one of the most elaborate affairs of the year. Although the collection was scheduled to be sold at a four-day auction in London on September 6, 7, 8 and 9, prior to that the items would be on display as part of a global show beginning in Tokyo on June 18 and 19, then in Sydney from July 1-4, New York from July 19-25, and Beverly Hills from July 29 to August 3, 1988. Elton had finally become so famous that he could send his belongings out on tour, and they would draw a crowd!

Among the items for sale were Gold records, pinball machines, the huge boots he had worn in the film *Tommy*, furniture, Tiffany lamps, pottery busts of Queen Elizabeth II,

Magritte paintings, a sea of hats, the Minnie Mouse and Donald Duck costumes, and an insane array of his gaudy eyewear and clothes. The incredible four-day auction brought in an astonishing $8,224,637. It became the most-talked-about auction event of the season.

It would not be like Elton to get rid of absolutely everything he owned. He did retain several of the things that he liked the most, including paintings by Francis Bacon, Patrick Procktor, and Brian Organ, twenty of his high-profile automobiles, some of his jewelry, his original scripts from Peter Seller's *The Goon Show*, and of course his 30,000 record albums. But by raising over $8 million by selling "The Elton John Collection," the rock singer had assuredly staged the most lucrative garage sale of the year!

Once Elton had assembled all of the items he was going to sell, he had them photographed. The resulting photo became the album cover art for his next album, the big "comeback" project, *Reg Strikes Back*.

Reg Strikes Back reunited Elton with producer Chris Thomas. After three albums with Gus Dudgeon, he went back to Thomas for his next trio of albums. *Reg Strikes Back* was released in June 1988 in the U.S., where it made it to Number 16, and July of that year in Europe, where it peaked at Number Three in Italy, Number Five in Switzerland, Number Eight in Norway, Number 13 in Australia, Number 18 in the U.K., Germany and Sweden. The album's most danceable single, "I Don't Wanna Go On With You Like This" became a huge Number One hit in Canada, peaking at Number Two in America, Number 16 in Australia, and Number 22 in Germany, and Number 30 in the U.K. "A Word in Spanish" hit Number Ten in Canada and Number 19 in the U.S. In America it was certified Gold in its first week of release and remained on the charts for almost five months.

According to the critics, *Reg Strikes Back* was a true attention-getter. Harold Goldberg in *Rolling Stone* claimed, "Okay, folks, here's the real comeback…. Elton John is back with urgent shouting and playful crooning… A throwback to his inspired pop rock of the '70s, *Reg Strikes Back* is cathartic for Elton John."[240]

Always a promoter, Elton immediately hit the road to publicize the new album. On June 8, 1988, Elton performed a 14-

song set at an AIDS benefit in Los Angeles, and from September to
October he had a 31-show concert tour across the United States.

That year, teenage singer Debbie Gibson was in the middle
of an unbeatable hot streak on the music charts in America. During
this era she placed five songs in the Top Ten, including the Number
One hits "Foolish Beat" and "Lost in Your Eyes." In doing so, she
became the youngest performer ever to write and record her own
Number One single and album. Since the 1980s, Gibson has
changed her stage name to the more adult "Deborah" and has
become an accomplished Broadway actress.

Gibson recalls, "Elton John invited me up on-stage to
perform with both he and Billy [Joel] at Madison Square Garden....
I couldn't believe it!"[233]

According to Gibson's publicist, David Salidor, "It was an
Elton John show at Madison Square Garden, and Billy Joel just
happened to be there.... I had arranged to get the tickets through
Tony King, who was working with Elton back then.... Tony also
gave us backstage passes. We went backstage to see Elton before the
show. Debbie was of course very excited about meeting Elton.
However, when we got backstage there was Billy Joel as well. Debbie
was thrilled, since these were her two biggest idols. During the
concert Billy got up onstage and performed with Elton. Then
Elton invited Debbie to join the two of them up on-stage while
they did 'Lucy in the Sky With Diamonds.' It was really an
unforgettable evening."[225]

Auctioning off "The Elton John Collection" had lifted a
weight in Elton's life. Now there were a couple more changes that
he wanted to make. In an effort to get free of the pressures of
owning the Watford Football Club, in 1988 he negotiated a
proposed £2 million deal for the sale of his controlling interest in
the Watford Football Club to Robert Maxwell. Although the deal
fell through, Elton explained, "Robert has an abrasive style to say
the least, but I got on well with him. With Watford I never intended
to up and off anyway, I just wanted to give the club a solid future
by putting it in the hands of Maxwell's company BPCC."[44]
Although he made light of the sale falling through, Watford was
becoming a drain on his time and energy.

The year's other huge pressure was his lawsuit with *The Sun*. Ultimately, on December 12, 1988, Elton won the suit against the publication, garnering both a public apology from *The Sun* and a financial settlement of $1.85 million. It seemed that *The Sun's* stories had depended on the honesty of its eyewitness, "Graham X." The mischievous lad overplayed his hand by naming specific dates that he supposedly supplied Elton with "rent boys," but he had named an event that took place in London on a date when Elton was out of the country. Elton's whereabouts were corroborated by his name appearing on the passenger list on the Concorde. Finally, "Graham X" broke down and confessed that he had made the whole story up.

That wasn't the only thing that broke down. After three years of marriage, the wedded union of Elton John and Renate Blauel came to end. Elton had realized within days of the wedding that this had been a huge mistake. Finally, the couple called it "quits." After they were officially divorced, Elton claimed, "The biggest regret I have about getting married is that I hurt someone who was a special person, one of the funniest, nicest, most attractive and fabulous people that I've ever met."[171]

Reportedly, Renate received a lovely cash settlement— estimated at $45 million—and a 17th-century cottage as a permanent residence of her own. Not only was that the end of their marriage, it was the end of their friendship as well.

On March 20, 1989, Elton launched his two-month tour of Europe. While performing in Paris, Elton collapsed onstage and had to seek medical treatment. However, he recovered and finished the show. While in Paris that week, he celebrated his 42nd birthday at a bash that cost a reported £200,000.

In the spring of 1989, Elton was back on the charts with his Aretha Franklin duet, "Through the Storm." Aretha was in the middle of a huge career resurgence, and she had been put in the recording studio with such diverse entertainers as George Michael, The Eurythmics, Keith Richards, James Brown, Whitney Houston, and The Four Tops. The Elton John duet showed both singers in fine form. However, Elton was later to complain that the song was patched together in the recording studio in post-production. He never even got to sing the song in person with Aretha. "Through the Storm" peaked at Number 16 in the U.S. and Canada, and at Number 41 in the U.K.

That year, Elton was also heard on the all-star 1950s/1960s homage album, *Rock, Rhythm & Blues*, along with Chaka Khan, Michael McDonald, and The Pointer Sisters. Elton's contribution to this Richard Perry-produced album was the Fats Domino song "I'm Ready."

On August 24, Elton participated in an all-star staging of The Who's rock opera *Tommy* at the Universal Amphitheatre in North Hollywood. In addition to Elton reprising his role of The Pinball Wizard, the cast included Patti Labelle as The Acid Queen, Phil Collins as Uncle Ernie, and Billy Idol as Cousin Kevin.

To commemorate his having signed with MCA Records, the company released *The Complete Thom Bell Sessions* for the first time. This time around it included all six of the tracks that Elton had recorded with Bell and The Spinners.

In August 1989, his thirty-first album, *Sleeping with the Past* was released. *Sleeping with the Past* found Elton studying the hits of Martha & The Vandellas, Aretha Franklin, Sam & Dave, Percy Sledge, Jackie Wilson, Marvin Gaye, Otis Redding, Ray Charles, and The Drifters, hoping to glean some sense of soulfulness for his singing. It made for a fascinating attempt at emulating the harmonies and soulful deliveries of these R&B legends. A lot of the songs were derivative of R&B classics. For instance, "Club at the End of the Street" directly mirrors Percy Sledge's "Dark End of the Street."

According to Elton at the time, he was finally experimenting with getting sober. "This is the first album I've made where I didn't really have any pressures hanging over me," he claimed. "When I started it, I knew my personal life was going to be sorted out."[238] *Sleeping with the Past* was written and recorded at Puk Studios in Denmark and at Air Studios in England with Chris Thomas producing.

Elton had a special feeling for all the work that Taupin put into the songs. He explained, "I dedicated *Sleeping with the Past* to Bernie, just because we were so happy working together. And I know Bernie was really thrilled with the way the album came out."[257]

Elton was not happy with MCA's promotion of the album, though. While onstage, Elton would announce that he refused to perform any of the material from his new album because MCA was not promoting it the way he wanted. This began an era of cancelled performances, cancelled interviews, and an overall health breakdown for the singer.

Although he complained about the way MCA was handling things, *Sleeping with the Past* has the distinction of being the biggest-selling Elton John album of the 1980s. The album made it to Number One in the U.K., Number Two in France and Australia, Number Six in Italy, Number Seven in Norway, Number Nine in Germany, and Number 23 in the U.S.

It yielded three hit singles. The song "Healing Hands" went to Number Eight in Canada, Number 13 in the U.S., Number 14 in Australia, and Number 45 in the U.K. "Club at the End of the Street" made it to Number 12 in Canada, Number 19 in Australia, Number 28 in the U.S., and Number 47 in England.

However, the real jackpot was the song "Sacrifice." It had taken twenty years of recording, but when it reached Number One in the UK, finally Elton John scored his first—and thus-far only—chart-topping solo single in his native country. It also made it to Number Seven in Australia, Number 18 in the U.S., Number 19 in Canada, and Number 36 in Germany.

From July to October of 1989, Elton was scheduled to tour North America. However, along the way, several of the 45 dates were cancelled because of his health. There was also a Pay-Per-View concert that was scheduled and then abandoned. All sorts of rumors spread like wildfire about Elton's poor health. Between his bulimia, his cocaine addiction, and his alcohol consumption, Elton was in horrifying shape. Toward the end of the tour, he threw a massive tantrum onstage, storming off and claiming that the evening's show would be the last concert he ever gave.

As he explained it, "I was sober when I recorded *Sleeping with the Past*—just. I went off the rails when I did the tour afterwards."[239] Indeed he did, since he collapsed onstage only a week into the tour.

One bright note for Elton at this time was his new boyfriend, Hugh Williams. Elton had met Hugh in Atlanta, where Williams was working at a Baskin-Robbins Ice Cream shop. They instantly hit it off, and before long, they were living together. In the beginning of their relationship they were totally co-dependent on each other's substance abuses and addictions. Elton had found the perfect live-in boyfriend and drinking buddy.

Looking back on this period, Elton was later to explain, "I was cocaine addicted. I was an alcoholic. I had a sexual addiction. I was bulimic for six years. I was all through being paranoid about my weight but not able to stop eating. So in the end I'd gorge myself, then deliberately make myself sick. For breakfast I'd have an enormous fry-up, followed by twenty pots of Sainsbury's cockles and then a tub of Häagen-Dazs vanilla [ice cream], so that I'd throw it all up again. I never stood still. I was always rushing, always thinking about the next thing. If I was eating a curry, I couldn't wait to throw it up so that I could have the next one."[207]

In January 1990, Elton was back on the road performing in Australia, New Zealand, and Tasmania. He did some stray concerts in America as well. However, something was clearly wrong with Elton. During this series of shows, he had a tendency to forget lyrics, and his piano playing was a bit off-tempo.

One of the top news stories sweeping America was the tale of Ryan White. Born on December 6, 1971, White was a hemophiliac who regularly had to have blood transfusions. After he was given tainted blood, in 1984 he was diagnosed with AIDS. When he was refused admittance to his school in Indianapolis, Indiana, due to AIDS paranoia, a lawsuit was filed. Treated horribly by their narrow-minded community, the White family had to relocate to escape persecution.

Elton John became one of a number of high-profile celebrities who came to the family's assistance, donating his time and his money to this heartbreaking case. On April 7, 1990, Elton performed at the *Farm Aid IV* concert at The Hoosierdome in Indianapolis. After singing "Daniel," and receiving a huge round of applause, he sat down at the piano and started to play "I'm Still Standing." In the middle of the song he forgot the words. To cover his tracks, he segued into his song "Candle in the Wind," which he dedicated to Ryan White.

This particular performance was an all-time low point for Elton. He had never been so out of it that he had forgotten the words to his songs, especially one he had been singing in concert for seven years.

Sadly, Ryan died the following morning from AIDS complications. Elton sang the song "Skyline Pigeon" at the funeral services. According to Elton, he did all that he could to be a supportive friend to Ryan. However, Elton himself was a bloated mess at the time and in desperate need of help as well.

Describing his interaction with Ryan and the White family, he recalls, "I spent quite a bit of time with them. When Ryan died I went to Indianapolis with Hugh, who I lived with then, to perform at Ryan's funeral. But if you look at the footage of me at the funeral you see how 'dead' I was. My hair was white. I was maybe 230 or 225 pounds, my eyes were dead. I was like a piano-playing Elvis Presley. I was so messed up. But the thing that happened to me as a result of seeing all that go down was that I started to see what really mattered, because of the experience of being with the Whites."[171]

He was very impressed and touched by the way in which the White family dealt with their tragedy. "God, those people had such dignity," Elton claimed. "For all that they'd suffered, there was no bitterness. And I'd had such blessings in my life and never properly appreciated them. I'd walk out of a hotel suite because I didn't like the flowers. I'm never, ever going to complain about anything again."[207]

Before he got down to the business of straightening out his personal life and addiction problems, Elton still had several career obligations. In May he had been booked at Donald Trump's Taj Mahal casino and resort in Atlantic City, New Jersey. Reviewing the show in *Rolling Stone* magazine, David Wild found, "There was a time when Elton John would have seemed the most appropriate rock star to play a casino. The flashy tours that marked his '70s commercial peak sometimes seemed a kitschy traveling circus, complete with plentiful props and countless costume changes. But in recent years, John has matured as a concert performer, smartly stripping down some of the goofy excesses and putting the emphasis back where it really belongs—on his impressive catalog of inspired pop songs."[241]

In July 1990, Elton and Bernie Taupin were in Los Angeles putting the final touches on the next album, a four-CD boxed set called *To Be Continued*.... In Beverly Hills, the pair met with Andy McKaie to retell their amazing story for the album's extensive liner notes. It was fitting that Elton tell his story at this time because he was truly at a crossroads in his life. That same month Elton went into the recording studio and recorded twelve new tracks with Don Was producing.

On June 30, 1990, Elton was one of the stars to appear at the Knebworth benefit in England. He performed along with Phil Collins, Paul McCartney, and Cliff Richard. The concert was also released as an album.

He was at the height of his cocaine addiction. Taking drugs is supposed to be fun. Was Elton having fun? "I did enjoy some of it, yeah," he claims. But he is quick to point out, "Towards the end I didn't 'cause I'd rented this house and I was upstairs just doing it on my own in my bedroom. I'd have to have half an ounce. Two or three days up at a time. George Harrison tried to help, and I just went: 'Woo, fuck off.'"[184]

Without a doubt, Elton John's life was falling apart by 1990. He knew that he needed help, but he didn't know how to go about it. It was his boyfriend Hugh Williams who put him on the right track. In fact, it was Hugh who checked himself into a clinic first. Elton's first reaction was not support or sympathy, it was sheer indignation.

As Elton explains, "I didn't know where to start until Hugh went into rehab, which was soon after we got back from Indianapolis. At first, I was so angry about it: 'How dare you go into rehab? How dare you try and get better and do something about your life?'"[171]

Hugh went to a treatment center in Prescott, Arizona. "I went to see Hugh there," Elton recalls. "We got there and I was told to write down three things that annoyed me about Hugh, and he was told to write down what he didn't like about me, what he thought I should change. I knew what was going to happen. I wrote these things down—I think they were: 'He doesn't put his CDs back in the case' and 'He's untidy,' and I couldn't think of anything more. We sat knee-to-knee, touching, and read mine out first. Then he read his out, and it must have been a page long. He was terrified. Knowing my temper, he thought I would just say, 'Fuck off! How dare you talk to me like that!' And I just sat there and I was shaking and I said to myself, 'You've got to stay here. You've got to hear the truth.' He said, 'You're a drug addict, you're bulimic.' Everything he said about me was true. And after he finished, I said, 'Yeah, you're right.' It was an incredibly brave thing for him to do. I sat there and I cried and I said, 'O.K., I need help.' And as soon as I said those three words, my soul came back, I could feel again, and I knew, from that point on, I was going to get better."[171]

Elton has always been an extremist. Whatever he does, he does one hundred and fifty percent, whether it is doing drugs, having wild parties, or alphabetizing his CD collection. It was the same with embracing sobriety. He dove into the deep end.

In July 1990, Elton John entered rehab. According to him, "Being so organized I phoned my doctor and said, 'I want to go into treatment as quickly as possible.' At the time, in 1990, the treatment centers weren't taking people who suffered from bulimia, alcoholism, and drug addiction together and dealing with all three issues at once. But they did find me a place in Chicago, in a hospital, and I went there. And I got the thirst for life back. I'd been given a second chance in life, which not many people get."[171]

Between the death of Ryan White, Hugh Williams entering rehab, and finally facing his own drug and alcohol abuses, for the first time in years, Elton was seeing things with clear eyes. "Since I got sober I haven't put myself into so many sexual situations where I could become HIV-positive, because I came through all that HIV-negative," he claimed.[171]

He was finally able to see how incredibly self-destructive and self-absorbed he had become. "I'm trying to break those patterns," he claimed in the 1990s. "I accept that I'm not going to change my personality overnight. It's getting better but you know the thing that's the hardest with me is that all my life I've craved love."[171]

Scotch, cocaine, and watching hours of gay porn. That had been Elton's life for years. And in time he had found that it was a hollow life at best. For all of his fame and all of the money he had amassed and spent, he was depressed, in ill health, and vastly unhappy. The doctors he consulted informed him that if he continued with his substance abuses, he would be dead in a few years. This was the big wake-up call for Elton. His biggest fear had been that he would end up like Elvis Presley: committing a slow suicide with all the drugs in his system. Elvis had died at the age of

42. Elton was now 43, and he had morphed into the person he had always feared he would become.

When he was ready to face his demons, Elton wanted an instant cure. The doctors told him that it would take a much greater period of time. As he recalls, "When they'd said, 'You've got to go into treatments for six weeks,' I'd replied, 'But I've got an album to do! I can't take six weeks off!'"[171]

But Elton knew he needed to take some time and realign his life. From July 1990, through the majority of the next year, that was exactly what he did. Says Elton, "When I came out of treatment, I took a year off. I'd never taken a year off in my life, but I realized, 'If I'm going to make progress in my life, I've got to do this.'"[171]

In the fall of 1990, Elton took up residence in a new London apartment. He was having Woodside remodeled, and he thought he would give city life a try again. He formally christened the new dwelling "Queensdale." No need to guess who the "queen" of the house was.

During this period, Elton took it upon himself to write letters of apology to everyone he knew whom he might have offended during his 14-year cocaine addiction. His mother and stepfather—Sheila and "Derf"—decided that they could return to England to live, since Elton had turned his life around.

In November 1990, MCA Records released the retrospective album *To Be Continued....* A four-CD set, it is truly the ultimate Elton package. If someone wanted to make a single Elton John album purchase, this should be it. *To Be Continued...* hits every era, every album, and several rarities and "B" sides. Elton dedicated the *To Be Continued...* boxed set to his boyfriend, Hugh Williams. After all, Hugh had saved his life.

To Be Continued... made it to Number 82 in the U.S. A couple of singles were released from the album. "You Got to Love Someone" made it to Number 33 in the U.K. and Number 43 in the U.S., and the song "Easier to Walk Away" made it to Number 63 in the U.K. In Europe the album was retitled *The Very Best of Elton John* and was released and hit Number One in England, Australia, France, Italy, Norway, Switzerland, and Sweden.

On November 11, 1990, Elton played his first post-rehab show. It was a benefit concert featuring Elton on the piano and Ray

Cooper's percussion work. Although he would spend the majority of the next year recovering from his years of drug and alcohol abuse, he was to make several guest appearances at benefits and different events.

As he took the stage that night for his first sober show, Elton realized that it was a whole new era for him. For him, this was the first time in 14 years that he had taken the stage without the benefit of cocaine or alcohol. It was the beginning of a whole new way of life for Elton John.

CHAPTER FIFTEEN

Like Candles in the Wind

Once he had gone through rehabilitation for alcohol, drugs, and bulimia, Elton John was ready for a new beginning. Does this mean that Elton checked himself out of the hospital in the summer of 1990, and everything was suddenly coming up roses for him? Far from it. It was a vast improvement, but sobriety alone didn't make the rest of the decade one big piece of cake. For him it was to be a time of new challenges, new career heights. However, there would also be new mistakes, new regrets, and several fresh unforeseen tragedies. The cocaine and booze were gone, but the drama that is Elton John remained fully intact.

Much of the drama Elton definitely caused himself. However, there were several things that were clearly out of his hands. In the next ten years he would lose several of the most important people in his life. At times it seemed to be one memorial service or tribute concert after another. Secure in his newfound sobriety, Elton John was going to remain stoic in the face of tragedy.

However, it was also an era of change and of much fun as well. On March 10, 1991, Elton appeared at the second annual benefit concert for The Rainforest Foundation. Sting hosts the charity event every year at Carnegie Hall. Elton performed his classic *Tumbleweed Connection* song "Come Down in Time" as a duet with Sting. He then spent his 44th birthday—March 25—onstage at a George Michael concert at Wembley Stadium in London. George and Elton performed a unique duet version of the song "Don't Let the Sun Go Down on Me." Fortunately, the whole concert was meticulously taped for possible future release.

On April 1, Elton made a surprise appearance at Rod Stewart's concert at Wembley Stadium. Not only did Rod not expect Elton to be there, but he also didn't suspect that Elton was going to appear in full drag: as the latest Mrs. Rod Stewart, Rachel Hunter. Hunter even helped Elton into his makeup that evening before his entrance. Elton performed the song "You're In My Heart" with Rod.

Elton was now spending more and more time in Atlanta, Georgia. One of the reasons was that Hugh was there. Another reason was that it was far away from his drug-filled past in New York and Los Angeles. On September 7, 1991, Elton took part in the 3.2 mile *From All Walks of Life* AIDS benefit walk in Atlanta.

In New York City, at The Four Seasons restaurant on October 16, Elton attended the launch party for the album *Two Rooms: Celebrating the Songs of Elton John & Bernie Taupin.* The songwriting duo was saluted in song on the album by several of their contemporary fellow-performers. The "A" list roster of rock stars included Eric Clapton, The Beach Boys, Jon Bon Jovi, Oleta Adams, Sinead O'Connor, Phil Collins, The Who, George Michael, Hall & Oates, Tina Turner, Rod Stewart, Sting, Kate Bush, Wilson Phillips, and Joe Cocker. Naturally, Elton couldn't help but make his own guest appearance on the album. On Sting's version of the song "Come Down in Time," the piano player is credited as being "Nancy Treadlight." Naturally, that is another one of Elton's female nicknames. The *Two Rooms* album went to Number 16 in the U.S.

On November 24, 1991, Freddie Mercury of the rock group Queen died from complications from AIDS. Although he was gay, Mercury never publicly admitted his sexuality. And he never admitted that he had been infected with AIDS, until a public statement he made the day before he died. Three days after Freddie's death, Elton was one of the mourners at Mercury's private funeral service. What happened to Freddie made a huge impact on Elton. It made him want to take a stand in the battle against AIDS. He began formulating ideas.

In the fall of 1991, George Michael approached Elton about an idea he had. He told his friend that he wanted to release the song "Don't Let the Sun Go Down on Me" as a single. Elton in turn did his best to talk him out of it, but George was convinced it would be a hit for them both.

Just to add a little bit of good karma to the song, George Michael decided to donate the proceeds from the single to charity. One half of the British single would go to The London Lighthouse, an AIDS charity; the other half would go to The Rainbow Trust, a children's charity. In America, The Boys & Girls Club of Chicago and The San Francisco AIDS Foundation would be the recipients.

As much of a long shot as the success of the single was, the George Michael and Elton John live version of "Don't Let the Sun Go Down on Me" became one of the biggest hit singles of either of their careers. It hit Number One in the U.K., the U.S, and Canada. It peaked at Number Three in Australia and Number Four in Germany.

Unfortunately, on December 15, 1991, Elton's father, Stanley Dwight, died at the age of sixty-six. Stanley had suffered for the past six years with heart problems including quadruple bypass surgery. He had ulcers, and he suffered from osteoarthritis which was severe enough eventually to keep him in a wheelchair. Still, with full knowledge of this, Elton refused to visit his dying father.

This is all part of the odd dichotomy that is Elton John. On one hand he is a generous man who gives tirelessly to charitable causes and to his friends. Yet, on the other hand, he could still not make amends with Stanley.

Earlier in 1991, Stanley's second wife, Edna, had gotten hold of Elton by telephoning John Reid. Elton talked to her while he was in France, and she told him of his father's fragile health. She implored him to come and visit as soon as possible. Edna was so confident that Elton would be coming that she prepared the spare bedroom for his arrival.

Not long afterward, Elton gave an interview with Sky Television, and he announced that when he was a child, he was actually afraid of his father. This was all that the media needed to investigate the whereabouts of Stanley. When a female reporter from *Sunday People* talked her way into the Dwight residence, she was able to obtain several statements from Stanley. The story that ran in the publication carried the headline: "Dying Dad's Love For Elton. He Sends Heartbreak Message To Star Through The People." To match *Sunday People*, competing paper The *Sunday Mirror* headlined their own story: "Anger of Elton's Dying Dad. Star Has Snubbed Us For Year." According to Edna Dwight, Elton phoned her and told her that he would not be coming to visit his dying father after all, as he was "annoyed" by the tabloids' coverage of the story. She claims, "He said, 'I'm not going to get involved in a slagging match,' and put the phone down. That was the last she heard from him." Edna was to later sadly explain, "We never wanted anything from him. Stan certainly never did—only a little of his time."[87] It was never to be.

On January 15, 1992, at the age of forty-five, Dee Murray died of a stroke, after battling skin cancer for eight years. His last appearance on one of Elton's albums was on *Reg Strikes Back*. When he died he left a wife and three children, and a mountain of medical bills that needed to be paid. To help out, Elton participated in a pair of tribute/benefit concerts for Dee at Nashville's Grand Ole Opry.

On March 12, Elton again performed at Sting's Rainforest Foundation benefit at Carnegie Hall. It was billed as *An Evening of Gershwin and Porter and Coward and....* One of the most unique things was Elton's new look. Suddenly he had a full head of hair. And it was a fuller head of hair than he had ever had, even as a child.

How was it that overnight he had gone from hat-covered and bald to suddenly having the dark, thick, healthy hair of a sixteen-year-old boy? Clearly, Elton's failed hair transplants of twenty years ago hadn't suddenly produced these millions of follicles. It was an elaborate hairpiece. His first "hair weave" cost a reported $27,000. It wasn't long before the jokes about Elton's "new hair" began to pop up in the press.

After a British journalist fired the first barbed comment, suddenly it was open season for the press to take shots at Elton's new hair. Did that hurt his feelings? "Oh, initially," he claimed. "I think *The Independent* said that 'Elton came out with a dead squirrel on his head,' which on reflection was very funny. I'm very happy with it and that's all that counts."[46]

It seemed that whenever Elton had a bombshell of an announcement to drop on the public, he did it on the pages of *Rolling Stone* magazine. Fourteen years after describing himself as "bisexual," the singer "came out" and proclaimed his homosexuality. Speaking to writer Philip Norman in its March 19, 1992, issue, the newly sober Elton explained, "I'm O.K. now. I've found someone I really love. I'm so in love, it's wonderful. I'm quite comfortable about being gay."[207]

He also claimed that it was Hugh who had brought him to this newly discovered sense of euphoria. "For the first time, I knew someone I wanted to be totally monogamous with. Before I only took hostages."[207]

Also in March of 1992, Elton left MCA Records for the second time and signed a new recording deal with PolyGram. He had liked the way they promoted the recent *Two Rooms* album, and he had been complaining about MCA for quite some time.

On April 20, an elite group of rock musicians gathered at Wembley Stadium for the concert: *A Tribute to Freddie Mercury*. In addition to having Elton on the bill, the all-star show included Guns 'N' Roses, Annie Lennox, David Bowie, Mick Ronson, Ian Hunter, Paul Young, Lisa Stansfield, George Michael, Roger Daltrey, and Robert Plant. In addition, most of the music that day was performed with the three remaining members of Queen: Brian May, John Deacon, and Roger Taylor.

Several of the performers sang their interpretations of songs that Freddie had made famous with Queen, including Roger Daltrey's "Innuendo," Annie Lennox and David Bowie dueting on "I Want to Break Free," and Elton's version of "The Show Must Go On." Elton also teamed up with Axl Rose for "Bohemian Rhapsody." However, the apex of the evening was a surreal camp rendition of "We Are the Champions" that Liza Minnelli performed.

At this show, the press noticed a new, slimmer Elton, who looked like he just walked out of the display window at a Versace store. It was his new look for the 1990s. That night Elton wore a crimson jacket and a Versace vest fastened with eight gold buckles.

In July 1992, Elton released his 35th album, *The One*. It was recorded at Studio Guillaume Tell in Paris and at Air Studios and The Townhouse in London with Chris Thomas producing. It was not an easy task this time around, since this was the first time in years that Elton had been in the studio when he wasn't fueled by cocaine.

According to John Reid: "He had a lot of fear going in to make the album because he hadn't made an album sober. We went into the studio the first day, and he lasted about twenty minutes and he said he couldn't do it."[248] However, once he "broke the ice," it became much easier.

Bernie Taupin was especially proud of the album, the music, and the way that Elton sounded. It was undisputedly, one of Elton's strongest albums—ever. So many of Elton's albums open with tepidly slow ballads. Not *The One*. It sets a great tone with the infectiously urgent sound of "The Simple Life." On that song he sings his heart out about the passionate discovery of a new life.

Another of the more dramatic songs on *The One* is the Elton John/Eric Clapton duet "Runaway Train." Both of these rock stars knew all too well that life sometimes veers dangerously out of control, like a runaway train. Since there was an Elton and Eric concert tour planned, the Rocket Man asked Bernie Taupin to compose the right song for the two of them to do together.

First of all, both men had come through their own separate drug addictions. And both of them had seen many of their friends die. In addition, Eric had very recently learned a lesson in how fleeting life could be. The death of his young son Conor in 1991 was still fresh in his mind. "Runaway Train" was the perfect piece for the duo to sing.

Recalls Taupin, "A lot of it has to do with the pain of losing. That sort of ties in with both Elton and Eric…. There's a redemptional quality about it…. They've both been through the mill and come back stronger than ever."[239]

One of the most effective songs on *The One* is "Emily," which contains some of Elton's most jazzy piano playing in ages. However, the most heartfelt performance on the album is "The Last Song," which is about a dying AIDS victim confronting his heterosexual father about his life as a gay man. It is one of the saddest and most touching of all of Elton and Bernie's songs together. According to Bernie, "Elton didn't suggest it. It was a big subject that's never been covered in a song before and I thought somebody should deal with it."[45]

As an album package, *The One* also featured a very different Elton John on the cover. Photographed by Patrick Demarchelier, Elton wore one of his expensive new hair weaves. His portrait is surrounded by a piece of art by Gianni Versace, which looks like one of the ultra-expensive scarves from the designer's collection.

During this era, Gianni Versace had become one of Elton's closest friends. The Italian designer was also a wealthy gay man, and together they had fun escapades at unpredictable destinations around the globe. The entire album package was designed by Versace and was as opulent as Elton John himself.

"Nowadays I'm fascinated with fashion," Elton claimed at the time, "because I think I understand the amount of work that goes into it and the amount of creativity involved in it. I have a great respect for anybody who designs clothes and continues to be successful, whether I particularly like their clothes or not. But I genuinely like the people who take the risks and people who are vibrant, like my friend Gianni Versace. That's why I wear Versace most of the time. I do like to wear other people's clothes, but I wear 85% Versace clothes because I just like them—they make me feel good. When I'm with Gianni, I'm with a soul mate. I get energy from him!"[171]

Elton even had Versace design the stage set for his *The One* tour. According to stage lighting expert George Masek, who worked on the tour, "What I heard about that, was that in the initial design meetings there was no place for the band, they were behind the set. Apparently, there was a little bit of concern on Elton's part about that: 'Where's the band?' And Versace said, 'They'll block set. If you can see the band, they will be in the way of my set.'"[269] Elton was truly in his heavy "Versace period."

According to music industry publicist David Salidor, "The album *The One*: it had artwork by Gianni Versace, lettering by Versace, Elton was wearing Versace clothes, and one of those crazy wigs of his. It looks like a gay wet dream."[81]

The critical response for *The One* was mixed. In *Rolling Stone* magazine, Jim Farber wrote, "Buying an Elton John album these days is like investing in a mutual fund: You won't get a huge pay-off, but you probably won't get burned either.... *The One* will ultimately be best remembered not for its music but for the first-ever cover shot of Elton's hair weave."[243] It seemed that as many people were talking about Elton's new hair as were talking about his music.

The One and its singles did quite well on the charts, returning Elton to Number One in several places. The album topped the charts in Germany, France, Italy, and Switzerland. It also hit Number Two in the U.K., Australia, and Norway; Number Eight in the U.S.; and Number 35 in Japan. The song "The One" hit Number One in Canada and in America on the Adult Contemporary chart, also making it to Number Four in Germany, and Number Nine on the U.S. Pop chart. "Runaway Train" made it to Number 31 in the U.K. and Number 41 in Germany. "The Last Song" hit Number Seven in Canada, Number 21 in the U.K., and Number 23 in Australia and the U.S. "The Simple Life" hit Number One on the Adult Contemporary chart in the States, Number Three in Canada, Number 38 in Germany, and Number 44 in the U.K. Elton was back on the charts in a big way.

Now it was time for Elton to give back to the world. In 1992 in America, and in 1993 in England, he established The Elton John AIDS Foundation (EJAF). According to its Web site, "EJAF focuses on supporting community-based prevention programs, harm reduction programs, public education to reduce the stigma of HIV/AIDS, advocacy to improve AIDS-related public policy, and direct services to persons living with HIV/AIDS."[25]

What was Elton's motivation for establishing this foundation? According to him, "I thought, 'Now maybe I've got a chance to do something about these horrible things that happen to everybody. By that time, of course, I'd lost so many more friends with AIDS and knew so many more people with HIV. I did a couple of benefits for people, but what I really wanted to do was to start my own foundation so that I could run things my way."[171]

Suddenly, in the 1990s, Elton was talking openly about his personal life as a gay man. After *Rolling Stone* published his quotes admitting to being homosexual, he never thought twice about mentioning it in public whenever he chose. Did he ever regret this latest disclosure about himself? "I got so many positive letters about it from people that were in situations far less fortunate than myself, in towns and little villages where it's very hard for people to come out," he claimed. "And I didn't realize that if I said something that it would help anybody."[43]

One of Elton's main supporters in his public "coming out" was Angela Bowie. According to her, "When Elton finally came out of the closet, he didn't just open the door, he ripped the lid off of it…. He put it out there, and 'got real.'"[100]

For Elton, by mid-1992 it was time for a new World Tour. He opened in Oslo, Norway, and proceeded on to Sweden, Denmark, Germany, Switzerland, Austria, France, and the Netherlands. From June 26-28, he and Eric Clapton played three nights of sold-out shows at Wembley Stadium in London. Then it was on to Belgium, Italy, and Portugal. On July 21, his show in Barcelona, Spain was broadcast by Britain's Radio 1, as a special 25th Anniversary celebration. On August 11, the North American leg of the tour opened in Atlanta, Georgia, at the Lakewood Amphitheatre. On August 21-22, Elton and Eric Clapton grossed an incredible $4,594,205 for two sold-out dates at Shea Stadium in Queens, New York.

In the next several months, Elton played everywhere from California to Tennessee to Colorado. On the 11th of September, he was one of the featured stars to perform on the *MTV Music Awards* telecast. He performed "The One" and a duet version of "November Rain" with Guns 'N' Roses. Then it was on to Illinois, Pennsylvania, and Massachusetts. In October, he was in New York City, selling out six shows to a grand total count of 113,406 people.

In October of 1992, Elton John and Bernie Taupin signed a publishing deal with Warner-Chappell Music, upon which they received a $39 million advance. According to Les Bider of Warner-Chappell Music, "John and Taupin are, to me, the George and Ira Gershwin of their time."[262]

The world tour continued through the United States to the last U.S. date in Los Angeles in November. That same month PolyGram Records released a two-CD, mini-boxed set entitled *Rare Masters* by Elton John. It was the long-awaited release of many of the rarities from his quarter century as a recording artist. It had oddities, including six pre-1970s recordings. Also on Disc One was the entire *Friends* soundtrack album, which had never been on CD before.

Next his world tour headed to Mexico City, Mexico, to set an attendance record at the Azteca Stadium. In two days, Elton played in front of 180,000 people.

As part of the new deal with PolyGram Records, PolyGram purchased the rights to Elton's entire pre-1976 catalogue. Then PolyGram bought out the Geffen Records Elton catalogue. With that they quit manufacturing the previous *Elton John's Greatest Hits III* and revamped it to become *Elton John Greatest Hits 1976-1986.* Plans were also underway to remaster and rerelease all of Elton's 12 original albums on CD, from *Empty Sky* to *Here and There*, with the original art intact.

In January 1993, Elton sold his interest in the Watford Football Club. It had been a great run for him, and it had provided him with a "centering" activity in his life when he really needed one. Now that he had kicked booze and cocaine, he was too busy putting his life together and running his AIDS foundation to be pouring any more time and money into the soccer team.

While continuing on his World Tour, in February and March of 1993, Elton was in Australia. Much to his surprise, his former boyfriend Gary Clarke had just announced that he was going to write a memoir about his lovelife with Elton John. To whip up some pre-publication publicity, Clarke granted a pair of interviews to the Australian tabloid, *Women's Week*, speaking of Elton's drug use, sex addiction, and childish tantrums.

While all of this was going on, television's *A Current Affair* aired an exposé on Elton's former wild life. In pre-taped footage, Elton discussed Gary's book, "I personally find it disappointing that Gary's done it, but I'm not going to let it destroy my life. My life back then was pretty damned bad. It was a box full of maggots in many ways.... I can't change it."[252]

In Melbourne, his third of three evening outdoor concerts took place on February 19. It was highly attended by humans, and unexpectedly—by hordes of black field crickets. The clean-and-sober Pinball Wizard gamely made it through two hours of music until one particular insect flew into his mouth mid-show. Flustered, Elton and the band left the stage, and after five minutes an announcement was made that the bug-ridden show was over. On April 27, 1993, Elton was one of the guests on the American television special, *Aretha Franklin: Duets*. The show, which included Rod Stewart, Gloria Estefan, and Bonnie Raitt, was taped on Broadway at New York City's Nederlander Theater. Elton sang a duet of "Border Song" with Aretha. The show aired on Fox-TV on May 9, and the profits from the live performance went to the Gay Men's Health Crisis, an AIDS organization.

Throughout April and May, Elton was again on tour in the United States. Then, from May into June, he was in Europe for a new series of shows. Since becoming sober, Elton had not only gotten his health and his energy back, he was nearly nuclear-powered. In June, he also performed in Israel, Greece, and Turkey.

The early 1990s was an era in the music business of superstar duet albums. Everyone from Frank Sinatra to Reba McEntire to Tony Bennett to Kenny Rogers to Ray Charles released albums comprised of celebrity duets. In Elton's case, it was a brilliant move.

The decision to do the *Duets* album found Elton in a very lively mode, as he began to plot out the guest stars and the kinds of songs he wanted to record. He also used several producers on this album. Although some fans were disappointed by the songs that Elton and his duet partners chose, *Duets* was undeniably the most "upbeat" and lively album that he released the entire decade. Who else but Elton could bring together such a diverse roster of singers, like Tammy Wynette, Leonard Cohen, k.d. lang, Bonnie Raitt, Little Richard, Don Henley, Gladys Knight, and even wildly exotic female impersonator RuPaul? And, what would the album be without his most famous duet partner of all: Kiki Dee?

Unfortunately, some of the performers whom Elton had wanted to record with were unavailable. This list included James Taylor, Neil Young, Axl Rose, Steve Winwood, and Bono of U2. He was able to invite several new young singers to appear with him on *Duets.* P.M. Dawn, Nik Kershaw, and Marcella Detroit all sang with Elton on the album. Elton's recent Number One duet with George Michael—"Don't Let the Sun Go Down on Me"—was included on the album as well.

The album recording sessions took place in eight weeks time, from July to August of 1993. John Reid said at the time, "It's quite amazing—the energy that shows in the album took place virtually by putting together a track a day for the first couple of weeks."[253]

According to Elton, "The reason I wanted to do it quickly is because there's not much spontaneity anymore in music. I wanted it to be done quickly so that we could have fun and the fun would translate into the CD."[254]

With regard to his duet partners, Elton claimed, "RuPaul was just fun to work with—I just chose a lot of people when I did my *Duets* album that would be nice to work with, like Leonard Cohen or Henley, because it's fun. The Aretha Franklin one wasn't very much fun because even though you're singing with Aretha

Franklin, I never met her until a year ago. We did it separately. And it was not in my key, so I had to have the balls squeezed and go for it."[46]

The producers who worked on *Duets* were also all selected for their distinctly different areas of expertise. Georgio Moroder was chosen to produce the '90s disco version of "Don't Go Breaking My Heart." Don Was, who had worked with both Elton and Bonnie Raitt separately, was a natural choice for their duet on "Love Letters." And Stevie Wonder produced and played all of the instruments on the Gladys Knight duet, "Go On and On." Several of the artists produced their own tracks as well, including Henley, Kershaw, Rea, and P.M. Dawn. Elton had always wanted to cover versions of some of his favorite Motown songs, which he did here. In addition, he and Bernie wrote new songs for his duets with Wynette and Little Richard. On one of the songs, "Duets for One," Elton wrote with Chris Difford of the group Squeeze.

After Elton and Tammy Wynette finished recording the song "What a Woman Needs," she asked him to autograph the sheet music as a souvenir for her. Elton took the pen and gladly complied by writing: "To the queen of country music from the queen of England." That was Elton, all the way!

When plans were made for Elton to record a new version of "Don't Go Breaking My Heart" with RuPaul, one of the things that they discovered was a shared love of Atlanta. According to RuPaul, "I moved to Atlanta in 1976 and left there 1987, having really done that town. Every square inch of Atlanta, Georgia, I have a story attached to it. It was my coming-of-age town."[268]

As a huge music collector, RuPaul also claims that he was more stunned at the idea of working with the legendary producer, Giorgio Moroder. "When he told me that Giorgio Moroder would be producing our record, I flipped more than it being with Elton John. I have always loved Elton John, but I just *fucking freaked* when I found out it would be Giorgio Moroder. I am the biggest Giorgio Moroder fan possible—there could ever be: Donna Summer, and Debbie Harry, and the soundtracks…. Elton was a breeze for me, but my nerves were on edge for Giorgio!" he insists.[268]

Listening to the finished recording it sounds like both singers are having a great time with each other in the studio. One of the things that most amazed RuPaul was the speed at which Elton works. Recalls RuPaul, "We did have a lot of fun. I was very intimidated by these two giants who I really looked up to. In the years that I've been recording, obviously, I sort of found my voice. I really hadn't then. I was very intimidated, and those two guys were ready to go in there and 'knock it out of the park,' and be done with it. I think we probably did it in under an hour."[268]

That same year, Frank Sinatra released his own *Duets* album, and it hit the top of the charts. However, the stars who recorded with him were not in the studio at the same time he was. Elton was determined not to do his album that way. One of the keys to the success of the songs on his album is the fact that all of the songs sound like they are unfolding spontaneously. RuPaul may have felt rushed in the studio at the time, but it gave the song immediacy. Ultimately, the "live in the studio" flavor worked in everyone's favor.

In November of 1993, when Elton John's *Duets* was released, it hit Number Three in Italy, Norway, and Switzerland; Number Five in the U.K., Number Ten in Germany, and Number 25 in the U.S. The song "True Love," with Kiki Dee was the album's biggest hit, making it to Number Two in England, Number 12 in Canada, Number 34 in Australia, Number 38 in Germany, and Number 56 in the U.S. "Don't Go Breaking My Heart" with RuPaul was a Number Seven hit in the U.K., Number 45 in Australia, Number 62 in Germany, and Number 92 in America. "Standing on Shaky Ground" with Don Henley hit Number 64 in Canada. And "Ain't Nothing Like the Real Thing" with Marcella Detroit made it to Number 24 in England.

As Elton's duet partners, RuPaul and Kiki Dee were really the winners on this album. In fact, "True Love" was the second most successful single of Kiki's career, topped only by the original version of "Don't Go Breaking My Heart." Their new song was produced by Narada Michael Walden, who is responsible for Elton's 1989 duet with Aretha Franklin, "Through the Storm."

The reviews were mixed for *Duets*, but they all seemed to agree that Elton was looking and sounding better than he had in years. Elysa Gardner in *Rolling Stone* wrote, "Unfortunately, little of the glorious schmaltz that made Elton John and his songwriting collaborator Bernie Taupin the Rodgers and Hammerstein of the rock era is evident on *Duets*...the album could have benefited from a little more of the overstated panache that has always been John's strong suit."[242]

In the *All Music Guide to Rock*, Stephen Thomas Erlewine found that: "Some of the material doesn't work in the duet format, and his partners occasionally don't mesh with his current and adult contemporary style...an ultimately disappointing record, even with the occasionally successful track, like the kitschy number with drag queen RuPaul."[96]

By now Elton's affair with Hugh Williams had ended, and they were living separate lives. Elton was actively looking for someone new in his life, and that someone was about to cross his path. On October 30, Elton met David Furnish, a 27-year-old who worked for Ogilvy & Mather, the advertising company. Furnish had originally worked in their Toronto office but transferred to London. While there, a friend left a message on his answering machine that would change his life. The message was an invitation to have dinner at Elton John's house. That was the beginning of Elton John's longest lasting love affair. Since that dinner party, Elton and Furnish have been together ever since.

On January 19, 1994, Elton was inducted into the Rock and Roll Hall of Fame. The rock star who did the official induction presentation was his new friend, Axl Rose. The event, which took place at The Waldorf Astoria Hotel in New York City, was a touching one for Elton. According to Axl that evening, "For myself, no one has been more of an inspiration than Elton John. When I first heard 'Bennie & The Jets,' I knew I had to be a performer."[250]

When Elton took the stage he proclaimed, "I'm not very good with words. I let all my expressions and my love and my pain and my anger come out in my melodies. I had someone to write my words for me. Without him, the journey would not have been possible. I feel cheating standing up here. Without Bernie, there wouldn't have been any Elton John at all."[250]

In the winter of 1993 to 1994, Elton was also busy promoting his single with RuPaul, "Don't Go Breaking My Heart." According to RuPaul, "It's my first real superstar convergence...! We jetted around Europe on this private plane promoting it. I'd never done that before. We hosted *The BRIT Awards* together, and we did a few television shows in Germany and San Remo. We performed it in San Remo, Italy."[268]

One of the things that RuPaul did while in England with Elton was to see the Rocket Man's massive and legendary record, single, and CD collection. "I went to his house in Holland Park, London," says RuPaul. "I went there, but the big collection of CDs is at his house in Windsor. He buys everything! He has this incredible sort of shelving system that wasn't like a dry cleaners has the racks of clothes, but it was this accordion-like closet system where you could pull out the huge drawers that were packed full of CDs. But these drawers were like floor-to-ceiling sort of closets. Sort of like a dresser drawer sitting on its side that goes from ceiling-to-floor."[268] When Elton and RuPaul hosted *The 13th Annual BRIT Awards* in London on February 14, they opened the event singing their international hit "Don't Go Breaking My Heart" to each other.

On April 9, Elton was one of the stars of the annual Rainforest benefit at Carnegie Hall. This year the event also featured Sting, James Taylor, Luciano Pavarotti, and Whitney Houston. He became close friends with Pavarotti and eventually recorded a duet version of his song "Live Like Horses" with Luciano for Pavarotti's own "duets" album, *For War Child.*

For Elton, much of 1994 was spent touring. Not only did he do a solo tour, but a unique teaming was born that year. After attempting to pair up with buddies like Rod Stewart and successfully doing it with Eric Clapton, Elton found a new touring partner who seemed like the perfect fit: Billy Joel.

Actually, the two men had known each other for quite some time. Billy recalls a chance meeting with Elton John in the 1970s. At the time they were the two most famous piano-playing rockers in the world. According to Joel, "The first time we met we were in Holland, at a hotel in Amsterdam. It was in the mid-'70s, and he was at his peak—it was the height of the Elton John era—and I was just starting out as 'the "Piano Man" guy.'... There were a thousand guitar players, but there were only two of us. The English piano player and the American piano player. And, seminally, rock & roll was not just guitar. Elton gave a funny-looking guy like me—and so many others—an opportunity to be a singer-songwriter."[52]

It was truly an inspired idea to put Billy Joel and Elton John together and create an entire concert event out of their pairing. In fact it was such a hit that the concert tour with these two piano men continued to be mounted for several years to come.

One of their first joint bookings was at Giants Stadium in East Rutherford, New Jersey, on July 22, 24, 26, 28-29, 1994. All five shows sold out at a reported box-office gross of $14,889,127.

One former Columbia Records employee remembers how successful the Elton and Billy tours were from the very start. Claims the source, "When the Billy Joel/Elton John collaboration was presented, the story that was told to us was that they were both sick of playing their old songs, so they would get together, play their songs, but also play each other's songs. And they did have an extraordinarily good time on that tour. And that was also one of the first times Billy stopped drinking, because Elton wasn't drinking or doing any drugs anymore."[228]

On September 7, 1994, after his first tour with Elton was completed, Billy appeared with James Taylor at a benefit at David's Island House on Martha's Vineyard in Massachusetts. The same month, Elton was out on the road solo as well. Elton's American concert dates in 1994 grossed over $56 million, and more than 1.2 million people had bought tickets to his shows.

Elton also got himself involved in a project that was quite unexpected. He had never really sought work scoring films. In fact, when he and Bernie had worked on *Friends*, two decades before, Elton swore he would never work in film again. He hated the process of writing music to fill an exactly timed block of screentime.

So he never sought out *The Lion King*, but it came to him and found him willing and interested in the challenge. As Elton recalls, "I kind of fell into it by accident."[172] Indeed, it was one of the best accidents that could have happened to him.

The project that was originally proposed was a full-length cartoon feature called *King of the Jungle*. It was in the development stages in 1991 when Michael Eisner and Jeffrey Katzenberg were at The Walt Disney Company, and they got in touch with lyricist Tim Rice. According to Rice, "They said to me, very kindly, 'Who would you like to do the music?' And Elton was my first choice.... I didn't think they could get him to be honest, but they did."[258]

When the offer to work on what became *The Lion King* came about, manager John Reid said to Elton, "If you don't do this, I'll kill you."[259]

Once everyone was aboard, the first thing to change was the title. Due to the fact that lions don't actually live in the jungle, it was renamed *The Lion King*. Cranky Elton John having the patience to write songs for a children's musical? This would have been unheard of in the late '70s and early '80s. But instead of being the laborious and frustrating process that Elton had remembered from *Friends*, he actually liked the idea of coming up with some lighthearted and inspiring songs for the film's animal characters. He found it much more fun than writing about some of the more somber topics he had tackled lately.

Elton had no clue how big a hit *The Lion King* was destined to become. According to him, "I remember David Geffen saying to me, 'You have no idea how big this movie will be!'... I mean, you know that a Disney cartoon is going to be successful, or good, because they spend four years making them. But I didn't know that this would turn out like it did. And I have to say that it was one of the most enjoyable experiences in my life, because it was a team effort.... It was amazing seeing the whole thing when it was finished. I was speechless."[171]

While *The Lion King* was being prepared for its summer release, on March 21, 1994, the night of the annual Academy Awards telecast, Elton John was one of the guest stars on television's *The Barbara Walters Special*. For the millions of viewers who tuned in, they saw Walters ask Elton to clarify his sexuality. "I am a homosexual man," Elton proudly proclaimed.[260]

When the film and soundtrack album for the film *The Lion King* was finally released in June 1994 in the U.S. and in Britain the following October, it became a huge success. One of the keys to its massive appeal was that it showcased Elton John and his music in a whole new arena.

The Lion King soundtrack album went to Number One in the U.S., Number Three in Australia, and Number Four in the U.K. The songs from the film also did astonishingly well. "Can You Feel the Love Tonight" hit Number One in Canada and on the American Adult Contemporary chart, Number Four on the U.S. Pop chart, Number Nine in Australia, Number 14 in the U.K. and Germany. Not only did the song top the chart in Canada, but it remained there for three months! "Circle of Life" hit Number Two on the U.S. Adult Contemporary chart, Number Three in Canada, Number Ten in Germany, Number 11 in the U.K., and Number 18 on the U.S. Pop chart. Thanks to *The Lion King* soundtrack, Elton John had his biggest hit album in years. It sold 15 million copies worldwide, garnered him five Grammy nominations, and the jackpot was far from over.

According to an astonished Elton, "The film of *The Lion King* really changed my musical life when it came out, because I'd never done anything like that before. Of course it became a juggernaut of a success."[172]

Thrilled with the current career upsurge he was receiving from the film and soundtrack, he claimed, "Nowadays, I get mobbed at airports by six year olds: 'We saw *The Lion King*!' To me that's great. That's what I wrote it for, for kids."[171]

Also in 1994, Elton was one of the featured stars on the album *The Glory of Gershwin*. An album tribute to the music of George and Ira Gershwin, it was produced by George Martin and featured the harmonica work of 80-year-old Larry Adler on all of the tracks. In addition to Elton, the album featured Cher, Elvis Costello, Meatloaf, Carly Simon, Sting, and a host of others. On *The Glory of Gershwin* Elton is heard singing "Someone to Watch Over Me" and "Our Love is Here to Stay."

On November 27, Elton began an 11-concert engagement at London's Royal Albert Hall, just "Reg" on piano and Ray Cooper on percussion. As the year 1994 came to an end, Elton could look back at a Number One album, a highly successful season of touring both solo and with Billy Joel, and a new career peak.

His first disc to be released in the U.K. on the new 1990s version of Rocket Records was his 39th album, *Made in England*. Recorded at Air Studios in Lyndhurst, England, this album represented another major set of changes for Elton. First of all, this was to be recorded with Greg Penny and Elton co-producing. In the band were his longtime mates Ray Cooper and Davey

Johnstone, joining Bob Birtch (bass), Guy Babylon (keyboards), and Charlie Morgan (drums). And for a quartet of the tracks—"Believe," "House," "Belfast," and "Cold"—Elton invited Paul Buckmaster to arrange and conduct the orchestra.

The album *Made in England* had a distinct and very vital tone to it. This was to be his first full solo album without Chris Thomas in a while. What was behind the producer change? And why did Elton choose this juncture to try and co-produce himself? "I've never been involved on the production side," he explained, "but on this album I ended up as co-producer with Greg Penny. I was there for every single note of music played. This time I sat there until I got the sound I wanted, whereas on some other albums I just said, 'O.K.! That'll do! That sounds fine.'"[171]

The first song on the album is "Believe," the dramatic ballad about gambling on love. According to Elton, that song carried the precise message he wanted to send out to his public at that time: "To me the song 'Believe' says strongly and loudly, 'I believe in love.' Things like religion can be so divisive. In theory it should be great; in practice it's completely destructive and divisive and breeds hatred. It's murderous, it's corrupt."[171]

One of the things that Elton was most pleased with was his ongoing friendship with Bernie Taupin. For the *Made in England* album, Elton insisted that Bernie come to England, to the recording studio, and they would create the entire set of recordings there—just like they used to do in the old days. Bernie was now married to his third wife, Stephanie Haymes, and together they were raising her two daughters. Living in the Santa Ynez Valley near Santa Barbara, California, he had found a new sense of peace.

When *Made in England* was released in March 1995, Elton was determined to do whatever he could to promote it. So, at midnight, the day it was due to be released, Elton and Bernie planted themselves at a table at Tower Records on Sunset Boulevard in Los Angeles to autograph copies of the album. Their efforts must have paid off, as the first week it was released it hit Number 13 in America's *Billboard* magazine, making it the highest debuting album Elton had released since *Blue Moves.*

Made in England hit the Top Ten in more than seven countries and ultimately sold four million copies. It made it to Number One in Switzerland, Number Two in France, Number Three in the U.K. and Norway, Number Four in Germany and Italy, Number Six in Australia, and Number 13 in the U.S. and Japan. "Believe" hit Number One in Canada and on the U.S. Adult Contemporary chart, Number 13 on the U.S. Pop chart, Number 15 in the U.K., and Number 23 in Australia. "Made in England" hit Number Five in Canada, Number 18 in the U.K., Number 48 in Australia, and Number 52 in America. "Blessed" reached Number Two on the American Adult Contemporary chart and Number Three in Canada, while "Please" peaked at Number 27 in Canada and Number 33 in England.

Critically, it was again a mixed bag. Peter Galvin in *Rolling Stone* wrote: "*Made in England* is a startlingly fine album, one that shows a newly committed artist tapping into the essence of his creative flow."[264]

William Rouhlman points out in the *All Music Guide to Rock*, "Lyricist Bernie Taupin is unusually personal…. John never works up much feeling for this concept, though he does come off alternately angry and solemn as the lyrics seem to require."[96]

On January 19, 1995, Elton was honored by AIDS Project Los Angeles (APLA) for his fund-raising efforts. Taking the stage at that event the Rocket Man claimed he was the event's "official gay recipient." He then pointed out about America, "This has been my second home for many, many years. This is where I 'came out,' in this country. I slept with half of it, and I came out HIV negative. I was a lucky, lucky person. It's my job to repay that debt."[261]

Elton made it clear that he had no intention of slowing down. In fact, he had just begun! According to him, "At the tender age of 48, which I will be on March 25 [1995], I realized that I've got a lot to do. I have so much more music to write, so much more to do for other people, so many things to do for myself. I feel like, for the first time in my life, I'm an adult."[171]

In January and February of 1995, Elton continued to tour with Ray Cooper, doing eight shows in Japan. After that Elton went back on the road with Billy Joel to revive their "Piano Men" performances. That year they found that they were consistently breaking attendance records wherever they went.

When the Academy Award nominations were announced in early 1995, Elton John and Tim Rice were nominated for an incredible three awards for their work on *The Lion King*, all in the category of Best Song Written for a Motion Picture. How funny that "Can You Feel the Love Tonight," "Circle of Life," and "Hakuna Matata" were all up for the same trophy! The non-Elton John songs that were nominated that year included a song called "Look What Love Has Done" from the film *Junior*, and "Make Up Your Mind" from *The Paper*.

Elton attended the gala Academy Awards on March 27, 1995, with his boyfriend David Furnish and his parents, Sheila and "Derf." In the middle of the live telecast, Elton had to get up onstage and perform "Can You Feel the Love Tonight."

Elton recalls, "Halfway through my performance, I started getting the jiggers, thinking about it, 'Well, the announcement's gonna be fairly soon,' and I was shaking in my seat."[266]

It was Sylvester Stallone who had the honor of reading off the name of the winning song, and it was "Can You Feel the Love Tonight." Onstage that evening, Elton proclaimed, "This is such an exciting night. I'd like to thank the Academy for this incredible honor, to Hans Zimmer, who did a wonderful job with the songs, to everybody at Disney, to my parents who are here tonight, to David, to John Reid, to my friends in Utah [vacationing Jeffrey Katzenberg], and everybody else who worked on this incredible project. I'd like to dedicate this award to my grandmother, Ivy Sewell. She died last week. She was the one who sat me down at the piano when I was three and made me play, so I'm accepting this in her honor."[267]

On April 13 and 14, the Billy Joel and Elton John *Face-To-Face* tour set new records at Joe Robbie Stadium in Miami, Florida. The box-office gross was $4,385,725 for the two dates at that venue, in front of a cumulative total of 103,694 concert fans. On July 30, Billy made an appearance at the Newport Rhythm & Blues Festival in Newport, Rhode Island, at the Fort Adams State Park.

Now in his mid-40s, Billy Joel completely turned his back on the idea of ever recording another new album of rock & roll music. Instead he filled his time with concert touring, recording an occasional single song or two for a soundtrack or a compilation album, and listening to and writing classical music. In his love life Billy found himself dating a series of different women. Although his career was at such a high pinnacle that he could afford to creatively coast on his laurels for the next couple of years, in his personal life he was undeniably in a steady downward spiral. During this era he was drinking Scotch and wine very heavily, and, by the beginning of the new century, he had noticeably begun to lose control of his life.

According to Billy Joel's drummer, Liberty DeVitto, this was also an era of some of Billy's heaviest drinking problems. "There is a photograph that a fan took during one of the Elton John/Billy Joel concerts which captures Billy drunk onstage, tripping over a monitor, and falling to the stage floor in the middle of the show. This took place at Giant Stadium in 1995." Says DeVitto, "Elton took Billy out to talk to him after that photo was taken."[229]

Throughout the 1990s the double star billing of Billy Joel and Elton John continued to be a draw. They often compared notes on songwriting. Billy told *The Performing Songwriter* magazine, "Elton gets lyrics from Bernie Taupin and says to me, 'See what you think.'... I'm going to go into the studio, and I'm going to see how Elton does it. Because he sees these lyrics and he writes music, which I think is fantastic. I'm exactly the other way. I'd like to write a piece of music and send it to Bernie and say, 'Here, you put some words to that.'"[230]

While on the road with Billy Joel, Liberty DeVitto claimed that Elton is one of the most down-to-earth stars he has ever worked with. "He's one of those people who have come to the fact of knowing who he is: 'This is what I am, and this is what I do. I am a pop star, musician, creative writer. I can't live without doing this.'" says Liberty.[231]

On May 9, 1995, Elton received a prestigious award from King Carl Gustav XVI of Sweden. He shared The Annual Polar Music Prize with classical conductor Mstislav Rostropovich. Each received a plaque and they divided $274,000 in awarded money. The Polar Music Prize is the highest honor a performer can be given from the King of Sweden.

From May 20 to July 8, 1995, Elton would spend his time touring Europe and Russia, hitting Moscow, Paris, Vienna, Stockholm, Oslo, Bologna, Copenhagen, Munich, and Monte Carlo, then from August 4 to October 22, Elton, complete with a full band, performed 36 dates in the United States.

While in Hamburg to play at the *Rock Over Germany Festival*, Elton had one of his classic onstage meltdowns. Pissed off about the pouring rain and the sound quality of the show, Elton bitched to the bewildered audience, "Welcome to paradise! Thank you for coming out and standing in the rain, but I ain't playing any of these festivals again!"[136] It was just another one of Reggie's bitchy little moments.

Elton John was busier than ever in 1995, and he seemed happier than he had been in ages. Did he feel that getting sober had changed his life? "Oh, Christ. It's changed completely," he claimed. "The boring, boring bit about getting sober and all that bit, that was four years ago and that changed my life completely. I can actually remember things now! Hahaha! Physically and mentally, my life is brilliant and I just wish I'd done it sooner."[46]

On the 1995 *Randy Newman's Faust* album, Elton is heard singing the song "Little Island." This clever "concept" album is loosely based on Goethe's novel about morality and the devil. Mr. John's role here is "Angel Rick." Also, in October of 1995, Elton was one of the featured performers included on the album *Tower of Song: The Songs of Leonard Cohen.* Cohen was one of Elton's all-time favorite singer/songwriters, and he gladly recorded his interpretation of one of Leonard's compositions. The LP also featured Cohen songs recorded by Billy Joel, Don Henley, Bono, Willie Nelson, Suzanne Vega, Sting, Peter Gabriel, and Trisha Yearwood. Elton's contribution was his recording of "I'm Your Man."

It was also in 1995 that PolyGram Records rereleased the original twelve Elton John albums. Each of them came complete with new liner notes by rock journalist John Tobler, sporting the original cover and interior art, and each including lyrics and detailed recording information. In addition, many of them featured bonus tracks, singles, and B-sides that were never included except on greatest hits albums (like "Philadelphia Freedom" and "Lucy in the Sky with Diamonds.")

In December 1995, Elton appeared on American television on the *VH1 Fashion Awards*. He performed his new single "Blessed," and he sang "The Bitch Is Back" with Tina Turner. Elton had been friends with Tina since they had both appeared in the film *Tommy* in the 1970s, and they consistently talked about working together. This was a rare duet from the two of them.

Having collaborated with Tim Rice so successfully on the film *The Lion King*, they decided to team up once again for the pop/rock adaptation of the Verdi opera *Aida*. With Elton writing the music, and Tim Rice providing the lyrics, suddenly Elton was going to be a Broadway composer. During this same period of time, *The Lion King* was also being adapted for the Broadway stage, and there were three new songs that Elton had to write for that as well.

Ever since Elton and David Furnish had become a couple, they had been quite a compatible pair. One of the things that set Furnish apart from Elton's previous love interests was the fact that he had his own life and his own ambitions. David wanted to get involved in filmmaking, and since he was now living with Elton John, who would make a more perfect documentary subject? David had been filming Elton in several settings for several months, and finally, on July 6, 1996, the public got to see a new view of the Pinball Wizard in *Tantrums and Tiaras*. The footage included one of Elton's last visits to see his Grandma Ivy, other revealing at-home footage, and naturally, a real tantrum.

In September 1996, MCA Records released the album *Elton John: Love Songs*. Since the company had purchased the rights to most of Elton's most significant recordings, they were free to "mix and match" an assortment of them and create new albums of "hits." *Love Songs* was comprised of older ballads like "Your Song," "Blue Eyes," and "Daniel," and some new tracks like "Circle of Life" and "Sacrifice." Elton even went into the studio and recorded two new songs: "No Valentines" and "You Can Make History (Young Again)."

The album made it to Number One in Chile and New Zealand, Number Two in Italy, Number Four in the U.K, Number Seven in Australia and Germany, Number 12 in Japan, and Number 24 in the U.S.

The year 1996 ended with the announcement that Elton was on Queen Elizabeth's New Years Honors List. He was subsequently awarded a Commander of the Order of the British Empire (CBE) for his years of charitable work and artistry. This was the traditional precursor to Knighthood.

The year 1997 was going to witness Elton John standing even further in the spotlight than he had ever been before. And for once, several of his most high-profile moments were not his doing at all—they just sort of unfolded. Sadly, he would experience the sudden and unexpected deaths of two of his dearest friends.

Everything started out as fun and games. March 25, 1997, was Elton John's elaborately festive 50th birthday party. His huge party was held in London on April 6. The event was quite the extravagant gala, in the form of a costume ball. Birthday-boy Elton dressed as Louis XIV straight out of the 18th century French royal court, complete with a three-and-a-half foot tall silver wig. His ostrich feather-lined train was so long—15 feet—that it required attendants to carry the end of it.

Elton's costume was so large that he and David Furnish had to arrive in a van, and they required a hydraulic lift to get them out of the vehicle and onto the pavement. Elton's gigantic wig had a sailing ship affixed on top of it. The press photographers had a field day getting a shot of Sun King Elton and Furnish, who was dressed as his courtier.

The gala party was meticulously planned by Elton's right hand man, Bob Halley, who kept many of the details of the event secret from his famous employer. It was attended by a glittering crowd of 600 partiers, including Andrew Lloyd-Webber, designer Jean-Paul Gaultier, Billy Joel, Charlie Watts of The Rolling Stones, and Boy George as the disc jockey. Joel and Watts both chose to wear World War II U.S. military uniforms. Shirley Bassey came dressed as Cleopatra, Lulu dressed as a 1920s flapper, John Reid was a swan, Paul Young was a swashbuckler, and Molly Meldrum came in full drag looking like someone's fairy godmother. Even Elton's parents got into the spirit of the evening, with Sheila as Queen Elizabeth II and "Derf" as the Duke of Edinburgh.

On April 30, Elton was once again at Carnegie Hall for the Rainforest Foundation benefit with Bonnie Raitt and Shawn

Colvin. He performed the song "Abide With Me," and a pair of Motown classics, The Temptations' "My Girl" and Mary Wells' "My Guy." The number was met with a lot of laughs, as Elton camped it up onstage singing about his "guy."

In early May, Elton and Billy Joel flew to Melbourne, Australia, where they were paid a million dollars apiece for two shows on May 9 and 10. Together they were there to open the Crown World of Entertainment center, and their concerts were for an audience of by-invitation-only guests.

Elton had several other projects in the works at the same time. He had already composed a reported two dozen songs for the new show *Aida*, was preparing his next album, and was now at work on songs for the forthcoming cartoon feature *The Road to Eldorado*. Fortunately, he had the ability to write a song in less than an hour.

In 1997, there was a bizarre murder case in America. There had been a recent series of murders of gay men, in various places, and they seemed to be committed by the same man. Police identitified Andrew Cunanan as the serial killer. As crazed Cunanan's final crime spree, he flew to Miami. In a bizarre set of circumstances, on July 15, 1997, Cunanan shot and killed Gianni Versace in front of his Miami mansion. Cunanan then shot and killed himself at another location in the Miami area. It was a huge tragedy.

Elton was stunned and deeply saddened at the news. When he arrived with David Furnish for Versace's funeral in Milan, Italy, on July 22, 1997, who did he instantly run into? Princess Diana.

Friends with Diana for many years, as Elton recalls, he and Diana had recently had a bit of disagreement. They had not spoken for a couple of months. "We did have a little falling out earlier in the year over a charity event," he explained. "We did write each other letters which neither of us responded to. It was only after the tragic death of Gianni Versace that we actually spoke," he claimed. "But we never stopped loving each other.... I think it was a test of friendship but every friendship goes through a rocky period."[255]

According to him, at the funeral, "She asked if she could sit next to me because she came on her own, which was a tremendous gesture for her to come. And I was—it was a very emotional day for me, because Gianni and I were extremely close. As soon as I saw her, I breathed a sigh of relief, even though I was with David, who's my partner. And we were like, 'Oh, God, thank God you're here,' you know? When I started crying and she put her arm around me, and she was—that's exactly what she was like. She was such a caring—she's a very calming person."[265]

Press photos show a saddened Elton seated between Diana and Furnish in the church at the funeral. The photos ran in newspapers around the world. Through tragedy, Elton's friendship with Diana was suddenly back on track.

For Elton, Versace's passing was another painful illustration of how fleeting life is and how it is meant to be enjoyed every minute. He recalled his friend: "Gianni used to say, 'Elton, there is no time to sit down! You must see this church. You must see this beautiful painting in the museum.' He taught me so much. He said, 'Take it all in. We're not here very long.' I don't hide from life anymore."[279]

Although he was in shock over Versace's murder, afterward Elton had no choice but to return to his committments. On August 8, 1997, Elton gave a concert in Monte Carlo, Monaco, as part of the annual Red Cross Ball. Princess Grace began the event in 1958, and it was a huge gala. The concert was held at The Monte Carlo Sporting Club.

Elton John was in Nice in the south of France on Sunday, August 31, when he learned that Princess Diana had been killed in a horrible car accident in Paris. When the news spread, it seemed that the whole world went into mourning. Elton was stunned beyond belief.

All news stopped that didn't center around the accident site in Paris or what was going on in London. The area in front of Buckingham Palace became a blanket of flowers as thousands and thousands of mourners came to pay their condolences in the only way they knew. All time seemed to stop between the Sunday when she died and the Saturday of the funeral. Finally plans began to formulate, and Elton became an integral part of them. Elton, who had returned to England, telephoned Bernie in California to tell him that he had been asked by Buckingham Palace to perform at the funeral on September 6. He wanted to talk to Taupin about composing a tribute to the Princess. Then he mentioned to Bernie that the English radio stations were playing "Candle in the Wind" as a Diana tribute. According to Bernie, "I thought he said, 'Let's rewrite the lyrics or at least some of the lyrics to "Candle in the Wind."' What he actually meant, I later learned, was, 'Could we write something new that was similar to "Candle in the Wind?"' I just totally misunderstood him on that initial phone call."[256]

Taupin continued, "My reaction was like somebody putting a hand around my heart and squeezing it, because I felt an immediate sense of intense pressure." It took him two hours to rework the song and tailor it for the occasion. "I tried to write it from a nation's standpoint and not as a singular person paying tribute. I felt it was very important that it sounded like it was coming from the people.... I wanted to make this one sound like an 'Everyman's tribute.'"[256]

For Elton, singing the new "Candle in the Wind" in front of untold millions around the world was one of the most stressful things that he had ever done. He wanted to keep his composure and get through the song perfectly. "When I started singing and playing, I suddenly realized this was it. I was fairly composed all the way through and I sang it well. But at the beginning of the last verse my voice cracked and I was really chock-full of emotion and I had to close my eyes and grit my teeth and get through it," he recalls.[255]

Like that line from "Your Song," when Elton sings "my gift is my song," the song that he sang that day was to be his gift to his friend. Right after the funeral, Elton went into the studio with Sir George Martin, and they recorded the song as a further tribute to Princess Diana. Martin had a few ideas for Elton, which he followed. "He suggested I did a piano and a voice live, and I did two takes," Elton explained. "The second take was really, really good. I did some harmonies on it and he added some string quartet and some woodwind," Elton explained.[255]

Elton also decided that the sales proceeds from the single raised would go to the Princess Diana Fund. He said at the time, "We could raise a substantial amount of money for the Princess's Foundation, I hope between £5 - £10m."[255]

Watching the funeral on television from New York City, Bernie claimed that he was "moved beyond words" by Elton's performance that day. However, perfectionist that he was, he claimed, "The quality of the [live recording and feed] was not as good as people think. When you hear the single, I think you'll agree it surpasses the original version."[256]

When the single was released, it instantly became the Number One song around the world: in Britain, the U.S., France, Holland, Germany, Switzerland, Ireland, Italy, Belgium, Austria, Norway, and Japan. By the time it finished its run on the charts, it surpassed the previous record of the best-selling song ever—Bing Crosby's "White Christmas."

Although Elton was happy about the record sales, it couldn't compete with the sense of loss that he felt for Diana. What would he miss the most about her? "Her sense of humor and her wicked laugh and her teasing and her flirting—but also her compassion and her sincerity. I think her greatest physical attribute were those eyes. They flirted with you, they were sorrowful and they were laughing. She had those beautiful eyes."[255]

Speaking to Barbara Walters on the television show *20/20*, Elton claimed that Diana had: "A feeling of love for people, compassion, humor, sadness. She could connect with everybody. She made everyone feel special. And that, you know, the Royal Family has been kind of, through centuries and centuries, remained aloof from that. And they're brought up to—in a different way from everybody else. And Diana broke the mold."[265]

While the song about Diana was still Number One, on September 23, 1997, the 41st Elton John album, *The Big Picture*, was released. The album did well on the charts, and it had clearly gotten swept up in all of the excitement and coverage that Elton had received from "Candle in the Wind, 1997." *The Big Picture* hit Number One in Switzerland and Italy, Number Two in Norway and Sweden, Number Three in the U.K. and Canada, Number Five in Australia, Number Eight in Germany, and Number Nine in the U.S.

The single for "Candle in the Wind, 1997" also carried the song "Something About the Way You Look Tonight," which was included on *The Big Picture*. To promote the album, Elton sang "Something About the Way You Look Tonight" on every American television show he could including *The Tonight Show with Jay Leno, Oprah Winfrey, The Late Show with Conan O'Brien*, and *Rosie O'Donnell*.

Although "Something About the Way You Look Tonight" technically made it up to Number One along with "Candle in the Wind, 1997," the song was not very memorable. The two subsequent singles—"Recover Your Soul" and "The River Can Bend"—pulled from *The Big Picture*, made it into the Top 40 in Great Britain but seemed to fizzle everywhere else.

The press reviews for *The Big Picture* were lukewarm at best. David Wild in *Rolling Stone* wrote, "Far from edgy or groundbreaking, *The Big Picture* nonetheless offers another lovely view of why this madman from across the water is still standing, and standing proudly at that."[244]

According to Bernie Taupin, though, the worst album Elton and he recorded was 1997's *The Big Picture*. Proclaims the lyricist, "The production is abysmally cold and technical. We wrote some decent songs, but most of it was shit, y'know. We've made some horribly crappy records, but then so have a lot of our contemporaries. You're not gonna plant roses continually. There's gonna be plenty of weeds in between."[158]

Elton was kept busy that fall with his *The Big Picture* Tour of America opening in Atlanta, Georgia, on October 8, and continuing through November 22 in Memphis, Tennessee. While he was on the tour, on October 8 he was a guest on Fran Drescher's television show *The Nanny*, appearing as himself. On November 13, 1997, the Broadway version of *The Lion King* opened and became a huge box-office smash. By December he was back in England and Scotland for a series of seven concerts, ending at Wembley Arena in London on the 20th of the month.

At the end of 1997, Elton wrote a check for $20 million for the Princess Diana Memorial Fund. His recording of "Candle in the Wind, 1997" was now the biggest-selling international single ever, ultimately selling over 37 million copies. In Canada, it sat at Number One for an incredible 47 weeks, spending an astonishing three years in the Top Ten.

As 1998 began, it became official that Elton John would be royally knighted by Queen Elizabeth II. On February 24, 1998, Elton, his parents, and David Furnish were present at Buckingham Palace for the official knighthood ceremony. From this point forward, it was no longer Elton John, Pop Star— it was Sir Elton Hercules John.

Elton spent much of 1998 touring. From January 21 to February 21 he was in the United States, starting off in Biloxi, Mississippi, and ending in Los Angeles. On February 11, he was at Sotheby's Auction House in Beverly Hills, where the "Taupin and John" autographed, handwritten lyrics for the song "Candle in the Wind 1997" sold for $400,000. The proceeds went to the Lund Foundation, a charity started by Shari Disney Lund, the daughter of Walt Disney.

From March 4 to April 3 the Elton John and Billy Joel *Face-to-Face* tour resumed once again. Together the piano men went to Australia, New Zealand, and Japan. From April 17 to May 16, Elton returned to his *The Big Picture* tour of America. On April 27, 1998, Elton John took time to be one of the celebrity performers at the Ninth Annual Rainforest Foundation concert. The bill that night included Billy Joel, Sting, James Taylor, and Martha Reeves. According to Martha, "After the show that night, Billy had us all come over to his apartment for an impromptu party. Everyone from Sting to Elton to James, to Katie Couric, all came along with us."[232]

While on the surface everything had seemed to be running smoothly regarding Elton's massively successful career, his cash flow, and his business dealings, in reality it was not. A problem rose to the surface. In 1998, Benjamin Pell got his hands on a letter from Elton's accountants, Price Waterhouse, dated January 7, 1998. Pell has made it a hobby of his to discover embarrassing documents about the rich and famous, which he then sells to the press. He sold the letter to *The Mirror* in London, who in turn published it in their January 26 issue. Suddenly everyone was talking about the disastrous state of Elton's financial affairs. It seemed that the document claimed that Elton's "available headroom" flow of cash was due to run out on April 1, 1998. Elton was livid and called John Reid demanding to know what was going on and how these documents got in the hands of the media.

These revelations blossomed into a scandal, as the newspapers began delving into Elton's affairs. *The Mirror* ran a further story headlined "£527,859 in One Day," about one of Elton's most insanely expensive spending sprees. Elton demanded an audit of his finances to be conducted by KPMG. When they

completed their audit they found £20 million missing. The finger
seemed to point to John Reid and his business decisions. It seemed
that Reid had handed over control of John Reid Enterprises to a
man named Andrew Haydon, and suddenly millions were missing.
On May 11, 1998, Elton fired Reid, and Reid settled with Elton out
of court for $5 million. Finally, in January 1999, Elton took legal
action against both Price Waterhouse and Andrew Haydon to
recoup his £20 million.

With the legal actions, even more of Elton's finances came
under scrutiny, and once the press got hold of the details, they had
a field day. Particularly embarrassing was the fact that his crazy
spending sprees were now making headlines. It seemed that from
1976 through 1977 Elton went through £40 million, including
£293,000 for flowers alone. At one visit to a Versace store, he spent
an astonishing £250,000. Elton's court case would drag on until
April 11, 2001, at which time he lost and was forced to pay the court
costs of roughly £8 million.

Now that *The Lion King* was a musical on Broadway, he
was ready to launch his very own musical. On October 7, Elton
John's first original stage musical opened at The Alliance Theater
in Atlanta, Georgia. Initially billed as *Elaborate Lives: The Legend
of Aida*, it was written with Tim Rice—who by now was also "Sir
Tim Rice." The *Aida* saga would go through many refinements—
including a shortening of its title—before it opened on Broadway.

It was a high-profile time for Elton. On December 11, 1998,
he was in Oslo, Norway, for the Nobel Prize Ceremony. That night
he entertained the crowd by singing "Your Song" and "The Way
You Look Tonight." Elton was named "The All-Time Favorite
Musical Performer" at *The People's Choice Awards*, which were
broadcast from the Pasadena Civic Auditorium on January10, 1999.
And on the 22nd of that month Elton appeared on Britain's television
show *Friday Night's All Wright*, on which he showed off his newest
in an ever-changing cavalcade of hair weaves. From February 13 to
March 19, Elton launched a solo tour of the United States,
beginning in Roanoke, Virginia, and ending in Huntsville, Alabama.

On February 14, 1999, Valentine's Day, a cartoon version
of Elton appeared on the hit television cartoon *The Simpsons*.
During the show Elton is heard singing "Your Song" to the owner

of the Quickie Mart, Apu, and his wife Manjula. Also, making fun of Elton's famous tantrums, one scene shows him throwing a fit when the chandelier in his private jet doesn't meet with his approval.

Dusty Springfield had always been one of Elton's favorite singers, and he was crushed when she lost her battle against cancer on March 5, 1999. When Dusty was honored by the Rock and Roll Hall of Fame on March 15, it was Elton who officially inducted her into its roster of stars. It was a fitting way for him to commemorate her tragic death at the age of 59. At the presentation, he performed her song "I Only Want to Be With You." He jokingly said from the podium that night, "I love you Dusty. You are enough to turn a gay boy straight…well not really."[271]

On March 23, 1999, the album *Elton John and Tim Rice's Aida* was released. This concept album was Elton's idea of a marketing tool for the launch of their Broadway-bound musical *Aida*. He invited several of his rock, pop, and country star friends to bring to life different songs from the show. Stars who participated included Tina Turner, LeAnn Rimes, Shania Twain, Janet Jackson, Lenny Kravitz, The Spice Girls, James Taylor, Sting, and naturally Elton himself. One of Elton's performances was done as a duet with his old friend Lulu, on the song "The Messenger."

Reviewing the all-star *Aida*, Anthony DeCurtis in *Rolling Stone* gave the album qualified praise by claiming, "There is every reason to expect an insufferable kitschfest…against all odds, this pop opera is impressively satisfying on its own unpretentious terms."[280]

The album actually made it to Number 12 in Norway, Number 24 in France, Number 29 in the U.K., and Number 41 in the U.S. The duet between Elton John and LeAnn Rimes, "Written in the Stars," made it to Number 29 in the U.S. as a single. By placing that high on the charts, Elton had placed at least one song per year in the American Top 40 every single year for the last 30 years.

Oddly enough, Tim Rice was not very happy about that album. According to him, "I didn't think that particular album was successful. It was a bit of a mess. It was quite prestigious, but it didn't do that well. The cast album was much better, and that also picked up a Gold record."[88]

At the afternoon rehearsals for the telecast of the VH1 *Diva's Live '99* at The Beacon Theater, on April 13, 1999, Elton got into an argument with Tina Turner and threw one of his most dramatic tantrums. Everything had been going well between them. Tina had done a duet of "Proud Mary" at the *VH1 Fashion Awards* in 1995, and she had just appeared on the all-star *Aida* album. Now Tina and Elton had a duet concert tour in the planning stages for later that year. That was before the fireworks flew between them at The Beacon.

They were going to do a duet of Tina's song "Proud Mary." According to Tina, "I made a mistake when I needed to show him how to play 'Proud Mary.' The mistake is you don't show Elton John how to play his piano."[270]

Elton yelled at her, "You don't tell me how to play my piano!" According to Tina, "Oh, Lord. It just exploded. It was like the past slapping me back in the face, truly, before all of those people, when all I simply was trying to do was get an arrangement right. So then he stormed off. He just went into a rage, which he apologized for later. He said he was wrong."[270]

News of the afternoon argument traveled like wildfire and added a sense of anticipation to the event. The question was, "Would Elton and Tina get into it again before the night was over?"

The afternoon fireworks ended, and the evening's show opened with the planned Tina song "The Best," blending into a duet of "The Bitch Is Back" between Elton and Tina, ending with "Proud Mary," with Cher joining in to make it a trio. In addition, Elton performed his own solo version of the song "I'm Still Standing," and LeAnn Rimes joined him for their hit "Written in the Stars." Elton also performed a solo version of "Like Father Like Son" from *Aida*. The evening was a huge success. However, as far as Tina Turner was concerned, the concert tour with temperamental Elton was off. She wasn't putting up with his antics.

The rest of the year continued to be typically high profile for Elton. April 17, 1999, again found him at Sting's Rainforest Foundation benefit concert. From May to June he launched another American tour. From June to July he performed 13 European concerts solo. And from August to September, he performed throughout the British Isles.

Elton was at his house in Nice, France, playing tennis in July 1999, when he suddenly felt dizzy. Doctors diagnosed an irregular heartbeat and recommended a pacemaker. In a routine operation on July 9, Elton had the pacemaker installed and continued to go about his business and his busy schedule as though nothing had happened.

In August 1999, Elton released the album *The Muse*, a movie soundtrack. With this very classical-sounding film score, Elton was stretching out. The light comedy starred Albert Brooks, Sharon Stone, and Andie MacDowell. A mainly instrumental album, *The Muse* also includes Elton singing the theme song "The Muse" in two different versions, the second one with an upbeat remix by Jermaine Dupri. From September to December Elton was all over the globe performing in concert in such diverse places as Chicago, Illinois; Vancouver, Canada; and Albert Hall in London, England. On October 23, 1999, he played at the wedding reception for James Packer and Jodie Meares. Packer is the son of Australia's wealthy businessman, Kerry Packer, and for his two-hour concert, Elton was paid an astonishing $1.2 million in Australian dollars. Perhaps that would supply him with enough cut flowers and Versace clothes to last him for a while.

However, as 1999 ended, it was Elton's appearance and tantrum on the VH1 *Diva's Live '99* that lingered in people's minds, particularly Tina Turner's. In retrospect Tina claimed of Elton, "He's not like [Mick] Jagger or like some of the other people that's professional enough to give a bit when two people are working together to make it work. He's just very sensitive. Very, very sensitive. We wouldn't have been happy, I think."[270]

Onstage that April night in 1999, surrounded by several strong women, including Whitney Houston, Faith Hill, Mary J. Blige, LeAnn Rimes, Brandy, Cher, and Tina Turner, apparently it was Sir Elton John who was the most temperamental "diva" of them all.

CHAPTER SIXTEEN

Glitter and Be Gay

The dawning of the new century brought with it new challenges and multi-media projects for Elton John. In the year 2000 alone, he had Broadway plays in the works, films for which he had provided the music, new albums, sold-out concerts, and awards. Still happy with his partner David Furnish, Elton had love, fame, money, and power. What else could he want? Only one thing: more! And, he was about to get it.

In January and February of 2000, Elton had several stray concert performances in the United States, starting off with January 7 in Honolulu, Hawaii; then it was off to Atlanta, Georgia; Fayetteville, Louisiana; and finally an engagement at The Venetian Room at The Fairmont Hotel in San Francisco, California. While all of this was going on, *Aida* was being fine-tuned on the road, before it began previews at The Palace Theater on February 22. Elton was not always happy with the decisions that the producers and directors were making for the show, and as usual he had no problem expressing his opinion.

In February 2000, Elton pitched one of his famous fits at The Palace Theater. He made newspaper headlines after he abruptly exited a performance of *Aida* in a grand diva-like protest. He had been assured that the techno treatments of the songs "Another Pyramid" and "My Strongest Suit" would be cut from the play after he saw it in December. To his displeasure, they weren't.

Admitted Elton, "I was pissed off at the way they treated two songs, so I walked out to make a point. It may not be subtle, but I had to do it. It got fixed. I saw *Aida* twice last week, and it was as perfect as I thought it could be."[279]

Members of the cast, crew, and house staff on *Aida* witnessed Elton's many moodswings in person. A male Palace Theater staff member who wishes to remain anonymous—we'll call him "Robby" —got to see one of "Reggie's little moments" up close as Elton clashed with the producers.

According to Robby, "He can be a sweetheart but he can act like a three-year-old if he gets upset. I was working for *Aida* when they were in previews, and he threw a hissy fit during a performance *IN* the house, yelling at the stage and running up the aisles...it was classic, I wish I had a video camera!... I heard more crazy stories from cast members, but that was the only one I had witnessed."[277]

Elton was also reportedly quite flirtatious with the young boys who worked on the show and at the theater. Recalls Robby, "I probably should have slept with him when I had the chance. He certainly made it evident that he wanted to. But he was so overweight, and I just hated his breath. I thought he was a disgusting little piggy at the time. I was much thinner then, but then so was he!"[277]

On February 21, Elton was honored by the National Academy of Recording Arts and Sciences (NARAS) as their "Musicares" Person of the Year to commemorate his lifetime achievements. He received a Lifetime Achievement Grammy Award two days later.

On March 14, Elton's next album was released. It was the soundtrack for the film *The Road to Eldorado*, featuring songs by Elton and Tim Rice. Both the movie and the music it contained drew a lukewarm response.

Jeffrey Westhoff in Illinois' *The Northwest Herald*, claimed, "Katzenberg rehired his *Lion King* musical team of Elton John and Tim Rice to supply the songs for *The Road to Eldorado*, but the magic doesn't happen again. Most of the songs are so middle-of-the-road they are forgotten the moment they end."[271]

On March 23, *Aida* officially opened on Broadway. It turned out to be a huge hit, and it would successfully run until September 4, 2000. The critics loved it, and tickets sold like wildfire. Sir Elton John, with two shows in production at once on The Great White Way, was now suddenly "Broadway Elton." Thanks to the strange turn of events that had occurred when he was invited to contribute songs to *The Lion King* the movie, he had a whole new career writing for the stage and for films.

From March to April, Elton continued to tour America on what was called *The Medusa Tour*. It started out in Lakeland,

Florida, and ended up in Atlanta, Georgia. April 3 found him in
New York City where he was feted by The Gay and Lesbian Alliance
Against Defamation (GLAAD) at their 11th Annual Media Awards.
He was celebrated in song by several Broadway performers
including Deborah Gibson, Betty Buckley, Sam Harris, Jennifer
Holiday, Andrea McArdle, and Sandra Bernhart. Heather Headley,
from the cast of *Aida*, performed Elton's song "Easy as Life" as well.
The event was hosted by Nathan Lane and Christine Baranski.

On April 6, Elton was at The Hammersmith Ballroom in
Manhattan for the taping of the television special: *An All-Star
Tribute to Joni Mitchell.* Also on the show were Bryan Adams, Mary
Chapin Carpenter, Wynonna Judd, Chaka Kahn, James Taylor, k.d.
lang, Diana Krall, and Cassandra Wilson. That evening Elton
performed Joni's song "Free Man in Paris." According to Elton,
who is a huge Joni Mitchell fan, performing this sensitive song, with
Joni watching him from the audience, was more nerve-wracking
than playing in front of Queen Elizabeth II. The television special
aired on April 16.

While on a subsequent European tour, on June 4, 2000,
Elton was at Chatsworth House, in Derbyshire, England, when *The
Tony Awards*, for Broadway excellence, were handed out in New
York City. *Aida* was nominated in five categories including Best
Original Score (Elton John and Tim Rice), Best Performance by a
Leading Actress in a Musical (Heather Headley), Best Scenic Design
(Bob Crowley), Best Costumes (also Bob Crowley), and Best
Lighting Design (Natasha Katz). The show won in every category
except Costumes. Elton John was now not only an Academy Award
winner, but he was a Tony Award–winning Broadway composer
as well.

From October 18 to 21, Elton was back in America, where
he performed in Wilkes Barre, Pennsylvania, before returning to
New York City to headline an all-star *Greatest Hits* concert at
Madison Square Garden on October 20 and 21. The concerts were
taped for a live album and a DVD package. The album, *Elton John:
One Night Only*, was rush-released only a month later, in time for
the Christmas season.

A single disc, 18-track album, it encompassed his hits from
the 1970s, 1980s, and even "Sacrifice" and "Can You Feel the Love

Tonight" from the 1990s. The special guest appearances on the album include Kiki Dee on the hit "Don't Go Breaking My Heart," "Your Song" with Ronan Keating, "Sad Songs (Say So Much)" with Bryan Adams, "Saturday Night's Alright (For Fighting)" with Anastacia, and "I Guess That's Why They Call it the Blues" with Mary J. Blige. The album went to Number Seven in the U.K., Number 12 in Switzerland, Number 14 in Norway, Number 20 in Italy, Number 32 in Australia, and Number 65 in the United States.

In February 2001, at *The Grammy Awards* in Los Angeles, Elton John made headlines again, performing with rapper Eminem, whose anti-homosexual lyrics were notorious. Although gay rights groups heavily criticized Elton for this move, he delivered an impassioned performance with Eminem on the rapper's song "Stan."

Throughout 2001, Elton was kept busy with solo tour dates and his ongoing *Face-to-Face* touring with Billy Joel. On October 1, 2001, Elton released his first new studio album of the new millennium: *Songs from the West Coast.* In the summer of 2000, Bernie went to Nice, France, to visit his musical partner. As they sat on the balcony and looked out at the view, they made a pact with each other. "We said, it's not been fucking good enough," Elton claimed. "We made a vow with each other on that balcony: 'Let's start making albums we can be proud of again.'"[184]

According to Elton, he really took this album seriously. "Bernie and I had already written a load of lyrics and he brought some of them to Nice. I think the main decision was that we had to be really harsh on ourselves. We had to draw a line in the sand and say, 'By the time this album comes out, I'm going to be 54. I want to make a really strong, perfect album! The best album I can do at the time.' And I think with this album, we've already achieved that."[88] It was his first album almost entirely written in California.

As far as record sales, Elton John's career had cooled off a bit, yet he still did respectfully well, especially in England. According to him, "My records sell about four million copies around the world, which is very well, thank you very much. *Songs from the West Coast* was a very poor seller in America, about 600,000 copies."[187]

It was a storyteller's album. On it Elton and Bernie delved into the lives of several characters whom they had observed and who touched their lives. Much of what they came up with was deeply thought out and masterfully done. The song "American Triangle," about the death of gay student Matthew Sheppard, is especially poignant. And "Ballad of the Boy in the Red Shoes" embraces a death of an AIDS-infected dancer. As the album's standout vocal performance, Elton's singing on "I Want Love" is done with such raw honesty that it is one of the best songs he has ever recorded of any era.

In addition, there were several star cameos, including Stevie Wonder providing harmonica and clarinet on "Dark Diamond," the organ playing of Billy Preston on "I Want Love" and "The Wasteland," and harmony vocal support from Rufus Wainwright on "American Triangle."

Songs from the West Coast features some fascinating cover and interior art on the CD package. The CD cover depicts Elton, wearing a Versace jacket, sitting in a booth at a Los Angeles diner. However, as you open up the package, it is a clever panoramic shot of several other characters, both in the diner and outside the plateglass windows on the street. There are two police officers frisking a burly man, Elton's trusty assistant, Bob Halley. The grey-haired man peering into the windows at the far right is Elton's personal valet, Mile Lewiston. There is also a young man at the diner's counter in a cowboy hat, and it's Elton's boyfriend, David Furnish.

The reviews of the album were mixed. According to Barry Walters in *Rolling Stone*, "It don't always work when veteran rockers try to conjure their classic albums' old black magic. Going back to your roots and whatnot sounds good on paper, but your voice and reflexes change, recording techniques evolve and fashions shift. Maybe you've actually grown up, even if your audience hasn't."[282]

The album hit Number Two in the U.K. and Norway, Number Three in Italy, Number Seven in Australia and Switzerland, Number Eight in Sweden, Number 14 in Germany, and Number 15 in the United States. There were three singles released off of the album. "I Want Love" hit Number Six on the American Adult

Contemporary chart, and Number Nine in the U.K. Pop chart. "This Train Don't Stop There Anymore" made it to Number Ten on the U.S. Adult Contemporary chart and Number 24 in the U.K. "Original Sin" peaked at Number 18 on the American AC chart and Number 39 in the U.K.

The videos filmed to promote the three singles from *Songs from the West Coast* were all unique cinematic pieces. For "I Want Love," Elton decided that he didn't want to be in it. Instead, he asked actor Robert Downey Jr. to play him. While a camera moved in front of him, Downey lip syncs while he walks from room to room in a deserted mansion. That worked so well, that for the video version of "This Train Don't Stop There Anymore" Elton was played by Justin Timberlake.

However, it is the video for "Original Sin" that is the most delicious train wreck of a video that Elton has ever done. In it he plays the father of a young girl, Mandy Moore. And, as his wife in the video, he has none-other-than Elizabeth Taylor. It also features look-alike actors playing Bette Midler, Sonny & Cher, Barbra Streisand, and Liza Minnelli. In it, Moore takes a *Wizard of Oz*-like voyage to Elton performing in a 1976 concert. When Dorothy-like Moore returns to the present day, Elton, as her father, announces, "Who is this Elton John anyway? Not some goddamn fudge-packer I hope!"

His international touring in the fall of 2001 took him to such diverse places as Madison Square Garden on October 20 for the post-9/11 benefit, *The Concerts for New York City*; to Mexico City, Mexico; Tokyo, Japan; Bangkok, Thailand; and the city/state of Singapore. On November 26, he was one of the stars to sing in London at the *Royal Variety Performance Show*. Among others on the bill were Cher and Jennifer Lopez.

Two days later, on November 28, 2001, Elton gave a special concert at the New York City rock venue, The China Club. It was part of an anniversary celebration for radio station WPLJ, the same station that had presented his *11-17-70* show 31 years before. To commemorate the date, Elton performed four songs on WPLJ, including "Ballad of the Boy in the Red Shoes," "I Want Love," and "This Train Don't Stop There Anymore," from the new album.

The year 2002 found Elton all over the globe once again starting January 13 in Washington, D.C., with Billy Joel. In addition, he continued to tour his solo act as well. The 2002 touring encompassed such places as Verona, Italy; Copenhagen, Denmark; Birmingham, England; and Dubai in the Arab Emirates.

In November of 2002 came the release of the two-CD set, *Elton John Greatest Hits 1970-2002*. It did well, hitting Number Three in the U.K. and France, Number Six in Australia and Norway, Number 12 in the U.S., Switzerland, and Sweden; and Number 13 in Italy, Number 18 in Canada, and Number 19 in Germany.

The year 2002 was not without its degree of tragedies though. On July 20, Gus Dudgeon and his wife Sheila were in their automobile on the M4, one of England's major highways, when they had a fatal accident. Elton attended the funeral services at St. Andrew's Church, Cobham, Surrey, and performed the song "High Flying Bird" in their honor.

On December 5, 2002, Elton made a guest appearance as himself on the top-rated comedy series *Will & Grace*. He followed the lead of several other media superstars, including Madonna and Cher, in dropping in on the fictional television characters of Jack, Will, Grace, and Karen. The plot has him in a restaurant where Will and Jack are dining and having an argument about the existence of a secret "gay mafia." When Will (Eric McCormack) dismisses the notion, he turns around to find Elton John seated at the next table.

On January 17, 2003, Elton was one of the performers onstage at Arrowhead Pond in Anaheim, California, as part of a tribute concert in his honor. That evening Jewel sang "Your Song," Michael McDonald performed "Take Me to the Pilot," Ray Charles interpreted "Sorry Seems to Be the Hardest Word," and even *Will & Grace's* Eric McCormack performed "Captain Fantastic & The Brown Dirt Cowboy." Elton himself closed the show, dueting with John Mayer on "Sacrifice" and performing an all-star version of "Crocodile Rock."

There wasn't a month of 2003 that did not find Elton John on tour somewhere. He was either on his own or performing the *Face-to-Face* shows with Billy Joel. According to Joel, his fashion sense and Elton's were at exact opposite ends of the spectrum. "Elton is what I would refer to as kind of an old-fashioned aristocracy English rock star," Billy claimed. "When you walk into Elton's dressing room, it's like the Taj Mahal—there are layers of glory, like the glory that was Rome. He's got 10 million shoes and a hundred pairs of glasses and beautifully multicolored outfits, and when he comes and visits me it's like he's going slumming. My dressing room looks like the back of a deli. We have some beer and some cold cuts. And then he looks in my wardrobe case, and he says, 'Let's see, what have we got? Black, black, black, black, black, charcoal, charcoal—Oooh, navy blue! How risqué!—black, black, black, black.' And then he leaves."[283]

On June 24, 2003, Elton performed in concert in Moscow, Russia, at The Kremlin Palace. Two days later, on June 26, he was back at home throwing his annual *White Tie & Tiara Ball* at his home, Woodside. He first threw The Ball in 1999 as a fund-raiser for The Elton John AIDS Foundation. An auction was held that raised £1,000,000 in 20 minutes. Among the auctioned items was a piano autographed by Elton and a dinner for ten with Elton and David Furnish.

Amidst his entire year of touring, just when it looked like Elton John was done having huge Number One hits, in 2003 the song "Are You Ready for Love" from his 1979 *Thom Bell Sessions* mini-album was suddenly released as a single, and it sailed up to the top of the charts in the United Kingdom. This effectively gave Elton John a Number One hit in each of the last four decades.

In 2004, Elton and Bernie contributed the song "The Heart of Every Girl" to the soundtrack of the Julia Roberts film *Mona Lisa Smile*. In America, the song hit Number 24 on the Adult Contemporary chart in *Billboard*.

The year 2004 kicked off with a concert in London on January 7, and then it was on to Atlanta, Georgia, to work on his 48th album. Next, Elton was in Las Vegas to perform eight shows at the Coliseum in The Caesar's Palace Hotel. Beginning in 2004, Las Vegas was to occupy a huge part of Elton's life for the next five years. It was there that he debuted *The Red Piano* show with wildly imaginative sets and visuals by David LaChappelle. *The Red Piano* show would run exclusively in Las Vegas on and off during the year for the next several years. It was staged in the room that had originally been built for Celine Dion's extravaganza of a show.

Celine ushered in the new "permanent fixture" mega-star shows in Las Vegas, followed by Elton John. It wasn't long before Barry Manilow, Cher, and Bette Midler all had similar long-running gigs in Vegas.

When Elton started playing his *Red Piano* show in Las Vegas, several of the reviewers wrote that it was a tailor-made career move for him. But was that a compliment or an insult? According to Elton, "One side of me said, 'Thanks a lot,' and the other said, 'Fuck you.' They always referred to me as the new Liberace in the early days because of the costumes and stuff. I was always 'anti' coming to Vegas. I never wanted to end up here. But it's a much hipper town than it used to be."[187]

His 48th album, *Peachtree Road*, was one of Elton's main focuses in 2004. For this album, Elton chose to co-produce it himself. He wanted to make it an album that shed a light on things he wanted to sing about, and he wanted to have full control of the music. Surprisingly, the album has a rather homogenized sound. Although it was a blend of ballads and up-tempo numbers, there was no real "sizzle" to the tracks.

One of the most amusing songs on the album is the song "They Call Her the Cat," which is about a "Delta queen" transsexual. Another successful song, "Freaks in Love," is a slow ballad about conviction and not listening to the public's opinion. "That's my favorite track on the album," says Elton.[187] While the album was produced by Patrick Leonard, Elton dedicated *Peachtree Road* to the memory of Gus and Sheila Dudgeon.

The press was relatively favorable. James Hunter in *Rolling Stone* wrote, "*Songs from the West Coast* returned Elton John to the piano tang, the discursive tunes and the chewy pop rock that made his '70s albums indestructible.... *Peachtree* highlights once again just how soulful John's music can be."[245]

Still, the public was not very interested or inspired when they heard *Peachtree Road*. The album never made it onto anyone's Top Ten list. In Canada and Switzerland it hit Number 11, Number 16 in Norway, Number 17 in the U.S., Number 21 in the U.K., Number 31 in Germany, Number 38 in Sweden, and Number 44 in Australia. There were three singles released off *Peachtree Road*. The first two only charted significantly in the U.K., where "All That I'm

Allowed (I'm Thankful)" hit Number 20 and "Turn the Lights Out When You Leave" hit Number 32. In America, the song "Answer in the Sky" reached Number Seven on the Adult Contemporary chart.

Elton was to lament about his 2004 album, "It is probably one of my lowest-selling albums of all time. It was disappointing everywhere in the world, so I have to hold my hands up and accept that the songs just didn't connect. I'm proud of *Peachtree Road*."[284]

There was a lot of Elton in the news in the last third of 2004. Most of it stemmed from his tantrum-like tirades in front of the press. In September, Elton got off of a plane in Taipei, Taiwan, where he was headed for a series of concerts. As he deplaned he was met by a group of aggressive paparazzi. Instead of being charming superstar Elton, he was in "cranky, pissy, obscenely vile" Reggie mode. Several weeks later he publicly admitted that he went a little off the deep end with his reactions. "The thing in Taiwan was unfortunate. We arrived at 12:15 at night, we were going through the terminal, and we were just ambushed. [The photographers] were pretty hostile. They were allowed to stay in immigration and photograph us. In the end you get tired and it's like, if they're going to say, 'Fuck off, out of Taiwan,' you're going to answer them back. This happened to Mel Gibson, it's happened to Robbie Williams; it seems to happen in Taiwan."[187]

Unfortunately for cranky Uncle Reg, the event was not only captured on still camera but it was also videotaped. The resulting footage of Elton having one of his famous meltdowns was all over television for several days. On October 4, 2004, Elton was at the *Q* magazine awards luncheon in London, which was also televised. This time his target was "The Material Girl" herself, Madonna. Never the strongest vocalist on the planet, Madonna has been suspected of using pre-recorded vocal tracks in concert, especially when she is performing her typically acrobatic dance routines onstage. The use of these pre-recorded vocal tracks became the subject of Elton's next public rant.

Getting up onstage, Elton said, "Madonna, Best Fucking Live Act? Fuck off! [crowd laughs and applauds] Since when has lip-syncing been live? [crowd applauds] Sorry about that, but I think anyone who lip-syncs in public, onstage, when you've been paid like 75 quid to see them, should be shot. Err…thank you very much. [crowd applauds] That's me off her fucking Christmas card list, but do I give a toss? No. Thank you very much."[188]

The award that the press could have given Elton after that outburst could have been: "The Crankiest Man in Show Business." In the next day's London papers, Elton was all over the headlines for his Madonna diatribe.

One of the funniest comments came from Liz Rosenberg, who is Madonna's publicist. According to Liz, "Madonna does not lip-synch nor does she spend her time trashing other artists." She further proclaimed, "Elton John remains on her Christmas card list whether he is nice…or naughty."[188]

Elton was amazed at all of the negative press he received because of his pronouncement. "The reaction to it was so hysterical," he said in amazement. "It was like I said I think all gays should be killed, or I think Hitler was right. I said someone was lip-syncing. I'm not afraid to speak my mind. I'm not going to mellow with age. I get more enraged about things as I get older because you see that these injustices go on."[187]

At the same *Q* magazine awards show, Elton took home the trophy for Best Classic Songwriter. When he was asked where the award would be displayed, he replied, "It will go with the other one in the staff room at Woodside. That's my house in Windsor. It's where the phone and fax are and it's where the dogs hang out."[189]

When it was pointed out that he had recently been spotted in public wearing an earring that was a diamond-studded penis, he explained, "I'm Elton John. That's nothing unusual for me. I'm a big fan of penises as I'm sure the world knows by now."[189]

Also in 2004, as a global debate over the issue of gay marriage erupted, Elton publicly announced that as soon as England recognized such unions, he would marry his longtime boyfriend David Furnish. When American President George W. Bush proposed a Constitutional Amendment to ban gay marriage, Elton didn't hesitate to jump into the fray. Said Sir Elton: "I thought, 'Well, if I've got a civil agreement, that'll be fine. But as soon as the President [George W. Bush] said 'No' [to gay marriage], I said, 'Right, I'm all for it.' I mean, how dare he say I can't marry David if I want to. You know the scene. If you're a gay couple, and one of them dies, the family steams in, takes everything, and the other half is just completely devastated. I've seen it happen maybe 50 or 60 times in my life. There's nothing the law can do about it and it's just savage. We live in the Twenty-First Century. And the things that religious organizations foist upon people are so Middle Ages."[187]

In December of 2004, Elton John received a Kennedy Center Honors award from President George W. Bush. Five are given a year, and this one was to honor Elton's body of work. Although he publicly opposed Bush's pronouncement about backing a constitutional amendment banning gay marriage, Elton chose to keep his mouth shut when in the President's presence. "You have to take the high ground," proclaimed Elton at the time. "You can't bring your political views into that arena. You have to be gracious." He also added, weeks before the Kennedy Center Honors ceremony, "David will be by my side."[187]

One of the most amusing looks at Elton John's life came in 2004 from writer Ian Gittins in Britain's *The Guardian*. According to Gittins, "Consider Sir Elton John, a man whose career can be seen as one gargantuan folly. Forever flouncing off baroque stage sets in frock coats and periwigs, or throwing heroic tantrums at miniscule setbacks, Pinner's Reg Dwight is nobody's idea of a level-headed icon. His sole saving grace is his utter shamelessness."[48]

Indeed, Elton was finally—and comfortably—growing into his own skin. In 2004 he claimed in his favorite voicebox publication, *Rolling Stone* magazine, "For me, this moment in my life is about trying to be true to myself."[285]

Bolstered by the success of *The Lion King* and *Aida* on Broadway, in 2004 and 2005 Elton was busy planning his next pair of entries to musical theater, *Billy Elliot* and *Lestat*. The decision was made to open *Billy Elliot* on London's West End and to open *Lestat* in New York City on Broadway. It was *Billy Elliot* which was the first to go into production.

The original film, *Billy Elliot*, was released in 2000 and was nominated for three Academy Awards. Written by Lee Hall and directed by Stephen Daldry, the movie told the story of Billy Elliot and his father, brother, and grandmother, who were caught up in the 1984 conflict between British coal miners and the Margaret Thatcher-run government. During these hard times, while the government attempts to break the miner's union, a local dance teacher discovers that young Billy has a natural talent for ballet dancing. There is a clash between the boy and his father. Ultimately, it is a story about discovering one's inner self, challenging convention, and letting creative expression rule. It was a touching tale which instantly grabbed Elton's attention. Furthermore, Billy's childhood best friend is a neighborhood boy who likes to dress up in women's clothes. In other words, *Billy Elliot* was tailor-made for Elton to bring to life musically.

"I'd seen the film," he recalls, "and I had to be helped out of my seat crying at the end of it. David, my partner, said, 'It would make a great stage musical,' and I said, 'Yeah, it would.'"[172] It wasn't long before the musical was in production with Elton's name attached.

Rather than turn the lyrics over to Tim Rice or Bernie Taupin, Elton recalls, "I said to Lee [Hall], who wrote the screenplay, 'You've got to write some lyrics.' He said, 'I've never written songs before,' and I said, 'Well, you're just going to have to have a go.' He wrote some lyrics that were brilliant, and I went to Atlanta with my band and went in a studio and wrote the whole thing in two weeks."[172]

Billy Elliot opened in March 2005, in London at The Victoria Theater. It proved to be a huge success with the critics and the ticket-buying public. The show was so successful that plans were set in motion for the Australian version of the show, and ultimately, the Broadway version as well.

To bolster the public's awareness of the music he had written for *Billy Elliot,* Elton went into the recording studio and recorded three of the tracks: "The Letter," "Merry Christmas Maggie Thatcher," and "Electricity." The three songs became the "bonus tracks" on 2005's "Special Collector's Edition" of *Peachtree Road.* Released as a single in the United Kingdom, Elton's version of "Electricity" hit Number Three on the music charts there, giving him a second Top Ten hit for the decade.

On July 2, 2005, the Live 8 concert was broadcast by satellite from five different international cities, benefiting the starving population of Africa, much as the massively successful *Live Aid* concert had done in 1985. For this new staging of the event, Elton was onstage in Hyde Park in London along with an all-star list of performers including Mariah Carey, Coldplay, Annie Lennox, Madonna, Sting, U2, Robbie Williams, and Paul McCartney.

When Elton took the stage, he announced to an international audience of millions, "I'm glad to be here in general because when the *Live Aid* concert happened 20 years ago I was pretty much a self-obsessed drug addict. And although I was really pleased to be a part of a great day I really wasn't adult enough or mature enough to realize the full consequences of what we were doing then. Since then, of course, I have been 15 years sober and clean and I think I have grown up and matured a bit and started my own AIDS charity and have been in a huge battle to help AIDS patients ever since."[286]

Less than a month later, "Long" John Baldry died on July 21, 2005, at the age of 64, of respiratory illness. Baldry had moved to Vancouver in 1978, where he lived with his boyfriend, Felix "Oz" Rexach. He continued to record and perform up until the very end. That year, his two most famous albums—the Elton John/Rod Stewart–produced *It Ain't Easy* and *Everything Stops for Tea*—were rereleased on CD.

In all of his years as a rock star, there were few things that Elton had not done. He had never released a Christmas album, surprisingly. Instead of doing a conventional Christmas album, Elton decided to play "disc jockey" and compile his favorite rock and pop Christmas recordings. He called it *Elton John's Christmas Party*. With proceeds going to his AIDS charity, Sir Elton chose some interesting seasonal goodies like The Beach Boys' "The Man with All the Toys," The Pet Shop Boys,' "It Doesn't Often Snow at Christmas," and Jimmy Buffett's "Christmas Island." Elton's "Step into Christmas" opens the album, and the final track is his new recording with Joss Stone, "Calling it Christmas."

On December 21, 2005, Elton became the first rock star to have been married to a woman and then to a man. England officially recognized a union between two members of the same sex under their new "Civil Partnership Act" on that day. Witnessed by Sheila and "Derf," Elton Hercules John and David Furnish were officially joined as a couple in the United Kingdom at the Windsor Guildhall.

In grand Elton style, that night he hosted a huge party at Woodside. The guest list included Lulu, Ringo Starr, Cilla Black, Donatella Versace, Hugh Grant, Michael Caine, Claudia Schiffer, Liz Hurley, Ozzy and Sharon Osbourne, and David Beckham and his Spice Girl wife Victoria.

The year 2006 began for Elton with a series of *Red Piano* shows in Las Vegas, from January to April. On April 25, Elton's latest Broadway offering, *Lestat,* had its official opening on Broadway. The two Anne Rice books that it was based on were a huge success. The film version of the books, *Interview with the Vampire*, was a box-office success starring Tom Cruise and Brad Pitt. Unfortunately, the musical, which Elton wrote with Bernie Taupin, turned out to be one monstrous disaster.

The original homoerotic novels, *Interview with the Vampire* (1976) and *The Vampire Lestat* (1985), by Ann Rice, are wildly imaginative and were popular books for humanizing the vampires. There was no question that when studly Lestat bites Louis on the neck, the two men were involved in a deeply personal sexual act.

Unfortunately for everyone, the Broadway musical of *Lestat* didn't work on any level. Even fans of the Ann Rice books were lost in this jumble of a play. The two books span the 1700s to 1985. If planned correctly, the time span could have been delightfully staged, but the history was inadequately capitalized upon.

Several huge segments of that plot were truncated, and others were not developed properly. Even in a vampire story, the audience has to have some sense of sympathy for at least one of the characters. In the 1994 film, *Interview with the Vampire*, the audience had compassion for Louis and Claudia. Here there was none.

The one flash of excitement in this confusing production was the Louisiana-style number in Act II, when the action moved from France to New Orleans. As a musical play, Elton and Bernie chose to use their songs to move the exposition of the plot, instead of making them excitingly expressive moments that developed the characters and punctuated the action. All of the songs were too wordy, and one was left to exit the show after two hours with not one single show-stopper. Where was the big "Hello, Dolly" number? Hell, even "Hello, Vampire" would have done it.

The final stake in the heart of the play was the fact that there weren't any known performers in the production. *Lestat* opened at The Palace Theater on Broadway on April, 25, 2006, and closed on May 28, 2006. Not even curious die-hard Elton fans could keep this joyless neck-biting musical afloat.

After the show closed Elton claimed, "It was a huge disappointment to me, because it was the first musical I had written with Bernie, and it's some of the best things we've done, but it just didn't work. One day the music will actually appear by itself with me doing it."[172]

Much of May, June, and July of 2006, Elton toured the globe, doing shows in Russia, Germany, France, Ireland, and England. On July 2, he was in London at Royal Albert Hall, entertaining gay Europe at the EuroPride Concert 2006. David Furnish presented the Rocket Man by announcing: "I'd like to introduce my husband: Sir Elton John."

In September, Elton played before concert crowds in such diverse places as Lithuania, Poland, England, the United States, and Canada. On the 19th of the month he released his next studio album, the concept piece: *The Captain & The Kid*. It was based on an idea of Bernie Taupin's. If their album *Captain Fantastic & The Brown Dirt Cowboy* had told the story of Elton and Bernie up to 1975, how about a new album about what had happened to them since? It seemed like a creative concept on paper. However, it only achieved moderate success.

When Bernie and Elton got together, the music flowed out of them very organically. According to Elton, "It was the quickest album we'd done since the '70s. Twenty days, writing and recording. The pressure was off. No red light."[184]

The majority of the ten tunes unfold as long narrative poems. Without following the lyrics to figure out what Elton is singing about, the songs fail to capture the imagination immediately. That doesn't mean that there isn't a lot of fun in this album, because there is a sense of humor to much of it. For instance, on "Just Like Noah's Ark," Bernie amusingly handed Elton lyrics about the drag revue The Cockettes and the rock star, penis-replicating duo, The Plaster Casters.

The Captain & The Kid has the same dark-toned musical style that *Captain Fantastic & The Brown Dirt Cowboy* contained. However, this time around, the music is not nearly as dynamic. There are no "hooks" in the choruses, and none of the tracks stand out as surefire hits.

In *Mojo* magazine, David Buckley reviewed *The Captain and The Kid*, calling it: "The continued comeback of The Queen Mum of Pop."[186]

Christian Hoard wrote in *Rolling Stone*, "*The Captain and the Kid* is the third album in a career-resurrecting run that began in 2001, when Elton John took the novel approach of sitting down at a piano and writing songs that sound a lot like Elton John…. And that's more than good enough."[287]

The album did moderately well. It hit Number Six in the U.K., Number Ten in Canada and Switzerland, Number 18 in the U.S., Number 25 in Germany, and Number 37 in Australia. There were two singles pulled from it. The only successful one was "The Bridge," which made it to Number 19 on the American Adult Contemporary chart.

As *The Captain & The Kid* hit the world's music charts, Elton spent the rest of 2006 on tour all over the globe. Stops included appearances in Australia, Switzerland, Canada, and Caesar's Palace in Las Vegas.

In the beginning of 2007, Elton continued to present *The Red Piano* show, tour about the United States, and even give a free concert on the Copacabana Beach in Rio De Janiero, Brazil. Then when March 25, 2007, rolled around, Elton spent his 60th birthday on a stage he should feel at home on by now: Madison Square Garden. It was a gala concert, filmed for a DVD to be titled, *Elton 60: Live in Madison Square Garden.*

Without a doubt, one of the best "live" recordings that Elton had made in ages is the bonus disc to this boxed-set. Although his voice is a bit gruff, his singing crackles with emotion. Hearing him sing this version of "Sixty Years On" with longtime bandmates Nigel Olsson and Davey Johnstone onstage with him on his 60th birthday, is especially riveting.

In addition, another Elton John album appeared on the charts: his next "greatest hits" package. This time around it was

called *Elton John: Rocket Man/Number Ones.* A single disc with
12 legitimate Number One hits and five additional Elton classics,
it came packaged with a DVD which included five songs taped at
The Red Piano show and five of his other videos. The album was a
huge Top Ten hit for him in five countries, hitting Number Two in
the U.K., Number Three in Norway, Number Six in Sweden,
Number Nine in the U.S., and Number Ten in Australia. It also
made it to Number 13 in Switzerland.

On July 1, 2007, Elton was one of the performers at *The
Concert for Diana,* held at Wembley Stadium, to commemorate the
tenth anniversary of the passing of Princess Diana of Wales. He
performed a quartet of his hits: "Your Song," "Saturday Night's
Alright (for Fighting)," "Tiny Dancer," and "Are You Ready for
Love." Also on the bill that night were Rod Stewart, Lily Allen,
Duran Duran, Nellie Furtado, Joss Stone, and Bryan Ferry.
Throughout the rest of the year, Elton's international touring
continued to take him to an exotic list of places including Kiev,
Russia; Malmö, Sweden; Baden-Baden, Germany; Odense,
Denmark; Madrid, Spain; Moscow, Russia; Glasgow, Scotland;
Paris, France; Riga, Latvia; and even Sioux Falls, South Dakota. On
December 13, 2007, Elton was in Sydney for the Australian opening
of his hit musical *Billy Elliot,* which continued to play successfully
in London. The next stop for the play was to be Broadway.

Elton started out 2008 with a quartet of concerts in South
Africa, in Cape Town, Durban, and Johannesberg. That was
followed by a concert in Abu Dhabi, Arab Emirates. On February
24, he was in West Hollywood to host what was billed as *Elton John
& David Furnish's 16th Annual EJAF Academy Awards Viewing
Party,* held at The Pacific Design Center. Elton and his band
performed, along with special musical guests Mary J. Blige and Jake
Shears of The Scissors Sisters.

On May 28, 2008, Elton performed his first concert in the
state of Alaska at The Sullivan Arena in Anchorage. He had now
performed in 49 out of 50 states. That same month he also gave
concerts everywhere from Perth, Australia, to Pensacola, Florida.

On June 2, 2008, Elton John and singer Lily Allen hosted
GQ magazine's *Fashion Awards* at London's Royal Opera House.
The award winners were secondary to the onstage sparring between

61-year-old Sir Elton, and 23-year-old Allen. Allen drank champagne onstage and started slurring her speech, showing signs of being inebriated. She announced, "...now we reach a very special point in the evening," at which point Elton jumped in and quipped, "What, you are going to have another drink?"

Allen, who was dressed in a ladylike, full-length gown, fired back, "Fuck off Elton! I'm 40 years younger than you.... I have my whole life ahead of me."

Not one to be outdone, Sir Elton proclaimed, "I could still snort you under the table."[288]

Several people were given awards that evening, including Led Zeppelin, who received an Outstanding Achievement Award for their recent comeback concert. However, in the next day's newspapers, it was Elton and his antics with Lily Allen that got all the press.

In July 2008, Ben & Jerry's Ice Cream announced that they were debuting a "limited edition" ice cream in Elton's honor called Goodbye Yellow Brickle Road. A chocolate ice cream base with bits of peanut butter cookie dough, butter brickle [crunchy butter toffee], and white chocolate chunks, it was only available from July 18-25 in Ben & Jerry's stores, with proceeds going towards Elton's AIDS Foundation. Part of the reason for the special ice cream flavor at that time was that Ben & Jerry's was a Vermont-based company, and Vermont remained the only state in the American union where Elton had never performed. His July 21, 2008, concert at Champlain Valley Expo Center in Essex Junction, Vermont, effectively changed that. What everyone really wanted to know was: "Just how many cartons of Goodbye Yellow Brickle Road did Elton eat that week?"

June 9, 2008, saw the release of deluxe and expanded versions of the albums *One* and *Tumbleweed Connection*. Each one contained bonus tracks, rare recordings, demos, and even BBC broadcasts of some of his most beloved songs.

On October 20, 2008, Elton appeared on American television's *The Today Show* to plug *Billy Elliot*, which was due to open on Broadway on November 13. After a brief interview with Elton by Matt Lauer, the three alternating lead actors who played the title role in the show performed a trio version of the show's signature song, "Electricity."

In an interview with New York's *Time Out* magazine around the same time, Elton discussed his connection to *Billy Elliot*, "At the end, when his father was in the box at Covent Garden and Billy came out in Matthew Bourne's *Swan Lake*, it meant that his father saw him at the height of his career—when he became everything he hoped he'd be and sacrificed for. My dad never saw me at my height when I became a star. I missed that from my father, and it really hit home."[172]

The show was already a big hit in London and Sydney. However, that was not a guarantee that it would strike a chord with American audiences and tough Broadway critics. According to Elton, "The show is about hard times. So I think people will identify with what's going on on-stage economically, and that's something we have going for us. Still, we have to translate that into people wanting to come and see it."[172]

In his November 11, 2008, appearance on the American television show *The View*, Elton promoted *Billy Elliot* and talked about his involvement in the play. The hostesses of the show, Whoopi Goldberg, Joy Behar, Sherri Shepherd, and Elizabeth Hasselbeck were all seated in a semi-circle. When Elton seated himself on the sofa between the hostesses of the show he looked stuffed into his clothes and highly uncomfortable. Throughout the interview he seemed ill-at-ease and rarely smiled.

During the segment, Elton told the show's hostesses that he was touched when he first saw the *Billy Elliot* film. He revealed that he was especially impressed at how Billy's father became supportive of his son's career. Elton again claimed that his own father never saw him perform at the height of his career.

Then the young actor Kiril Kulish—as the character Billy Elliot—performed the "showstopper" from the musical, the song "Electricity." Unfortunately, it didn't really work as well out of the context of the play. At the end of the show, Elton brought out his two dogs, Marilyn and Arthur. He appeared to be anything but a rock star. Instead he looked more like a fussy, slightly cranky, middle-aged gay man with a pair of canines on a leash.

The night of Tuesday, November 11, Elton hosted *An Enduring Vision*, the 7th Annual Elton John AIDS Foundation Benefit at Cipriani Wall Street. His special guest for the evening was Gladys Knight. The gala raised $2 million for his charity.

That evening, while everyone was giddy about the November 4th Presidential election of Barack Obama, members of gay America were still stunned by the passage of controversial Proposition 8, banning gay marriage in California, and similar measures that passed in Arizona and Florida. Elton had his own opinions.

At the AIDS Foundation benefit in New York, Elton proclaimed to a reporter for *USA Today*, "What is wrong with Proposition 8 is that they went for marriage. Marriage is going to put a lot of people off, the word 'marriage'.... I don't want to be married. I'm very happy with a civil partnership. If gay people want to get married, or get together, they should have a civil partnership.... You get the same equal rights that we do when we have a civil partnership. Heterosexual people get married. We can have civil partnerships."[275] That ruffled some feathers.

On the Web site www.gay.com, Clark Hamlyn took offense and wrote, "Newsflash—Sir Elton: gay marriage exists already in countries across the globe, and DID exist in California until it was taken away. And while we're all thrilled that you are happy with your civil partnership, it's just not going to cut it for us."[275]

The excitement was far from over. It finally reached a peak with the November 13 Broadway opening of *Billy Elliot*. Elton had no idea how the play would be received. That night at The Imperial Theater, a star-studded crowd including Rosie O'Donnell, Kevin Spacey, Barbara Walters, Mario Cantone, Lynn Redgrave, Natasha Richardson, John Stamos, Billie Jean King, Deborah Cox, fashion designer Valentino, Anna Wintour, Roger Waters of Pink Floyd, film producers Brian Grazer and Ron Howard, and New York City Mayor Michael Bloomberg were in attendance.

Would American audiences understand the musical and embrace it? Judging by the standing ovation and the enthusiastic applause from the crowd that night, the answer was a resounding "yes!"

As the show came to a close, the cast took the stage for the opening night curtain call, and Elton came out to take a bow dressed in a flouncy ballet tutu. Dr. Stephen Tay was in the audience opening night to witness it. He amusingly claimed, "I was there that night, and I saw Elton in the tutu. Let me tell you, he has much better legs than Tim Curry in *Rocky Horror Picture Show*!"[285]

The American press reviews for *Billy Elliot* were mainly glowing. Roger Friedman on *Fox News Online* wrote, "You could be a fan of Elton John's for the last—yes—38 years and still not be prepared for his gigantic Broadway hit, *Billy Elliot*...[which] opened last night in New York to the most amazing thing: a standing ovation in the middle of the show."[273]

Ben Brantley in the *New York Times* claimed, "Tough and insistent...this show both artfully anatomizes and brazenly exploits the most fundamental and enduring appeal of musicals themselves."[274]

It was Charles McNulty, theater critic for the *Los Angeles Times* who hated it. In his review, headlined "*BILLY ELLIOT* MUGGED ON BROADWAY," he claimed, "There's a thin line between a mega-hit and a mega-mediocrity."[276] Still, there was no question, with *Billy Elliot*, Elton John had another Broadway hit on his hands.

Throughout late 2008, Elton began touring again with *The Red Piano* show. In November and December, he took the show to Berlin, Birmingham, Munich, Hamburg, Cologne, Helsinki, Stockholm, Oslo, Manchester, Liverpool, London, and Paris.

On December 1, 2008, it was announced in *New Musical Express* that Elton John was due to record his next album with a new producer at the helm: Mark Ronson. Ronson had recently come to prominence due to his work with Amy Winehouse on her Grammy Award–winning, multimillion-selling 2006 *Back to Black*. That album had made Winehouse an instant star, and critics loved the snappy retro-Motown sound of the music, especially on the song "Rehab." This sounds exactly like the kind of move that Elton needs to make at exactly the right time. The sound quality of his post-2000 albums could use some flair and excitement.

On December 4, 2008, Elton's partner David Furnish was presented one of the "Man of Style Awards" by Project Angel Food, L.A., at its Divine Design gala fundraiser. Project Angel Food provides meals to those afflicted with HIV/AIDS.

According to Furnish, his good luck charm is a lock of his boyfriend's hair. "I have around my neck a little tiny locket and it has a lock of Elton's baby hair and a picture of him as a baby," he says. "I wear it for important occasions, when I climbed Mt.

Kilimanjaro and on airplanes. It's a talisman of sorts that makes me feel protected, like I have got a piece of him with me all the time."[173]

Sporting a shaggy, blond hair weave on his head, Elton John performed with his *Red Piano* show at the O2 arena in London on New Year's Eve 2008. Wearing a black suit jacket embroidered with musical notes, he helped 17,000 partying patrons welcome in 2009. Part of the concert, including his performance of the song "Tiny Dancer," was broadcast in America as well.

Elton John has been back and forth with his involvement with his beloved Watford Football Club over the last couple of years, to the point where he can run hot or cold by the week. He was made the soccer team's Honorary President, but in 2008 he got into a feud with Watford's former chairman Graham Simpson and walked out in a snit. In early 2009 he was reportedly back with Watford, though.

On January 6, 2009, it was announced that Elton John's newest animated feature would be *Gnomeo & Juliet*, loosely based on Shakespeare's *Romeo & Juliet*. It is the first full-length cartoon feature that he has worked on since *The Road to Eldorado* in 2000, and the very first one he is doing with Bernie Taupin. Elton is producing it together with his boyfriend David Furnish, in association with Baker Bloodworth and Steve Hamilton Shaw. *Gnomeo & Juliet* is to be released in 2011, from Starz Animation in Toronto, Canada, in association with Miramax Films.

Elton started out 2009 with January concerts in Venezuela, Columbia, and Mexico. Then in February it was off to finish the last of his Las Vegas shows with his *Red Piano* extravaganza. That same month, Elton paired up again with his "Piano Man" friend, Billy Joel, for a revival of their *Face-to-Face* concerts. Dates for those are set up to run into 2010.

When he began his career in the 1960s and 1970s, Elton John desired fame. He achieved fame, and at several points, his fame nearly destroyed him. The fact that he was overweight, not classically good looking, and was losing his hair, all eroded his self confidence. He was gay and had to pretend that he was not. And to mask all of his pain, he turned to excessive amounts of alcohol and even attempted suicide. Yet, he is someone who has come through the storm, emerging stronger and more self-confident than ever before.

In spite of the personal demons that Elton has faced, there have been some unresolved issues which he never really faced. One of those had to do with his biological father, Stanley Dwight. In his *Billy Elliot* interviews Elton consistently claimed that his father never saw him at his creative height. That is not 100% accurate. He gave Stanley and Edna and their four boys front-row seats to his Liverpool shows back in 1973 when he was already a big star. He even went to their home with John Reid for a meal. What happened after that? What caused the ill feelings between father and son? Only Elton knows.

According to his stepmother, Edna, it's Elton who is at fault. The fact that Elton refused to visit his dying father, nor attend his funeral, was very telling. In 2005, *Blender* magazine tracked down Elton's half-brother, Geoff Dwight. Geoff, who is 20 years younger than Elton, lost all respect for the former Reggie Dwight when the superstar was a no show at his dad's funeral. Geoff claimed, "In the end, I think it came down to money. My dad was never impressed, while Elton was obsessed by it."[289]

Elton attends his friends' funerals, even performs in front of millions of viewers at funerals. Yet, his own father's memorial seemed to hold no importance to him. Everyone has "unresolved issues," and Elton is no different.

What is undeniable is his incredible talent, which continues to display itself. Who would have thought, when *Goodbye Yellow Brick Road* was Number One on the charts, that three decades later, the public would still be anticipating the next Elton John album, let alone awaiting the next Elton John Broadway musical, or the next Elton John movie.

Elton John and Bernie Taupin are already the longest-running, most successful songwriting team in the history of popular music. And, they still work together on a cavalcade of projects. Though Taupin has working with other performers—creating Number One hits for Starship ("We Built This City") and Heart ("These Dreams"), for example—he will forever be linked with Elton.

Of all their songs together, the one that personifies them the most, as a duo, is still "We All Fall in Love Sometime." According to Sir Elton, "Out of all the songs we've ever written that one sums up our relationship the best. We love each other and we're not close to each other, but I can't imagine my life without him in it. And I never see him. Astonishing."[184]

When he was a teenager in England, Elton spent countless hours in his room listening to records by The Supremes, The Four Tops, and Dusty Springfield. He grew up to be someone whom those very same stars admired. According to Duke Fakir of The Four Tops, "Elton is one of the most awesome talents out there: his piano playing, and his songwriting, and his delivery. He is so unique in the way he does sing, and I love his voice. He is a very, very talented person. He has all the talent it takes, and evidently he loves the business. He is still there, and he is still pumping it out."[131]

Since she last saw Elton John in the 1980s, Angela Bowie knows that he has done admirable things with his life and has used his celebrity status to make positive changes in society. According to her, "Who knew that Elton John, the international pop star for four decades, he of the outrageous costumes and assorted fashionable and wild spectacles, would curry favor at court and become the troubadour for a modern day princess: Princess Diana? Who knew that a wonderful, bold and inventive keyboard player would be knighted and favored by the most powerful woman in the world: Queen Elizabeth of England?... Elton John emerged a stronger and more determined role model for many young people."[278]

He certainly has the respect of his fellow rock superstars. Bono of the rock group U2 claims, "Elton is the Louis XIV of pop. He is my *Roi Soleil* [Sun King] of pop music and he takes up the entire road as far as I'm concerned. I can sing high or I can sing low, but Elton is right there in the middle of the road and you can't get past him."[190]

Tim Rice further sings his praises by stating, "Elton is truly one of the great musicians of the Twentieth Century, and his magnificent voice is as important an ingredient in his success as his peerless songs are."[221]

With as much admiration as Elton has received for his musical talent, he has certainly received just as much press coverage for what he wears. Whether it is a lime green sport coat, a Minnie Mouse costume, or something so insanely garish it looks like it was plucked from Josephine Baker's dressing room, Sir Elton makes headlines for his fashion statements wherever he goes.

According to David Furnish, "He asks me to help him get dressed, and pick out which ties and shirts match, but he has his own sense of style, which is much more exuberant than mine. He can pull it off because he has the larger-than-life personality.... I don't know another man who can wear color like Elton does."[173]

Undeniably, Elton John and David Furnish do march around like a pair of male peacocks. They dress expensively, and outrageously, and delight at it. Let's face it, every day with Elton is a costume party.

However, Jimmy Greenspoon insists, "With Elton it's all about the music. He can be wearing street clothes, or standing there in the Donald Duck outfit, it doesn't matter. It's the music that makes Elton John a star."[210]

In their private life, Elton and David Furnish are almost inseparable. Elton also remains very close with his mother and stepfather. He travels all over the world with his pet dogs. Over the years he has had, and outlived, so many dogs that he has a dog cemetery at Woodside. According to him, "There are all these little headstones, with names like Bruce and Brian. Anyone looking at them might think they were old boyfriends I'd have bumped off."[207]

Elton loves to be as outrageous as possible at all times. He makes broad and bombastic statements, and he speaks his mind whenever he wants—and people listen. He also loves peppering his statements with expletives. He is a man who—upon occasion—has gone so far as to have described himself as being "a silly cunt." Insists a gleeful Sir Elton, "'Cunt' is probably my favorite word. It is the best word in the English language!"[184]

For the early years of his life Elton was a neurotic work-in-progress. When he was not yet twenty-five years old, he was a gigantic hit-making music legend. However, he was not prepared to be thrust into the glare and public scrutiny that goes with the territory. As he recalls, "I had this huge successful career and then this very unsure private life. I really didn't sort out my personal persona until I got sober."[184]

Through it all, Elton has lived something of a charmed life. He has taken chances, and he has made several mistakes, and yet he has survived unscathed. If you take into consideration some of the maladies that other gay rock stars have suffered, Sir Elton has been very lucky. Although he lived his life very close to the edge, he didn't die young like Freddie Mercury. He hasn't been arrested for his sexual dalliances like George Michael. After his initial burst of mega-superstardom, Elton could have faded away into obscurity, only surfacing amidst a new scandal like Boy George.

What Elton does have going for him is a sense of himself, a great deal of "ego," and a professional respect for himself. He is perfectly happy with living life close to the edge, without ever going over the edge.

The very idea of retirement from performing is repugnant to him. "They can't seem to pension me off. They can't pension off The Rolling Stones or Pink Floyd or Eric Clapton. I love seeing young people come up, but how dare anyone suggest that The Stones are old and boring or that Joni Mitchell is incapable of writing new songs because she's over 50? That's crap," he says defiantly. [279]

He is an Academy Award winner, a Grammy Award winner, a Kennedy Center Honors recipient, and his own Queen knighted him. The album *Elton John's Greatest Hits* alone has sold 24 million copies worldwide. For Elton John, it has been quite a career, and still he and his career continue to grow and evolve.

If Elton had to sum up his career in one statement, what would that be? According to him, "An overview of my career is usually…glasses…homosexuality…Watford Football Club… tantrums…flowers. But the music was pretty phenomenal, y'know."[184]

And what does he think of himself as a person? According to the frank and scandalous Rocket Man himself, "I'm the most famous 'poof' in the world!"[249] Yes indeed, Elton, that you are.

Is Elton John a musical genius? Definitely. Is there more great music coming from Elton? Years worth; he isn't the type of guy to sit around and remain idle. Is Elton something of a "mad genius?" Absolutely! A genius nonetheless. He is a bawdy, creative original. He has an unquenchable thirst to create music, and that's what makes Elton tick. He is a brilliant composer and a rock & roll original. In addition to that, he is also a bit of a spoiled child, a diva, and an incredibly intuitive artist. When he stands up and proclaims in front of a crowd of thousands of screaming fans that "The Bitch is back," in reality, he never went away. Without question, the world's most flamboyant, most outrageous, and most bitchy rock star on the planet truly is: Sir Elton John.

QUOTE SOURCES

1   "Elton Storms the States," *Melody Maker,* by Richard Williams, September 26, 1970

2   "Elton John," *Rolling Stone,* by John Mendelssohn, November 12, 1970

3   "Elton John Steams 'Em Up," *Rolling Stone,* November 12, 1970

4   "Elton John: The Record Rise of a Superstar Called Reg," by Peggy Valentine, *Disc and Music Echo,* 1971

5   "Elton John: *The Tumbleweed Connection,*" by Peggy Valentine, *Sounds,* 1971

6   "This is Your Song: The Elton John Interview" by Mick McGrath and Mike Quigley, *The Georgia Straight,* April 11, 1971

7   "Bernie Taupin: The B-Side of Elton John," by Steve Turner, *Beat Instrumental,* February 1972

8   "Step Right Up and Feel the Man's Muscles: *Honky Château,*" by Charles Shaar Murray, *Creem,* June 1972

9   "Elton John: Don't Shoot Me I'm Only the Piano Player," by Steve Turner, *Beat Instrumental,* January 1973

10   "The Elton John Story: Final Part," by John Tobler, *Zig Zag,* April 1973

11   "Elton John: Don't Shoot Me I'm Only the Piano Player," *Let it Rock,* April 1973

12   "What Do Bowie, Elton, and Mantovani Have in Common? [Gus Dudgeon]," by Harold Bronson, *Music World,* June 1, 1973

13   "Elton John: Starship Trouper," by Jerry Gilbert, *Sounds,* September 15, 1973

14   "Elton's Finest Hour!," by Chris Charlesworth, *Melody Maker,* September 15, 1973

15   "Elton John at the Hollywood Bowl – July 1973," by David Resin, *Rolling Stone,* October 11, 1973

16 "The Elton John Career," by Richard Cromelin, *Phonograph Record*, November 1973

17 "Elton John Steps Into Christmas," by Chris Welch, *Melody Maker*, November 24, 1973

18 "Elton John: Goodbye Yellow Brick Road," by Wayne Robins, *Creem*, January 1974

19 "Elton John: *Caribou*," by Chris Welch, *Melody Maker*, June 15, 1974

20 "Elton John: The Short Hero," by Charles Shaar Murray, *NME*, July 6, 1974

21 "Elton John: *Caribou*," by Bud Scoppa, *Photographic Record*, August 1974

22 "Elton John: *Greatest Hits*; Randy Newman: *Good Old Boys*; Pete Atkin: *Secret Drinker*," by Simon Frith, *Let it Rock*, January 1975

23 "Elton John: Hammersmith Odeon, London," by John Tobler, *ZigZag*, January 1975

24 "Elton John: Hammersmith Odeon, London," by Chris Welch, *Melody Maker*, January 4, 1975

25 "The Life and Times of Elton John, Part 1," by Charles Shaar Murray, *NME*, February 22, 1975

26 "Elton John, Part 2: They Laughed When I Stood Up to Play the Piano," by Charles Shaar Murray, *NME*, March 1, 1975

27 "Elton John, Part 3: Maybe it's Because I'm a Socialist," by Charles Shaar Murray, *NME*, March 8, 1975

28 "Elton John: *Captain Fantastic and The Brown Dirt Cowboy*," by Greg Shaw, *Phonograph Record*, June 1975

29 "Elton John: I Want to Chug, Not Race," by Caroline Coon, *Melody Maker*, June 21, 1975

30 "A Million Dollar Friendship: An Interview with Gus Dudgeon," by Jon Tiven, *Circus Raves*, August 1975

31   "Elton John: *Captain Fantastic and The Brown Dirt Cowboy* (MCA)," by Wayne Robins, *Creem*, August 1975

32   "Elton John: *Rock of the Westies*," by Charles Shaar Murray, *NME*, October 25, 1975

33   "Elton John: *Captain Fantastic and The Brown Dirt Cowboy*," by John Tobler, *ZigZag*, November 1975

34   "Elton John: *Rock of the Westies* (MCA)," by Ben Edmonds, *Phonograph Record*, November 1975

35   "Elton John: Ol' Four Eyes is Back," by Vivien Goldman, *Sounds*, May 8, 1976

36   "Elton John: He's Got the Whole World in His Hands," by Charles Charlesworth, *Melody Maker*, August 14, 1976

37   "Elton John: *Blue Moves* (Rocket)," by Mick Brown, *Sounds*, October 23, 1976

38   "Elton John: *Blue Moves*," by Bud Scoppa, *Phonograph Record*, November 1976

39   "Elton John: *Blue Moves*," by John Tobler, *ZigZag*, December 1976

40   "The Real Elton John Stands Up—'Hoorah!,'" by Phil Sutcliffe, *Sounds*, December 18, 1976

41   "Elton John: Concert in Central Park," by Roy Trakin, *Musician*, September 1980

42   "Elton John: *Jump Up!* (Geffen)," by Gene Sculatti, *Creem*, August 1982

43   "The Fall and Rise of Reginald Dwight," by Chris Salewicz, *Q*, December 1986

44   "Elton John: You've Got to Laugh…," by Phil Sutcliffe, *Q*, August 1988

45   "Bernie Taupin: Him Indoors," by Robert Sandall, *Q*, July 1992

46   "Elton John," by Mat Snow, *Q*, January 1995

47   "Elton John: Sound Your Funky Horn," by Cliff Jones, *Mojo*, October 1997

48   "How Sir Elton Recovered His Cool," by Ian Gittins, *The Guardian*, 2004

49   "Bernie Taupin: Bernie Taupin (Elektra)," by Lester Bangs,
     Phonograph Record, March 1972

50   "Patti LaBelle & The Belles [sic]: Tiles, London," by Bill Millar, *Soul
     Magazine*, June 1966

51   "Kiki Dee: The Life Story of a Hot Girl," by Bob Wolfinden, *NME*,
     October 5, 1974

52   "The Immortals—The Greatest Artists of All Time: 49, Elton John,"
     by Billy Joel, *Rolling Stone*, April, 15, 2004

53   "The Rise of Ziggy Stardust: David Bowie's Version of Camp Rock,"
     by Henry Edwards, *After Dark*, October 1972

54   "Oh, You Pretty Thing," by Michael Watts, *Melody Maker*,
     January 22, 1972

55   "Elton John: The *Playboy* Interview," by David Standish & Eugenie
     Ross-Leming, *Playboy*, January 1976

56   "Elton John, The Troubadour," by Robert Hilburn, *Los Angeles
     Times*, August 1970

57   "Elton John: It's Lonely at the Top/Captain Fantastic Reveals
     Secrets of Songwriting, Rock Stardom…and Who He's Sleeping
     With," by Cliff Jahr, *Rolling Stone*, October 7, 1976

58   "Elton John," by Charles Shaar Murray, *NME*, January 1974

59   "Elton John: No Future," by Stephen Holden, *Rolling Stone*,
     January 25, 1979

60   "On The Elton John Watch," by Ken Tucker, *Rolling Stone*, July 24, 1980

61   "Elton John New Rock Talent," by Robert Hilburn, *Los Angeles
     Times*, August 27, 1970

62   "Elton John: After Three Gold Albums and the Praise of Dylan,
     Leon and Millions, What Can He Say But' Thank You' and
     Occasionally 'Fuck Off, Norman,'" by David Felton, *Rolling Stone*,
     June 10, 1971

[63] "Elton John: The *Rolling Stone* Interview," by Paul Gambaccini, *Rolling Stone*, August 16, 1973

[64] Author's telephone interview with Lamar Fike, October 1, 2008

[65] "Elton John Tells All to Our Lisa," by Lisa Robinson, *The Chicago Sun-Times*, July 18, 1976

[66] "Elton John to Lily Allen: 'I Could Still Snort You Under the Table," by Korin Miller, *New York Daily News*, September 3, 2008

[67] "Elton John," by Nik Cohn, *New York Times*, August 22, 1971

[68] "Elton John" *Circus*, December 1970

[69] "Elton (Hercules) John," *Current Biography*, March 1975

[70] "…And in Elton John's Case," by Lynn Van Matre, *The Chicago Tribune* "Arts and Fun" section, November 10, 1974

[71] "The Story of Elton's Life," edited by Danny Fields, Randi Reisfeld and Pat Wadsley, *Elton* fan magazine, 1975

[72] "Why Elton Didn't Commit Suicide," by Darryl Flynn, *Pageant*, November 1975

[73] "Elton John," by Tony Parsons, *The Daily Telegraph*, April 8, 1995

[74] "Honest John," by Nigel Farndale, *The Sunday Telegraph Magazine*, September 14, 1997

[75] "Neil Tennant Interviews Elton John," *Interview*, Jaunary 1998

[76] "Elton John: The *Billboard* Interveiw," by Timothy White, *Billboard*, October 4, 1997

[77] "Elton John: Five Years of Fun," by Robert Hilburn, *Record World*, January 31, 1976

[78] *To Be Continued…*, Elton John and Bernie Taupin interview by Andy McKaie for album liner notes, MCA Records, 1990

[79] "Interview with Elton John," by Larry King, CNN Television Transcript, airdate: March 15, 2008

80   "Interview with Elton John," by Larry King, CNN Television
Transcript, airdate: January 25, 2002

81   Author's telephone interview with David Salidor, October 11, 2008

82   *Me, Myself and I*, video documentary, VH1 television network, 2008

83   Receipt from Hodges & Johnson's music store, Romford, Essex,
England, dated February 26, 1963

84   Letter from Stanley Dwight to Edna Clough, dated December 2,
1962, personal collection of Edna Clough Dwight

85   Letter from Stanley Dwight to Edna Clough, dated December 17,
1962, personal collection of Edna Clough Dwight

86   Letter from Reginald Kenneth Dwight to Stanley Dwight, circa
1963, personal collection of Edna Clough Dwight

87   *Sir Elton*, by Phillip Norman, Carrol & Graf, Avalon Publishing
Group, New York , New York, 2001

88   *Elton: The Biography*, by David Buckley, Chicago Review Press, 2007

89   Author's telephone interview with Kenneth Reynolds, October 13, 2008

90   Review of the single "Come Back Baby," of *Record Retailer and
Music Industry News*, July 22, 1964

91   Author's conversation with Bill Wyman, Maya Bar, Monte Carlo,
Monaco, July 30, 2008

92   *Don't Block the Blessings: Revelations of a Lifetime*, by Patti
LaBelle with Laura B. Randolph, Riverhead Books, a division of
G.P. Putnam's Sons, New York, New York, 1996

93   *It Ain't Easy: Long John Baldry and the Birth of the British Blues*,
by Paul Myers, Greystone Books, Douglas & McIntyre Publishing,
Vancouver, Canada, 2007

94   *Elton John in His Own Words*, by Susan Black, Omnibus Press,
London, England, 1993

95   Elton John on NBC-TV's *The Today Show*, interview with Matt
Lauer, October 20, 2008

[96] *All Music Guide to Rock*, edited by Vladimir Bogdanov, Chris Woodstra, and Stephen Thomas Erlewine, Backbeat Books, San Francisco, California, 2002

[97] Liner notes for the CD version of *Empty Sky*, by John Tobler Rocket Records, 1995

[98] Author's telephone interview with Sarah Dash, October 17, 2008

[99] Author's e-mail statement from Race Taylor, October 31, 2008

[100] Author's in-person interview with Angela Bowie, Mark Bego's living room, Tucson, Arizona, July 24, 2008

[101] Author's telephone interview with Danny Hutton, August 26, 2008

[102] "Still Captain Fantastic," by Leslie Bennetts, *Vanity Fair*, November 1997

[103] *The Complete Motown Singles, Volume 10: 1970*, CD package liner notes essay entitled "I'm Here to Change the Records" by John Reid as told to Adam White, Motown Records, 2008

[104] *Elton John: Deluxe Edition*, CD liner notes, by John Tobler, Mercury/Chronicle / Rocket Records, 2008

[105] "Russ Regan: The Man Who Brought Elton John to America," by Eliot Sekuler, *Record World*, January 31, 1976

[106] *Fire and Rain: The James Taylor Story*, by Ian Halpern, Mainstream Publishing, Edinburgh, Scotland 2001

[107] "John Reid Tells His Side of the Story," by Eliot Sekuler, *Record World*, January 31, 1976

[108] "Weston Describes the Troub Engagement," *Record World*, January 31, 1976

[109] "The Many Faces of Elton John," by Ellen Mandell, *Good Times*, originally printed circa 1970 / 1971, reprinted June 21, 1988

[110] *It Ain't Easy*, by John Baldry, album reissue liner notes by Sid Griffin, Warner Brothers Records, 2005

111   *Touch*, by The Supremes, album liner notes by Elton John, Motown Records, 1971

112   *Everything Stops for Tea*, by John Baldry, album reissue liner notes by Sid Griffin, Warner Brothers Records, 2005

113   "Elton John," by David Felton, *Rolling Stone*, June 10, 1971

114   *11-17-70*, by Elton John, album reissue liner notes by John Tobler, Rocket Records, 1995

115   Author's e-mail statements from Tom Cuddy of WPLJ-FM radio station in New York City, November 8, 2008

116   *Tumbleweed Connection*—Deluxe Edition, by Elton John, album reissue Liner notes by John Tobler, Rocket Records, 2008

117   *Madman Across the Water*, album review by Alec Dubro, *Rolling Stone* magazine, January 20, 1972

118   "Taupin Speaks through Elton John's Mouth," by Patrick Snyder, syndicated *Rolling Stone*, Fall 1977

119   *Off the Record: An Oral History of Popular Music*, by Joe Smith, edited by Mitchell Fink, Warner Books, 1988

120   *Everything Stops for Tea*, by John Baldry, album, Baldry's own adlibs on the recorded track "You Can't Judge a Book," Warner Brothers Records, 1972

121   *Taupin*, album review by Alan Richards, *Crawdaddy* magazine, 1972

122   *Honky Château*, album reissue liner notes by John Tobler, Rocket Records, 1995

123   *Don't Shoot Me I'm Only the Piano Player*, album reissue liner notes by John Tobler, Rocket Records, 1995

124   *Everything Stops for Baldry*, by Mike Ledgerwood, Disc, June 3, 1972

125   "Gladys Knight Shows Up For Elton John," by Rush & Molloy, *The New York Daily News*, November 13th 2008

[126] "Kiki Dee: 'He Put the Music in Me," by Mike Harris, *Record World*, January 31, 1976

[127] "Tony King Salutes 'A Competent Piano Player,'" *Record World*, January 31, 1976.

[128] *Goodbye Yellow Brick Road*, album review by Stephen Davis, *Rolling Stone*, November 22, 1973

[129] *Rolling Stone: The 500 Greatest Albums of All Time*, by the editors of *Rolling Stone* magazine, Wenner Media, New York, New York, 2005

[130] "In Hard Times, Born to Pirouette," by Ben Brantley, *The New York Times*, November 14, 2008

[131] Author's telephone interview with Duke Fakir of The Four Tops, July 16, 2008

[132] *Goodbye Yellow Brick Road*, album reissue liner notes by John Tobler, Rocket Records, 1995

[133] Author's interview with Jimmy Greenspoon, Don Schula's Steakhouse, New York City, September 1, 2005.

[134] "Finally Elton's Varied Sound Is in the Pink," by Lynn Van Matre, *The Chicago Tribune*, August 27, 1973

[135] "His Hobby's a Prickly Subject," *Jackie* magazine, London, 1969

[136] *His Song: The Musical Journey of Elton John*, by Elizabeth J. Rosenthal, Billboard Books, Watson-Guptill Publications, New York City, 2001

[137] *Caribou*, album reissue liner notes by John Tobler, Rocket Records, 1995

[138] "Elton's Albums: An Appraisal," *Record World*, January 31, 1976

[139] "The Songs of Elton and Bernie: A Musical Monument to the '70s," by Eric Van Lustbader, *Record World*, January 31, 1976

[140] "*Caribou*—Elton John's Rocky Mountain Orgasm," by Steven Gaines, *Circus*, 1975

[141] "*Elton & Tommy*," edited by Danny Fields, Randi Reisfeld and Pat Wadsley, *Elton* fan magazine, 1975

142 *Supreme Faith: Someday We'll Be Together*, by Mary Wilson and Patricia Romanowski [including sections by Mary Wilson and Mark Bego], Harper Collins, New York City, 1990

143 *The Elton John Story*, John Lennon interview, KOPA-FM radio station, Scottsdale, Arizona, broadcast fall of 1982

144 *Elton John, Bernie Taupin, Gus Dudgeon and Others*, radio interview by Paul Gambaccini, 1976

145 Elton John radio interview with Andy Peebles, December 28, 1980

146 *Captain Fantastic & The Brown Dirt Cowboy*, album reissue liner notes by John Tobler, Rocket Records, 1995

147 "Elton's Next Album," by Paul Gregutt, *The Weekly of Metropolitan Seattle*, October 26-November 1, 1977

148 Author's interview with May Pang, Jayia Thai Restaurant, New York City, September 25, 2008

149 Author's telephone interview with David Stanley, October 3, 2008

150 "Elton's Tour Ends: Tears, Lennon, and Whatever Gets You Through the Night," by Ed McCormack, *Rolling Stone*, January 2, 1975

151 "The Talk of the Town," *The New Yorker* magazine, December 23, 1974

152 "Tripping on the Traces of Elton John," by Henry Edwards, *After Dark*, March 1976

153 Review of *Captain Fantastic & The Brown Dirt Cowboy*, by Jon Landau, *Rolling Stone*, July 17, 1975

154 "Will Cher Be a Long Playing Single?" by Kay Gardella, *The New York Daily News*, February 9, 1975

155 "Cher's TV Clothes Cost Up to $30,000 a Week," by Robert G. Smith, *The National Enquirer*, June 24, 1975

156 "Cher and Cher Alone," a review of *The Cher Show*, by Harry F. Waters, *Newsweek*, 1975

157 *Cher*, television variety show, CBS-TV, February 16, 1975

158 Author's interview with Arthur Brown, New York City, 1975

159 "The Bash," a review of the *Tommy* film debut party, *Time*, March 31,1975

160 *Leonard Maltin's 1998 Movie & Video Guide*, by Leonard Maltin, Signet Books, New York, New York, 1997

161 *Elton John: Tantrums and Tiaras*, a documentary by David Furnish, 1997

162 "A Piece of The Rock of the Westies," by Patrick Snyder, *Rolling Stone* December 4, 1975

163 Review of Elton John at The Troubadour, by Robert Hilburn, *The Los Angeles Times*, 1975

164 *The Daily Mail*, London, England, 1976

165 "The Elton John Band," a review by Ben Edmonds, *Rolling Stone*, November 20, 1975

166 "…and a Star on Hollywood Boulevard," by Julia Orange, *Rolling Stone*, December 4, 1975.

167 *Elton, My Elton*, Gary Clarke, Smith Gryphon Publishers; London, England, 1995

168 "Annals of Pop: He's a Little Bit Funny," by Ian Parker, *The New Yorker*, August 26-September 2, 1996

169 "Elton Jilted Me," by Wensley Clarkson and Tony Bushby, *The Sunday Mirror*, February 19, 1994

170 "Diary," by William Hickey, *The Daily Express*, February 13, 1984

171 "Elton John: 150% Involved," by Ingrid Sischy, *Interview*, April 1995

172 "Back to Broadway," by Kate Taylor, *The Wall Street Journal*, November 7, 2008

173 "He's His Own Man," by Booth Moore, *Los Angeles Times*, November 30, 2008

174 *The Truth Game*, French television show, February 1986.

[175]   Author's conversation with Bill Wyman at The Monte Carlo Sporting Club, Monaco, August 1, 2008

[176]   "Elton John: Rock's Captain Fantastic," including material by David DeVoss, *Time* magazine, July 7, 1975

[177]   "Elton John MK II," by Phil Sutcliffe, *Juke*, April 15, 1977, reprinted from an earlier issue of *Sounds*

[178]   Here and There album review from *Blender* magazine's Web site, "The Guide" at www.blender.com, 2008

[179]   "Elton Takes a Dive," by Ken Tucker, *Rolling Stone*, September 23, 1976

[180]   *Blue Moves* album review, by Ariel Swartley, *Rolling Stone*, December 30, 1976

[181]   "Prude of the Week," by Sorel, *The Village Voice*, November 15, 1976

[182]   "Correspondence, Love Letters, and Advice," *Rolling Stone*, November 4, 1976

[183]   "Elton John No Longer Views Life Through Crazy Glasses, Darkly: He's a New and Different Man," by Fred Hauptfuhrer, *People*, 1977

[184]   "Fantastic Voyage," by Tom Doyle, *Mojo*, Ocbober 2006

[185]   Author's interview with Jack Donaghy, New York City, December 12, 2008

[186]   "A Life Less Ordinary," by David Buckley, a review of *The Captain and The Kid*, *Mojo*, October 12, 2006

[187]   "The Rocket Man Blasts Off," by Dave Karger, *US* magazine, November 5, 2004

[188]   "Ouch! Elton's Madonna Spat in Full," *Q* magazine, December 2004

[189]   "Elton John: More Danger and Excitement for Him, Please," *Q* magazine, December 2004

[190]   "Elton Vs. Bono," *Q* magazine, December 2004

[191]   "Crowd of 400,000 Sets Record for Park," *New York Times*, September 14, 1980

192 "Elton's Comeback Ignites On-Stage but Not on Record," a review of *Victim of Love*, by Martha Hume, *US* magazine, November 27, 1979

193 "Flamboyant, Vulnerable Star Was in Eclipse Last Two Years," by John Rockwell, *New York Times*, May 23, 1979

194 "Leningrad's Young People Mob Elton John," *New York Times*, May 23, 1979

195 Liner notes on the single version of the single "Song for Guy," Rocket Records, 1978

196 "Elton John Wow's 'em—to Put it Mildly—Back in the U.S.S.R.," by Jim Gallagher, *The Chicago Tribune*, May 1979

197 "Rock Concert: Elton John in Central Park," by Robert Palmer, *New York Times*, September 14, 1979

198 Author's interview with Richie Cannata, Cove Sound Studios, Glen Cove, New York, October 18, 2005

199 Author's interview with David Salidor, January 6, 2009

200 Elton John radio interview with Andy Peebles, December 28, 1980

201 "Elton John Almost Back," by Steve Pond, *Los Angeles Times*, July 5, 1981

202 "Two Icons of Rock Music," by Robert Palmer, *New York Times*, May 31, 1981

203 Review of *The Fox*, by Stephen Holden, *Rolling Stone*, August 6, 1981

204 Review of *Victim of Love*, by Stephen Holden, *Rolling Stone*, December 13, 1979

205 *Jump Up!* re-issued album liner notes, by John Tobler, Rocket/Universal Records, 2003

206 Author's e-mail from Randy Jones, January 23, 2009

207 "The Rebirth of Elton John," by Phillip Norman, *Rolling Stone*, March 19, 1992

208 Review of *Jump Up!*, by Parke Puterbaugh, *Rolling Stone*, May 27, 1982

209   Author's telephone interview with Beth Wernick, September 2, 2008

210   Author's telephone interview with Jimmy Greenspoon, January 3, 2009

211   *Rocket Man: Elton John From A-Z*, by Claude Bernardin and Tom
      Stanton, Praeger Publishers, Westport, Connecticut, 1996

212   Author's telephone interview with Duncan Faure, January 8, 2009

213   Author's telephone interview with "Anonymous Source,"
      January 8, 2009

214   *Too Low For Zero*, reissued album liner notes, by John Tobler,
      Island/Mercury/Rocket Records, 1998

215   *Too Low For Zero*, album review by Don Shewey, *Rolling Stone*,
      June 9, 1983

216   *Breaking Hearts*, album review by Peter Puterbaugh, *Rolling Stone*,
      August 16, 1984

217   *Ice on Fire*, album review by Rob Hoerburger, *Rolling Stone*,
      January 30, 1986

218   "Elton John: Staying in Touch," by Roy Trakin, *Hit Parader*,
      November 1983

219   Account of the Cartier junket, by Christopher Wilson, *Daily
      Express*, 1983

220   Elton John radio interview with Scott Muni, May 22, 1985

221   *The Elton John Scrapbook*, by Mary Ann Cassata, Citidel Press,
      Kensington Books, New York City, 2002

222   "Pop Albums," by Ken Tucker, *The Philadelphia Inquirer*,
      November 23, 1996

223   Elton John radio interview with Andy Peebles, October 17, 1986

224   "Elton John is Back, With More Flash Than Fire," by Jim McFarlin,
      USA Today, August 19, 1986

225   Author's conversation with David Salidor, July 14, 2006.

226 "Interview: Liberty DeVitto, Drummer for Billy Joel," by Don Zalaica, *LiveDaily* (internet news service), March 14, 2001

227 "Billy Joel," by Timothy White, *Billboard*, December 3, 1994

228 Author's interview with an unnamed source, and former Columbia Records employee, New York City, September 30, 2005

229 Author's interview with Liberty DeVitto, New York City, March 9, 2006

230 "Billy Joel: Scenes from a Musical Life," by Bill DeMain, *The Performing Songwriter*, January/February 1996

231 Author's interview with Liberty DeVitto, in a conference room at the offices of Clear Channel Radio, New York City, October 1, 2005

232 Author's interview with Martha Reeves, on the phone, March 19, 2006

233 Author's e-mail from Deborah Gibson, July 11, 2006

234 *The Andy Warhol Diaries*, by Andy Warhol, edited by Pat Hackett, Warner Books, New York City 1991

235 "First Note Sound in Tour De Force," by Pat Bowring, no publication cited, as quoted in *His Song*

236 *Sunday People*, London, January 11, 1987

237 "Elton's Lust for Bondage," *The Sun*, London, February 25, 1987

238 Elton John and Bernie Taupin radio interview with Roger Scott, August, 26, 1989

239 *Two into One*, Elton John and Bernie Taupin, August 31, 1992, as quoted in *His Song*

240 *Reg Strikes Back*, album review by Harold Goldberg, *Rolling Stone*, October 6, 1988

241 "A Winning Bet," by David Wild, *Rolling Stone*, June 28, 1990

242 *Duets*, album review by Elysa Gardner, *Rolling Stone*, December 9, 1993

243 *The One*, album review by Jim Farber, *Rolling Stone*, September 3, 1992

[244]   *The Big Picture*, by David Wild, *Rolling Stone*, October 16, 1997

[245]   *Peachtree Road*, by James Hunter, *Rolling Stone*, November 25, 2004

[246]   *Live in Australia*, album review by Brian Chin, *The New York Post*, 1987

[247]   "Dee Murray 1946-1992," *Rolling Stone*, March 5, 1992

[248]   "Elton John's Menagerie of Dreams," by Robert Hilburn, *Los Angeles Times*, as quoted in *His Song*

[249]   "GLAAD Continues to Watch Media," by Dennis McMillian, *The San Francisco Bay Times*, April 5, 2007

[250]   The Rock and Roll Hall of Fame, speech by Axl Rose, The Waldorf Astoria Hotel, January 19, 1994

[251]   Web site for The Elton John Foundation, information accessed on January 14, 2009

[252]   Elton John television interview with David White, *Real Life*, February 1993

[253]   Elton John, John Reid, and others, television interview, *The Beat File*, Japan, 1994

[254]   Elton John radio interview, 105 Network, Italy, November 1993

[255]   "Elton's Song Set to Raise £10 M," The BBC Online, September 8, 1997

[256]   "Relighting 'Candle' for Di," by Robert Hilburn, *Los Angeles Times*, September 14, 1997

[257]   "Elton John: The *Billboard* Interview," by Timothy White, *Billboard*, October 4, 1997

[258]   "Singing Animals are Only Human," by Larry Nager, *The Philadelphia Daily News*, July 6, 1994

[259]   Elton John and others, *The Lion King, A Musical Journey*, ABC-TV, June 15, 1994

[260]   Elton John on *The Barbara Walters Special*, ABC-TV, March 21, 1994

[261]   Coverage on *Show Biz Today*, CNN-TV, January 20, 1975

262   "Elton and Bernie Renew Pub Tie," by Irv Lichman, *Billboard*, November 14, 1992

263   Author's telephone interview with Crystal Waters, July 18, 1980

264   *Made in England*, album review by Peter Galvin, *Rolling Stone*, May 5, 1995

265   Elton John interview by Barbara Walters, *20/20*, ABC-TV, September 5, 1997

266   Elton John interview, *Extra*, WCAU-TV Philadalphia, March 28, 1995

267   *The Academy Awards* telecast, March 27, 1995

268   Author's telephone interview with RuPaul, October 30, 2008

269   Author's telephone interview with George Masek, November 10, 2008

270   "Tina Bids Farewell," by Daniel Schorn, www.CBSnews.com, December 25, 2005

271   Review of *The Road to Eldorado*, by Jeffrey Westhoff, *Northwest Herald* [Illinois], June 19, 2002

272   Review of *The Road to Eldorado*, by Mike Halverson, *The Sacramento News & Review*, May 31, 2001

273   "Elton John Taps Out Broadway Smash," by Roger Friedman, *Fox News Online*, November 14, 2008

274   "In Hard Times, Born to Pirouette," a review of *Billy Elliot*, by Ben Brantley, *New York Times*, November 14, 2008

275   "Elton John Pooh-Pooh's Gay Marriage, by Clark Hamolyn, www.gay.com, November 14, 2008

276   "Billy Elliot Mugged on Broadway," by Charles McNulty, *Los Angeles Times*, November 14, 2008

277   Author's internet interview with anonymous *Aida* staff member, identified as "Robby," November 1, 2008

278   Author's e-mail from Angela Bowie, January 7, 2009

279 "Elton John," *USA Today*, March 31, 2000

280 *Aida* album review by Anthony DeCurtis, *Rolling Stone*, April 1, 1999

281 Author's telephone interview with Charles Moniz, January 19, 2009

282 *Songs From the West Coast*, and album review by Barry Walters, *Rolling Stone*, September 17, 2001

283 "The Unusual Habits of Elton John," by Mim Udovitch, *Rolling Stone*, November 8, 2001

284 "Elton John" in *The Telegraph*, London, as quoted in *Elton: The Biography*, 2007

285 "Sir Bitch is Back," by David Wild, *Rolling Stone*, November 25, 2004

286 Elton John onstage at *Live 8*, broadcast from Hyde Park, London, England, July 2, 2005

287 *The Captain & The Kid*, album review by Christian Hoard, *Rolling Stone*, September 18, 2006

288 "Elton John and Lily Allen in War of Words at *GQ* Awards," by Vernoica Schmidt, *TimesOnLine*, U.K., September 3, 2008

289 "Rock's Most Embarrassing Siblings," by Ben Mitchell, *Blender*, October 2005

290 Author's conversation with Alice Cooper, Phoenix, Arizona, March 3, 2009

291 "Elton John's Gorilla Suit Prank Terrified Iggy," www.contactmusic.com, September 7, 2005

BIBLIOGRAPHY

Bernardin, Claude; Stanton, Tom. *Rocket Man*. Westport, Connecticut: Praeger Publishing, 1996.

Black, Susan. *Elton John in His Own Words*. London, England: Omnibus Press, 1993.

Bogdanov, Vladimir; Woodstra, Chris; and Erlewine, Stephen Thomas. *All Music Guide to Rock*. San Francisco, California: Backbeat Books, 2002.

Bego, Mark. *Billy Joel: The Biography*. New York City: Thunder's Mouth Press, 2007; London, England: JR Books, 2008.

Bego, Mark. *Cher: If You Believe*. Boulder, Colorado: Taylor Trade Publishing, 2001.

Bego, Mark. *Jackson Browne: His Life and Music*. New York: Citadel Press, Kensington Books, 2005.

Bowie, Angela, with Carr, Patrick. *Backstage Passes*. New York: Cooper Square Press, 2000.

Buckley, David. *Elton: The Biography*. Chicago, Illinois: Chicago Review Press, 2007.

Cassata, Mary Ann. *The Elton John Scrapbook*. New York: Citadel Press, Kensington Books, 2002.

Clarke, Gary. *Elton, My Elton*. London, England: Smith Gryphon, 1995.

Editors of *Rolling Stone* magazine. *Rolling Stone: The 500 Greatest Albums of All Time*. New York: Wenner Media, 2005.

Halpern, Ian. *Fire and Rain: The James Taylor Story*. Edinburgh, Scotland: Mainstream Publishing, 2001.

Labelle, Patti, with Randolph, Laura B. *Don't Block the Blessings: Revelations of a Lifetime*. New York: Riverhead Books, a division of G.P. Putnam's Sons, 1996.

Maltin, Leonard. *Leonard Maltin's 1998 Movie & Video Guide*. New York: Signet Books, 1997.

Myers, Paul. *It Ain't Easy: Long John Baldry and the Birth of the British Blues*. Vancouver, Canada: Greystone Books, Douglas & McIntyre Publishing, 2007.

Norman, Phillip. *Sir Elton*. New York: Carrol & Graf, Avalon Publishing Group, 2001.

Rees, Dafydd; Crampton, Luke. *VH1 Music First Rock Stars Encyclopedia*. New York: DK Publishing, 1999.

Rosenthal, Elizabeth J. *His Song: The Musical Journey of Elton John*. New York: Billboard Books, Watson-Guptill Publications, 2001.

Smith, Joe; edited by Fink, Michael. *Off the Record: An Oral History of Popular Music*. New York: Warner Books, 1988.

Whitburn, Joel. *Top Pop Albums 1955-1985*. Menomonee Falls, Wisconsin: Record Research Books, 1985.

Whitburn, Joel. T*op Pop Singles 1955-1996*. Menomonee Falls, Wisconsin: Record Research Books, 1997.

Wilson, Mary; Ronanowski, Patricia [including sections by Mary Wilson and Mark Bego]. *Supreme Faith: Someday We'll Be Together*. New York: Harper Collins, 1990.

ELTON JOHN

DISCOGRAPHY

Over the years there have been countless international versions of Elton John albums and singles. While this discography contains the most pertinent information, in reality a full and complete international discography could easily occupy its own book. The album information below takes into consideration the tally favored by the ultimate discography man himself: Elton John. For instance, Elton considered the 1970 British version of *Empty Sky* to be a different album than the 1975 U.S. and international versions of the same vinyl album. In that way, when it came time to release the 1980 album *21 at 33*, he could legitimately use that title to signify the fact that he had released 21 albums by the time he reached the age 33.

ALBUMS:

	Year	Title	U.S. Weeks Chart on U.S.		U.K. Weeks Chart on U.K.	
			Peak	Chart	Peak	Chart
1.	1969	*Empty Sky* [U.K only]	- -	- -		
2.	1970	*Elton John*	4	51	5	22
3.	1971	*Tumbleweed Connection*	5	37	2	20
4.	1971	*Friends* (Film Soundtrack)	36	19	-	-
5.	1971	*11-17-70* [U.S.] / *17-11-70* [U.K.]	11	23	20	2
6.	1971	*Madman Across the Water*	8	51	41	2
7.	1972	*Honky Château*	1	61	2	23
8.	1973	*Don't Shoot Me I'm Only the Piano Player*	1	89	1	42
9.	1973	*Goodbye Yellow*				

		Brick Road	1	103	1	88
10.	1974	Caribou	1	54	1	18
11.	1975	Elton John: Greatest Hits	1	107	1	84
12.	1975	Captain Fantastic and the Brown Dirt Cowboy	1	43	2	24
13.	1975	Empty Sky [U.S. Version]	6	18	-	-
14.	1975	Rock of the Westies	1	26	5	12
15.	1976	Here and There	4	20	7	7
16.	1976	Blue Moves	3	22	3	15
17.	1977	Elton John: Greatest Hits, Vol. 2	21	20	6	24
18.	1978	A Single Man	15	18	8	26
19.	1979	The Thom Bell Sessions	51	18	-	-
20.	1979	Victim of Love	35	10	41	3
21.	1980	21 at 33	13	21	12	13
22.	1981	The Fox	21	19	12	12
23.	1982	Jump Up!	17	33	13	12
24.	1983	Too Low for Zero	25	54	7	73
25.	1984	Breaking Hearts	20	34	2	23
26.	1985	Ice on Fire	48	28	3	23
27.	1986	Leather Jackets	91	9	24	9
28.	1987	Live in Australia	24	41	70	7
29.	1987	Elton John: Greatest Hits, Vol. 3	84		-	-
30.	1988	Reg Strikes Back	16	29	18	6
31.	1989	Sleeping With the Past	23	53	1	42
32.	1990	To Be Continued	82	13	-	-
33.	1990	The Very Best of Elton John	-	-	1	
34.	1991	Two Rooms [Tribute Album With Appearance by Elton]	18			
35.	1992	The One	8	53	2	18
36.	1992	Rare Masters				
37.	1993	Duets	25	22	5	18
38.	1994	The Lion King (Movie Soundtrack)	1	88	-	-
39.	1995	Made in England	13	46	3	14
40.	1996	Love Songs	24	76	4	48

No.	Year	Title				
41.	1997	Big Picture	9	23	3	23
42.	1999	Elton John & Tim Rice's Aida	41	7	29	2
43	1999	The Muse (Movie Soundtrack)				
44.	2000	The Road to Eldorado (Movie Soundtrack)	63	8	-	-
45.	2000	One Night Only	65	18	7	13
46.	2001	Songs from the West Coast	15	24	2	34
47.	2002	Greatest Hits 1970-2002	12	67	3	54
48.	2004	Peachtree Road	17	10	21	8
49.	2006	The Captain & The Kid	18	6	-	-
50.	2006	Elton John's Christmas Party	-	-	-	-
51.	2007	Rocket Man: Number Ones	9	2	-	-

SINGLES:

	Year	Title	U.S. Chart Peak	Weeks on U.S. Chart	U.K. Chart Peak	Weeks on U.K. Chart
1.	1968	"I've Been Loving You'	-	-	-	-
2.	1969	"Lady Samantha"	-	-	-	-
3.	1969	"It's Me That You Need"	-	-	-	-
4.	1970	"Border Song"	92	5	-	-
5.	1970	"Rock & Roll Madonna"	-	-	-	-
6.	1970	"Your Song"	8	14	7	12
7.	1971	"Friends"	34	9	-	-
8.	1971	"Levon"	24	10	-	-
9.	1972	"Tiny Dancer"	41	7	-	-
10.	1972	"Rocket Man"	6	15	2	13
11.	1972	"Honky Cat"	8	10	31	6
12.	1972	"Crocodile Rock"	1	17	5	14

13.	1973	"Daniel"	2	15	4	10
14.	1973	"Saturday Night's Alright (For Fighting)"	12	12	7	9
15.	1973	"Step Into Christmas"	-	-	24	7
16.	1973	"Goodbye Yellow Brick Road"	2	17	6	16
17.	1974	"Candle in the Wind"	-	-	11	9
18.	1974	"Bennie & The Jets"	1	18	37	5
19.	1974	"Don't Let the Sun Go Down On Me"	2	15	16	8
20.	1974	"The Bitch Is Back"	4	14	15	7
21.	1974	"Lucy in the Sky with Diamonds"	1	14	10	10
22.	1975	"Philadelphia Freedom"	1	21	12	9
23.	1975	"Someone Saved My Life Tonight"	4	13	22	5
24.	1975	"Island Girl"	1	15	14	8
25.	1976	"Grow Some Funk of Your Own"	14	11	-	-
26.	1976	"Pinball Wizard"	-	-	7	7
27.	1976	"Don't Go Breaking My Heart" [duet with Kiki Dee]	1	20	1	14
28.	1976	"Sorry Seems to Be the Hardest Word"	6	14	11	10
29.	1977	"Bite Your Lip"	28	6	28	4
30.	1977	"Crazy Water"	-	-	27	6
31.	1978	"Ego"	34	8	34	6
32.	1978	"Part Time Love"	22	10	15	13
33.	1978	"Song For Guy"	110	1	4	10
34.	1978	"Funeral For a Friend" / "Love Lies Bleeding"	-	-	-	-
35.	1979	"Mama Can't Buy You Love"	9	18	-	-
36.	1979	"Victim of Love"	31	10	-	-
37.	1979	"Johnny B. Goode"	-	-	-	-
38.	1980	"Little Jeannie"	3	31	33	7
39.	1980	"Sartorial Eloquence" [U.K. Title]	-	-	44	5
	1980	"Don't Ya Wanna Play This Game No				

#	Year	Title				
		More" [U.S. Title]	39	12	-	-
40.	1980	"Harmony"	-	-	-	-
41.	1980	"Dear God"	-	-	-	-
42.	1981	"I Saw Her Standing There"	-	-	40	4
43.	1981	"Nobody Wins"	21	13	42	5
44.	1981	"Just Like Belgium"	-	-	-	-
45.	1981	"Chloe"	34	13	-	-
46.	1982	"Empty Garden"	13	17	51	4
47.	1982	"Blue Eyes"	12	18	8	10
48.	1982	"Princess"	-	-	-	-
49.	1982	"Ball and Chain"	-	-	-	-
50.	1982	"All Quiet on the Western Front"	-	-	-	-
51.	1983	"I'm Still Standing"	12	16	4	11
52.	1983	"Kiss the Bride"	25	12	20	7
53.	1983	"I Guess That's Why They Call It the Blues"	4	23	5	15
54.	1983	"Cold as Christmas (In the Middle of the Year)"	-	-	33	6
55.	1984	"Sad Songs (Say So Much)"	5	19	7	12
56.	1984	"Passengers"	-	-	5	11
57.	1984	"Who Wears These Shoes"	16	14	50	3
58.	1984	"In Neon"	38	13	-	-
59.	1984	"Breaking Hearts (Ain't What It Used to Be)"	-	-	59	3
60.	1985	"Act of War" [duet with Millie Jackson]	-	-	32	5
61.	1985	"Wrap Her Up" [featuring George Michael]	20	14	12	10
62.	1985	"That's What Friends are For" [with Dionne Warwick, Gladys Knight & Stevie Wonder]	1	23	16	9
63.	1986	"Nikita"	7	18	3	13
64.	1986	"Cry to Heaven"	-	-	47	4
65.	1986	"Heartache All Over the World"	55	8	45	4

66.	1986	"Slow Rivers"	-	-		44	8
67.	1987	"Flames of Paradise" [duet with Jennifer Rush]	36	13		59	3
68.	1987	"Your Song" [live]	-	-		85	1
69.	1987	"Candle in the Wind" [live]	6	21		5	11
70.	1988	"Take Me to the Pilot" [live]	-	-		-	-
71.	1988	"I Don't Wanna Go on With You Like That"	2	18		30	8
72.	1988	"Mona Lisas and Mad Hatters"	-	-		-	-
73.	1988	"Town of Plenty"	-	-		74	1
74.	1988	"A Word in Spanish"	19	13		91	1
75.	1989	"Through the Storm" [duet with Aretha Franklin]	16	11		41	3
76.	1989	"Healing Hands"	13	15		45	5
77.	1990	"Sacrifice"	18	17		1	15
78.	1990	"Club at the End of the Street"	28	16		47	3
79.	1990	"You Gotta Love Someone"	43	13		33	4
80.	1990	"Easier to Walk Away"	-	-		63	2
81.	1991	"Don't Let the Sun Go Down On Me" [duet with George Michael]	1	20		1	10
82.	1992	"The One"	9	22		10	8
83.	1992	"Runaway Train" [duet with Eric Clapton]	-	-		31	4
84.	1992	"The Last Song"	23	20		21	4
85.	1993	"Simple Life"	30	16		44	2
86.	1993	"True Love" [duet with Kiki Dee]	56	12		2	10
87.	1993	"Don't Go Breaking My Heart" [duet with RuPaul]	92	2		7	7
88.	1994	"Ain't Nothing Like the Real Thing" [Duet with Marcella Detroit]	-	-		24	4
89.	1994	"Can You Feel the					

		Love Tonight"	4	26	14	9
90.	1994	"The Circle of Life"	18	20	11	12
91.	1995	"Believe"	13	20	15	7
92.	1995	"Made in England"	52	10	18	5
93.	1995	"Blessed"	34	20	-	-
94.	1995	"Please"	-	-	33	3
95.	1996	"You Can Make History (Young Again)"	70	17	-	-
96.	1996	"Live Like Horses" [duet with Luciano Pavarotti]	-	-	9	6
97.	1997	"Candle in the Wind – 1997"[tribute to Princess Diana]	1	42	1	24
98.	1998	"Recover Your Soul"	55	20	16	3
99.	1999	"If the River Can Bend"	-	-	32	2
100.	1999	"Written in the Stars" [duet with LeAnn Rimes]	29	10	10	8
101.	2000	"Someday Out of the Blue"	49	15	-	-
102.	2001	"I Want Love"	110	1	9	10
103.	2002	"This Train Don't Stop Here Anymore"	-	-	24	4
104.	2002	"Original Sin"	-	-	39	2
105.	2002	"Your Song" [duet with Alessandro Safina]	-	-	4	10
106.	2003	"Are You Ready For Love" [Remix]	-	-	1	14
107.	2004	"All That I'm Allowed (I'm Thankful)"	-	-	20	5
108.	2004	"Turn the Lights Out When You Leave"	-	-	32	2
109.	2005	"Electricity"	-	-	4	1

Acknowledgments

Catherine Bailey

Linda Bego

Kirsten Borchardt

Gary Brooker

Carlene Carter

Alice Cooper

Brad DeMeulenaere

Micky Dolenz

Lamar Fike

Chris Gilman

Harry Haun

Danny Hutton

Tony King

George Masek

Charles Moniz

May Pang

Kenneth Reynolds

Justin Ross

David Salidor

Dan Smetanka

David Stanley

Derek Storm

Crystal Waters

Beth Wernick

Bill Wyman

Bob and Mary Bego

Cindy Birdsong

Angela Bowie

Richie Cannata

Darby Connor

Sarah Dash

Liberty DiVitto

Abdul "Duke" Fakir

Duncan Faure

Jimmy Greenspoon

Bobby Hedglin

Randy Jones

Marcy MacDonald

Scott Mendel

Mark Olsen

Tony Panico

Jeremy Robson

RuPaul

Andy Skurow

Mark Sokoloff

Marsha Stern

Henrietta Tiefenthaler

Harry Weinger

Mary Wilson

ABOUT THE AUTHOR

MARK BEGO is a professional writer who is called "The Number One Best-Selling Pop Biographer" in *Publisher's Weekly* and has been referred to in the press as "The Prince of Pop Music Bios." He has authored over 52 published books involving rock & roll and show business. He has penned two *New York Times* bestsellers, a *Los Angeles Times* bestseller, and the *Chicago Tribune* bestseller *Dancing in the Street: Confessions of a Motown Diva* written with its subject, Martha Reeves of the beloved recording group Martha & The Vandellas.

His biographies have included the life stories of some of the biggest stars of rock (Elvis Presley, Michael Jackson, Madonna, Bonnie Raitt, The Doobie Brothers, and Three Dog Night), soul (Aretha Franklin, Martha Reeves & The Vandellas, Tina Turner, and Whitney Houston), pop (Sonny & Cher, The Monkees, Sade, and Barry Manilow) and country (George Strait, Patsy Cline, Alan Jackson, and Vince Gill). He has also written about film and television stars (Rock Hudson, Julia Roberts, Leonardo DeCaprio, Will Smith, Matt Damon, and The Marx Brothers).

In 1984, he released his biography of Michael Jackson, entitled *Michael!* It spent six weeks on the *New York Times* bestseller list and was published in six foreign language editions.

The following year, in 1985, Bego wrote the million-selling *Madonna!* about the pop icon. He has also written books with Micky Dolenz of The Monkees (*I'm a Believer*), Debbie Gibson (*Between the Lines*), and Jimmy Greenspoon of Three Dog Night (*One is the Loneliest Number*).

In 1998, Bego wrote the biography *Leonardo DiCaprio: Romantic Hero.* It spent six weeks on the *New York Times'* bestseller list. He is frequently seen on television speaking about show business, on such shows as *Entertainment Tonight, Biography,* and *True Hollywood Story.* When Michael Jackson suddenly died in June 2009, Mark made three appearances on www.ABCnews.com, discussing Michael's sad death and commentating at his funeral.

In 2008, he published *Billy Joel: The Biography* with JR Books, and then his 51st pop culture book, written with Randy

Jones of The Village People, entitled *Macho Man*. His website is www.MarkBego.com.

Mark released four books in October 2009: in addition to *Elton John: The Story,* he released a memoir with Ruth Mueller called *One Minute Before Midnight, Whitney Houston: Die Biography* (in German), and *Tina Turner: Die Biography* (in German).